To Chinese History.

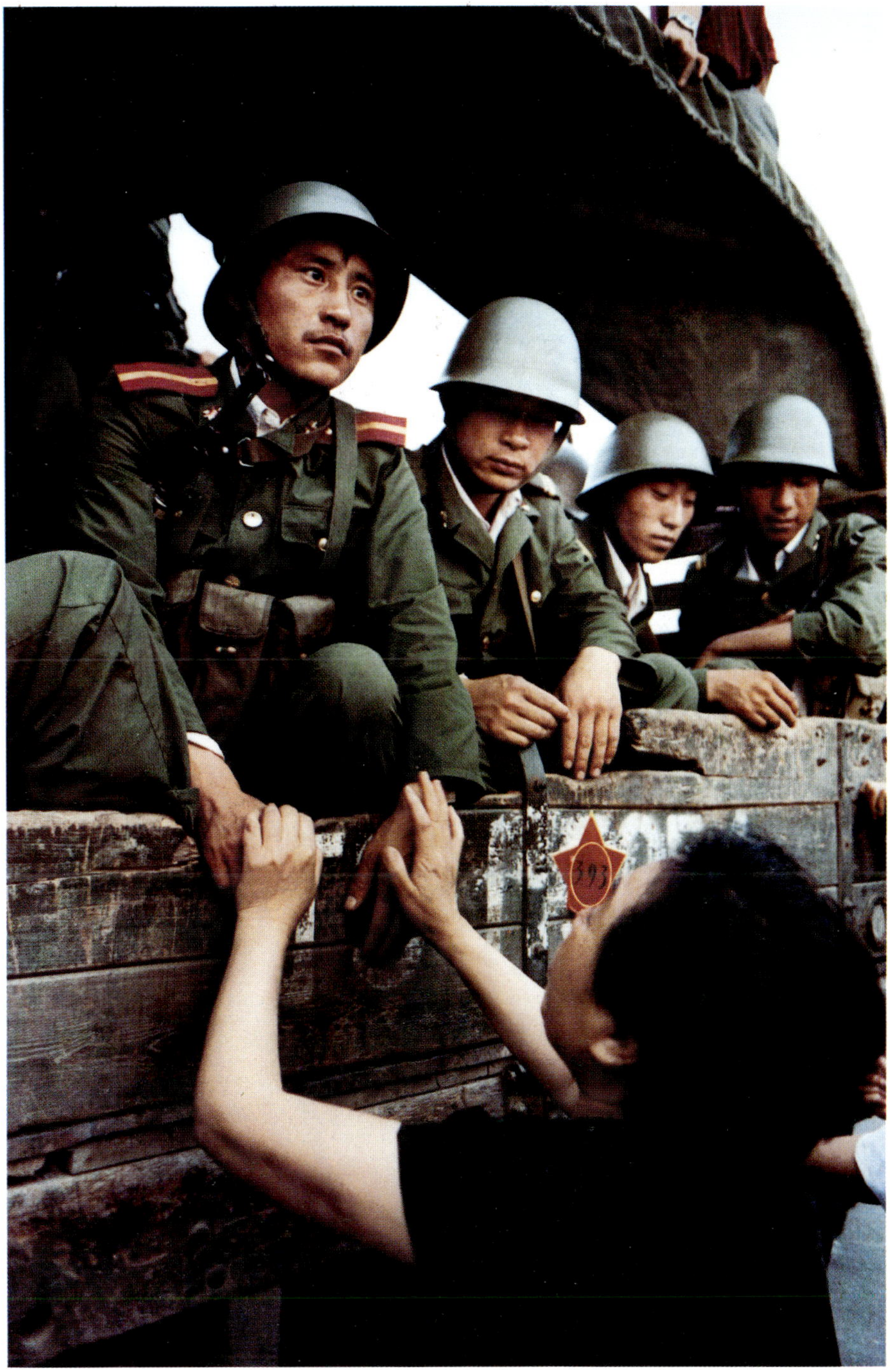

© David C. Turnley, 1989. Kodak Ektapress Gold 400 professional film

you to its core. And holds you hostage to its honesty. LESSON № 1:
Never compromise your ideals.

THE PHOTO GALLERY & WORKSHOP HANDBOOK

Jeff Cason

images
PRESS INC.

The Photo Gallery & Workshop Handbook

Library of Congress Catalog Card Number: 90-084934

Jeff Cason
The Photo Gallery & Workshop Handbook

ISBN: 0-929-667-08-5

About the Author:

Jeff Cason is the author of the *Photo Marketing Handbook* also published by Images Press. His previous experiences as Publicity Director for RCA Records, and Director of Promotion and Publicity for *Dance Magazine* and the defunct entertainment magazine, *AfterDark*, has allowed him the opportunity of working with a variety of outstanding photographers in the U.S. and Europe. He currently resides in New York City.

Graphic Design and Typography by Ray Noonan, ParaGraphic Artists, NYC
Cover Design by Valerie English

Published by Images Press, 7 East 17th Street, New York, NY 10003
Printed and bound in the United States of America

Contents

Acknowledgments

The author gratefully acknowledges the able assistance, and the persistence, of researchers Ellen Hoo and Judy Chan.

Thanks, once again, to Jackson Chong, computer wizard extraordinaire, for his long-distance dedication.

And an especially heart-felt thanks to the following photography professionals who generously provided their time and wisdom:

Jim Baker, *Anderson Ranch Arts Center*
Ben Breard, *Afterimage*
Terri Costantino, *Gallery 44*
Marnie Gillette, *San Francisco Camerawork*
Ted Hartman, *The Minneapolis Institute of Arts*
Marita Holdaway, *The Benham Gallery*
Daile Kaplan, *Swann Galleries*
Jim & Chris McLarty, *East Africa Photographic Workshops*
John Smith-Amato, *Synchronicity Space*

Introduction

The decision to produce this handbook came about through an awareness of a flourishing marketplace which offers an infinite variety of educational and exhibition opportunities to the photographer; albeit in a seemingly *haphazard* manner. Many photographic publications or journals devote extremely limited editorial space, sometimes bolstered by small advertisements in the back pages, to information on workshops and galleries. Thus, photographers seeking to expand their photographic education and experience are generally left to search futilely for information with which to locate a suitable workshop or gallery situation. The principle goal of the *Photo Gallery & Workshop Handbook* then is to cohesively present as much of this information as is possible in one place, providing photographers, photo-lovers, and anyone interested in the art of photography with a one-stop photography resource book.

Those of us who are members of the "baby-boom" generation, as well as those who have come after, have watched our world appear to shrink as universal communication systems have advanced our lifestyles into a fast-forward mode. We children of the electronic age have had the opportunity to travel regularly and easily to exotic locations that the "Joe Average" of previous generations only dreamed about. As a result, today's photographers and photo-enthusiasts have an unlimited panorama of photography-related activities and events from which to choose.

When research for this volume commenced there were many obvious places to begin. But it became clear almost immediately that many of the available resource books and publications contained extremely out-dated, vague, or limited information. Thus our research team embarked on an international scavenger hunt to find the most up-to-date gallery addresses and workshop offerings. With modest pride and sweated brow we are able to say that the majority of the information contained in this handbook comes directly from questionnaires completed by representatives of the galleries, museums, and workshops included in the listings sections.

The *Photo Gallery & Workshop Handbook* has been designed to provide helpful information to photographers, both novice and established, who are seeking to exhibit their work or perhaps expand their knowledge or experience by attending a workshop or photo-tour. In most instances, the galleries included here have provided us with pretty specific information regarding what type of material they are looking to exhibit. For the photographic spectator, and those interested in learning about photo-collecting, the extensive listings also offer a comprehensive run-down of galleries specializing in photography, as well as information on the permanent collections of many of the world's leading museums. Also for photo collectors the conversation with Swann Gallerie's Daile Kaplan offers invaluable insight into the world of photography auctions.

Workshops also continue to evolve, and if the information supplied to us via our questionnaires is a true barometer, there is almost no destination too far off the beaten path and no photographic subject left unattended. The options available to workshop and photo-tour participants run the gamut in price, time, location, and instruction.

Finally, what we're hoping to provide with the *Photo Gallery & Workshop Handbook* is a kind of "clearing-house" of photographic activity. As you will see while reading the listings, geographically we're all over the place. So, if your plans include attending a two-week workshop photographing the wildflowers of the Alpine Mountains, you will also be able to use the galleries and museums listings to locate local photographic outlets in which to while away your leisure hours. But whatever your destination, or inclination, we hope we have provided you with a useful reference tool that will help you on your way to reaching your photographic goals!

From Here

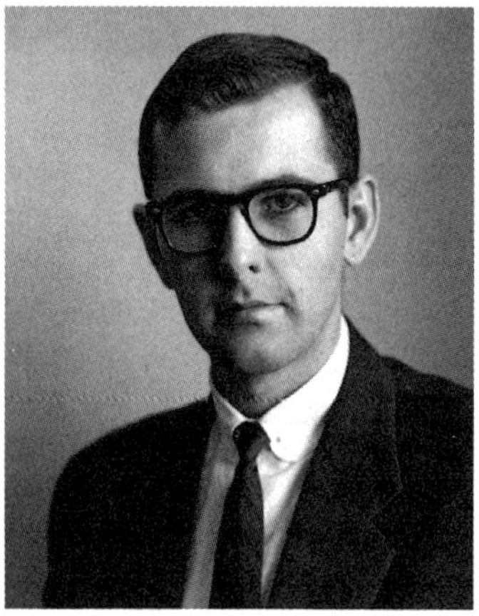

Uelsmann, Jerry '57

Photographic Technology, Men's Dorm (President), Delta Lambda Epsilon. Photographic Students Association, Camera Club.

Who'd have ever guessed that this clean-cut kid from Detroit would turn out images of such uncompromising quality and mystical impact? Actually, anybody who watched him closely at RIT. Because even

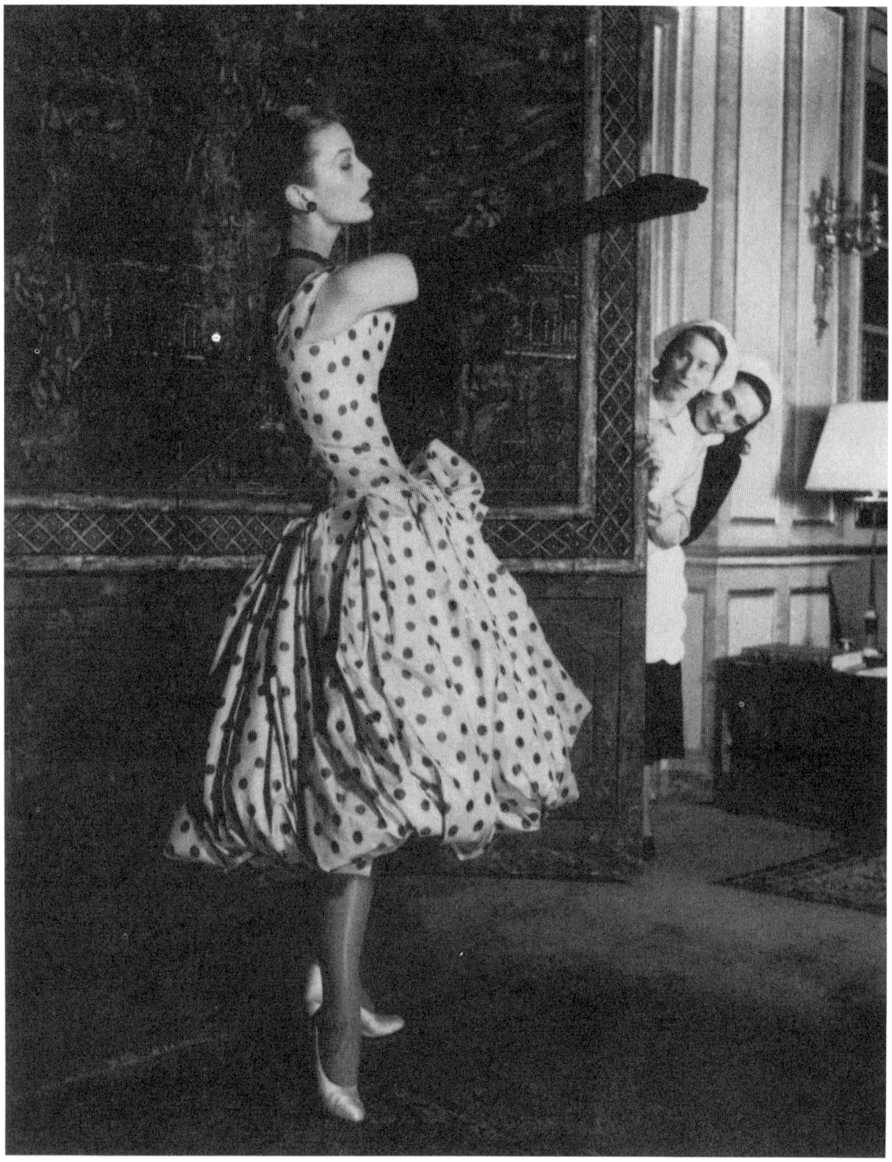

Louise Dahl-Wolfe. American (1895-1989). Mary Jane Russell in Dior Dress. *1950. Gelatin silver print. Gift of Helen Cummings Ziegler. Photograph Courtesy of the National Museum of Women in the Arts.*

Part I:
Galleries, Museums, and Auctions

The Photographic Art Market: The State of an Art

As the United States and other members of the global village have bunkered-down for the latest economic recession, it is obvious to predict that the photographic art market will be seriously affected. Signs of conservative spending at recent auctions point toward a bottoming-out of what appeared to be ceilingless prices paid for the works of the master photographers during the eighties.

The good news is, as those who regularly follow the trends of the photographic art market might already know, that photography, in comparison to other mediums, will almost certainly continue to be affordable and accessible in the nineties. Pop-star Graham Nash's extensive photo collection sold at a record-breaking $2.4 million at Sotheby's New York auction house in the spring of 1990. However, by autumn photographic auctions held at both Sotheby's and Christie's, as reported by *The New York Times*, earned little more than 50% of what was expected and many lots remained unsold. The Christie's autumn auction did garner $126,500 for a 1920's Rayograph by Man Ray which was a record for an auctioned photograph. Another record-setting price was achieved at the October Sotheby's auction when $99,000 was offered for an Alfred Stieglitz portrait of Georgia O'Keeffe, making this the highest price paid for a photograph by Stieglitz at auction. As the recession looms, it appears likely that top dollar will continue to be paid for rare vintage works by the masters. However, as photography has only in the recent past been generally accepted as fine art by the tradition-bound arbiters of the art world, prices in most instances have not yet escalated to the out-of-reach heights found in some of the other areas of the art market. But with heavily bankrolled museums and arts institutions now actively in the photography collecting game, competition is escalating to new heights. And if the economic forecast turns favorable, the sky may yet become the limit. A painting by an acknowledged master, such as Monet or Pisarro, which finds its way to the auction house is probably not within reach of the majority of art consumers. But a modern print by a classic photographer such as Cartier-Bresson or Berenice Abbot can be surprisingly affordable given the right circumstance.

A photographer friend who specializes in runway-fashion and travel photography, and who has had, until recently, little experience purchasing photographic art, attended the *Greta Garbo Benefit Auction and Reception* held by Sotheby's in New York City in late 1990. Fascinated by the Garbo mystique and attracted to the event more as voyeur than buyer, the friend discovered several photo-portraits of the star by the legendary photographer, and Garbo confidant, Cecil Beaton. Learning she could proffer a silent bid for the modern print created especially for this benefit event, she did so and promptly forgot about it. Several weeks passed and responding to a telephone call, she learned that not only had she placed the accepted bid but she was the only one who hadn't yet picked up her treasure. Subsequently, she became the owner of a beautiful photograph by a favorite artist, and as the auction benefited a variety of educational charities, her purchase was also a nice tax-deduction. Not a bad track-record for a first photo auction. The price? *Less than $1,000.*

Undoubtedly most people do not have such luck the first time around and many aren't even aware that photographic art of every variety is available and within reach. Prices are erratic in the photography market, even during times of economic stability. As you would when making any major purchase, whether it be a new automobile or television, it is imperative that you study the market and learn the buying and selling trends. But then, success can be measured in many ways. Some buyers are content owning a second rate print by a beloved or master photographer regardless of the price or the market value. While others are just as happy owning a piece that speaks directly to them even if to no one else. Of course, the best scenario is a favorite photograph, purchased at a good price, by an unknown who suddenly becomes the "next big thing." Acknowledgment of one's own fine eye is often the best reward for many of us.

Reviewing top prices achieved in recent years provides a barometer of sorts to understanding the fluctuations of the photo-art market. A big success story, although certainly a sad and ironic one, is that of Robert Mapplethorpe. Without question a success before his death from AIDS, the notoriety surrounding the exhibition of his work, *The Perfect Moment*, first in Washington, D.C., and then at Cincinnati's Contemporary Arts Center, has pushed prices for his work into the $40,000 range. Other contemporary photographers such as Cindy Sherman, William Wegman, and the Starn Twins are now also priced above $20,000.

Shopping for fine photography can be as complicated or as simple as you make it. If you have done your homework and you know what you are looking for, perhaps developing a relationship with a good private photo dealer is your next step. If you are considering starting a photography collection it is essential for you to attend auctions, galleries, and museum exhibitions regularly. The more you are able to learn about the marketplace the more insight you will have in establishing your own collection.

Auctions are not necessarily for everyone, at least when it comes to making your initial photography purchases. But they are certainly for anyone interested in keeping up with the movement patterns and the prices of the photography market. Also most auction houses offer a well researched catalogue of the material to be auctioned accompanied by estimates the images are expected to bring during the big event. A well produced catalogue can be the single most important source for a quick education in photo-collecting.

Another source of education readily available to many of us are local museums, libraries, art institutions, and historic societies. Many leading national and regional museums own priceless permanent collections which, while not always available to the public, can usually be viewed if an appointment is secured in advance. Some of these establishments maintain private viewing rooms and if the photographs themselves can not be handled, the images belonging to the collection can usually be viewed via an optical-disc or micro-film system.

Understanding the scope of the photographic community and appreciation of the historic development of the art of photography are essential fundamentals in learning to operate within the wide world of the photographic art market.

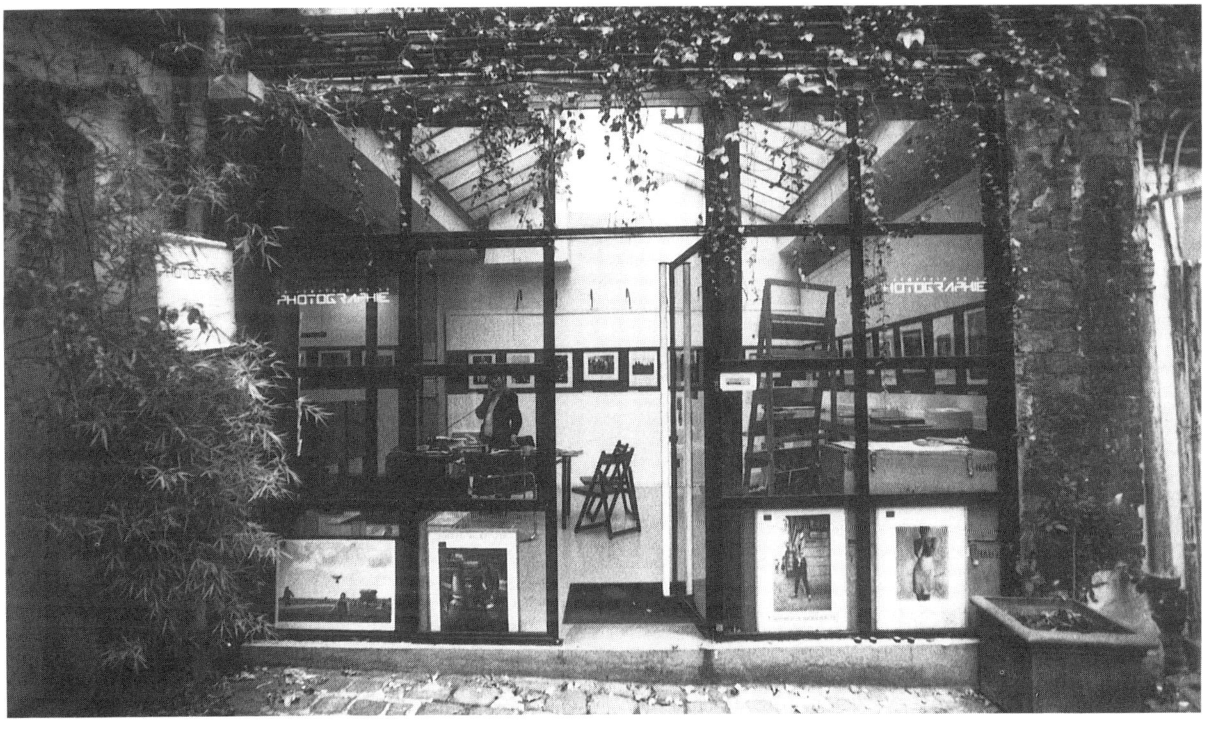

Photograph by Scott Halleran

Comptoir de la Photographie is a showcase for contemporary photography in Paris, France.

Tales from the Auction House: Swann Galleries

New York City's Swann Galleries is perceived by many to be the country's leading photographic auction house. Although not devoted exclusively to the auctioning of photographic works and literature, and perhaps not as well known for record-breaking sales as the world famous Sotheby's and Christie's, Swann enjoys a reputation as an arbiter of new trends in the marketplace.

TRENDS & THE CHANGING AUCTION CLIMATE

Curator-historian, Daile Kaplan, is head of the photography department at Swann Galleries, and the author of *Lewis Hine In Europe: The Lost Photographs.* Previously she was the director of the Historical Photo Collection of the United Methodist Church which has a respository of 200,000 photographs. She has been on the job for just over one year - a topsy-turvey year, rife with economic uncertainty that has seen both historic, record-breaking sales as well as an abundance of masterful work remaining unsold at leading auction houses around the world.

Overseeing the photographic auctions from her unique vantage point has provided Kaplan with a front-row seat to the erratic market patterns at the leading auction houses' buying and selling wars. "In light of the fact that there were a lot, a lot of photographs offered in the October auctions, I think that all of the houses have decided to be more selective and offer images that are literally 'cutting-edge'," offers Kaplan. "We had virtually 600 lots and approximately 450 of them were photographs or photographic collections. That's an area that Swann has pioneered. Where Sotheby's and Christie's tend to offer 'blue-chip' master-work images, we offer collections - whether they're 'news' collections, 'circus' collections, 'New York' collections, 'celebrity' collections. That kind of material is becoming very desirable, so that's an area where we will continue to go."

Kaplan also forsees a continued interest in the work of the legendary photographer of Native American subjects, Edward Curtis. "I think focus will continue on Edward Curtis's photogravures, which interested me alot. Obviously it is Native American material and there is always interest in that kind of imagery. However, the Curtis images are not original photographs, rather photo-mechanical reproductions, or photogravures in this case. They are very beautiful, very handsomely produced, and yet there has never been that strong a market for 'groups of images', which is to say, not the entire portfolio. We were offering selections of images that were based on thematic considerations...so that was a good sign."

As in most other areas of popular culture, it is next to impossible to guess what might launch a new trend and the photographic art world is no exception. Is the renewed interest in photography of the Civil War era due in part to the success of the acclaimed PBS television series, *The Civil War,* or the popular film, *Dances With Wolves*? Is it a coincidence that Man Ray's work is setting records at auction while a glamorous retrospective of his work is traveling the world's museums? Kaplan generally takes the trends in stride, "There are always waves or trends in any market. So, for example, at a certain point there may be tremendous interest in a body of work by a photographer and later on, as a supply of images becomes available, there is less of an interest. But if it is a master photographer, like an Ansel Adams or Berenice Abbot or Eugene Atget, I don't think that one need worry that the market will crash-out. But there is a situation of continued introduction of new material in the market, and decisions will be made based on both aesthetic and market interests."

It is especially important to be able to pinpoint new trends if you are a beginner collector and economics dictate that you spend your money wisely. Take time to procure and study the auction house's catalogue before attending the auction. Afterwards, request the

"Prices Realized" information sheet for a real education in photographic auctions. With some experience under your belt, like Kaplan, you'll have soon developed a sense of what material is in demand. "One of the areas that I've been surprised to see do extremely well is celebrity photography. In our spring sale we had an early photograph of Marilyn Monroe by Philippe Halsman that sold for $3,300. This was a record-breaking price for that image. In the fall sale we had a very unusual piece, a large color print that Frank Sinatra shot of the Ali-Frazier fight. It was published in *Life* when the fight took place. There are these oddities that continue to crop up because so many famous performers and cultural figures are interested in photography and so one never knows what will walk in the door."

PHOTOGRAPHIC LITERATURE

Other new trends were evident at recent photo-auctions such as the strong interest in the works from the "Photo-Secessionists", Eastern European photography, PhotoJournalism, and Photographic Literature. The "Photo-Secessionists" were a society of art photographers, organized in 1902 and led by the legendary Alfred Stieglitz. Other founding members included John G. Bullock, William B. Dyer, Gertrude Kasebier, Edward J. Steichen, and Clarence H. White, among others. The group was devoted to winning recognition for the pictorial photography movement in America and Europe.

Much previously unseen work from post-war Eastern European photographers is also becoming more available as the Iron Curtain swings further open. And photo-journalism, or work that illustrates cultural history and was perhaps first seen publicly when published in magazines such as *Life* or *Look* is receiving a lot of attention. But the foremost trend for Swann has been the interest in "photographic literature." Daile Kaplan speculates on the trend of the moment: "We have broken records in terms of photographic literature, and there is a continued interest in

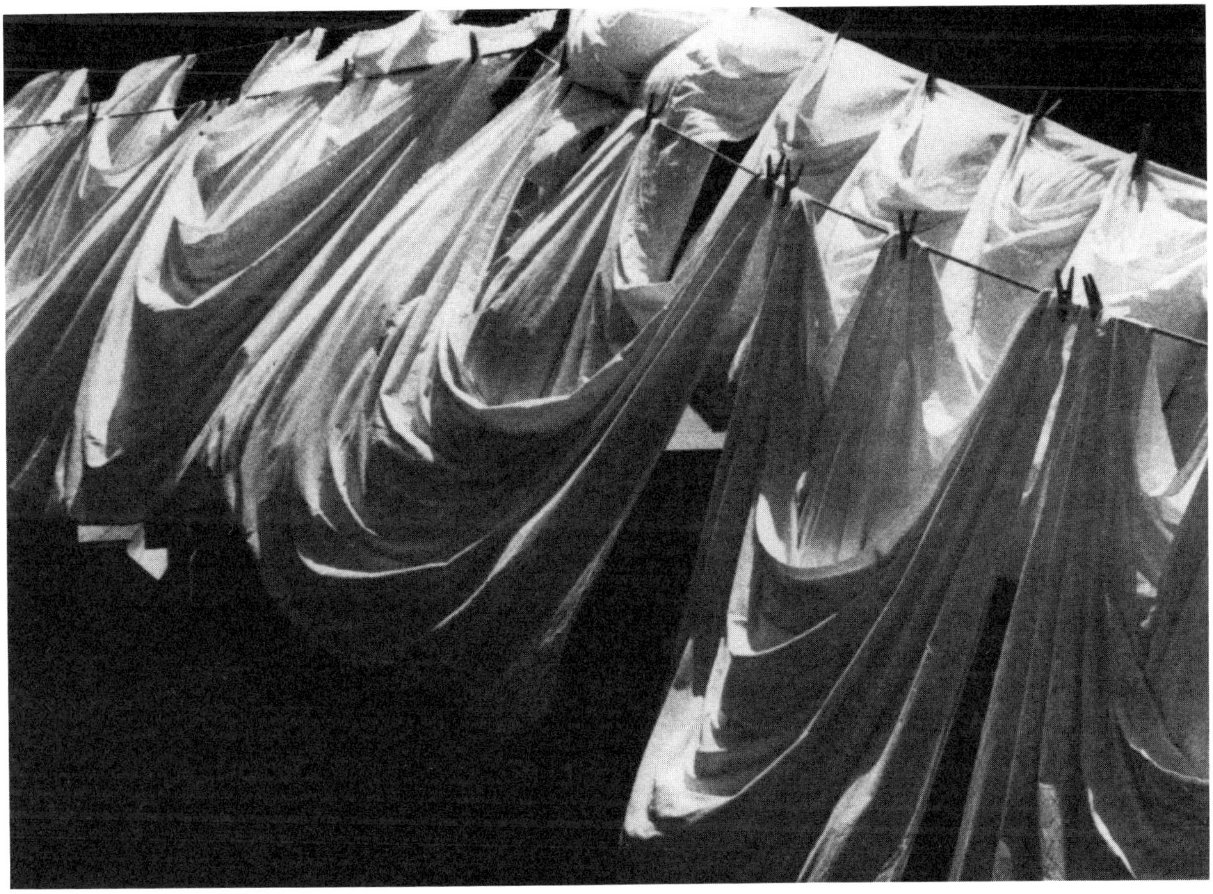

Photograph courtesy of The Swann Galleries

Ralph Steiner's Drying Clothes, *a signed silver print from the 1950s, is an example of one type of photographic art featured at Swann Galleries' auctions.*

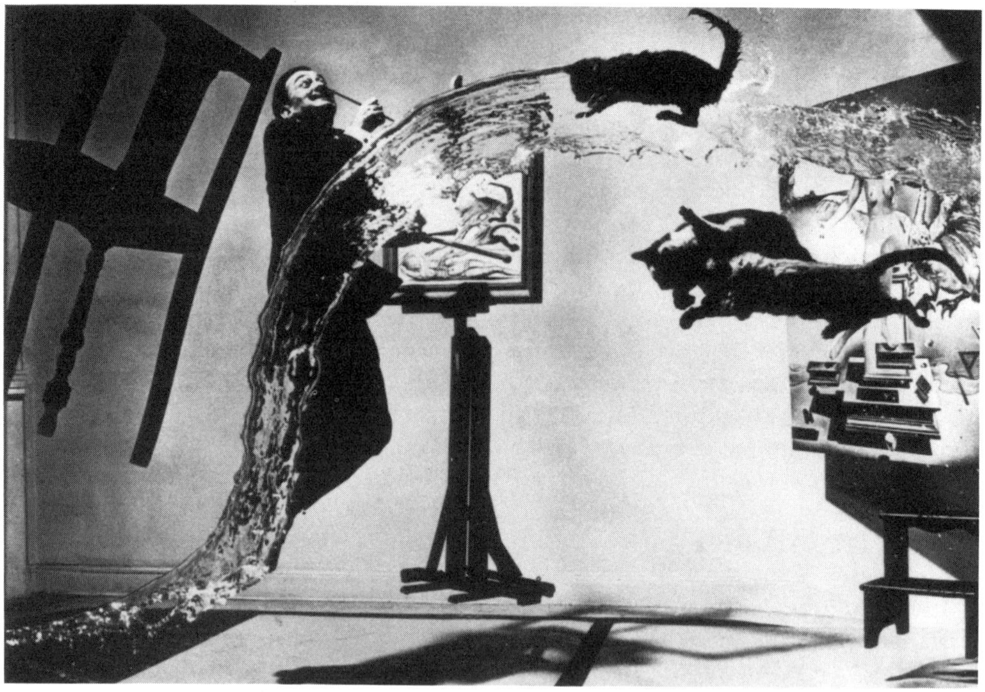

Photograph courtesy of The Swann Galleries

Philippe Halsman's famous photograph Dali Atomicus *is more popular than ever and continues to command attention at photography auctions.*

books. Some of the classics, which appear in almost everyone of our sales, continue to go up in value. There was a period when we were offering less photographic literature and more photographic images, but I've gotten so many requests for more books that we will continue to do that."

Two of the classic books to which Kaplan refers are Paul Strand's 1967 2nd edition of *The Mexican Portfolio* and *Moments Preserved*, an Irving Penn volume, first produced in 1960. The Strand book, one of 1000 numbered copies, brought $2,860 at auction (estimated to bring from $1,500/2,500). The 1st edition Penn, brought $660 (estimated at $400/500). The Strand sale was a record-breaker. According to Kaplan even facsimile editions of vintage photographic literature can command high prices. "*The Pencil of Nature,* William Henry Fox-Talbot's book published about 1842, is probably the first volume of photographic literature. The last time an original copy came up for auction, a dealer named Hans P. Kraus, Jr. created a facsimile edition which sells for about $1,000. The original sells for $40,000, or $50,000, or $60,000, depending on the condition."

Will photographic literature become the last affordable photo-art? "One of the advantages, I think, of a novice collector coming to Swann is that we offer material that might be called the lower end of the spectrum. For example, in the area of photographic literature where we set a record on the sale of the Strand portfolio, it is possible to buy books for as little as $100. That market seems to be very stable and, in fact, escalating, whereas, the other market of 19th and 20th century photographs is definitely going through a transition after the escalation of the '80s."

THE AUCTION HOUSE EDUCATION

Why attend a photography auction? Not only is an auction perhaps the quickest way of educating oneself in maneuvering the photographic art market, but the setting is one of instant gratification on several levels. First, as a potential owner of the work on view at the auction exhibition, you will be able to handle and closely inspect the image. Secondly, attending an auction you will quickly learn current market values. Kaplan whole-heartedly advises attending auction previews. "One of the delightful elements of going to a preview, or the exhibition, is to see the panorama of materials. Ordinarily, there is never an opportunity to see that type of survey of images or literature. During the 150th anniversary of photography it was one

thing where every museum had their show. But one would never think of an auction house as a museum setting, where, in fact, if you want to learn about photography, if you want to see the kinds of materials that are out there, and that are associated with photographers, I don't think there is any better place. In an auction house, you can take the photograph off the wall, you can handle it. Of course, in a museum you'd be arrested if you tried to do that. So there is the hands-on element, which is a good source of educational background."

What advice would Kaplan offer a novice buyer? "*Always examine a print.* Clearly the condition of a print impacts considerably on the investment and thus the price the print might finally realize."

Is timing everything? "The one misconception that people make is that once a photographer's name is splashed all over the newspaper, then the novice collector or the young collector, may feel justified in making a purchase of that photographer's images. But clearly, that is the time when the images might be at the *higher* end of the market. I would suggest to any collector to read alot, get a firm background in what photography is about, and go with your instincts. In other words, try to make choices that represent what *you* are interested in, but based on an educational kind of selection."

Is it necessary to win the state lottery to afford photographic art? "There are modern prints that you can purchase by Cartier-Bresson or Andre Kertez for $400-600. It is important to remember that these are not vintage prints, but there are plenty of images out there that one can purchase for under $1,000 by master photographers. Again, its important to bear in mind if you are going to start collecting, there is everything for everybody's budget!"

COLLECTORS FORECAST

Will the well run dry or will the prices be driven beyond the sky? Daile Kaplan predicts optimistically: "There are always wonderful items out there, and depending upon what comes up for auction, and what people in the audience and community are interested in, there is always the strong possibility of record-breaking or record-setting auctions. In that respect I feel optimistic because one of the great things about photography is the wealth of material out there. And while we do not offer as many 'blue-chip' items as Sotheby's or Christies, I would like to think that we are in a situation where we are offering the next wave of collectibles, whether it is photo-journalism or vernacular imagery. When a Stieglitz photograph sells for $99,000, when a Man Ray goes for over $100,000, we are reaching that parity with the art market. Clearly there are master photographers whose work will continue to command prices where they will eventually reach the million dollar realm and reach a par with a Van Gogh. That may not happen in *our* lifetime, but who knows what historical or social trends will factor in on that. There are so many things to bear in mind.

What it eventually boils down to, the auction world, the auction market, is a social construction of value. What is happening here determines what price an image will achieve. And that's the fascinating part of it...trying to second guess what is going to happen, trying to understand, trying to forsee all the different factors!"

The Swann Galleries are located at 104 East 25th Street, New York, New York 10010. (212) 254-4710.

The major photography auctions are held twice annually, in April and October, by the following leading auction houses:

Sotheby's (212) 606-7240
1334 York Avenue
New York, New York 10021

Sotheby's (213) 274-0340
308 North Rodeo Drive
Beverly Hills, California 90210

Sotheby's (44) 71-493-8080
34-35 New Bond Street
London W1A 2AA, England

Sotheby's (33) 1-4266-4060
3 Rue de Miromesnil
75008 Paris, France

Christie, Manson, & Wood (212) 606-0490
502 Park Avenue
New York, New York 10022

Christie's (44) 71-839-9060
8 King Street, St. James's
London SW1 Y6QT, England

Butterfield & Butterfield (415) 861-7500
220 San Bruno Avenue
San Francisco, California 94103

Butterfield & Butterfield (213) 850-7500
7601 Sunset Boulevard
Los Angeles, California 90046

Chart of Prices Realized

The following examples from the Swann Galleries' October 1990 auction of 19th & 20th century photography illustrate the types of photographic art available at auction. The numbers in parentheses refer to the estimated price-range a piece is expected to bring at auction. The following number is the actual price achieved.

PHOTOGRAPHIC LITERATURE

Berenice Abbott: *Greenwich Village, Today & Yesterday* (1949) First Edition. (150/200) $193

Ansel Adams: *My Camera in the National Parks* (1950) Signed First Edition. (250/350) $358

Henri Cartier-Bresson: *The Decisive Moment* (1952) First American Edition (300/500) $385.

Paul Strand: *The Mexican Portfolio* (1967) One of 1000 numbered copies, signed by Strand (1,500/2,500) $2,860

Camera Work Magazine: #22 The Steichen "Autochrome" Number (1908) Illustrated with 3, 4-color halftones (600/900) $550

ALBUMS, COLLECTIONS, AND STEREOS

Circus: A collection of 420 cartes-de-viste, cabinet cards, postcards of circus performers with descriptions. (1870s) Albumen, printing-out paper and silver prints. (2,000/3,000) $2,420

Civil War: Group of 178 cartes-de-viste of officers, including Sherman, Farragut, Goldsborough, etc., and notables such as Edwin Booth, Tom Thumb, and Henry Clay. (1860s) (600/900) $2,200

Egypt: "On The Nile," an album with 22 cyanotypes of genre and landscape views. (1890s) (400/600) $935

World War II: A limited edition album for members of the American Top Brass, with 75 silver prints depicting the war, in a leather folio. (1940s) (2,000/3,000) $4,400

American West: Group of 13 stereographs by Watkins, Jackson, and Haynes. (1870s-80s) (600/900) $330

PHOTOGRAPHS

Ansel Adams: *Mt. Moran*, signed silver print, 1960s. (1,000/1,500) $935

Ansel Adams: *Portfolio VII*, group of 12 photographs of the West: 11 toned silver prints; one original Polaroid Land photograph; numbered and signed, 1976. (25,000/35,000) $24,200

George N. Barnard: *The Rebel Defenses of Atlanta*, albumen print with inscription, 1863-64. (400/600) $715

Henri Cartier-Bresson: Portrait of Edward Weston, silver print, for *Harper's Bazaar*, 1947. (1,000/1,500) $550

Philippe Halsman: *Dali Atomicus*, silver print, numbered, 1981. (1,000/1,500) $1,320

Man Ray: Portrait of Constantin Brancusi, silver print, signed, 1931. (4,000/6,000) $7,150

Roy Schatt: James Dean, silver print, signed, 1954. (600/900) $1,760

Ralph Steiner: *Drying Clothes*, silver print, signed, 1950s. (800/1,200) $1,430

James Van Der Zee: *Daddy Grace*, silver print, 1930s. (600/900) $825

Weegee: *Portrait of Transvestite Robber*, silver print, 1940s. (700/1,000) $523

The following selections are from the 1990 Butterfield & Butterfield photography auctions:

Henri Cartier-Bresson: *The Decisive Moment*, published 1952. (300/400) $275

Paul Strand: *The Mexican Portfolio*, 20 photogravures, signed and numbered, 1930s. (1,000/1,500) $1,430

Mathew Brady: Portrait of President Ulysses S. Grant, albumen print, 1869. (800/1,000) $990

Helmut Newton: *Charlotte Rampling, Arles*, gelatin silver print, signed, 1973. (600/800) $1,320

Alfred Steiglitz: *Winter-Fifth Avenue*, photogravure from *Camera Work* Number 12, 1905. (500/700) $935

Cindy Sherman: Untitled Self Portrait, gelatin silver print, signed and numbered, 1975. (1,000/1,500) $1,100

Edward S. Curtis: *Aphrodite (The Spirit of the Sea)*, blue-toned gelatin silver print, circa 1920. (2,500/3,000) $2,475

Richard Avedon: *Andy Warhol, Artist, New York City*, gelatin silver print, numbered, 1969. (1,500/1,800) $16,500

Laura Gilpin: *Navajo Family*, gelatin silver print, signed, 1950s. (800/1,200) $2,200

Henri Cartier-Bresson: *Rue Mouffetard*, gelatin silver print, 1954. (2,000/2,200) $4,675

George Platt Lynes: Yul Brynner, gelatin silver print, 1942. (500/700) $770

Imogen Cunningham: *The Unmade Bed*, gelatin silver print, signed, 1957. (6,000/9,000) $12,100

Judy Dater: *Imogen & Twinka*, gelatin silver print, signed and numbered, 1974. (1,200/1,800) $1,320

George Hurrell: Joan Crawford, gelatin silver print, signed and numbered, circa 1938. (500/700) $605

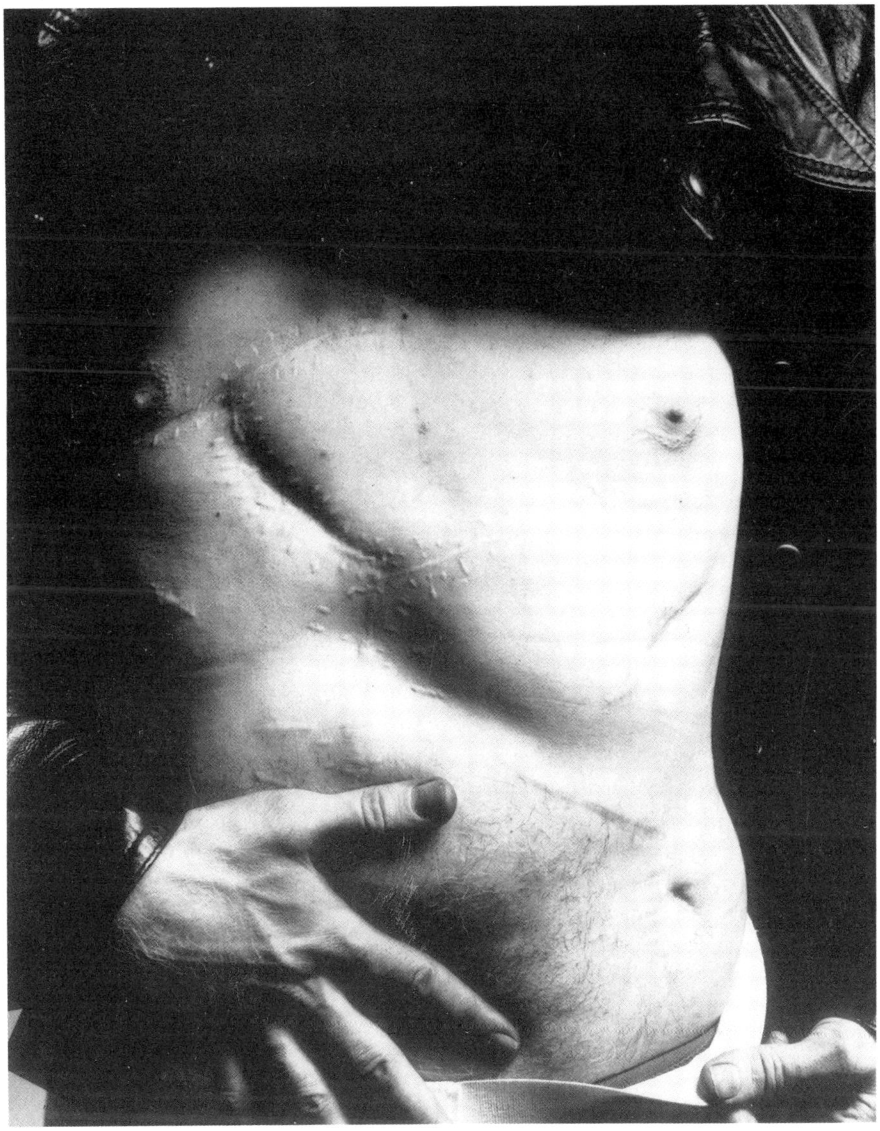

Photograph courtesy of Butterfield & Butterfield

Richard Avedon's Andy Warhol, Artist, NYC *from 1969 and printed c. 1975, was one of the hot properties at a Butterfield and Butterfield auction. The photo, which features Warhol's wounds from an assassination attempt, was expected to bring from $1,500/1,800. The image ultimately achieved $16,500!*

Presenting Your Portfolio

Sometimes there is a lot to that over-used adage "you only have one opportunity to make a first impression." Although most members of our over-analyzing society would like to think themselves beyond making value judgments based on first impressions, the fact remains that first impressions are generally instinctive reactions. With that in mind, try to remember in searching for a gallery or exhibition space for that first show, that a lack of information or an improperly planned attack may not allow for a second impression.

All galleries, from the local community exhibition spaces to the famous world-class names, maintain individual standards with regard to the type of art they want to exhibit and the manner in which the art will ultimately be displayed. As will become clear upon reading the entries in the gallery listings section of this handbook, curators, managers, and gallery owners are generally quite specific as to the type of material they are interested in reviewing and the manner in which they prefer it be submitted. *Although there are no submission rules written in stone,* there are some standard guidelines that generally hold true. The best thing you can do for yourself is to listen to the professionals.

First, if a gallery indicates it is open to reviewing your portfolio and they view material only in slide format, one page of twenty slides is appropriate. Twenty may not seem like a lot to you, but keep in mind that gallery personnel are well experienced in reviewing portfolios and if they're interested in what they see, you will be asked to show them more. Of course, it is sometimes tough to choose your own most outstanding work and tougher still to second guess what the viewer, probably a total stranger, is looking for. The best approach is to choose material that does not illustrate your growth as a photographer, but that illustrates a theme or emphasizes a unique creative direction. For example, if you've photographed a series of abandoned movie houses, this will provide a theme and perhaps give the reviewer an idea for your exhibition. However, most reviewers will expect for *you* to have a clear concept in mind for your exhibition.

Some reviewers are not interested in viewing slides at all and will only view work in print format as it is meant to be viewed hanging on a wall. (In most cases unframed, and sometimes even without matting.) Although the approach should be the same as presenting your work in slide format, keep in mind that if the gallery requests submitted prints be high quality, finished pieces, that is exactly what they will expect to see. Also keep in mind that this endeavor is probably going to cost you quite a bit more than submitting work in slide format unless you also happen to be a talented printer!

As you read the gallery listings you might come across an entry that seems to be written directly to you. Unfortunately, that entry may be for a gallery in Costa Mesa, California and you may reside in Des Moines, Iowa. The gallery requests that all submissions contain a maximum of twenty slides and be accompanied by a resume, artist's statement and press-clippings. Okay, you have had two exhibitions in Des Moines already, and you've even received some favorable reviews, and you think now is the time to branch out. But how will you deliver your portfolio to California?

An important rule in submitting your work anywhere is to not lose control of original slides, negatives, or art work. The only time *original* slides or art should be shown is when you are going to accompany the portfolio for the review or you are retrieving the material on the same day. Obviously every situation will not allow your being there, and some gallery curators prefer to view work without the participation of the artist. For this reason, time should be spent on finding and establishing a relationship with a quality slide duping house or printer which will enable you to furnish the reviewer with samples that are truly representative of the original material. The importance of your relationship with the duping or printing technician should not be underestimated. This new best-friend is going to ensure that the blues and magentas in your dupes are true, the contrast intact, and that your whites are clean.

Now that you have gotten used to the idea that your portfolio may be traveling without you and you are confident that your dupes or work prints are of good quality, all you need do is deliver the goods. If you are dropping your portfolio off at a local gallery, you will have already been furnished with a time schedule. However, once you have confirmed, via telephone or letter (the gallery will usually let you know the preferred mode of communication), that the gallery in Costa Mesa will welcome the opportunity to review your photographs, you now must choose the best method of shipping the portfolio. Federal Express, U.P.S., and, yes, even the U.S. Post Office's Express Mail service can provide insured, prompt delivery of your portfolio. Not only do you have the option of insuring the portfolio, you will have the security of a signed delivery receipt. But don't relax yet - you will also have to work out details for the return of the portfolio. A little communication with the gallery will probably allow for return delivery via the same method. *Do not assume that the gallery will provide return shipment!*

A brief word about the information accompanying the portfolio. Resumes are almost always requested and should only contain basic personal information, and succinct background information regarding previous exhibitions and related photographic endeavors. Some reviewers are interested in an "artist's statement." Generally this is a brief essay clearly communicating the photographer's theme, which in turn should be illustrated by the accompanying photographs. Not only will the statement help sell the exhibition idea, should you receive a show it will aid the gallery personnel in "talking-up" your work. Press-clippings are also of interest to reviewers and should naturally be included. (Unless of course, they're negative, in which case you probably no longer have them!)

If you have gotten as far as submitting your portfolio to a prospective gallery, you've taken that first giant step. Hopefully, you've taken that step with a dose of reality. Yes, it can be a hard, cruel, competitive world out there and perhaps your first experience will not be a positive one. Some reviewers may offer little, if any, comments on your work and others may go so far as to schedule an appointment to discuss your portfolio in detail. Always approach a gallery or museum as a learning experience. Few photographers are granted an exhibition with their first portfolio review. However, many photographers have received helpful, important guidance and direction from the criticisms and wisdom of experienced curators.

Equally important is doing one's "homework" before contacting a gallery or exhibition space. There are numerous ways to keep up with the evolving photography scene. Become familiar with the exhibition trends featured in museums and galleries. Read the many photographic magazines which cover the photographic art market. Attend shows in local and regional galleries and learn about the type of photography the galleries are known for exhibiting. Above all, don't waste the time of the gallery reviewer. *Remember, the first impression could be the only impression!*

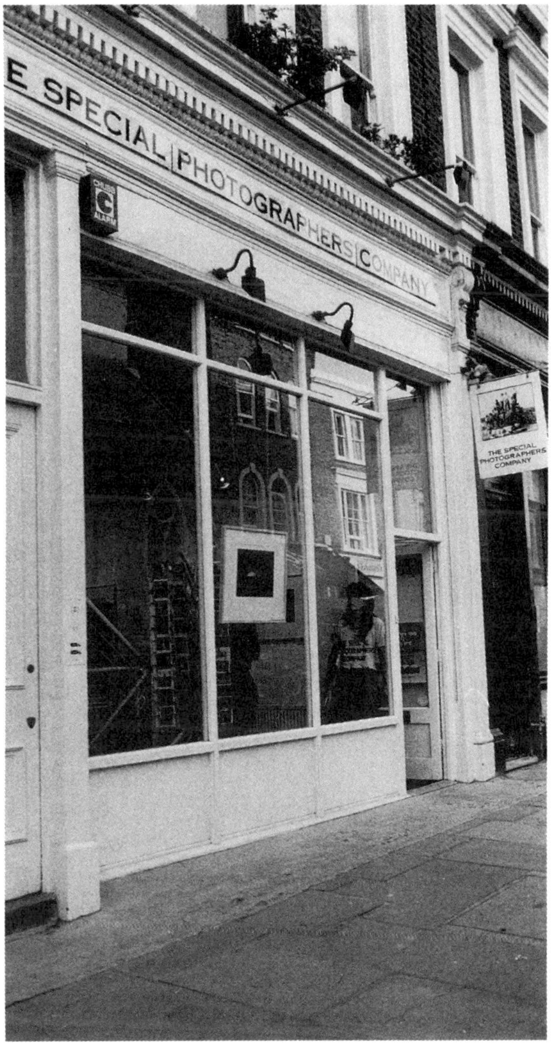

Photograph by Peter L. Gould

London's The Special Photographer's Company regularly presents a broad spectrum of photographic art.

The Professionals Speak: Words of Wisdom from Curators and Gallery Owners

In hopes of providing an informative and timely overview on the photographic gallery and exhibition world, I asked a select group of art professionals their opinions on a variety of topics pertaining to the experience of exhibiting photography.

The gallery directors and curators, and their comments offered here, represent a typical, yet broad, cross-section of experiences. The speakers represent photographic showcases as diverse as arts institutions, fine art galleries, and experimental exhibition spaces. Geographically, they represent the north, south, east, and west, and Canada too. And although the topics put before them are fairly general, you will find the responses, in some cases, as varied as the organizations and regions they represent.

Ben Breard
AFTERIMAGE GALLERY
Dallas, Texas

Ben Breard opened Afterimage in 1971 after receiving his master's degree in photojournalism. Afterimage was one of the first fine art galleries devoted exclusively to photography.

FINDING A GALLERY: "First know the kind of work a gallery handles; the kind of photographers. By that I mean, some of them handle only 'big names.' You have to get that kind of information first."

PORTFOLIOS: "Should contain only the very best work. Not the work that the photographer *thinks* will

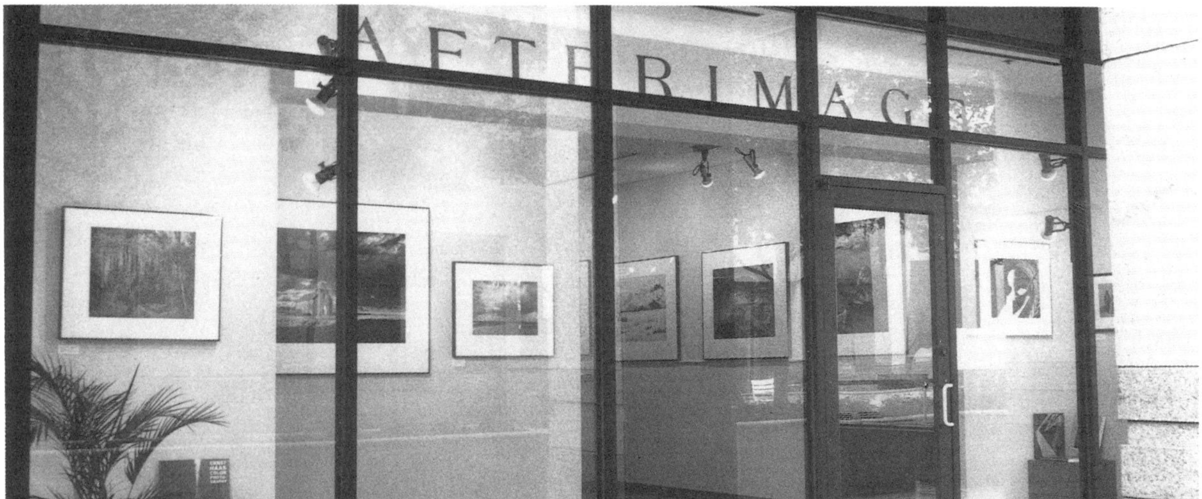

Photograph courtesy of Afterimage Gallery

Afterimage Gallery, Dallas, was one of the first galleries in the U.S. to exclusively exhibit photographic art.

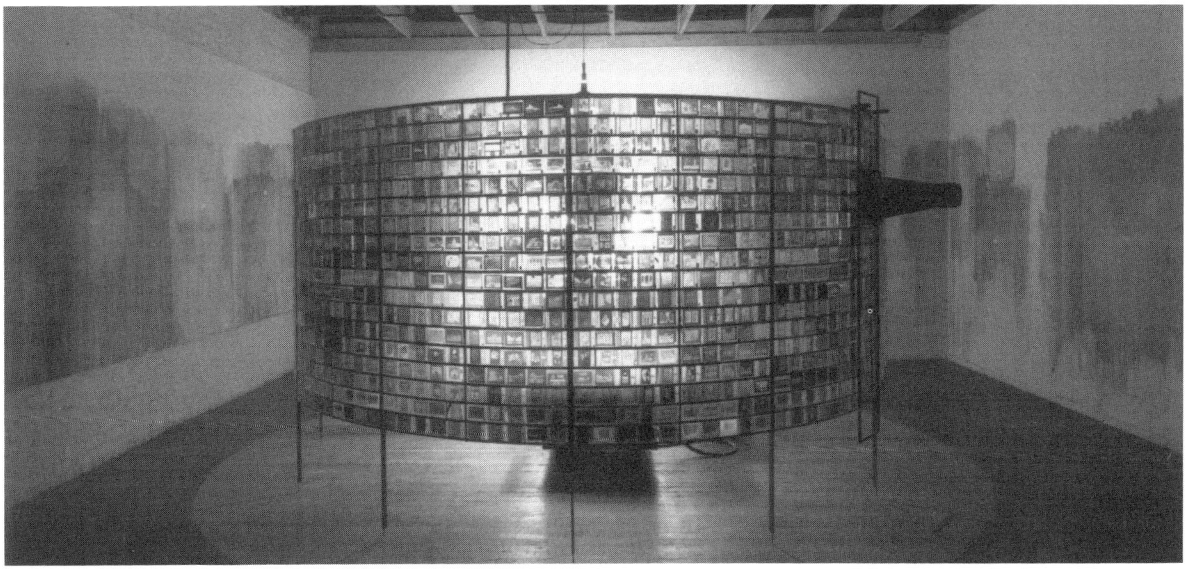

San Francisco Camerawork presents a variety of photography such as the mixed-media installation pictured here, Subjective Archives, *by Bruce Tomb and John Randolph.*

sell the best. It shouldn't be more than 15 or 20 images."

PORTFOLIO MISTAKES: "The biggest mistake that people make is that they can't edit. I've had people show me portfolios with a hundred images and it just dilutes the work. The other thing is that they're not ready yet - they're not good enough yet. I don't like to use that phrase, but they sometimes just need more years. They don't have a big enough inventory of good pictures."

THE OUTSTANDING PORTFOLIO: "I see maybe 6 to 10 a year. But that doesn't mean I accept the work. Many times it's not that different from somebody we already have or its just not saleable. Maybe that number is a little low."

THE EXHIBITION EXPERIENCE: "The reward of exhibiting work is the satisfaction that other people are looking at it, and hopefully appreciating it...more than just your immediate family or professors. Also there may be some monetary gain but not necessarily. It also keeps you *motivated.* In preparing for a show you have to work hard to get those prints out. Another advantage of being in a gallery is that gallery directors can recommend a photographer's work to other dealers. When someone comes in and shows me their work and resume and it mentions that they're carried by various galleries, that lets me know that they're more professional as opposed to a resume that just lists college shows."

PHOTOGRAPHIC TRENDS: "In this part of the country we get more landscape work than most places. There are some trends that are national trends but they may not be exhibited around here. For example, post-modern or set-up scenes."

THE PHOTOGRAPHY BUYER: "We have customers all the way from very sophisticated collectors down to people buying their first prints. Usually something nice and colorful. Also corporations that mostly buy for decor. We sell quite a lot of the new guys like Christopher Burkette from Oregon who does 20 x 24 C-chromes. He was down at *Fotofest* and nobody had ever heard of him. He carried his portfolio around and now he's carried by several galleries all over the country. Also we sell a lot of the old French guys: Doisneau, Ronis - they're real popular here. Their modern prints are well priced. 19th century vintage prints - nobody cares two flips for that here - it doesn't sell at all."

Marnie Gillette
SAN FRANCISCO CAMERAWORK
San Francisco, California

Marnie Gillette is the Executive Director of Camerawork, a post she has held for the past 7 years. She was also involved with the well-known, now defunct, Light Gallery of New York City and previously held the position of Curator of Exhibitions at the Center for Creative Photography in Tucson.

FINDING A GALLERY: "First they must find a gallery that would be interested in their type of work. We get a lot of people coming in here that don't even

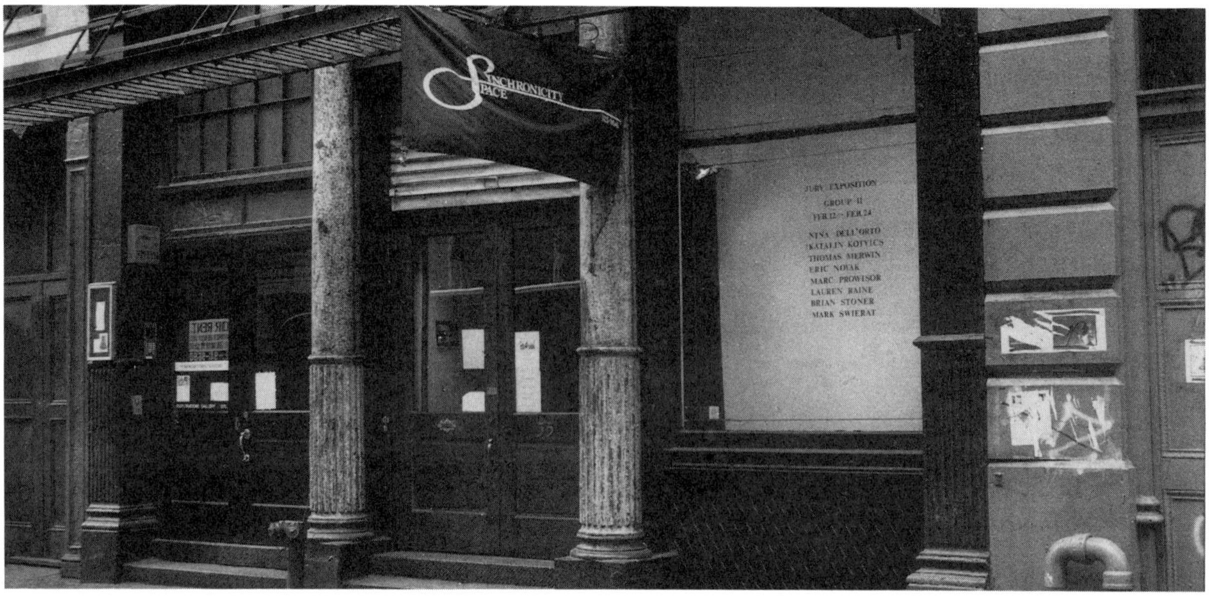

Photograph by Barbara Rosen

Synchronicity Space is one of the many unique exhibition spaces which have garnered New York City's Soho district world notice.

know that Camerawork is non-profit and that we don't represent people. So basically, first people should research ahead of time before they even approach a gallery."

PORTFOLIOS: "A good portfolio should include about 20 prints, and it should usually entail one body of work so that it shows a strength through several images, not a diversity of images, style, technique. Once you've seen the initial body of work you can get further into discussions of what they've done in the past or what they hope to do in the future. Really, they should just take their strength in one area."

PORTFOLIO MISTAKES: "When you're meeting with somebody and they have four portfolio boxes, that's a little much usually for someone to want to concentrate on and look through. Thats why I think it should be a tight portfolio of about 20 prints."

THE OUTSTANDING PORTFOLIO: "We have slides submitted to us and probably out of that work we may show 10 people out of 300 bodies of work that we see. We're constantly looking at work. Then we have a committee that looks through the material. As far as unique and different work, there's a lot of good work out there."

THE EXHIBITION EXPERIENCE: "I think the primary value is for the photographer, him or herself, to see their work displayed all at one time and to see how it has evolved and to learn from that experience. Secondly they get feedback from other people. But initially, the most important thing is for the photographer to really view it all in one place and really take a critical look at it for themselves, and see what they're creating and what will be the next work that they do."

PHOTOGRAPHIC TRENDS: "Quite a bit of work we've seen recently has to do with individuals and identity, and its much more personal than work that I've seen in the last two years. People seem to be turning more to the personal - a lot of individual expression."

THE PHOTOGRAPHY BUYER: "We just sell one or two prints per year. Sales are really not our purpose. Our purpose is for *education* as a non-profit gallery. So we show more emerging artists, or work that is experimental. For instance we wouldn't have a show of Robert Mapplethorpe's work and not because of the content or anything, but because he's just so well-known. Our position is that we're trying to help other artists have an exhibition space."

John Smith-Amato
SYNCHRONICITY SPACE
New York, New York

John Smith-Amato is the Director of Synchronicity Space, a gallery for painting and drawing which also frequently features photography. An exhibited painter, Smith-Amato has taught at Columbia University and also currently teaches at Synchronicity Space. The gallery is located in New York City's Soho district.

FINDING A GALLERY: "He or she should first prepare a selection of 4 x 5 transparencies. Primarily its the preparation. First thing when you walk into a gallery you should have your presentation ready and really professional for the sake of clarity. The gallery owners usually know what they're looking for, or the direction they're going, and they'll want to make sure that the work is going to fit-in in that direction. One of the things I like to look at is 4 x 5 transparencies."

PORTFOLIOS: "Not just contacts! Some finished product should be included just to show the growing relationship between when an original shot was taken and the developing, so the gallery owners can see for themselves the progression of the work - to see how it grew to the finished product. That's really important; especially if you're dealing with a knowledgeable gallery."

PORTFOLIO MISTAKES: "One thing I think, is that they should be there for the presentation. *I think it's a big mistake to leave your work and then expect someone to give it the kind of attention that is necessary.* You can forego scheduling and timing, and whatever personal things, to go along with whatever scheduling is made available. There is too much that goes on of a personal nature at a presentation."

THE OUTSTANDING PORTFOLIO: "Maybe one out of every 8 to 10. I make a referral if a particular work doesn't fit into my direction. I make phone calls for them. Regardless of the direction, they should, of course, pay attention to the galleries for awhile before they make their presentations. But they should never hesitate to walk into a gallery to show their work."

THE EXHIBITION EXPERIENCE: "In the photographic world there is a large amount of work and with an exhibition they can see where they are. They can get a quick understanding of where they're coming from and where they're going."

PHOTOGRAPHIC TRENDS: "Believe it or not, I'm starting to see greater objectivity come back into it. There was a glut for awhile of over-technique, over-involvement by the photographer. Now they're starting to back off and allowing the image the full space. It seems like they're becoming more objective again, rather than tampering with the image. There seems to be more attention to *aesthetics*."

THE PHOTOGRAPHY BUYER: "They're still buying and looking toward the original, and the buyers of photography are coming from the middle class. They would love to be buying paintings, but if they find photography that is painterly, then it seems to sell."

Marita Holdaway
BENHAM GALLERY
Seattle, Washington

Marita Holdaway, (along with partner Lisa Sharamitaro) was inspired to open Benham Gallery after reading a book by Ansel Adams. The gallery which is devoted exclusively to photography also sponors the annual International Invitational Photography Exhibition. Holdaway is also a working commerical photographer who specializes in publicity photography and head-shots for actors and actresses.

FINDING A GALLERY: "Probably the best thing to do is to start making phone calls and checking to

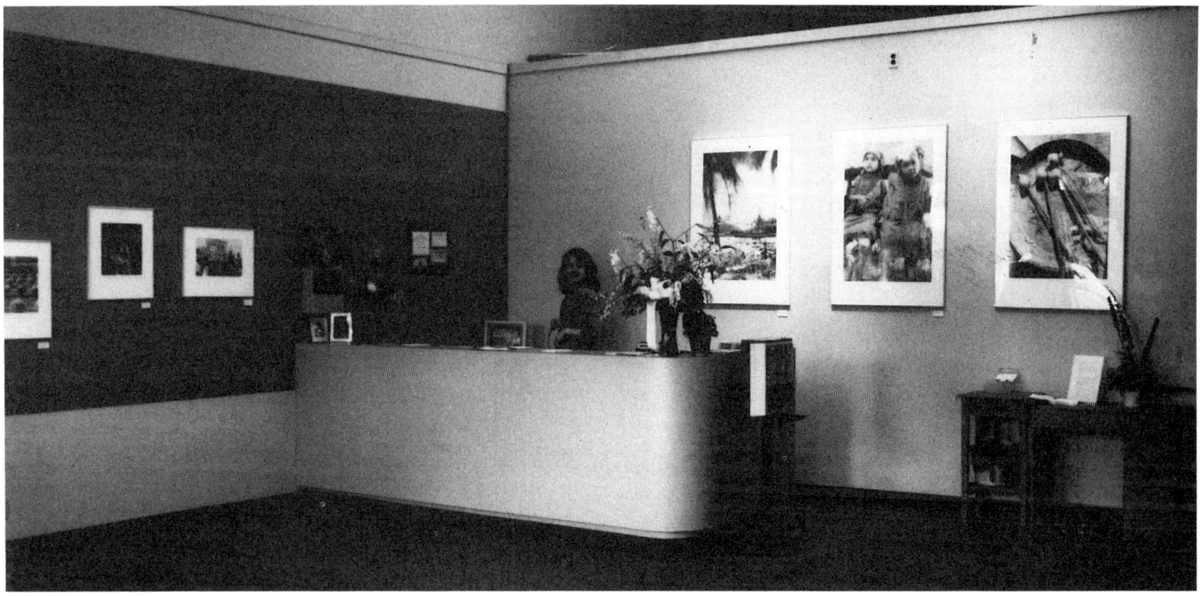

Photograph courtesy of Benham Studio Gallery

Seattle's Benham Studio Gallery is devoted to showcasing the work of promising new talent.

see if the gallery has any openings, as far as shows, and what they require for portfolio review. They should go directly and find out what the gallery is all about."

PORTFOLIOS: "A good portfolio should have a strong sense of the photographer's feeling. A person should be able to look through a portfolio and be able to tell that the photographs are done by the same photographer. A lot of photographers will bring in portraits, and landscapes, and streetscenes, and studio work, and that's not really what we're looking for for a show. We're looking for something that has *continuity* through the entire layout of it. When someone walks into the gallery to see a show, we want them to look at an image and be drawn to the next image, and the next image, etc. And that usually is accomplished by having some sort of continuity in a show."

PORTFOLIO MISTAKES: "Showing all their work. We review portfolios twice a year and ideally they should come in and show us what they have as an idea for a show. That would be the material we want to see. But some people get confused and they bring in everything. And we ask, 'Well, what is your show?' If they don't have an idea of what personal kind of thing they are into doing, or what they are trying to put together, then we can't show their work."

THE OUTSTANDING PORTFOLIO: "When we review portfolios we probably see anywhere from 20 to 30 per session. Usually, our experience is we get 8 to 10 worthwhile portfolios and we can only schedule 6. We schedule half a year at a time. We show really diversified types of photography. The majority of our photographers are local people and they are up-and-coming - they've had just a very few shows or they've never had a one-person show."

THE EXHIBITION EXPERIENCE: "The value of an exhibition would just be the experience of having an entire show up in a comprehensive setting and the exposure that comes from the experience. We are not a big sales gallery; we're more of an exhibition gallery."

PHOTOGRAPHIC TRENDS: "We probably see more street photography. Like cityscapes, usually featuring people in everyday settings. Like documentary style, and not necessarily very pretty. That's what we're seeing the most of. Other than that it's various other things."

THE PHOTOGRAPHY BUYER: "We don't really depend upon selling photographic work to keep the doors open, so it allows for us to show people who don't necessarily have a sales reputation. Like Duane Michaels, or any photographer who has a reputation. If you show their work you're gonna sell just because of the name. But we can show people who are more contemporary, that are just starting, and it allows them to get exposure. We usually sell about one piece or two pieces per exhibit. It's usually the most striking piece as far as the content and feeling of the photograph. They're not generally buying the real calm flower photograph or cityscene. It's usually a little more challenging. We just had an international exhibition and we sold about 7 prints of this one photograph by Austrian photographer Matthias Hermann called "Mr. Prof. Willi Schmidt." It's a photograph of this very distinguished looking gentleman behind the wheel of the very first Jaguar that came off the rack; but the technique and feeling of the photograph was so incredible that it just bowled people over. That's been the most successful photograph we've had."

Ted Hartman
MINNEAPOLIS INSTITUTE OF THE ARTS
Minneapolis, Minnesota

Ted Hartman started out at the Minneapolis Institute of the Arts as staff photographer and 20 years later rules as photography curator for the department which he helped create. Hartman regularly curates exhibitions from the permanent collection which travel to a regional community of arts organizations and small museums.

FINDING A GALLERY: "The artist needs to be pretty informed about what a gallery or museum typically shows. What their profile is, if you will. It's crazy to send a certain kind of work to a gallery that has, for instance, no track record in showing, say, historical work or museum that doesn't do anything with contemporary photography."

PORTFOLIOS: "In our case the first level of contact is a portfolio of slides, a succinct distillation of the work that you feel is at the center of what you as a photographer are about - and not try and second guess and sort of play the audience or play the game of second-guessing; trying to slant the work to fit what you think the gallery is looking for. Be *confident* in your own work and your own vision, and select those pictures that are very much to the point about how you see yourself as an artist photographer. *Don't try to cover all the bases."*

PORTFOLIO MISTAKES: "It would certainly be a mistake, and it rarely happens anymore, that people just send 8 x 10 prints. Or it's all over the map - a selection which needs to be lean and modest, instead

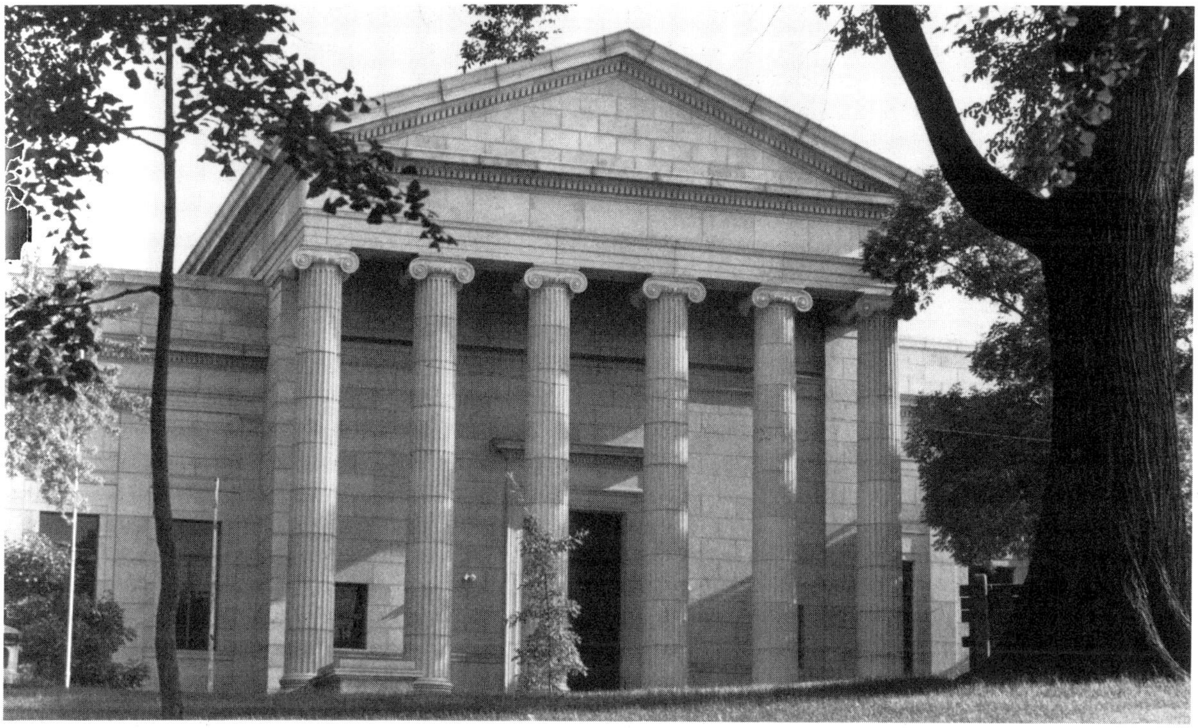

Photograph courtesy of The Minneapolis Institute of the Arts

The Minneapolis Institute of the Arts was one of the first American museums to build a photography collection.

it's all over the map. It needs to be really focused in terms of point of view. More is not better. Less is better. Current work. It's all well and good to see early work, but what are you doing *now*?"

THE OUTSTANDING PORTFOLIO: "Seeing work that is worthy of exhibition is one thing. The capacity of the gallery or the museum to fit all of that into an exhibition year, or calendar, is another proposition. There's always far more deserving artists and potential exhibitions than there is time to do it. That's what is tough on this side of the proposition - *simply because the work is deserving doesn't assure that it's going to get shown*. There are always lots of other priorities. Museums, for instance, need to balance their exhibition program between shows from the permanent collection and shows that are organized by other institutions - historical, contemporary, - and unless it's a gallery devoted to one particular point-of-view, say the work of younger photographers, any given artist's work must fit in somehow, and be considered against the larger needs. Most artists just can't be all that aware of the process. So understanding that there are alot of things that need to be taken into account by the gallery director or museum curator; being informed about museum practice, getting to know curators, and how they operate, etc. That familiarity will allow the photographer to be a little more realistic about what to expect. It's unreasonable to think that just because you call up or send your portfolio that something's going to happen. That ain't real life. We receive tons and tons of unsolicited stuff, to the point where there's no way we can write a personalized, sensitive comment. I think that's the case at most museums. Artists seem to be very much into a system now and they're very systematic in sending the same material to a lot of different places. It's a shot in the dark and I think that artists have to realize it's a shot in the dark. The only thing I can assure people of is that work will be, indeed kept, filed, considered, and reviewed. And if it is pertinent, we will contact the artists and pursue this. In either case, whether it's a potential exhibition, or purchase, or both."

THE EXHIBITION EXPERIENCE: "The opportunity to get a sense of how your work is perceived by an audience and from either the curator or gallery director. Getting that kind of feed-back, whether it contradicts or confirms what you think you're doing. Having an opportunity to have an audience."

PHOTOGRAPHIC TRENDS: "I'm very reluctant speculating about trends. But it's pretty evident; all you have to do is look through gallery listings of current exhibitions to realize that there are cycles and waves of work. That is, there's a lot of very trendy stuff. That's always going to be the case, what's fashionable. Currently there's alot of work that looks just like the Starn Twins or just like Cindy Sherman or Bruce Webber or Robert Mapplethorpe. Those are kind of predictable, and it's pretty rare to see something that's very strong but not trendy. There's also quite a resurgence of interest, I've noticed, in the last couple of years in a kind of photojournalistic image. Heavily manipulated work, journalistic kind of work and autobiographical, and, of course, landscapes are persistent."

THE PHOTOGRAPHY BUYER: The Minneapolis Institute of the Arts does not sell photography.

Terry Costantino
GALLERY 44
Toronto, Canada

Terry Costantino is Associate Director of Gallery 44, a photographic gallery devoted to expanding the boundaries of the art. A graduate of Ryerson Polytechnical with a BAA in Media Studies with Still Photography Option, Costantino was also part of the team behind the now defunct magazine, Photo Communique.

FINDING A GALLERY: "In our particular case we're part of an artist-run network of galleries across Canada. There is a mandate for all of the galleries, and also there are submission requirements, deadlines, and all of that sort of thing. So one could use the available information and do it that way and find a suitable gallery. In photography there are very few dealers and commercial galleries, so most photo-artists would be associated with a gallery that is not specifically photography. In terms of public galleries, the situation, as far as I understand it, is still kind of they come to you. So in terms of getting in at the ground floor, it would be the artist run center's network."

PORTFOLIOS: "We prefer to look at slides at least in the beginning. We have three submission deadlines a year and we take in slides. We like a written statement about the work. We prefer to look at work that can be viewed as a body of work, whether it be on a specific topic, or in a specific area of photography. It should also include a detailed slide list that gives the original dimensions of the work, the medium, and a good CV, something concise but inclusive. Some people do like to give us prints and that's okay, but we prefer not to have them in the first round. If we're really interested in someone's work, of course, we'll either go to their studio or have them come in and show us a portfolio. A really important thing in terms of our submissions is the written documentation. It can be the downfall. As much as we'd like to believe that work can stand on its own, a well-written, not too lengthy, artist statement helps a lot. Because in our case we're not seeing the artist, we're seeing only this representation they're sending us. How we choose our shows is through an exhibition selection committee and it goes through several rounds where we start off with small groups so that we can discuss the work at length and then we have a faster meeting with a larger group. So it is really important to be clear in all your materials."

PORTFOLIO MISTAKES: "I think the biggest mistake people make is in not looking at other photographs and not realizing the intent of the specific gallery that they're applying to. If your work is obviously unsuitable, then we recognize that right away and we can't spend a lot of time on it. Sometimes the quality of the presentation - such as making it very clear - is this a work print or do you consider this an exhibition quality print?"

THE OUTSTANDING PORTFOLIO: "We have 10 exhibitions per year. Some of those are group. Then we 2 or 3 person shows and then solo exhibitions. We try to vary that so through the year we could show as many as say, 20 to 25 artists. With exhibition deadlines we're probably looking at 40 to 100 portfolios at each round. So percentage wise what makes it into the gallery is quite small. And personally, the amount of striking work, work with a concept where the meaning and the technical ability have come together to make the work outstanding is not a lot. It's probably 3 out of 40, maybe not even that."

THE EXHIBITION EXPERIENCE: "It gets your name out in front of many people. It helps establish you to some degree as a professional artist which can help you in many other ways. You can establish yourself as a business, as an artist. You can apply for grants, etc. But it's sort of contingent on the fact that as an artist you do show your work. So the promotional aspect is very important. I would hope feedback from people if you're able to be there; positive feeling about your own work; and the will to continue, are the benefits."

PHOTOGRAPHIC TRENDS: "We're having an exhibition of work from Quebec which the curator has divided into two areas she calls: 'Autobiography' and 'Subject-Object-Subtext,' and there are pretty prominent trends displayed here. The trend grows out of the '60s documentary tradition, but it presents the personal through this tradition and hopefully universalizes it to some degree. So the work is highly personal, yet conceptual at the same time. Also, and I don't know why this is, but the work tends to be almost black on black. It's very difficult to view some of it just because it's so dark and there could be glare and lighting problems, etc. But it's also very interesting technique that hasn't been used all that much. I think we've just come through a heavy period of self-portraiture, and I don't know if that's over or not. I don't seem to be seeing as much of it as I did. And a slight resurgence of interest in landscape."

THE PHOTOGRAPHY BUYER: "We do sell work if the artist wants us to and it's an accessible size. We never sell, for instance, photography such as an installation piece. We define photography in the broadest sense. So if there's any photographic element in the piece, or if it's photographically derived then we would consider it. Our mandate is to push the boundaries of photography. So we would show what we consider the traditional genres, but it must be offering something new to the viewer. That's what people who frequent our gallery expect. And why I wish more of the artists who bring their portfolios to us would come to the gallery and realize the type of work we're showing. So normally we would not show the traditional portraiture or landscape unless it somehow leaped beyond the norm in some way. Our patrons are pretty consistent."

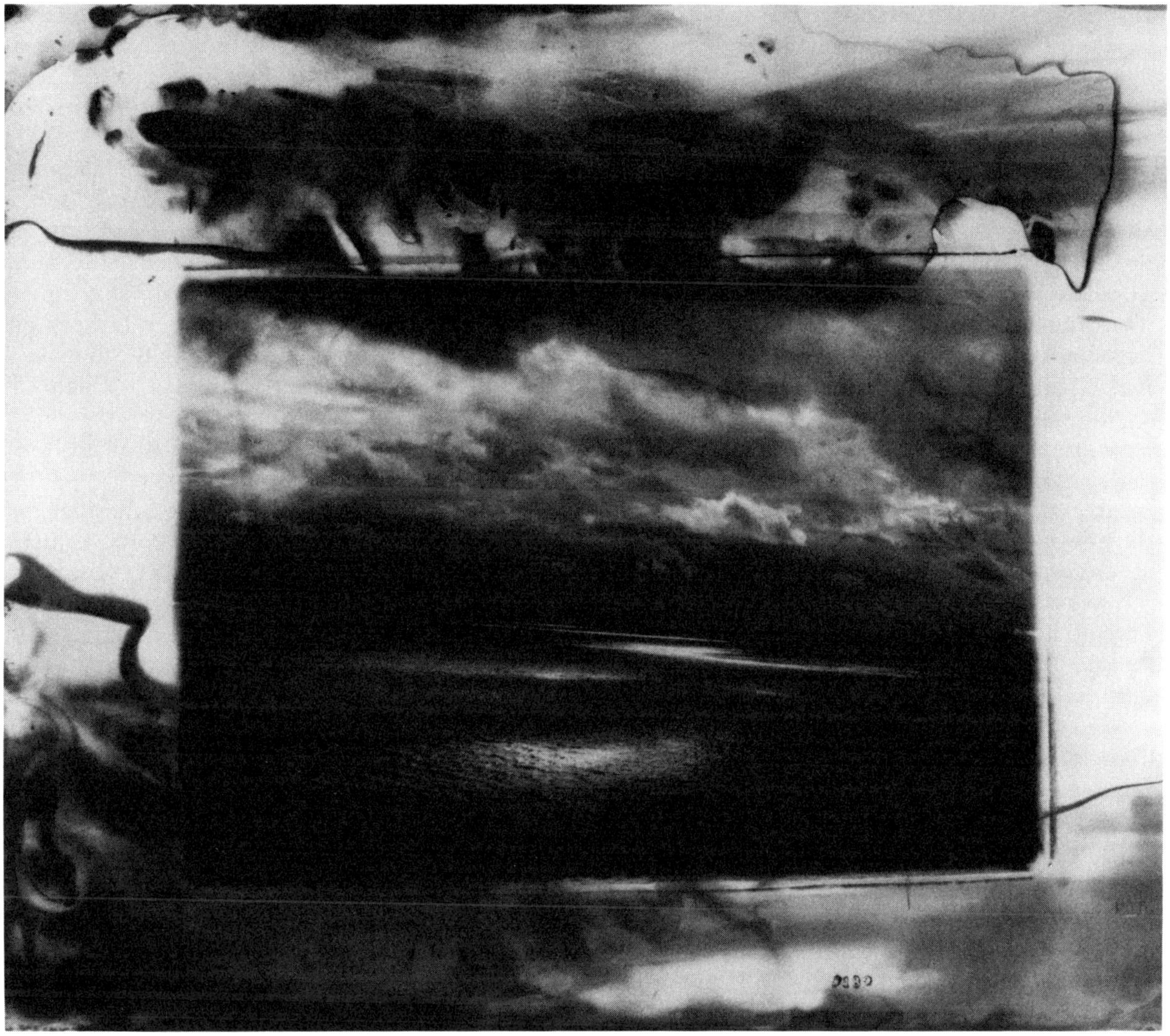

Photography courtesy of Gallery 44 Centre for Contemporary Photography

#482 *from the exhibition* Dynamic Title: Autobiography, *by Gallery 44 founding member Verant Richards (1951-1988), was featured in a posthumous retrospective at the Toronto gallery.*

Gallery & Museum Listings

The majority of the galleries and museums listed in this section have completed questionnaires which have provided us with the information contained in the individual entries. The listings have a two-fold purpose: they are intended to be used as a "meeting place" or "introduction service" for photographers and gallery owners, and also as a guide to museum collections and the outstanding galleries worldwide which regularly showcase photographic art.

Most of the entry information is self-explanatory, but because the information provided may be crucial for those seeking to connect with the right gallery, some explanation is in order. Attempts have been made to offer as much information as possible within the confines of a limited space. However, it is inevitable that sometimes information is lost (or confused) in the translation - in this case that could be from French, German, Polish, and yes, even English!

As you read the entries, it will become quite clear that galleries are exhibiting many different types of photographic art; and thus there are many different interests and guidelines. If you are a photographer reading these listings to find the gallery that might be right for you, please remember that it is in your own best interest to read closely and try to follow the dictates of the submission guidelines. *Above all, do not waste your time and that of the gallery director by approaching a gallery or exhibition space that is clearly not appropriate.*

If you are perusing the entries as a spectator, remember to check the gallery or museum's exhibition schedule before planning a visit to insure that photography is being exhibited. Keep in mind when planning a museum visit that collection material is not always on display, and even though photography from the permanent collections may be available in a private viewing room, prior arrangements must usually be made to provide access.

All of the galleries included here do not necessarily exhibit photography exclusively or regularly. However, from our research we have found that more and more galleries are beginning to offer photography exhibitions periodically. Also, in an attempt to illustrate the accessibility of photographic art, we have democratically included a wide range of galleries and exhibition spaces from the little-known community galleries to the powerful and celebrated career-making galleries. In other words, any gallery actively engaged in the marketing of photographic art we have attempted to include in this handbook. Without a doubt, photography is available to the masses as never before.

In addition to basic location and contact information, each gallery listing attempts to provide an overview representative of the on-going efforts of the gallery. Full attention should be given to the "submission requirements" and "photographer's expenses" areas, as these sections serve as indicators of the economic commitment one might have to make. The key to the symbols next to the gallery name is as follows: ✯ is for Non-Profit, ✔ means the gallery is open to reviewing portfolios, and ▲ means the gallery also functions as a private dealer.

It is also important to apply a little logic when deciding upon which galleries to contact. Just as a gallery director generally has an idea of how he or she wants the gallery to appear visually, you have probably also visualized how you would like to see your images exhibited. Lighting, space limitations, and gallery involvement are all areas which should not be overlooked. As you read the entries, note whether a gallery is non-profit, and understand that that can be a plus or minus depending upon your own perceptions of what you want to accomplish. Non-profit can mean that the gallery functions with extremely limited funds or it can mean that the gallery enjoys a special status which allows it to accept gifts from private sources who are happy to subsidize the arts for a nice tax write-off.

Special services offered by galleries run the gamut. Some galleries are only able to provide you with wall space and lighting for six weeks and that's it. Others provide artist referral services, corporate sales consultations, elaborate marketing and promotional campaigns, and glamorous opening receptions. Read between, under, and all around, the agreement lines before you sign anything. While it may be true that all these wonderful things do exist and are possible, you may find that *your* economic involvement is necessary to pull them off. In reality, most galleries are generous and have only your best interests at heart as they, too want a successful exhibition. But remember, it will be your work hanging on the walls and the value of your involvement can not be underestimated.

Although there are some museum listings which indicate that portfolios are welcomed for review, most of the museums included here offer important and unique photographic collections. Many of them create exhibitions which periodically display the works owned by the museum. Many of the museums also offer photography lectures and seminars, and invite your participation in their special events which often include photo fairs and exhibitions by regional artists. Do not overlook these special events as they may offer a good opportunity to have your work seen and reviewed by professionals.

Please note that all local telephone numbers, with the exception of those for the U.S. and Canada, are preceded by country and city codes. North American numbers are preceded by the area code only.

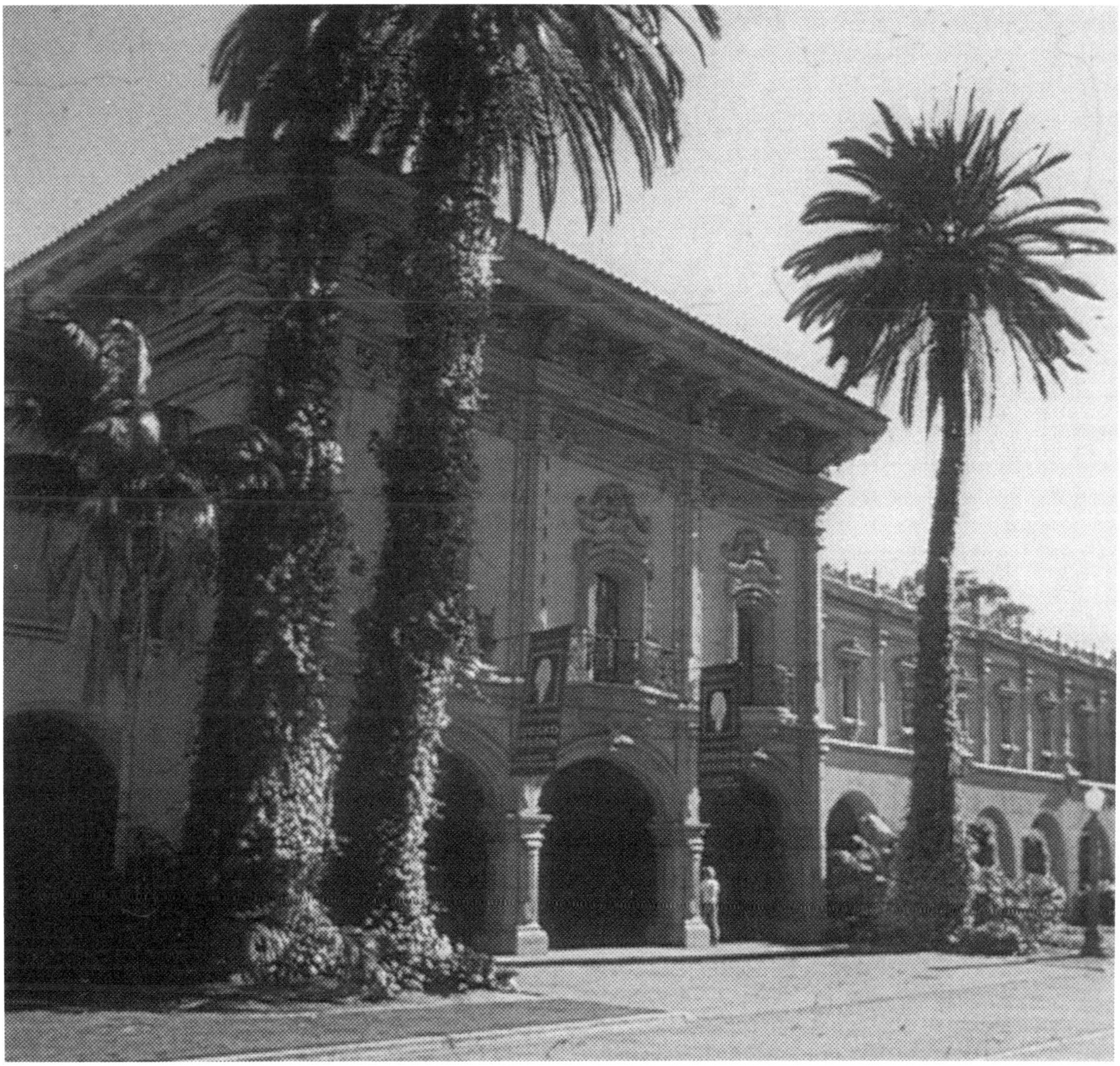

Photograph courtesy of The Museum of Photographic Arts

The Museum of Photographic Arts, in the magnificent Balboa Park, overlooks the city of San Diego and the Pacific Ocean.

U.S. Galleries and Museums

ALABAMA

BIRMINGHAM MUSEUM OF ART ✔☆

2000 Eighth Avenue North
Birmingham, Alabama 35203
205-254-2565 *Fax:* 205-254-2714
Contact: Trudy Wilner Stack, Photography Curator

The Museum of Art presents 6 photographic exhibitions annually and has an active exhibition, acquisition, and education program in photogaphy. A support group, *The Photography Guild*, collects work of historic importance and contemporary relevance. The museum also hosts important traveling exhibitions such as *In Our Time: The World As Seen By Magnum Photographers* which is scheduled to hit Birmingham in the summer of '91.

Requirements: High quality, fine art photography can be submitted by mail or dropped off at the curator's office. Contact directly for more information.

ARIZONA

NEW EXPOSURE CATALOG ✔

4807 North 70th Street
Scottsdale, Arizona 85251
602-990-2915
Contact: Susan Brahocki

New Exposure Catalog produces two fine art photography exhibitions annually in addition to its two catalogues. The folks at New Exposure view black and white and color fine art photography for the possibility of including the work in one of their catalogues.

Requirements: Sample prints, slides, resume, and prices may be sent along with a SASE.

Expenses: Shipping, framing, and the cost of print production are some of the costs which may be incurred by the photographer.

ETHERTON/STERN GALLERY ✔▲

135 South 6th Avenue
Tucson, Arizona 85701
602-624-7370 *Fax:* 602-792-4569
Contact: Terry Etherton or Michael Stern

The Etherton/Stern Gallery exhibits art in all media but with an emphasis on photography. The gallery, which mounts 8 exhibits annually, is probably the largest photo gallery in the southwest and maintains an inventory ranging from 19th century American and European to post-modern photography.

Requirements: Slides or prints should be offered for review.

Size: 3,000 square feet.

Lighting: Quartz track.

Services: The gallery actively promotes its shows in various media and hosts receptions for all its exhibits.

Expenses: Expenses vary and usually include some shipping and matting.

CENTER FOR CREATIVE PHOTOGRAPHY ✔☆

University of Arizona
Tucson, Arizona 85721
602-621-7968 *Fax:* 602-621-9444
Contact: Victor La Viola, Curator, Education

The Center for Creative Photography has one of the leading photographic collections in the world and contains more than 50,000 photographs in addition to galleries, photographers' archives and research facilities. The archives of Ansel Adams, Richard Avedon, Louise Dahl-Wolfe, Andreas Feininger, Paul Strand, and other master photographers are housed at the center.

Requirements: Finished quality prints, either mounted or unmounted, may be offered for review.

Size: 5,000 square feet and 340 linear feet.

Lighting: Incandescent track.

Services: The photographers' archives form the richest source of research material available on the history of photography; the library includes more than 10,000

monographs, periodicals, and catalogues; printviewing from the collection is available.
Expenses: Photographer's expenses are negotiable.

OLD PUEBLO MUSEUM ✔★

7401 North La Cholla Boulevard
Tucson, Arizona 85741
602-742-2355 *Fax:* 602-797-0936
Contact: Diane M. Johnson, Director

Tucson's Old Pueblo Museum is an innovative art facility housed within the walls of Foothills Center, a shopping mall. The design and architecture evokes the beauty of the southwest to which the museum is devoted. Photography is exhibited regularly.
Requirements: Write for the exhibition proposal requirements. Recent shows which featured photography were *Timeless Images From Arizona Highways, Cactus!,* and *Space Photography.*
Size: 150 running feet or 5,000 square feet.
Services: Tours, workshops, and lectures by exhibited artists are some of the special services offered. Advertising and mass mailings promote the museum's shows.
Expenses: Production and one-way shipping are the expenses incurred by the photographer.

ACREY'S GALLERY

431 Highway 179 A-8
Sedona, Arizona 86336
602-282-2983

Acrey's Gallery showcases the work of fine art photographer Jack Acrey who specializes in images of the west, wildlife, landscapes and people. The gallery also does custom archival matting and framing.

CREEKSIDE GALLERIES

At Artesania Plaza, 251 Highway 179
Sedona, Arizona 86336
602-282-1465
Contact: Monica Beeler or Debra Schumacher

Although Creekside Galleries exhibits a variety of visual art mediums, the gallery represents the work of two outstanding photographers, Gary Ladd and Michael Fatali who specialize in photographing the spectacular landscapes and nature of the southwest.

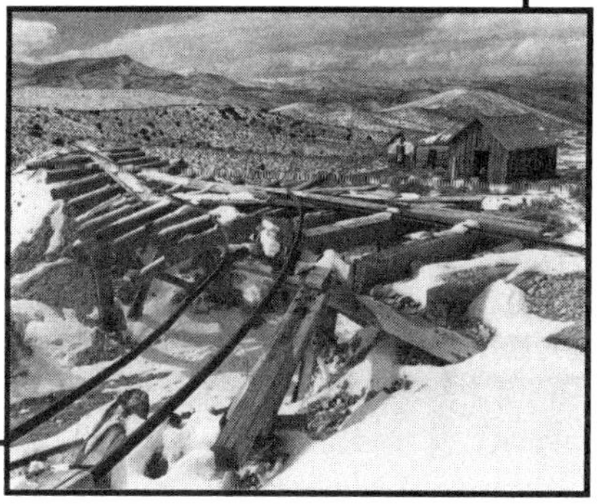

"Tracks"
Silver Print

LOU DESERIO GALLERY
Sinagua Plaza, Hwy 89-A #15
Sedona, Arizona 86336
602-282-9433

The Lou DeSerio Gallery is devoted exclusively to the fine-art photography of Mr. DeSerio who is one of the foremost color landscape photographers of today. A student of Ansel Adams, DeSerio has taught at Mesa Community College and has published a book called *A Last Look,* which is a record of the west's vanishing ghost towns.

TATE GALLERY
671 Highway 79
Sedona, Arizona 86336
602-282-1822

Photographer Dave Tate opened his gallery in Sedona in the spring of 1990. Formerly a specialist in architecture and interior design photography in Newport Beach, California, Tate has turned to landscape photography which he accomplishes with a Horseman 45FA view camera. Tate also shows the work of other photo artists in his gallery.

ARKANSAS

ARKANSAS ARTS CENTER
10th & Commerce
Little Rock, Arkansas 72203
501-372-4000
Hours: Monday-Saturday 10-5; Sunday 12-5.

The Arkansas Arts Center usually offers several photography related exhibitions each year as well as the annual *Prints, Drawings, and Photographs* show. The center also sponsors traveling exhibitions of original works from their permenent collection.

CALIFORNIA

MUSEUM OF CONTEMPORARY ART
250 South Grand Avenue / California Plaza
Los Angeles, California 90012
213-621-2766
Admission: $4.00
Hours: Tuesday-Sunday 11-6; Thursday evenings until 8:00. Closed Monday.

The Museum of Contemporary Art and its offshoot, The Temporary Contemporary, offer a wide variety of photography-related programs in addition to regularly exhibiting photographic art. The Museum also hosts a support group, the *Photo Council,* and maintains a permanent photography collection. The collection recently was enlarged by a gift from the estate of celebrated Los Angelean photographer Max Yavno with a donation of approximately 200 vintage and contemporary prints documenting California. Check both MOCA and The Temporary Contemporary (located at 152 North Central Avenue; 213-621-2766) for their schedules of photographic events.

WOMAN'S BUILDING ✔✯
1727 North Spring Street
Los Angeles, California 90012
213-221-6161
Contact: Executive Director

The Woman's Building is a public center for female culture and was established in 1973 by artist Judy Chicago and others. The center regularly presents photographic art in its two galleries and offers programs, lectures, and workshops to the general public.
Requirements: A sheet of 20 slides with a biography, a statement, and additional information can be submitted accompanied by a SASE.
Size: 20'x 50' in the Front and Cafe galleries.
Services: The center offers a bookstore, a slide library and archives, and classes and workshops. Promotion of the center's exhibitions is through the membership calendar, press releases and show announcements.

L.A. CENTER FOR PHOTOGRAPHIC STUDIES ✔✯
1048 West 6th Street
Los Angeles, California 90017
213-482-3566
Contact: Suzy Kerr

LACPS is a community arts organization committed to "an artistic vision which promotes progressive thinking in the arts." As such, LACPS is interested in work which explores the boundaries of photography within a political, social, or cultural context.
Requirements: A minimum of 20 slides and resume with a proposal may be submitted to the center.
Size: 11'x 35'.
Lighting: Track and flood lights.
Services: In addition to exhibitions, installations, and lectures, the center publishes the bi-monthly *LACPS Calendar* and the photographic journal *Frame-Work* 3 times annually. The center promotes its activities via the local and national art media.

Key: ✔ = Portfolios Reviewed
✯ = Non-Profit Organization
▲ = Private Dealer

LOS ANGELES COUNTY MUSEUM OF ART

5905 Wilshire Boulevard
Los Angeles, California 90036
213-857-6000
Admission: $3.00
Hours: Tuesday-Friday 10-5; Saturday & Sunday 10-6; closed Monday.

The Los Angeles County Museum of Art frequently hosts major traveling exhibitions. In 1990 the museum was the recipient of over 170 photographic works from the collection of singer/musician Graham Nash, many of which have already been exhibited at the facility. The collection includes work from such contemporary American and European photographers as Mary Ellen Mark, Rafael Vargas, Marilyn Bridges, Robert Flynt, and others.

CURE GALLERY ✔

8022 Melrose Avenue
Los Angeles, California 90046
213-653-3877
Contact: Marc Erlandson or Phil Miller

The Cure Gallery is one of L.A.'s outstanding art showcases on the Melrose Avenue strip. Presenting 12 to 14 shows annually in all media, the gallery regularly features contemporary photographic art.

Requirements: Photographs can be presented in person or via the mail.
Size: 1,000 square feet.
Lighting: Track.
Services: The gallery gives 10% to the artist's choice charity every month. The gallery's mailing list and advertising is used to promote exhibitions.
Expenses: Framing, shipping, and part of advertising costs are expenses which may be paid by the photographer.

G. RAY HAWKINS GALLERY ▲

910 Colorado Avenue
Santa Monica, California 90046
213-394-5558

The G. Ray Hawkins Gallery was for many years a popular mainstay of L.A.'s Melrose Avenue gallery scene but has recently relocated to the heart of the newly thriving Santa Monica Colorado Avenue gallery area. Established in 1975, the highly regarded pioneering photographic gallery continues to exhibit trend-setting work as well as representing several artists and important estates. The gallery is also a licensed auction house.

Services: The gallery offers a private search service for photography collectors.

SOUTHWEST MUSEUM

234 Museum Drive
Los Angeles, California 90065
213-221-2163
Admission: $4.00
Hours: Tuesday-Sunday 11-5; closed Mondays and major holidays.

The collections of the Southwest Museum, the oldest museum in Los Angeles (established in 1907), represent the Native American cultures from Alaska to South America. The museum frequently exhibits both historical and contemporary photography depicting Native American and related themes. The museum also maintains an extensive research library containing over 100,000 photographs which can be viewed via video disc. The museum's permanent collection contains several important portfolios of early Western photography by Orlando S. Goff, David F. Barry, and Frank B. Fiske. Goff was responsible for the first portraits of Northern Plains Indian Warriors, among them Sitting Bull.

The following galleries in Los Angeles and southern California also exhibit and sell photographic art:

Andrea Ross 213-453-6662
2110 Broadway
Santa Monica, California 90404

The Art Scene 619-483-2740
4150 Mission Beach Boulevard
Pacific Beach, California 92109

Artist Space at Southfair 619-755-1662
2010 Jimmy Durante Boulevard
Del Mar, California 92014

Ayzenberg Gallery 213-652-0814
665 N. La Cienega Boulevard
Los Angeles, California 90069

B-1 Gallery 213-392-9625
2730 Main Street
Santa Monica, California 90405

Blum Helman 213-451-0955
916 Colorado Avenue
Santa Monica, California 90401

Boritzer/Gray Gallery 213-392-8399
3110 Main Street #100
Santa Monica, California 90405

Circle Gallery 619-296-2596
2501 San Diego Avenue
San Diego, California 92110

Couturier 213-933-5557
166 N. LaBrea Avenue
Hollywood, California 90036

Ettinger Gallery 714-497-3309
2222 Laguna Canyon Road
Laguna Beach, California 92651

Fahey-Klein Gallery 213-934-2250
148 N. LaBrea Avenue
Hollywood, California 90036

Irvine Fine Arts Center 714-552-1018
14321 Yale Avenue
Irvine, California 92714

Jan Kesner (▲) 213-938-6834
164 N. LaBrea Avenue
Hollywood, California 90036

Linda Cathcart 213-451-1121
924 Colorado Avenue
Santa Monica, California 90401

Los Angeles Municipal Art Gallery 213-485-4581
4804 Hollywood Boulevard
Hollywood, California 90027

Lyceum Galleries 619-274-2632
Horton Plaza
San Diego, California 92101

Meyers/Bloom Gallery 213-829-0062
2112 Broadway
Santa Monica, California 90401

O.B. Contemporary Gallere 619-222-1965
5005 Niagara Avenue
Ocean Beach, California 92107

Options/The Alternative Gallery 619-239-0511
744 G Street, Suite 102
San Diego, California 92101

Pense Gallery 213-393-0069
908 Colorado Avenue
Santa Monica, California 90401

Peter Fetterman (▲) 213-393-0069
908 Colorado Avenue, Suite B
Santa Monica, California 90401

Photo Impact 213-461-0141
931 N. Citrus Avenue
Los Angeles, California 90038

Richard Green 213-828-6666
2036 Broadway
Santa Monica, California 90401

Saxon-Lee Gallery 213-933-5282
7525 Beverly Boulevard
Hollywood, California 90036

Shoshana Wayne Gallery 213-451-3733
1454 Fifth Avenue
Santa Monica, California 90401

Stephen Cohen 20th Century Photographs (▲)
213-654-1890
8277 Fountain Avenue
Los Angeles, California 90046

Stephen White Gallery of Photography (▲)
213-934-3547
7319 Beverly Boulevard
Los Angeles, California 90036

Wildlife Gallery 714-494-7456
1259 S. Coast Hwy
Laguna Beach, California 92651

J. PAUL GETTY MUSEUM

17985 Pacific Coast Highway
Malibu, California 90265
213-459-7611
Admission: Free
Hours: Tuesday-Sunday 10-5. Parking reservations are required. Closed Monday.

The Getty, housed in a recreation of a first-century Roman country villa in a garden setting overlooking the Pacific Ocean, contains an extensive collection of 19th and 20th century American and European photographs in addition to its many other treasures. In 1984 the museum founded its Department of Photographs with the acquisition of several major collections including those of Samuel Wagstaff, Arnold Crane, Bruno Bischofberger, and others. Since 1986 the museum has presented over 16 photographic exhibitions and continues to acquire important photographs for its collection.

PALOS VERDES ART CENTER ✔✯

5604 West Crestridge Road
Rancho Palos Verdes, California 90274
213-541-2479
Contact: Exhibition Committee

The Palos Verdes Art Center located west of Los Angeles and just south of LAX, shows fine art and photography. Photography classes and an on-going classic film series are also available at the center.

Requirements: Six slides with a resume may be presented to the exhibition committee.
Size: 1,200 square feet.

Services: The center promotes exhibitions through direct mail, artist receptions, and the media.
Expenses: Framing.

NORTON SIMON MUSEUM OF ART
411 West Colorado Boulevard
Pasadena, California 91105
818-449-6840
Admission: $4.00
Hours: Thursday-Sunday 12-6.

The Norton Simon Museum of Art contains 30 galleries and a sculpture garden and features seven centuries of European art from the Renaissance to the 20th Century. The museum regularly exhibits photographic art and owns a large collection of rare prints by Frederick Sommer which were selected and donated by the photographer in 1965.

THE HUNTINGTON
1151 Oxford Road
San Marino, California 91108
818-405-2100
Admission: Donation
Hours: Tuesday-Saturday 1-4:30; Sunday by reservation.

The Huntington, located on the out-skirts of Los Angeles close to Pasadena, is one of the country's leading cultural and educational centers. The institution contains an outstanding research library, a 130 acre botanical garden, and an art collection featuring such treasures of 18th and 19th British and French art as Gainsborough's *Blue Boy* and Lawrence's *Pinkie*. The Huntington Library has over 300,000 photographs in its collections, primarily historical and covering the American West, California history, early Los Angeles, and Native American heritage. The "photographic art" collection contains approximately 1,500 images by Adams, Weston, Carleton Watkins, Willard Van Dyke, and others.

ORLANDO GALLERY ✔
14553 Ventura Boulevard
Sherman Oaks, California 91403
818-789-6012
Contact: Philip Orlando or Robert Giwo

The Orlando Gallery exhibits contemporary art work and will view sample works from new photographers working in a contemporary mode.
Requirements: Slides with resume may be submitted.
Size: 2,000 square feet.
Lighting: Track.
Services: The gallery engages in the standard promotional activities.
Expenses: Varies from show to show.

MUSEUM OF PHOTOGRAPHIC ARTS
1649 El Prado, Balboa Park
San Diego, California 92101
619-239-5262
Admission: $2.50
Hours: Daily 10-5; Thursdays until 9.

Commandeering a prominent postion in Balboa Park's cultural complex, Casa de Balboa, the Museum of Photographic Arts has become one of San Diego's most popular and important attractions since opening its doors in 1983. Presenting as many as eight major exhibitions annually, the Museum also maintains an impressive permanent collection which is especially strong in contemporary photographs and daguerreotypes. Two shows which originated at MOPA and are traveling now are *Revelaciones: The Art of Manuel Alvarez Bravo* and *The Duane Michaels Show*. Upcoming presentations for '91 and '92 include: *Paul Strand & Ansel Adams: Native Land & Natural Scene* and *Nicolas Nixon: Pictures of People*.

LARKSPUR FINE ARTS
457 N. Palm Canyon Drive
Palm Springs, California 92263
619-325-3142
Contact: William Hilligoss

Palm Springs' Larkspur Fine Arts Gallery is devoted to exhibiting the photographic art of Edward S. Curtis. Curtis spent more than 35 years photographing and documenting the vanishing race of the Native Americans. The company has also produced a 20 volume video series of Curtis' work with each volume devoted to a different Native American tribe.

CALIFORNIA MUSEUM OF PHOTOGRAPHY ✔★
University of California
Riverside, California 92521
714-787-4787 *Fax:* 714-787-4792
Contact: Jonathon Green, Director or Edward W. Earle, Curator

Located one hour east of Los Angeles, the California Museum of Photography was established in 1973 and, with its recent move to a new facility, the museum now maintains the largest photography exhibition space on the west coast. The CMP houses 4 temporary galleries, 2 permanent galleries, an interactive "please touch" gallery, a museum store, and for researchers, an archive which includes the renowned *Keystone Mast Collection of Stereographs*.

Requirements: The museum is interested in "cutting-edge" contemporary, historical, and some video work. A one-page selection of slides accompanied by supportive material and a SASE may be offered for review.
Size: There are 4 galleries of 600 to 2,500 square feet.
Lighting: Tungsten/halogen.
Services: Lectures, films, workshops, and special events are scheduled regularly. The museum offers guided tours to groups and the research facilities are available by appointment.
Expenses: There is no fixed policy regarding expenses.

SUSAN SPIRITUS GALLERY ✔

3333 Bear Street #330
Costa Mesa, California 92626
714-549-7550
Contact: Susan Spiritus

Contemporary American and European photography is shown in 10 new exhibitions each year in the Susan Spiritus Gallery. The gallery, which can be found south of L.A. in the coastal town of Costa Mesa, has been in the business of selling photographic art since 1976.
Requirements: Material presented for review should be matted archivally. Do not send or show framed work.
Size: 1,100 square feet.
Lighting: Halogen.
Services: The gallery maintains a framing service. The gallery promotes exhibitions via announcements.
Expenses: Shipping both ways is paid for by the photographer.

BC SPACE ✔

235 Forest Avenue
Laguna Beach, California 92651
714-497-1880
Contact: Mark Chamberlain

Laguna Beach, which offers an active gallery scene, is an easy drive south from the heart of Los Angeles via the Santa Ana Freeway. Among the galleries in the area, BC Space is one of southern California's preeminent contemporary art/photography outlets. In keeping with its "cutting-edge" reputation, the gallery is interested only in viewing material that is issue-oriented, fresh, and contemporary.
Requirements: Slides must be accompanied by resume and SASE.
Size: 1,500 square feet.
Lighting: Tungsten.
Services: The gallery promotes exhibitions through mailing lists and press-releases.
Expenses: The photographer pays for shipping and occasionally shares in the costs of announcements and receptions.

SANTA BARBARA MUSEUM OF ART

1130 State Street
Santa Barbara, California 93101
805-963-4364
Hours: Tuesday-Saturday 11-5; Thursday until 9; Sunday 12-5.

The Santa Barbara Museum of Art regularly exhibits photographic art. 1991 will feature *Ansel Adams: Classic Images,* a collection of work which was selected by Adams that ranges from early views of Yosemite to portraits of his contemporaries such as Georgia O'Keeffe and Alfred Stieglitz. Also on view in 1991 will be an extensive look at *Soviet Photography* and set for 1992 is *The First Hundred Years of California Photography.*

CENTER GALLERY

San Carlos & Ninth Avenue
Carmel, California 93921
408-625-5181

Located in Carmel's Sunset Cultural Center, the Center Gallery is an off-shoot of The Photographic Center of Monterey Peninsula. Since opening in 1988, the Center Gallery has featured traveling national exhibits, regional group shows, and an annual member's exhibition.
Requirements: The gallery mainly exhibits photography by regional artists. Contact directly for submission information.

WESTON GALLERY ✔

6th Avenue & Dolores
Carmel, California 93921
408-624-4453 *Fax:* 408-624-7190
Contact: Gail Gibson, Director

The Weston Gallery in Carmel is located south of Monterey and north of Big Sur on the Pacific coast. Named in honor of the legendary nature photographer, Edward Weston, the gallery mounts several solo shows annually as well as many group exhibitions.
Requirements: Call for an appointment or submit slides with accompanying resume.
Services: The gallery offers private and corporate consultation and sales and participates in major art fairs. National and international advertising and catalogues and brochures are used to promote the Weston Gallery.

Expenses: Shipping and matting are the photographer's expenses.

MONTEREY PENINSULA MUSEUM OF ART ✔☆

559 Pacific Street
Monterey, California 93940
408-372-5477 *Fax:* 408-373-4907
Contact: Richard W. Gadd, Assistant Curator of Photography

The Monterey Peninsula Museum of Art presents approximately 4 shows featuring photography each year. The museum is interested in photography that is regionally, historically, or contemporary oriented.
Requirements: One page of sample slides with a resume and other relative material may be offered for review.
Lighting: Track.
Services: The museum's events are publicized in the local and regional media.
Expenses: The photographer pays for matting and framing his work.

ELEONORE AUSTERER GALLERY ✔

540 Sutter Street
San Francisco, California 94102
415-986-2244 *Fax:* 415-986-2281
Contact: Eleonore Austerer

The Eleonore Austerer Gallery exhibits international contemporary art and 20th century mastergraphics. The gallery is interested in reviewing the work of established photographers only.
Requirements: The gallery will view quality samples.
Size: 4,800 square feet.
Lighting: Halogen and incandescent.
Services: The gallery specializes in debuting foreign artists who have already become known in their homelands.
Expenses: Expenses are variable.

SAN FRANCISCO MUSEUM OF MODERN ART

401 Van Ness Avenue
San Francisco, California 94102
415-863-8800
Admission: $4.00
Hours: Tuesday-Friday 10-5; Saturday & Sunday 11-5; Thursday evenings to 9.

Located in the Civic Center of San Francisco, the Museum of Modern Art features a variety of photographic exhibitions yearly. 1991 will offer: *Florence Henri: Artist-Photographer of the Avant Garde,* the first major U.S. showing of the artist's work; *Linda Connor,* an exhibition by a local artist whose work focuses on ritual grounds and sacred temples of Nepal, France, Ireland, and Hawaii; *Josef Koudelka,* the Czech photographer's images of Gypsy life in eastern Europe; *Lisette Model,* a retrospective of the American photographer will include work not previously exhibited; and *The Duane Michaels Show,* the traveling retrospective of the commercial photographer's work.

SAN FRANCISCO CAMERAWORK ✔☆

70 Twelfth Street
San Francisco, California 94103
415-621-1001
Contact: Marnie Gillett, Director

San Francisco Camerawork was founded in 1974 in response to the needs of the Bay Area photographic community. Camerawork is committed to presenting experimental work which expands the definition of photography and is engaged in an on-gong campaign to develop an audience for innovative emerging artists.
Requirements: Sample slides, a statement from the artist, and a SASE can be presented for consideration.
Size: 97 square feet and 68 running feet.
Lighting: This 3rd floor space utilizes natural light via the skylite.
Services: Exhibiting artists receive a honorarium. Among many special services are workshops, two annual lecture series, "Open Forum" which is a portfolio review for members and the public, a reference library, and a bookstore.
Expenses: Exhibited photographers generally do not incur expenses.

MICHAEL SHAPIRO GALLERY ✔

250 Sutter Street, 3rd Floor
San Francisco, California 94108
415-398-6655 *Fax:* 415-398-0667
Contact: Michael Shapiro

The Michael Shapiro Gallery exhibits black and white photography of the 20th century.
Requirements: Submit 10 to 12 examples of your best work.
Size: 1,000 square feet.
Lighting: Halogen.
Services: The gallery offers framing and photo conservation services and uses standard gallery promotion.
Expenses: Matting and shipping are paid for by the photographer.

HOLOS GALLERY ✔

1792 Haight Street
San Francisco, California 94117
415-221-4717 *Fax:* 415-221-4815
Contact: Gary Zellerbach, President

San Francisco's Holos Gallery has specialized in holograms - 3-D photo images made with lasers - since 1979. Photographers with appropriate material can contact the gallery.

Requirements: Slides with a resume are required for review.
Size: 600 square feet.
Lighting: Halogen.
Services: The gallery has a world-wide wholesale distribution of holograms. The gallery hosts opening receptions and sends press releases and direct mail pieces to its clients.
Expenses: Framing is the only expense for the photographer.

THE OAKLAND MUSEUM

1000 Oak Street
Oakland, California 94607
415-273-3401
Hours: Wednesday to Saturday 10-5; noon to 7 Sunday; closed Monday, Tuesday.

The Oakland Museum maintains an extensive photography collection which contains work of both historic importance and artistic merit - from the earliest photographs illustrating the California Gold Rush to Edward Curtis' turn-of-the-century documentation of the vanishing Indians of North America. The museum's collections also contain the largest number of Dorothea Lange's photographs and negatives, early portfolios of Ansel Adams, and acquisitions of the celebrated Bay Area photographers group known as "f/64". While not limited to west coast photographers exclusively, the museum continues to exhibit progressive work from California artists working in a contemporary direction.

The San Francisco area galleries and museums listed below frequently present photographic exhibitions:

Artspace 415-626-9100
1286 Folsom Street
San Francisco, California 94103

Beau Bo 415-621-2469
206 Filmore Street
San Francisco, California 94103

Capp Street Project 415-626-7747
270 14th Street
San Francisco, California 94103

Eye Gallery 415-431-6911
1151 Mission Street
San Francisco, California 94103

Fraenkel Gallery (▲) 415-981-2661
55 Grant Avenue
San Francisco, California 94108

Intersection For The Arts 415-626-2787
446 Valencia Street
San Francisco, California 94110

Kimball's East 415-658-2555
5800 Shellmound Street
Emeryville, California 94608

Paul M. Hertzman, Inc. (▲) 415-626-2677
P.O. Box 40447
San Francisco, California 94140

Pro Arts 415-763-4361
461 Ninth Street
San Francisco, California 94115

Rena Bransten 415-982-3292
77 Geary Street
San Francisco, California 94108

Robert Koch Gallery (▲) 415-421-0122
49 Geary Street
San Francisco, California 94108

Scott Nichols Gallery (▲) 415-788-4641
P.O. Box 330030
San Francisco, California 94133

Southern Exposure Gallery 415-863-2141
401 Alabama
San Francisco, California 94110

Thomas V. Meyer Fine Art (▲) 415-
169 25th Avenue
San Francisco, California 94121

University Art Museum 415-642-1438
2625 Durant Avenue
Berkeley, California 94720

Ursula Gropper Associates (▲) 415-331-2414
10 Laurel Lane
Sausalito, California 94965

Vision Gallery (▲) 415-621-2107
1155 Mission
San Francisco, California 94103

MOUNTAIN LIGHT PHOTOGRAPHY, INC.

1483 A Solano Avenue
Albany, California 94706
415-524-9343 *Fax:* 415-524-5009
Contact: Marcia Roberson

Mountain Light Photography exhibits the works of renown landscape photographer Galen Rowell exclusively. Rowell, who initially captured the public's interest as a mountain-climbing photographer, has produced many photo books which are sold in the gallery along with posters of his work.

DE SAISSET MUSEUM

Santa Clara University
Santa Clara, California 95053
408-554-4528
Admission: Free
Hours: Tuesday-Sunday 11-4; closed Monday.

De Saisset Museum, operated by Santa Clara University, regularly exhibits photographic works and has featured the photography of Edward Weston, Cay Lang, and Victor Landweber in recent years. In addition to famous works in the permanent collection by Ansel Adams, Imogen Cunningham, and Weston, the museum is the recipient of the estate of the late photography gallery pioneer Helen Johnston. The estate, containing many important works which debuted in the legendary Focus Gallery in San Francisco from 1966 to its closing in 1985, has been divided between De Saisset, the San Francisco Museum of Modern Art, and The Oakland Museum.

COLORADO

DENVER ART MUSEUM

100 West 14th Avenue Parkway
Denver, Colorado 80204
303-575-2794
Admission: $3.00
Hours: Tuesday-Saturday 10-5; Sunday 12-5; closed Monday.

Denver Art Museum regularly exhibits photographic art and maintains the Shwayder Photography Gallery expressly for that purpose. Recent exhibitions include *Perpetual Photos* the television-photography images of Allan McCollum and *Walls of Time: The Rock Art of Canyon de Chelly,* large scale photographs by Bill O'Connor and David DeHarport of the rarely seen canyon art. In 1990 the museum acquired nearly 1,000 rare photographs from the *Daniel Wolf Collection of Photography.* At a cost of $1.5 million, the 19th century American landscape photography by pioneer photographers Eadweard Muybridge, Carleton Watkins, and others, represents one of the finest photographic documentations of the early West.

GINNY WILLIAMS GALLERY ✔

299 Fillmore Street
Denver, Colorado 80206
303-321-4077 *Fax:* 303-394-3060
Contact: Ginny Williams or Robbie Williams

The Ginny Williams Gallery offers 10 or 11 photographic exhibitions each year and is interested in showing contemporary photography and photographically related material.
Requirements: Contact for appointment. Slides are suitable.
Size: 5,000 feet.
Lighting: Track lighting.
Services: The gallery features a library and hosts lectures. Promotional services include reception, print advertising, and press-releases.
Expenses: Transportation.

Photographic art can also be found through the following Denver galleries and private dealers:

Camera Obscura Gallery 303-623-4059
1309 Bannock Street
Denver, Colorado 80204

Payton Rule 303-293-9080
1736 Wazee Street
Denver, Colorado 80202

CONNECTICUT

WADSWORTH ATHENEUM

600 Main Street
Hartford, Connecticut 06103
203-278-2670
Admission: $3.00
Hours: Tuesday - Sunday 11-5; admission is free on Thursday.

Centrally located in downtown Hartford, the Wadsworth Atheneum Museum maintains a contemporary art collection devoted to artists with local ties. Photographer Ellen Carey is represented in the collection with several color polaroid works.

REAL ART WAYS ✔★

56 Arbor Street
Hartford, Connecticut 06106
203-232-1006
Contact: Anne R. Pasternak, Curator

Real Art Ways presents approximately 10 exhibitions annually in all media.

Requirements: Slides with biographies and SASE for review should be sent to the gallery. Open to both new and established artists.
Size: 800 square feet.
Lighting: Spotlights.
Services: Announcements, invitations, brochures, and a calendar are some of the services offered by the gallery.

GOLDSMITH GALLERY ✔

845 Boston Post Road
Madison, Connecticut 06443
203-245-7800
Contact: Yvonne P. Goldsmith

The Goldsmith Gallery, located outside of New Haven on the Long Island Sound, specializes in the fine arts. The gallery, currently mounting one photographic exhibition annually, will view work from new photographers. Realism and impressionism are subjects of interest to the gallery.

Requirements: Slides accompanied by a resume can be submitted.
Size: 2,500 square feet.
Services: The gallery promotes via direct mail and newspapers.
Expenses: Freight and reproduction materials are the photographer's expenses.

ARTSPACE ✔★

70 Audubon Street
New Haven, Connecticut 06518
203-772-2377
Contact: Barbara A. Harder, Coordinator

Artspace is a not-for-profit center for visual, literary, and performing arts. The center was devised as an outlet for artists from diverse backgrounds to display their innovative talents. Artspace mounts 10 exhibitions each year and is interested in a wide variety of excellent and innovative art.

Requirements: Submissions in slide format are preferred. Resume and back-up information should be included.
Size: 1,600 square feet.
Services: Artspace offers curating, installation, and design assistance. The gallery promotes its activities to over 3,000 via a mailing list.
Expenses: Expenses are negotiable. The gallery receives 30% commission on all sales.

DELAWARE

GALLERY 913, UNIVERSITY OF DELAWARE ✔★

913 Market Street Mall
Wilmington, Delaware 19711
302-573-4488 *Fax:* 302-573-4479
Contact: Phyllis N. Townsend

Gallery 913 at the University of Delaware in Wilmington exhibits photography exclusively. Only 30 miles from Philadelphia and 65 from Baltimore, the gallery presents 6 to 8 exhibitions each year.

Requirements: Portfolios should contain a minimum of 20 slides and be accompanied by a resume.
Size: 61 linear feet.
Lighting: Track lighting.
Services: The gallery covers the costs of receptions, image cards, and mailings and uses posters, direct-mail and the local media to promote exhibitions.
Expenses: The major expense to photographers is framing.

VISITOR CENTER ✔★

Federal Street
Dover, Delaware 19903
302-739-4266
Contact: Dominique Coulet or Kristen Presta

Dover, Delaware's Visitor Center is interested in exhibiting photography of the state and by the state's photographers.

Requirements: Slides should be submitted for consideration.
Size: 25′x 25′.
Lighting: Indirect and spotlights.
Services: The center's P.R. officer organizes press conferences with the artists.
Expenses: Shipping, reception, and invitations.

DISTRICT OF COLUMBIA

ANSEL ADAMS COLLECTION

Wilderness Society/1400 I Street N.W.
Washington, D.C. 20005
202-833-2300
Admission: Free
Hours: Monday-Friday, 10-5.

The estate of Ansel Adams bequeathed seventy of the photographer's most important landscape photographs to the *Wilderness Society* where they are kept on permanent display.

NATIONAL MUSEUM OF WOMEN IN THE ARTS

1250 New York Avenue, N.W.
Washington, D.C. 20005
202-783-5000
Hours: Monday-Saturday 10-5; Sunday 12-5.

Situated between the White House and Convention Center, the National Museum of Women In The Arts is centrally located in Washington's museum district. The NMWA offers the single most important collection of art by women in the world and with its permanent collection provides a comprehensive survey from the 16th century to the present. In 1987 NMWA presented its first photography show, *Louise Dahl-Wolfe: A Retrospective Exhibition,* a comprehensive view of work by the fashion photographer long associated with *Harper's Bazaar.* Since that time the museum has continued to feature both historic and contemporary photography and has maintained a permanent collection containing 100 Dahl-Wolfes and more.

CORCORAN GALLERY OF ART

17th Street & New York Avenue N.W.
Washington, D.C. 20006
202-638-1439
Admission: Free
Hours: Tuesday-Sunday 10-4:30, Thursday until 9; closed Mondays.

Recognized internationally as a major center of American art, The Corcoran Gallery of Art includes photography in its permanent collection and occasionally organizes major exhibitions which subsequently travel the U.S. and beyond. In the works, and scheduled for a 1992 debut, is *Song of My People,* a documentation of the pain and joy of life in Black America by 50 leading African-American photographers. The Corcoran's permanent collection, like the photography exhibitions it offers, contains both classic and contemporary and everything in-between. The Corcoran is located one block from the White House and is within walking distance of many of the major art attractions in the capital city.

TARTT GALLERY ✔▲

2017 Q Street N.W.
Washington, D.C. 20009
202-332-5652 *Fax:* 202-462-1019
Contact: Jo Tartt, Jr.

The Tartt Gallery annually mounts 5 to 10 shows featuring contemporary and 19th century masters. The gallery also has a special interest in emerging artists.

Requirements: Contact directly for information regarding submission requirements.
Size: There are 3 floors, each 800 square feet.
Lighting: Standard.
Services: The gallery promotes its exhibitions via the local media and mailings.
Expenses: Expenses are negotiable on a case by case basis, but the artist usually pays for shipping, matting, and framing.

THE LIBRARY OF CONGRESS

10 First Street S.E.
Washington, D.C. 20540
202-707-5000
Admission: Free
Hours: Monday-Friday 8:30-9:30; Saturday 8:30-6.

The Library of Congress' *Prints and Photographs Division* contains over 9 million images, including a *Master Photographs Collection* of 4,000 original works by noted photographers. Important historic photography is on view continuously and visitors can view an optical disc featuring 40,000 works from the library's collection. The library also maintains an extensive Matthew Brady collection and a complete collection of *Look Magazines*. Beyond photography, the Library of Congress, often referred to as the "Nation's Library," features unique permanent exhibitions covering everything from such priceless treasures as the Library's copy of the Gutenberg Bible to a copyright exhibit starring Barbie & Ken.

ARTHUR M. SACKLER GALLERY

1050 Independence Avenue, S.W.
Washington, D.C. 20560
202-357-2700
Admission: Free
Hours: Daily 10-5:30.

Another of the Smithsonian Institution's galleries, the Sackler showcases Asian and Near Eastern art and serves as host to major international exhibitions. The gallery shares with the nearby Freer Gallery a research library and collection which contains a broad visual documentation of a number of Islamic subjects, the *Carl Whiting Bishop Collection* of early 20th century photographs of China, and a photographic collection of the Dowager Empress Cixi (1835-1908). The periodic temporary photography exhibitions are generally historic in nature such as *Antoin Sevruguin: Photographs of Iran,* turn of the century images on display through June 1991.

NATIONAL PORTRAIT GALLERY
8th & F Streets, N.W.
Washington, D.C. 20560
202-357-2700
Admission: Free
Hours: Daily 10-5.

The National Portrait Gallery, which is part of the Smithsonian Institution, only received authorization from congress to acquire photography in 1976. Since that time important historical portraits such as a 1843 daguerreotype of John Quincy Adams, the first president to be photographed, and the only original print of Alexander Gardner's "cracked plate" negative of Abraham Lincoln have been acquired. The extensive collection of photographic portraiture exceeds 8,500 images. The Gallery regularly presents special exhibitions such as *Camera Portraits: Photographs From the National Portrait Gallery, London* and *Lincoln's Contemporaries: Photographs By Mathew Brady,* scheduled for '91-92.

NATIONAL GALLERY OF ART
Fourth Street at Constitution Ave N.W.
Washington, D.C. 20565
202-737-4215
Admission: Free
Hours: Monday-Saturday 10-5; Sunday 11-6.
Extended summer hours.

The National Gallery of Art, located a short walk down Pennsylvania Avenue from the Capitol Building, came about by a joint resolution of Congress in the late '30's and although supported on a daily basis by federal funds, the building and art therein are gifts from private citizens. Although the National Gallery does not maintain a space exclusively for exhibiting photography, the gallery does curate major traveling exhibitions such as the recent *On The Art of Fixing A Shadow: 150 Years of Photography* and the upcoming centennial retropective, *Paul Strand.* The National Gallery has also been the recipient recently of important works by Walker Evans (*Subway Series*), Stieglitz, and Strand.

Other galleries showing photography in the Washington, D.C. area are:

Jones Troyer Fitzpatrick Gallery (▲) 202-328-7189
1614 20th Street N.W.
Washington, D.C. 20009

Kathleen Ewing Gallery (▲) 202-328-0955
1609 Connecticut Avenue
Washington, D.C. 20009

Marie Martin Fine Art Photography (▲)
301-907-0371
7301 Delfield Street
Chevy Chase, Maryland 20815

Middendorf Gallery (▲) 202-462-2009
2009 Columbia Road N.W.
Washington, D.C. 20009

Sandra Berler Fine Photographic Prints (▲)
301-656-8144
7002 Connecticut Avenue
Chevy Chase, Maryland 20815

Spectrum Gallery 202-333-0954
1132 29th Street
Washington, D.C. 20007

Washington Center for Photogaphy 703-821-5301
1609 Connecticut Avenue N.W.
Washington, D.C. 20009

FLORIDA

JACKSONVILLE ART MUSEUM
4160 Boulevard Center Drive
Jacksonville, Florida 32207
904-398-8336
Hours: Tuesday-Friday 10-5; Saturday and Sunday 1-5. Closed Monday.

The Jacksonville Art Museum has featured major exhibitions of the work of Cartier-Bresson, Kertesz, Hockney, and other internationally known photographers during the last few years. The museum's own permanent photography collection contains many contemporary works by Robert Mapplethorpe, William Wegman, Larry Clark, and Jay Shoots. A selection of classes and workshops are offered on a seasonal basis.

GREAT SOUTHERN GALLERY ✔
910 Duval Street
Key West, Florida 33040
305-294-6660
Contact: Dick Moody

The Great Southern Gallery is a fine arts gallery showcasing art by Florida artists and photographers.
Requirements: Submissions are by appointment only via telephone. Slides or prints with resume can be submitted if an appointment is accepted.
Size: 3,000 square feet.
Lighting: Track lighting.

Services: Custom framing and art supplies are available at the gallery. Local advertising and postcard mailings promote the gallery's shows.
Expenses: Shipping, framing, and matting are some of the costs which may be incurred by the photographer.

CENTER FOR THE FINE ARTS

101 West Flagler Street
Miami, Florida 33130
305-375-1700
Admission: $3.00
Hours: Tuesday-Saturday 10-5; Sunday 12-5; Thursday evenings to 9.

Miami's Center for the Fine Arts presents many of the outstanding touring exhibitions courtesy of regional corporations and arts organizations. The center also provides a showcase for state artists as in the exhibition *Fact & Fiction: The State of Florida Photography.*

PETER DREW GALLERY ✔

Crocker Center, 5050 Town Center Circle
Boca Raton, Florida 33486
407-391-4348
Contact: Linda T. Fleetwood

The Peter Drew Gallery in Boca Raton, just north of Miami, offers fine art photography. Currently the gallery represents two photographers all year long as well as various others on an invitational basis.
Requirements: Emerging and established artists should first call for an appointment. Unsolicited slides must be accompanied by SASE for return. Cover letter, resume, and press clippings must accompany transparencies or slides.
Size: 2,800 square feet.
Lighting: Mixed lighting.
Services: Special services include artist submissions to public institutions and corporations, updates on competitions, and appraisals for work represented by the gallery. To promote their exhibitions the gallery lists shows in 12 Florida based calendars.
Expenses: Framing and shipping to the gallery are the primary expenses. Upon acceptance the work must be prepared for exhibition in regard to professional matting, framing, etc.

Key: ✔ = Portfolios Reviewed
✯ = Non-Profit Organization
▲ = Private Dealer

FLORIDA CENTER FOR CONTEMPORARY ART ✔✯

1722 East 7th Avenue
Tampa, Florida 33605
813-248-1171
Contact: Betty Napolitan

Florida Center for Contemporary Art hosts from 6 to 9 exhibitions annually, usually featuring the work of artists from the southeast.
Requirements: Photographers at all levels can submit slides for consideration.
Size: 2,000 square feet.
Lighting: Track.
Services: Direct mail campaigns and press releases are used to promote the exhibitions. The center also pays honorariums and offers a juried member's show.
Expenses: Photographer's expenses are variable.

BRAD COOPER GALLERY ✔

311 South Howard Avenue
Tampa, Florida 33606
813-251-6105
Contact: Brad Cooper

The Brad Cooper Gallery is a fine arts gallery.
Requirements: New and established photographers may submit 1 sheet of slides for review.
Size: 675 square feet.
Lighting: Track lighting.
Services: The gallery sells art to corporations and collectors.

CLAYTON GALLERIES ✔

4105 South MacDill Avenue
Tampa, Florida 33611
813-831-3753
Contact: Cathleen C. Clayton

The Clayton Galleries provide a showcase for contemporary Floridian and regional artists. Both new and established photographers may contact the gallery to show work.
Requirements: Slides with a resume and a SASE may be offered.
Size: 2,000 square feet.
Lighting: Halogen, individually controlled spotlights.
Services: The gallery offers art consultation for corporate and private collections. Direct mail and regional print media are used to promote exhibitions.
Expenses: Shipping to and from the gallery.

STEIN GALLERY ✔

3105 Bay to Bay Boulevard
Tampa, Florida 33629
813-831-9987
Contact: Barbara Hill, Director

Although not exclusively a photography gallery, Tampa's Stein Gallery is an enthusiastic exhibitor of photographic work. The gallery mounts 8 exhibitions annually of contemporary art in all media.

Requirements: A portfolio of information should be sent to the gallery for review including a packet of current slides, resume, price range, articles, and a SASE.
Size: 2,200 square feet.
Lighting: Halogen.
Services: The Stein Gallery offers a variety of special services including curatorial assistance, slide presentations to corporate and private collectors, free lectures in the gallery, and promotion of the artist.
Expenses: Photographer's expenses include shipping both ways, framing, and the cost of producing slides and dupes.

ST. PETERSBURG MUSEUM OF FINE ARTS

255 Beach Drive NE
St. Petersburg, Florida 33701
813-896-2667
Admission: $2.00
Hours: Tuesday-Saturday 10-5; 1-5 Sunday.

St. Petersburg's Museum of Fine Arts is one of the south's most highly regarded fine arts museums and frequently exhibits photographic art such as the recently held Elliott Erwitt retrospective and Weegee's Greenwich Village photos from the '40s and '50s. The museum's permanent photography collection contains mid-nineteenth century daguerreotypes, calotypes and albumen prints, as well as a variety of 20th century contemporary images by photographic greats such as Paul Strand, Alfred Stieglitz, Arnold Newman, and Imogen Cunningham. The museum also has an organization of photography lovers, The Friends of Photography, who sponsor lectures and other activities by noteworthy photographers.

GEORGIA

HIGH MUSEUM OF ART

1280 Peachtree Street, N.E.
Atlanta, Georgia 30309
404-892-HIGH
Admission: $4.00
Hours: Tuesday-Saturday 10-5; Sunday noon to 5; closed Mondays.

The High Museum of Art is located in mid-town Atlanta and is part of the Robert W. Woodruff Art Center complex that also houses the Atlanta Symphony Orchestra, the Alliance Theatre Company, and the Atlanta College of Art. The museum, which is one of the south's most prominent fine arts facilities, maintains a photography collection of almost 3,000 19th and 20th century images by American and European masters. Photographic exhibitions traveling to the High Museum during 1991-92 include: *The New Vision: Photography Between The World Wars, Ralph Eugene Meatyard: An American Visionary,* and *This Sporting Life, 1878-1989,* images of sports and culture curated by the museum.

ILLINOIS

BACKDROP - AN ART GALLERY ✔

845 West Armitage
Chicago, Illinois 60005
312-404-7799 *Fax:* 708-253-2184
Contact: Lisa or Kris Hanson

The Backdrop maintains two locations. The second and larger gallery is in the Chicago suburb of Arlington Heights at 15 East Campbell Street. Both galleries mount several new exhibitions each year featuring art in all media.

Requirements: Slides should be accompanied by a resume.
Size: The Chicago gallery is 750' and Arlington Heights is 1,200'.
Services: The gallery offers commercial and home art consultation and advertises in the national and local art media.
Expenses: Shipping to the gallery.

MARY AND LEIGH BLOCK GALLERY

1967 Sheridan Road
Evanston, Illinois 60208
708-491-4000

The Mary & Leigh Block Gallery, which is administered by Northwestern University, frequently showcases photographic art and also maintains an impressive permanent collection which features 196 photographs by the legendary master W. Eugene Smith.

Key: ✔ = Portfolios Reviewed
★ = Non-Profit Organization
▲ = Private Dealer

RIVERWALK GALLERY ✔✮

443 West Aurora Avenue
Naperville, Illinois 60540
708-369-3443
Contact: Michele Rocush

Riverwalk Gallery is located just northwest of Chicago near the town of Aurora. The gallery, situated on the banks of the DuPage River, overlooks a historic quarry and has been designed to blend the art inside with the beauty of the natural setting. The gallery mounts 7 or 8 shows each year encompassing art in a variety of mediums.

Requirements: Submissions must include a minimum of 5 slides or photographs with a resume.
Size: There are two rooms: 33'x 35' and 24'x 25'.
Lighting: Track.
Expenses: Shipping and travel expenses are paid for by the photographer.

THE CHICAGO PUBLIC LIBRARY CULTURAL CENTER

78 East Washington Street
Chicago, Illinois 60602
312-346-3278
Hours: Monday-Thursday 9-7; Friday 9-6; Saturday 9-5; closed Sunday.

The *City of Chicago Department of Cultural Affairs* in conjunction with the Chicago Public Library presents more than 500 free programs and exhibitions annually in this European-styled landmark building. The cultural center regularly features both vintage and contemporary photographic exhibitions.

THE ART INSTITUTE OF CHICAGO/ PHOTO COLLECTIONS ✔✮

Michigan Avenue at Adams Street
Chicago, Illinois 60603
312-443-3663
Contact: Photography Department

The Photography Department of the Art Institute of Chicago reviews portfolios every Tuesday. Work regarding the history of photography is of great interest to the institute which mounts approximately 14 exhibitions annually.

Requirements: Portfolios are received on Tuesdays. However, an appointment must be made prior to drop-off. Portfolios are returned on the day of drop-off. Out-of-town photographers unable to leave portfolios may call to see if special arrangements can be made.
Size: 400 square feet.
Services: There is a photography study room available. The photographic exhibitions are promoted via museum publications and press-releases.

MUSEUM OF CONTEMPORARY PHOTOGRAPHY

Columbia College, 600 South Michigan Ave
Chicago, Illinois 60605
312-663-5554
Hours: Weekdays 10-5; Saturday 12-5.

The Museum of Contemporary Photography was founded by Columbia College Chicago in 1976 to exhibit, collect and promote contemporary photography, making it unique in the midwest for its exclusive commitment to the medium of photography. The museum features an on-going series of exhibitions, lectures and panel discussions, a permanent collection of American work, the *Midwest Photographers Project Print Study Room*, and traveling exhibitions curated at the museum. Themuseum often features socially significant work complimented by video and lecture presentations such as the recent exhibition *Raising Issues About Representing AIDS* with photos by Alon Reininger and Linda Troeller.

NORTHERN ILLINOIS UNIVERSITY ART GALLERY ✔★

212 West Superior, Suite 306
Chicago, Illinois 60605
312-642-6010
Contact: Peggy Doherty

Chicago's Northern Illinois University Art Gallery mounts 12 contemporary shows annually of art in all media. The gallery will view slides from developing and established photographers.
Requirements: Slides will be reviewed if accompanied by SASE.
Size: 2,000 square feet.
Lighting: Tungsten track lighting.
Services: Exhibitions are promoted via newspaper listings, gallery guides, and ads in local art journals.
Expenses: Shipping is the primary expense for the photographer.

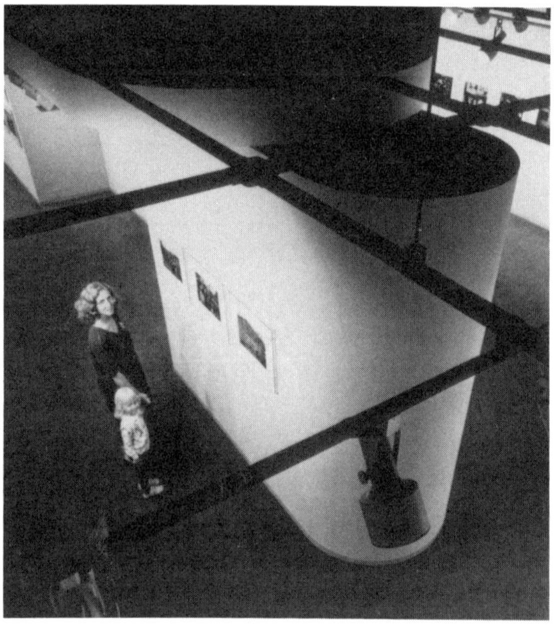

Photo by William G. Frederking

Chicago's Museum of Contemporary Photography was founded by Columbia College in 1976. Pictured here are the museum's east and west galleries.

CATHERINE EDELMAN GALLERY ✔

300 West Superior
Chicago, Illinois 60610
312-266-2350 *Fax:* 312-266-1967
Contact: Catherine Edelman

The Catherine Edelman Gallery is one of Chicago's most enduring and prominent art galleries. The gallery specializes in exhibitions of contemporary photography.
Requirements: Slides with press-clippings and resume may be submitted via the mail. Please include a SASE.
Size: 1,100 square feet.
Lighting: Halogen track lights.
Services: The gallery actively engages in all the standard promotional activities.
Expenses: Shipment one-way, matting, and announcement card mailing costs are the photogapher's expenses.

EHLERS CAUDILL GALLERY LTD. ✔▲

750 North Orleans, Suite 203
Chicago, Illinois 60610
312-642-8611
Contact: Shashi Caudill or Carol Ehlers

Chicago's Ehlers Caudill Gallery annually mounts between 6 and 8 photographic exhibitions. The gallery is interested in contemporary and historical photography that challenges the definition of the medium.
Requirements: Slides must be accompanied by a resume and a SASE.
Size: 1,500 square feet.
Services: The gallery promotes via newspapers and art magazines.

AXIS PHOTO PLUS ✔

5225 South Harper
Chicago, Illinois 60615
312-955-3278
Contact: Ed Pate

The Axis Photo Plus Gallery exhibits all types of photographic art in color and b/w.
Requirements: Submit one page of slides, a one paragraph bio, and a sample 5x7 b/w print suitable for postcard reproduction.
Size: 500 square feet.
Lighting: Track with spotlights.
Services: Darkroom rentals and one-hour photo finishing are available. Press releases are sent to all the Chicago newspapers.
Expenses: Reception costs and 50% of announcement card costs are the photographers.

ARTEMISIA GALLERY ✔☆

700 North Carpenter
Chicago, Illinois 60622
312-226-7323

Artemisia is a women's artist cooperative which is able to mount as many as 60 shows annually in its five exhibition spaces. The gallery exhibits the work of emerging and alternative artists of both sexes in a variety of media. The gallery also is dedicated to presenting major female artists whose work has not been shown previously in Chicago. Some well-known names who have exhibited at Artemisia are Alice Neel, Phyllis Bramson, and Judy Chicago.

Requirements: A page of 10 labeled slides with a resume and support material should be sent to Artemisia for review.
Size: 3,000 square feet throughout 5 rooms.
Lighting: Track.
Services: The gallery provides educational services to the art community. Exhibited artists have use of the gallery's mailing list, label service, and bulk mailing permit.
Expenses: The photographer pays a rental fee and for the announcements.

RANDOLPH STREET GALLERY ✔☆

756 North Milwaukee
Chicago, Illinois 60622
312-666-7737
Contact: Peter Taub

The Randolph Street Gallery mounts 7 shows annually of a contemporary and innovative nature.

Requirements: Slides can be submitted for review.
Size: 25′x 50′.
Lighting: Indoor flood lights.
Services: An honorarium is offered to the artists. Standard promotional efforts are employed.

The following galleries, museums, and private dealers in the Chicago area also offer photographic exhibitions:

Baruch Gallery (▲) 312-944-3377
40 E. Delaware Place
Chicago, Illinois 60611

Carl Hammer Gallery 312-266-8512
200 W. Superior
Chicago, Illinois 60610

Collected Image (▲) 312-334-6336
4865 N. Magnolia
Chicago, Illinois 60640

Edwynn Houk Gallery (▲) 312-943-0698
200 W. Superior
Chicago, Illinois 60610

Museum of Contemporary Art 312-280-2660
237 E. Ontario
Chicago, Illinois 60611

Peace Museum 312-440-1860
430 W. Erie
Chicago, Illinois 60610

Prairie Lee Gallery 312-266-7113
301 W. Superior
Chicago, Illinois 60610

Printworks Ltd. 312-664-9407
311 W. Superior
Chicago, Illinois 60610

Sazama Gallery 312-951-0004
300 W. Superior
Chicago, Illinois 60610

Steven Daiter (▲) 312-549-1553
722 W. Grace
Chicago, Illinois 60613

Terra Museum of American Art 312-664-3939
666 N. Michigan
Chicago, Illinois 60611

INDIANA

INDIANAPOLIS ART LEAGUE ✔☆

820 E. 67th Street
Indianapolis, Indiana 46220
317-255-2464 *Fax:* 317-254-0486
Contact: Julia Muney, Exhibitions Curator

Although not exclusively a photographic gallery, the Indianapolis Art League does present a few photo shows each year. The League is interested in contemporary work from Indiana and midwestern artists, both new and established.

Requirements: Slides accompanied by resume and cover letter are preferred. Slides are kept for permanent reference.
Size: 1,200 square feet and 150 running feet.
Lighting: Incandescent track lighting.
Services: The League offers the services of a full-time public relations/marketing director. Additionally, there is an artist referral service and corporate consultations.
Expenses: Framing and transporation of the work.

KATHRYN A. TODD FINE ARTS ✔

5356 North Hillside Avenue
Indianapolis, Indiana 46220
317-253-0250
Contact: Kathryn A. Todd

The Kathryn A. Todd Fine Arts gallery, which primarily exhibits nature and wildlife subjects, mounts several photographic shows each year.
Requirements: The gallery prefers to view photographs framed and matted.
Size: 1,800 square feet.
Lighting: Natural and florescent.
Expenses: Framing, matting, and shipping to the gallery are the photographer's expenses.

KANSAS

ARTFRAMES ✔

912 Illinois
Lawrence, Kansas 66044
913-842-1991
Contact: Linda Crabb

Artframes in Lawrence, Kansas, about one hour west of Kansas City, will view photography from both new and established photographers.
Requirements: Present framed work in person if possible. Otherwise contact directly with slide samples.

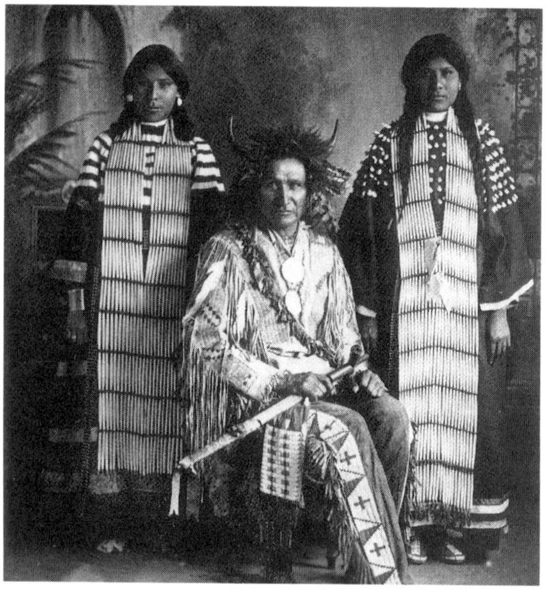

Photograph courtesy of the Southwest Museum

Vintage photography such as Red Fish & Daughters *by Frank B. Fiske is featured regularly at the Southwest Museum in Los Angeles.*

Services: Custom framing is available. The gallery promotes shows via local media and with mailings.
Expenses: Shipping (one-way) and framing expenses are the photographers.

KENTUCKY

LOUISVILLE VISUAL ART ASSOCIATION ✔

3005 Upper River Road
Louisville, Kentucky 40207
502-896-2146 *Fax:* 502-896-2148
Contact: John P. Begley, Director

The Louisville Visual Art Association mounts up to 12 contemporary themed exhibits annually featuring a variety of mediums. Interested photographers may submit sample slides for review.
Size: 150 running feet.

CARNEGIE ARTS CENTER ✔★

1028 Scott Boulevard
Covington, Kentucky 41011
606-491-2030
Contact: Arlene Gibeau

The historic Carnegie Arts Center offers 45 exhibits each year in its four galleries. Located in northern Kentucky across the Ohio River from Cincinnati, the center is housed in an outstanding Neo-French Renaissance structure built in 1902 and listed on the *National Register of Historic Places.*
Requirements: Although the center generally shows the work of tri-state residents (Kentucky, Ohio, Indiana), a *Call to Artists* is mailed in January requesting 10 slides for judging.
Size: 5,000 square feet in four gallery spaces.
Lighting: Track and natural light.
Services: Public Service Announcements, posters, invitations, local media, and membership mailings are utilized to present the center's activities.
Expenses: Mounting, framing, and transportation are the photographer's expenses.

TWO STREET STUDIO ✔

126 South Second Street
Paducah, Kentucky 42001
502-443-3927
Contact: Sarah Roush

Situated in the southwestern corner of Kentucky on the Ohio River, Paducah's Two Street Studio functions as an artist's gathering place as well as an active gallery which exhibits 8 to 10 shows annually. The studio is interested in mid-west regional contempory photography.

Requirements: Photographers should submit 16"x 20" prints, museum matted front and back, or in acid-free transparent envelopes.
Size: 2,000 square feet.
Lighting: Track.
Services: The studio promotes its activities via local radio interviews, announcements, and press releases. The studio also hosts poetry readings.
Expenses: Matting and framing, half the cost of color announcements, and travel costs are expenses incurred by the photographer.

LOUISIANA

GALLERY 630B ✔

636 Baronne Street
New Orleans, Louisiana 70113
504-529-7666
Contact: Marguerite Oestreicher

New Orlean's Gallery 630B can be found in the historic *French Quarter*, the heart of the city's artistic community. The gallery, not devoted exclusively to photography, primarily features the works of contemporary European and Latin American artists.
Requirements: 10 sample slides with resume and SASE can be submitted, clearly identified with name and address. The gallery currently represents a few photographers and generally handles large scale works in color. However, they are open to all quality work.
Size: 4,000 square feet.
Lighting: Halogen.
Services: The gallery offers curatorial and corporate services. Color invitations, gallery guide listings, and advertising are some of the promotional devices utilized.
Expenses: Freight to the gallery, framing, and all preparations necessary to ready the work for showing.

NEW ORLEANS MUSEUM OF ART

City Park
New Orleans, Louisiana 70179
504-488-2631
Admission: $4.00
Hours: Tuesday-Sunday 10-5. Closed Monday.

The New Orleans Museum of Art has been collecting photographic art seriously since 1973 and has garnered an international reputation as having one of the finest collections in the U.S. The more than 6,000 vintage photographs include 19th century travel photos, works from the Photo-Secession, American documentary photography, and work by members of Group f/64. Individual master photographers such as Ansel Adams, Margaret Bourke-White, Imogen Cunningham, Josel Sudek, Kertez, and others have been collected by the Museum to demonstrate the range of their art. The Museum, which is expanding its photography space, exhibits work from the permanent collection on a quarterly basis in the Laughlin Gallery.

Other outlets for photographic art in Louisiana are:

Arthur Roger Gallery 504-522-1999
432 Julia Street
New Orleans, Louisiana 70130

A Gallery For Fine Photography (▲) 504-568-1313
313 Royal Street
New Orleans, Louisiana 70130

MARYLAND

CHESAPEAKE GALLERY ✔✯

401 Thomas Run Road
Bel Air, Maryland 21014
301-836-4390
Contact: Marlene Barnes

The Chesapeake Gallery is located in Bel Air on the Harford Community College campus about twenty miles from Baltimore. The gallery exhibits fine art and historically significant collections.
Requirements: Fine art photographers should submit 15 to 20 samples slides with a resume.
Size: 30'x 40'.
Lighting: Track spots.
Services: Standard promotional activities are utilized to publicize the gallery.
Expenses: Framing and shipping (both directions) are paid for by the photographer.

ROSENBERG GALLERY, GOUCHER COLLEGE ✔✯

Dulaney Valley Road
Baltimore, Maryland 21204
301-337-6073 *Fax:* 301-337-6123
Contact: Helen Glazer, Exhibitions Director

The Rosenberg Gallery at Goucher College features contemporary art from the Maryland, D.C., and Virginia tri-state area. The gallery will review work from new photographers.

Requirements: Interested photographers should submit between 10 and 20 slides plus a resume and SASE. A brief statement is optional.
Size: 128 running feet.
Lighting: Incandescent track.
Services: The gallery is situated in the lobby of a performance and lecture hall complex which receives 65,000 visitors annually. The gallery promotes its shows via an extensive mailing list of over 10,000.
Expenses: Expenses are variable and can include framing, matting, and shipping.

SCHOOL 33 ART CENTER ✔★

1427 Light Street
Baltimore, Maryland 21230
301-396-4641 *Fax:* 301-625-2634
Contact: Madeline Irvine

School 33 Art Center specializes in contemporary visual art and mounts approximately 20 shows each year.
Requirements: Check directly with the center for the next application period. There is an annual call for Entries Prospectus.
Size: Gallery I is 1,240 square feet and II is 420 square feet.
Lighting: Track lighting.
Services: Press-releases, public service announcements, special events and an exhibition calendar are services of the School 33 Art Center.
Expenses: Shipping and framing work.

MASSACHUSETTS

WILLIAMS COLLEGE MUSEUM OF ART

Main Street
Williamstown, Massachusetts 01267
413-597-2429
Hours: Monday-Saturday 10-5; Sunday 1-5.

The Williams College Museum of Art offers one of the finest college museums in the country. An easy drive from both New York City (3 hours) and Boston (2 1/2), the museum emphasizes contemporary and modern art and its exhibitions rival those of major art institutions. Although the college museum owns a collection of photographic art by master photographers and often hosts important traveling exhibitions, local photographers are also regularly featured. The permanent collection contains groups of work by Kertesz and Bourne and portfolios by Walker Evans and Manuel Alvarez Bravo.

ROBERT KLEIN GALLERY ▲

207 South Street
Boston, Massachusetts 02111
617-482-8188

Boston's Robert Klein Gallery, which is one of the oldest east coast galleries specializing in photography, sells vintage 19th & 20th century and contemporary works.

LEE GALLERY ✔▲

119 Charles Street
Boston, Massachusetts 02114
617-729-4967
Contact: Mack Lee

The Lee Gallery exhibits vintage 19th and early 20th century photography.
Requirements: The gallery occasionally reviews portfolios. Matted prints are preferred for review purposes.

INSTITUTE OF CONTEMPORARY ART

955 Boylston Street
Boston, Massachusetts 02115
617-266-5152
Admission: $4.00
Hours: Wednesday & Sunday 11-5;
Thursday-Saturday 11-8.

Boston's Institute of Contemporary Art was established in 1936 as a non-collecting museum dedicated to presenting contemporary art in all media. The institute regularly presents a broad range of visual and performing arts activities including film screenings, television broadcasts, touring exhibitions and educational programs. In its earliest days the institute earned a pioneering reputation for presenting in the U.S. for the first time such innovative artists as Oskar Kokoschka and Edvard Munch. The tradition continues today as ICA hosts the controversial *Robert Mapplethorpe: The Perfect Moment.*

GALLERY SEVEN ✔

77 Rocky Neck Avenue
East Gloucester, Massachusetts 02130
508-281-6443
Contact: Patricia Weiler, Gallery Manager

Gallery Seven is located north of Boston in Gloucester and exhibits gelatin silver prints exclusively. The gallery also offers workshops in gelatin silver printing by Joseph Flack Weiler, as well as critiques of fine art photography.
Requirements: Telephone for an appointment.

HARVARD UNIVERSITY ART MUSEUMS FOGG ART MUSEUM

32 Quincy Street
Cambridge, Massachusetts 02138
617-495-9400
Admission: $4.00
Hours: Tuesday-Sunday 10-5; closed Monday.

Of the three Harvard University Art Museums, the Fogg, opened to the public in 1895, is the oldest and contains outstanding collections of photographs, prints, and drawings. The Fogg also houses the Harvard Fine Arts Library which contains a leading research collection and more than a million photographs and slides of works of art. Photographic exhibitions mounted by the Fogg are unusually innovative such as *Photographic Techniques in Art Conservation and Research* which explored the ways in which photography is used as a tool in art conservation and art detection. The Fogg's collection is also noted for its contemporary photography and its work in experimental media.

PHOTOGRAPHIC RESOURCE CENTER ✔★

602 Commonwealth Avenue
Boston, Massachusetts 02215
617-353-0700
Contact: Stan Trecker or Anita Douthat

The Photographic Resource Center at Boston University was launched in 1976 as the photographic showplace of New England. Annually the center presents 5 or 6 major shows as well as numerous smaller ones. With a current membership of over two thousand, the PRC attracts major artists such as William Wegman, Lee Friedlander, and Hiro as participants in its lecture series. The PRC also houses the Aaron Siskind Library of over 3,000 non-circulating photographic books.

Requirements: Photographers offering innovative, contemporary work may send slides for consideration by the Programming Committee.
Size: Main gallery is 28′ x 40′ plus two 50′ hallways.
Lighting: Tungsten track lighting.
Services: The PRC sponsors workshops and open portfolio nights. The center also produces two publications: *Newsletter* and a journal entitled *Views*.

The following galleries and museums in Boston regularly show photographic art:

Andrea Marquit Fine Arts 617-859-0190
207 Newbury Street
Boston, Massachusetts 02116

Boston Anthenaeum 617-227-0270
10 1/2 Beacon Street
Boston, Massachusetts 02108

Howard Yezerski 617-426-8085
186 South Street
Boston, Massachusetts 02111

MIT Museum 617-253-4444
265 Massachusetts Avenue
Boston, Massachusetts 02139

Zoe 617-536-6800
207 Newbury Street
Boston, Massachusetts 02116

MICHIGAN

DETROIT INSTITUTE OF ARTS

5200 Woodward Avenue
Detroit, Michigan 48202
313-833-7962
Admission: Free
Hours: Wednesday-Sunday 9:30-5:30; closed Monday and Tuesday.

The Detroit Institute of Arts has been at the forefront of American fine arts museums in collecting photographic art during the last two decades. The museum's Albert & Peggy de Salle Gallery of Photography is continually in use showing recent acquisitions such as the 1990 exhibition of works by distinguished African American photographers James Van DerZee, P.H. Polk, Roy DeCarava, and others. The permanent collection contains more than 7,000 images from the mid-19th through 20th century including surrealist, documentary, and pictorialist work. Special exhibitions often are complimented by guest lectures by such well-known speakers as Susan Sontag and *New York Times* photography critic Andy Grundberg.

MINNESOTA

JON OULMAN GALLERY ✔

Wyman Bldg, 7th Fl, 400 First Avenue N
Minneapolis, Minnesota 55401
612-333-2386
Contact: Jon Oulman

The Jon Oulman Gallery exhibits art in all mediums. The gallery will view material from photographers in slide format and accompanied by biographical information and SASE.

M C GALLERY ✔

400 1st Avenue North
Minneapolis, Minnesota 55401
612-339-1480 *Fax:* 612-339-1484
Contact: M.C. Anderson

The M C Gallery offers 16 contemporary shows annually.

Requirements: The gallery is open to viewing work from both new and established photographers.
Size: Two rooms totaling 3,500 square feet.
Lighting: Track.
Services: The gallery aids in framing and hanging shows, advertises in the appropriate magazines, and sends brochures to its extensive mailing list.
Expenses: Presentation costs and half of shipping costs.

WALKER ART CENTER

Vineland Place
Minneapolis, Minnesota 55403
612-375-7577
Admission: $3.00
Hours: Tuesday-Saturday 10-8; Sunday 11-5; closed Monday. Free Thursday.

Minneapolis' popular Walker Art Center presents an on-going film/video series, performance art, a lecture/education series, and temporary art/photography exhibitions regularly. The center also owns an impressive photography collection including works by Berenice Abbott, as well as Ansel Adams, Lee Friedlander, and Brett and Edward Weston.

THE MINNEAPOLIS INSTITUTE OF ARTS ✔✯

2400 Third Avenue South
Minneapolis, Minnesota 55404
612-870-3109 *Fax:* 612-870-3004
Contact: Ted Hartwell, Curator of Photography

The Minneapolis Institute of the Arts offers 4 major photographic exhibitions annually. The institute was one of the first museums in the U.S. to build a photography collection and today the collection numbers almost 10,000 images and includes works by master-photographers Stieglitz, Steichen, Evans, and Adams. In addition to hosting important traveling exhibitions, the institute also curates in-house such recent exhibitions as *Sylvia Plachy's Unguided Tour.*

Requirements: The institute in interested in all forms of creative photography. In person offerings should be originals. If contact is via the mail, submit only slides.
Size: 150 running feet.

ICEBOX GALLERY ✔

2401 Central Avenue N.E.
Minneapolis, Minnesota 55418
612-788-1790
Contact: H.M. Christopherson

The Icebox Gallery mounts 8 photographic exhibitions annually.

Requirements: Resumes with letters and SASE should accompany sample slides. Thought provoking themes are preferred.
Size: 750 square feet.
Lighting: Halogen.
Services: Local advertising and direct mail are used to promote the gallery. Quality framing is also offered.
Expenses: Invitations and mailing costs.

MISSOURI

SAINT LOUIS ART MUSEUM

Forest Park
St. Louis, Missouri 63110
314-721-0072
Admission: Free
Hours: Tuesdays 1:30-8:30; Wednesday-Sunday 10-5; closed Mondays.

The first municipally-supported art museum in the U.S., the Saint Louis Art Museum, is housed in the only permanent structure created for the 1904 World's Fair. The massive building, designed by noted architect Cass Gilbert, was put to good use during the museum's recent photography celebration *The Developing Eye: 150 Years of Photography From St. Louis Collections,* in which the museum was able to relinquish 18 separate galleries exclusively to photography. The Saint Louis Art Museum has an outstanding record for exhibiting photographic art. In addition to hosting many of the celebrated traveling exhibitions and internally curated shows, the museum sponsors an on-going photo/lecture series.

MORGAN GALLERY

819 Walnut Street, Scarritt Arcade
Kansas City, Missouri 64106
816-556-9446
Contact: Dana Crick Schupp, Photography Curator

The Morgan Gallery has just recently initiated a new fine art photography division. Contact them directly for information regarding portfolio reviews and exhibition schedules.

NELSON-ATKINS MUSEUM OF ART
4525 Oak Street
Kansas City, Missouri 64111
816-561-4000
Hours: Tuesday-Saturday 10-5; Sunday 1-5. Closed Monday.

The Nelson-Atkins Museum of Art maintains a permanent photographic collection with works by Edward Weston, Walker Evans, and Alfred Stieglitz and often exhibits shows curated by Hallmark Cards such as the recent *George N. Barnard, Photographer of Sherman's Campaign.* The museum also offers periodic adult education classes on photography. 1991 photographic exhibitions will include *Clarence John Laughlin: A Retrospective, Walker Evans: American Photographs,* and *Revelaciones: The Art of Manuel Alvarez Bravo.*

NEBRASKA

JOSLYN ART MUSEUM
2200 Dodge Street
Omaha, Nebraska 68102
402-342-3300
Admission: $2.00
Hours: Tuesday-Saturday 10-5; Sunday 1-5; Thursday evenings until 9.

The Joslyn Art Museum has served as a premier center for the visual arts since 1931. The museum's fine arts collection houses works from antiquity to the present, with a special emphasis on 19th and 20th century European and American art. The museum frequently hosts major traveling photography exhibitions such as recent major retrospectives of Karsh and Cartier-Bresson, the first major retrospective of Czech-American pictorialist D.J. Ruzicka, and the upcoming *I Dream A World* portraits of black women who changed America by Pulitzer Prize-winner Brian Lanker. The museum's permanent collection contains a large number of Native American photographs by F.A. Rinehart and Edward S. Curtis.

SHELDON MEMORIAL ART GALLERY
University of Nebraska
Lincoln, Nebraska 68588
402-472-2461
Admission: Free
Hours: Tuesday-Saturday 10-5; Sunday 2-9; Thursday-Saturday evenings 7-9.

The collections of the Sheldon Memorial Art Gallery document the development of American art from the 18th century to the present. The photography collection is particularly comprehensive, containing more than 1,500 significant prints both historical and contemporary in nature. The gallery also frequently hosts major traveling exhibitions as well as shows curated internally. 1991 exhibitions include the *James Enyeart Collection* and *Contact: Photojournalism Since Viet Nam* which will showcase the documentary work of photographers of the well-known Contact Press agency.

NEW JERSEY

HAYDEN PHOTOGRAPHY ✔
326 Washington Street #4C
Hoboken, New Jersey 07030
201-963-7081
Contact: Kathleen Hayden

Hayden Photography, located minutes from Manhattan via the Lincoln Tunnel, is a small gallery which offers two exhibitions annually. The gallery is generally interested in viewing black and white photography and pinhole photography.

NEW MEXICO

ALBUQUERQUE MUSEUM ✔☆
2000 Mountain Road NW
Albuquerque, New Mexico 87104
505-243-7255 *Fax:* 505-764-6546
Contact: Ellen Landis, Curator

The Albuquerque Museum mounts between 5 and 8 exhibits annually. Photography from emerging and

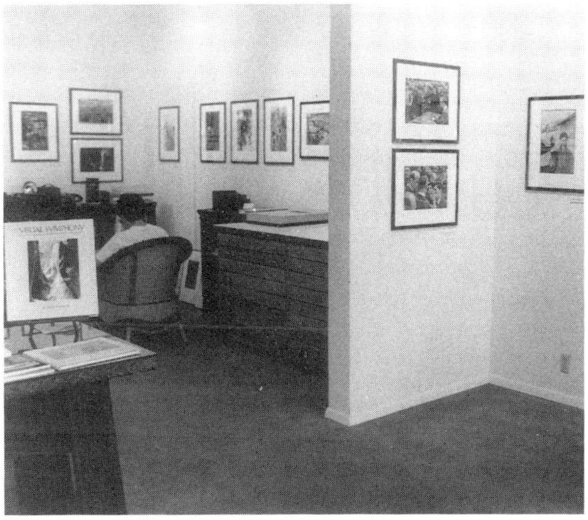

Photograph by Peter L. Gould

The Andrew Smith Gallery, in Santa Fe, specializes in American photography of the 19th & 20th centuries.

established photographers can be presented for consideration.
Requirements: Submit matted prints only after making contact with the curator.

ANDREW SMITH GALLERY, INC. ▲

76 E. San Francisco Street
Santa Fe, New Mexico 87501
505-984-1234 *Fax:* 505-983-2428
Contact: John Boland, Associate Director

The Andrew Smith Gallery specializes in fine American 19th and 20th century photography. The gallery represents a large number of photographers and was not reviewing new work at press time.

Other galleries in the Santa Fe area showing photographic art are:

Elaine Horwitch Galleries 505-988-8997
129 West Palace Avenue
Santa Fe, New Mexico 87501

Santa Fe Lightsource 505-980-9540
100 E. San Francisco Street
Santa Fe, New Mexico 87501

Scheinbaum & Russek, Ltd. (▲) 505-988-5116
328 Guadalupe, Suite M
Santa Fe, New Mexico 87501

NEW YORK

CARDOZO SCHOOL OF LAW/YESHIVA UNIVERSITY ✔✯

55 5th Avenue
New York, New York 10003
212-790-0310 *Fax:* 212-790-0345
Contact: Dean's Office

Perhaps an unexpected location for photography viewing, the Benjamin N. Cardozo School of Law mounts 5 shows annually. Photographers at all levels may submit samples of their work for consideration following written communication with the Dean's Office.
Expenses: Mounting and removing the exhibition materials.

Key: ✔ = Portfolios Reviewed
✯ = Non-Profit Organization
▲ = Private Dealer

LOWENHERZ GALLERY AT CAMERA CLUB OF NY ✔✯

853 Broadway
New York, New York 10003
212-260-7077
Contact: Gail Fischer, Exhibitions

The Lowenherz Gallery offers upcoming minority artists and others the possibility of a first New York show. The gallery is exhibiting approximately 9 shows each year of social commentary and cutting-edge photography. Because the gallery features the work of artists before they are recognized by the art world, prices are at a very affordable level for collectors.
Requirements: One sheet of 20 slides accompanied by a SASE and support material may be sent to Ms. Fischer for review.
Size: Roughly 20′ x 30′.
Lighting: Spots.
Services: Local advertising, press releases, and direct mail campaigns are utilized to build awareness of the gallery and its artists.
Expenses: All exhibition expenses are paid for by the photographer unless a grant is obtained.

PUCHONG GALLERY ✔

36A Third Avenue
New York, New York 10003
212-982-1811
Contact: Melvin Dennis

The Puchong Gallery is one of the most popular photographic galleries in New York City. The 13 exhibitions mounted annually present contemporary and experimental photography.
Requirements: Prints, supplemented by slides can be presented for consideration.
Size: 400 square feet.
Lighting: Halogen tracks.
Services: The gallery promotes shows by advertising in *Photography In New York* and its own tabloid publications. Press-releases are sent to the media.
Expenses: Basic promotional expenses such as advertising, reception, etc., are the photographer's. Expenses are variable per exhibition.

UNION SQUARE GALLERY ✔✯

118 E. 17th Street
New York, New York 10003
212-777-8393
Contact: Todd Weinstein

The Union Square Gallery, situated in Manhattan's burgeoning Flatiron district, features the *Ernst Haas Viewing Room.* Established in 1980 by Todd Weinstein who worked with Haas for many years, the gallery

has shown such photographic artists as Louis Stettner, Ed Grazda, Maggie Steber and Eugene Richards. The gallery is interested in viewing work from emerging and known artists.
Requirements: The gallery director recommends becoming familiar with the gallery and its style to see if it's an appropriate space to show your work.
Size: 200 square feet.
Lighting: Track with halogen.

FRANK BERNARDUCCI GALLERY ✔
560 Broadway
New York, New York 10011
212-334-0982
Contact: Frank Bernarducci

The Frank Bernarducci Gallery mounts about 10 shows annually of which 3 are devoted to photography. The gallery also represents several photographers.
Requirements: Work samples in slide format only may be presented.
Expenses: All expenses are variable depending on individual exhibition needs. Generally, the costs include framing, some mailing, half of the advertising, and transportation.

HELIO GALLERIES ✔
588 Broadway, 4th Floor
New York, New York 10012
212-966-5156 *Fax:* 212-260-1928
Contact: Joseph S. Sipos

Helio mounts 14 exhibits annually and also sponsors photography competitions.
Size: 5,000 square feet.
Lighting: Halogen.
Services: The gallery offers art lectures.

LAURENCE MILLER CONTEMPORARY PHOTOGRAPHS ✔▲
138 Spring Street
New York, New York 10012
212-226-1220 *Fax:* 212-226-2343
Contact: Laurence G. Miller

The venerable Laurence Miller Gallery is located in the heart of Soho, New York City's gallery mall. Showcasing the best in contemporary and fine vintage photography, the gallery mounts 9 shows annually and still finds time to review the work of photo-artists. William Eggleston, Lee Friedlander, and Michael Spano are a few of the photographers the gallery currently represents. Classic photographs from Weegee, Arbus, Stieglitz and Winogrand can also be found here.

Requirements: The gallery will review material from photographers on a seasonal basis. Contact first before submitting anything. After contact is made, slides must be accompanied by a SASE.
Size: 1,200 square feet.
Services: The gallery hosts opening receptions and uses the standard promotional machinery for exhibition publicity.

LIEBERMAN & SAUL ✔▲

155 Spring Street
New York, New York 10012
212-431-0747 *Fax:* 212-925-3491
Contact: Julie Saul or Nancy Lieberman

Lieberman and Saul present 9 contemporary and vintage photography exhibitions each year.
Requirements: Slides with resume and a SASE may be submitted via the mail
Size: 1,200 square feet.
Lighting: Track.
Services: The gallery promotes its exhibitions via advertisements and mailings.

MIN/LOWINSKY GALLERY ✔

584 Broadway
New York, New York 10012
212-226-5440 *Fax:* 212-226-5442
Contact: Sarah Hoe Sterling, Director

Simon Lowinsky began as an art dealer in San Francisco in the late sixties and, after relocating to the eastcoast, opened his gallery in Soho in 1989. Known for having an outstanding collection of vintage photographs, the gallery sells prints by classic photographers such as Man Ray, Kertesz, Mapplethorpe, Weston, and Imogen Cunningham. In late 1990 the gallery merged with Tokyo's Min Gallery and will now also promote the work of Japanese artists in the U.S.
Requirements: The gallery only reviews work which has been recommended. Vintage photographs can be offered by appointment.
Size: 1,800 square feet.
Services: The gallery advertises in leading photographic and art journals.
Expenses: Framing and publicity photos are the expenses of the photographer.

Key: ✔ = Portfolios Reviewed
★ = Non-Profit Organization
▲ = Private Dealer

MOTEL FINE ARTS ✔

167 Spring Street
New York, New York 10012
212-925-0205 *Fax:* 212-941-5491
Contact: Nina Chernik

Motel Fine Arts exhibits photographic art exclusively. The gallery is located in Soho.
Requirements: Finished prints can be offered for review.
Size: 2,000 square feet.
Lighting: Track.
Services: The gallery sometimes finances artistic projects.

MULTI MEDIA ARTS GALLERY ✔

580 Broadway, Suite 504
New York, New York 10012
212-966-4080
Contact: Chana Benjamin, Director

The Multi Media Arts Gallery offers 6 photographic exhibitions each year. The gallery also hosts a photography group which exhibits twice annually. The gallery is interested in new work that is non-sexist, non-racist, and non-violent in b/w or color.
Requirements: Prints or slides can be submitted.
Size: 11′ x 14′.
Lighting: Halogen spots.
Services: The gallery consults corporations and collectors on art purchasing. Press releases and listings promote the shows.
Expenses: There is a $35 membership fee in addition to the costs for reception, announcements, insurance and advertising.

NEW MUSEUM OF CONTEMPORARY ART

583 Broadway
New York, New York 10012
212-219-1222
Admission: $3.50
Hours: Wednesday-Sunday 12-6; Friday & Saturday until 8. Closed Mon-Tuesday.

The New Museum of Contemporary Art is located far from the busy byways of the traditional Manhattan museum scene. And we're not just talking physically! Unlike many museums, the New Museum's "semi-permanent" collection is retained for 10 years only, insuring that the art on view remains "contemporary." Created in 1977 as the only museum in New York devoted exclusively to the art and ideas of our time, The New Museum provides an arena for art that is experimental, non-traditional, or that might not otherwise receive a public viewing. Visit the New

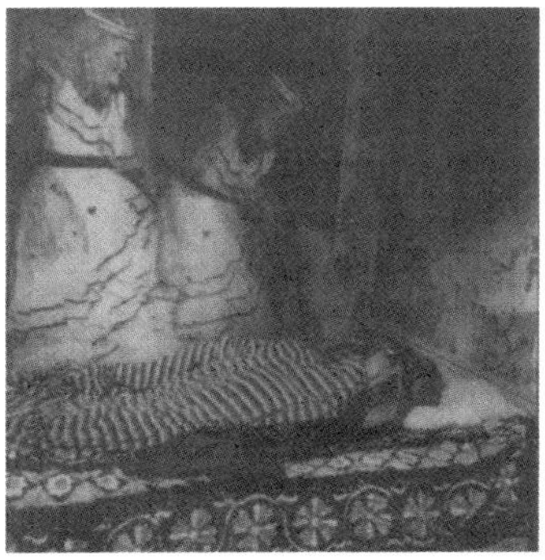

Pamela DeMarris

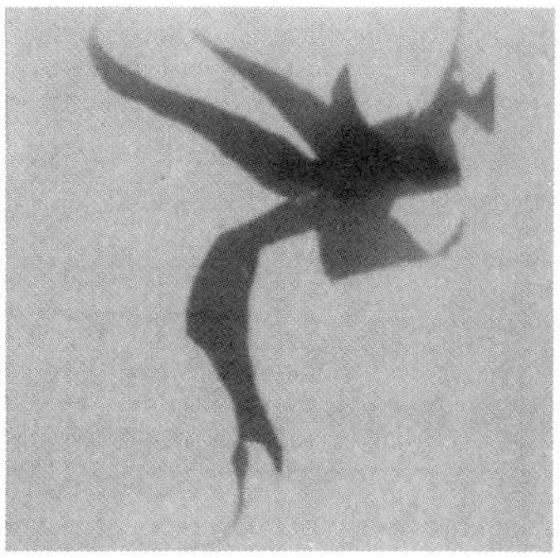

Eva Shaderowfsky

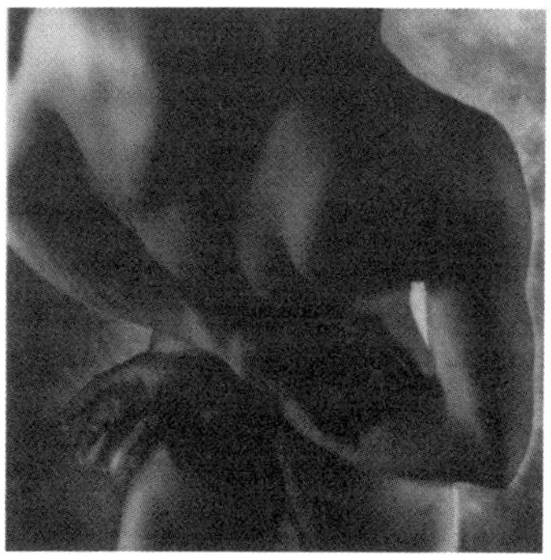

Charlie Pizzarello

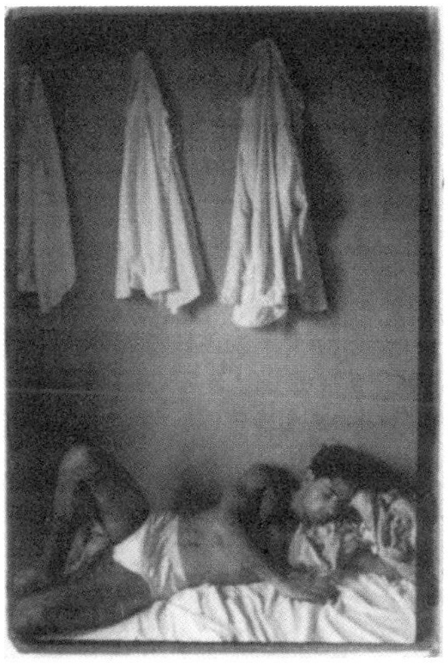

Bill Costa

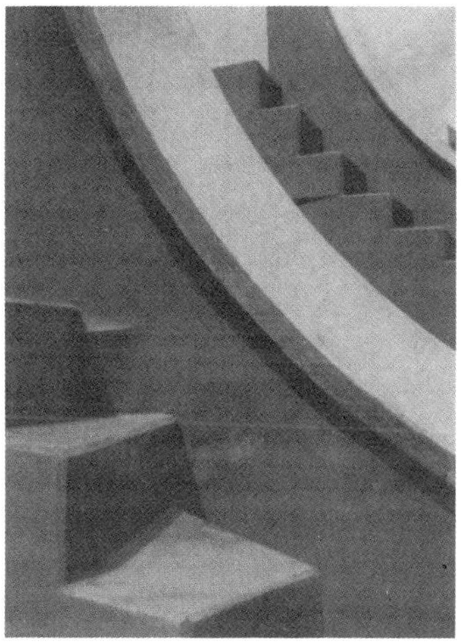

Barry Perlus

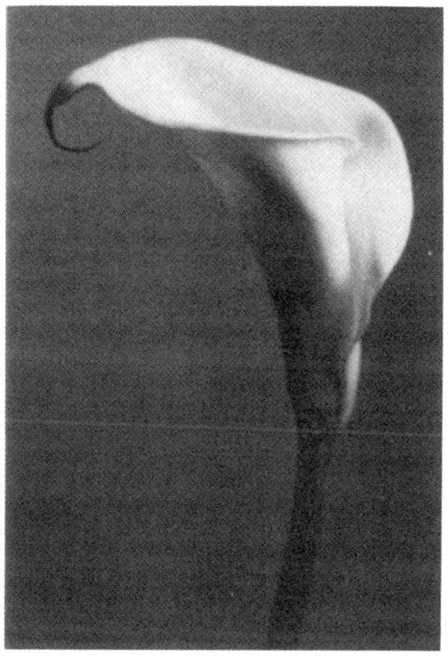

Anita Chernewski

PUCHONG FOLIOS

Puchong Folios, 36A Third Avenue, New York, N. Y. 10003 / Tel. (212) 481 - 0901

PUCHONG FOLIOS is a new review of fine art photography for connoisseurs and collectors. Removable multi-page folios illustrating featured artists are the heart of the publication, which will also include articles on collecting, printing media, laws governing reproducible artwork, critical analysis, commentaries, and reviews of photo exhibits with an international scope. (The photographs displayed above appear courtesy of the Puchong Gallery.)

Museum expecting to see innovative photography. The Museum also maintains an acclaimed education program and the *Soho Center Library*.

O.K. HARRIS WORKS OF ART ✔

383 West Broadway
New York, New York 10012
212-431-3600
Contact: Ivan C. Karp

O.K. Harris opened in Soho in 1969 and is one of the landmark galleries of the area. The gallery's prominent reputation lies in its demand for innovation of concept and maturity of technique. Photojournalism, urban documentation, and industrial documentation are the types of photography you might find in any of the 9 to 10 photography exhibitions the gallery mounts each year.

Requirements: Applicant photographers will be received in-person from Tuesday to Friday, 10-6, without appointment. 25 to 50 exhibition-size photos should be presented. Applicants can also mail 35mm slides with a SASE. Do not mail photographic prints!
Size: There are 4 exhibition spaces within the gallery.
Lighting: Variable.
Services: Lectures to student and fine arts organizations, a photographic archives of the gallery, and utilization of space for dancers, poets, and musicians are some of the services of O.K. Harris.
Expenses: Exhibitors incur the costs of shipping and framing.

ONE BOND/MASTERWORKS

One Bond Street
New York, New York 10012
212-614-9880 *Fax:* 212-477-8414
Contact: Michael M. Senft

The newly opened One Bond/Masterworks gallery presents 4 photographic exhibitions annually. The gallery primarily exhibits photography produced between the first and second World Wars.

OPSIS FOUNDATION ✔☆

561 Broadway, 10C
New York, New York 10012
212-966-8881 *Fax:* 212-966-8876
Contact: Frank Roth

The Opsis Foundation (Greek for sight or vision) was founded by film-maker Allan Albert to promote new contemporary photography. The foundation is especially interested in work that documents the world and its problems. The foundation and gallery are housed in the landmarked *Singer Building* in the heart of Soho. Exhibits change about every 5 to 8 weeks from September to June.

Requirements: Prospective photographers must call or write for an application to submit their work. Photographers must not have had a previous one-person exhibition in New York City. At least 10 and not more than 40 slides must accompany the application.
Size: 2,500 square feet.
Lighting: Spots and natural light.
Services: Matting and framing services are available for exhibited works. Each show receives an opening, and invitations and extensive media coverage are provided.
Expenses: Any additional advertising is paid for by the photographer.

PHOTOFIND GALLERY/HOWARD GREENBERG ▲

138 Spring Street
New York, New York 10012
212-334-0010 *Fax:* 212-941-7479
Contact: Howard Greenberg or Sarah Morthland

Photofind Gallery mounts 10 exhibitions yearly of fine vintage photographs. Their extensive inventory of works by photographic masters includes pictures by Berenice Abbott, Walker Evans, W. Eugene Smith, Roman Vishniac, and Lisette Model, among others. The gallery also represents and sells the work of many contemporary photographers.

STALEY-WISE ✔▲

560 Broadway, 6th Floor
New York, New York 10012
212-966-6223
Contact: Taki Wise or Etheleen Staley

The Staley-Wise Gallery, recently moved to this new location, presents 4 or 5 photographic exhibitions each year. Images illustrating fashion, style, and portraits are of interest to the gallery.

Requirements: Contact directly for information.

WARD-NASSE GALLERY ✔☆

178 Prince Street
New York, New York 10012
212-925-6951
Contact: Robert Curcio or Margot Norton

The Ward-Nasse Gallery is an artist run, non-profit gallery which was established in Soho in 1970. The gallery membership takes a very active part in all areas of the gallery's operation. 17 exhibitions are mounted annually, with a new one opening about every 3 weeks. True to its original concept, the gallery

prides itself on remaining an outlet for experimental art.
Requirements: Request an application form which can then be submitted with slides and biographical material.
Size: 2,000 square feet.
Lighting: Standard.
Services: The gallery maintains a slide library that is open to consultants. Members can also set up special viewings for clients. The gallery takes advantage of listings in many media outlets.

THE WITKIN GALLERY, INC. ★

415 West Broadway, 4th Floor
New York, New York 10012
212-925-5510
Contact: Evelyne Z. Daitz, Director

The Witkin Gallery enjoys a long-standing reputation as a showcase for fine art photography. Although the gallery is not devoted entirely to photographic art, 5 photography exhibitions are presented each year.
Requirements: The Witkin will only review the work of photographers who have been highly recommended by a curator, another gallery or a school. The director is interested in viewing high quality prints which illustrate a personalized point-of-view.
Services: The gallery maintains a book department where out-of-print, as well as current, books can be purchased.

FRANKLIN FURNACE ✔★

112 Franklin Street
New York, New York 10013
212-925-4671
Contact: Martha Wilson, Director

Franklin Furnace, "the Last Word in Museums", is one of Manhattan's genuinely experimental "alternative" spaces. Created in 1976 by artist Martha Wilson, the space is dedicated to the concept that "time" is the artistic medium of the 20th century. Temporal works of art such as artists' books, performance art, and temporary installations are collected and presented at the Furnace. Laurie Anderson, Eric Bogosian, and Karen Finley have all performed here.
Requirements: Franklin Furnace does review work from photographers. The deadline is April 1st for applications accompanied by slides.
Size: 1,500 square feet.
Services: Documentation and promotional services are offered by the organization.
Expenses: Announcement cards and framing are the artist's expenses.

HOME FOR CONTEMPORARY THEATRE & ART ✔★

44 Walker Street
New York, New York 10013
212-334-0272
Contact: Barbara Busachino

Home For Contemporary Theatre & Art shows the work of emerging artists in all media. Currently they are offering about 12 exhibitions annually.
Requirements: Slides may be submitted via the post.
Size: 18′x 22′.
Lighting: Track lighting.
Services: Free space and advertising.

MUSEUM OF HOLOGRAPHY ✔★

11 Mercer Street
New York, New York 10013
212-925-0581
Contact: Martha Tomko, Director or Sydney Dinsmore, Curator

Soho's Museum of Holography mounts between 2 to 10 exhibitions annually of holography and related laser technology.
Requirements: New and established holographers may present actual holograms with video, slide, and photographic documentation.
Size: 2,000 square feet.
Lighting: Halogen spot and flood.
Services: The museum offers group tours, demonstrations, workshops, educational video, related publications, and a gift shop. An in-house magazine is published called *Holosphere.*
Expenses: The artist is responsible for all framing and presentation expenses and sometimes accommodation.

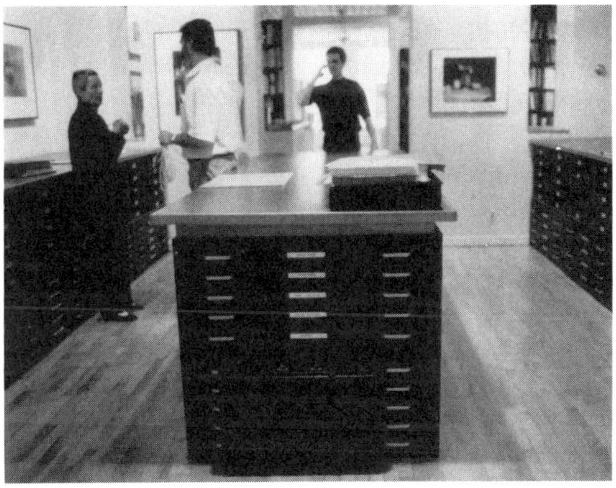

Photograph by Barbara Rosen

The Witkin Gallery in Soho is a showcase for fine art photography.

SOHO 20 ✔★

469 Broome Street
New York, New York 10013
212-226-4167
Contact: Eugenia C. Foxworth, Director

Soho 20 is a women's cooperative art gallery presenting 17 shows annually in all media. Established in 1973 as an alternative to the commercial gallery circuit, Soho 20 has continually expanded its goals and now exhibits Third World women artists, senior women artists, and emerging artists. The gallery is interested in viewing contemporary work from new and established female photographers.

Requirements: Write to Soho 20 for application information. Their application information and forms will supply you with extensive details for exhibiting and becoming a member.
Services: The gallery employs a public relations professional.

SYNCHRONICITY SPACE ✔★

55 Mercer Street
New York, New York 10013
212-925-8645
Contact: John Smith-Amato, Director of Fine Arts

Synchronicity Space annually produces about 22 exhibitions of which 3 or 4 are photographic in content. The gallery is interested in showing work which is representational to semi-abstract.

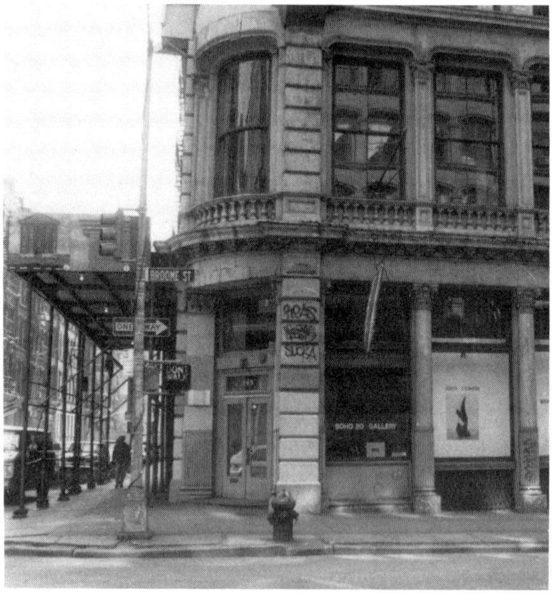

Photograph by Barbara Rosen

Soho 20 on Broome Street in Soho is a women's art cooperative.

Requirements: Work samples can be sent to John Smith-Amato or left for review.
Size: 1,500 square feet.
Lighting: Flood lights.
Services: The gallery creates press-kits for media use and utilizes the many free listings opportunities.
Expenses: A fee is charged for the gallery use. $800 for solo shows and $400 per artist for group shows of not more than 3 artists. Opening receptions, mailings, and insurance are other possible costs to the artist.

TOM CUGLIANI GALLERY ✔

508 Greenwich Street
New York, New York 10013
212-966-9006 *Fax:* 212-925-8792
Contact: Tom Cugliani

The Tom Cugliani Gallery exhibits art in every medium. The gallery will view work from developing and established photographers.

Requirements: Send slides with SASE.
Size: 1,500 square feet.
Lighting: Incandescent.

ROBIN RICE GALLERY ✔

325 West 11th Street
New York, New York 10014
212-366-6660
Contact: Robin Rice

Still-life photographer Robin Rice's newly opened gallery in Greenwich Village will be presenting 9 shows annually featuring contemporary fine-art photography exclusively. The gallery will review work illustrating an original style and is particularly interested in work produced via early 19th century processes.

Requirements: Contact by telephone before submitting material.
Size: 700 square feet with a 15 foot ceiling.
Lighting: Halogen.

NEW YORK PUBLIC LIBRARY

Fifth Avenue and 42nd Street
New York, New York 10018
212-221-7676
Admission: Free
Hours: Gallery hours: Monday-Saturday 10-6; closed Sunday.

Perhaps the most celebrated library in the world, New York City's Public Library is both an outstanding research facility and a landmark tourist stop. In addition to the library's 32,000,000 item collection, the structure also houses several galleries and exhibition spaces regularly featuring photography both as documentation and art. Recent exhibitions devoted to photography have included: *The View From Space: American Astronaut Photography, 1962-1972* and *Berenice Abbott, Photographer: A Modern Vision*. The New York Public Library Photography Collection contains over 50,000 fine art and documentary images and 72,000 stereographs of 19th century travel views, the social sciences, and more.

MUSEUM OF MODERN ART

11 West 53rd Street
New York, New York 10019
212-708-9480
Admission: $6.00
Hours: Daily 11-6; Thursday evenings until 9:00; closed Wednesday.

MOMA's photographic collection began in 1930 with the gift of a Walker Evans photograph from Lincoln Kirstein. In 1937 The Museum of Modern Art presented America's first critical survey of the history of photographic art with the exhibition *Photography: 1839-1937*. In 1940 the museum's Department of Photography was established and today oversee's a permanent collection of over 20,000 photographs and the many major traveling exhibitions which begin at the MOMA. MOMA's *Edward Steichen Photography Center* encompasses 6 small galleries plus a gallery for temporary exhibitions and the museum also houses a Photography Study Center. The annual *New Photography* show offers the work of undiscovered artists.

BONNI BENRUBI FINE ART PHOTOGRAPHS ✔▲

148 East 74th Street
New York, New York 10021
212-517-3766 *Fax:* 212-288-7815
Contact: Bonni Benrubi or Melissa Hotchkiss

Bonni Benrubi Fine Art Photographs, in Manhattan's upper eastside, is interested in vintage American as well as contemporary photography. The dealers will review work from both developing and established artists.

Requirements: Slides with a SASE may be submitted.
Services: The gallery has matting, framing, and insurance services.

JANET LEHR INC. ✔▲

891 Park Avenue
New York, New York 10021
212-288-1802 *Fax:* 212-288-6234
Contact: Janet Lehr

Janet Lehr mounts 5 exhibits annually featuring work dating from 1839 to the present. Specializing in vintage 19th & 20th century images, the photography offered covers a wide range of subjects including fashion, the American West, documentary, Bauhaus, and others.

Requirements: Photographers can submit slides with biographical information included.
Size: 1,950 square feet.
Lighting: Low intensity halogen.
Services: The gallery maintains a mailing list of over 3,500 which it uses to publicize its artwork.

PRAKAPAS GALLERY ▲

19 East 71st Street
New York, New York 10021
212-737-6066 *Fax:* 212-734-2759
Contact: Eugene J. or Dorothy S. Prakapas

Prakapas Gallery, located in New York City's upper eastside, exhibits European modernist work as well as some contemporary work of a serious, experimental nature.

Requirements: The gallery will view photographers' work; however, new photographers by referral only.

WHITNEY MUSEUM OF AMERICAN ART

945 Madison Avenue
New York, New York 10021
212-570-3600
Admission: $5.00
Hours: Tuesday 1-8; Wednesday-Saturday 11-5; Sunday 12-6. Closed Monday.

The Whitney Museum of American Art was founded in 1930 by Gertrude Vanderbilt Whitney in celebration of the richness and diversity of American art created in this century. Today, 60 years later, the museum continues the visionary quest of its founder and has expanded to include four branches: a sculpture court and galleries at the Philip Morris headquarters on Park Avenue; a gallery at the Federal Reserve Plaza in the Wall Street area; mid-town galleries at the Equitable Center on Seventh Avenue; and the Fairfield County branch in Stamford, Connecticut. The Whitney does not have a photography department but does feature special photographic exhibitions regularly.

PACE/MACGILL GALLERY

32 East 57th Street, Ninth Floor
New York, New York 10022
212-759-7999 *Fax:* 212-759-8964
Contact: Peter Macgill, Director

The Pace/MacGill Gallery is one of the leading photography galleries in New York City. The gallery is currently hosting about 20 exhibitions each year showcasing contemporary photography.

NEW YORK PUBLIC LIBRARY - LINCOLN CENTER

111 Amsterdam Avenue at 65th Street
New York, New York 10023
212-870-1600
Admission: Free
Hours: Monday-Friday 12-6; Saturday 10-6; closed Sunday.

Not quite as well-known as the main branch on 42nd & Fifth, the New York Public Library at Lincoln Center is greatly appreciated by those who work in or are fascinated by the arts. The several galleries housed here regularly present photography as historical documentation and as art, generally in relation to dance, music, theater, or film. A recent exhibition devoted to dance photography *Round About The Ballet* offered images of dancers Nureyev, Markarova, and Kirkland by former official photographer to the Royal Ballet in London, Roy Round.

NEW YORK HISTORICAL SOCIETY

170 Central Park West
New York, New York 10024
212-873-3400
Admission: $3.00
Hours: Tuesday-Sunday 10-5; closed Monday.

The New York Historical Society is a distinguished research and education facility and the Society maintains extensive photographic documentation not only of New York City and state, but of the U.S. Established in 1804, the Society houses New York City's oldest museum and an outstanding research library. The museum frequently displays work from its permanent collection and temporary exhibitions such as *Charles Gilbert Hine: Impressions of a City* are regularly presented.

STUDIO MUSEUM IN HARLEM

144 West 125th Street
New York, New York 10027
212-865-2420
Admission: $2.00
Hours: Wednesday-Friday 10-5; Saturday-Sunday 1-6; closed Monday and Tuesday.

The Studio Museum in Harlem stands in the heart of the world's most celebrated black community and is easily reached by several subway and bus lines. The museum, which is the cornerstone of the community's rebirth and redevelopment, contains galleries, workshops and artist's studios, a museum shop, and an extensive permanent collection of work by leading black artists. In 1987 the Studio Museum became the first, and only, black museum to receive accreditation from the *American Association of Museums*. Devoted to collecting, documenting, and analyzing the art of Black America, the museum recently mounted an exhibition called *Home: Contemporary Urban Images by Black Photographers.*

THE JEWISH MUSEUM

1109 Fifth Avenue
New York, New York 10028
212-860-1888
Admission: $4.50
Hours: Sunday 11-6; Monday-Thursday 12-5; closed Friday and Saturday.

Showcasing 4,000 years of Jewish culture, New York City's Jewish Museum is located on *Museum Mile*, 5th Avenue at 92nd Street. Housed in one of the world-renowned avenue's striking turn-of-the-century mansions, The Jewish Museum contains historic Hebrew objects, religious artifacts from Europe and

Israel, and art in all mediums celebrating the Jewish faith. The museum frequently presents photographic exhibitions, generally historic or documentary in content. Recent photographic exhibitions have included Helene Hourmat's photos of her French-Moroccan Jewish family history and *A Day In The Warsaw Ghetto,* photos taken in 1941 and exhibited in the U.S. for the first time in 1990.

METROPOLITAN MUSEUM OF ART

82nd Street and Fifth Avenue
New York, New York 10028
212-879-5500
Admission: $5.00
Hours: Tuesday-Sunday 9:30-5:15; Fridays & Saturdays until 8:45. Shut Monday.

Heralded internationally as one of the most important art institutions in existence, The Metropolitan is the jewel in New York's collection of world-class art museums. In addition to the numerous collections encompassing every era, culture, and medium, the Met owns an impressive photographic collection which was donated by the Ford Motor Company in 1987 and contains over 500 photographs by a variety of stellar artists such as Man Ray, Stieglitz, Moholyg-Nagy, Brancusi and Magritte. Many of these pictures were exhibited at the Met in 1989 as part of the exhibition *The New Vision: Photography Between the Wars.* The museum is also the recipient of 600 photos from Stieglitz's personal collection.

INTERNATIONAL CENTER OF PHOTOGRAPHY ✔

1130 Fifth Avenue
New York, New York 10121
212-860-1777 *Fax:* 212-360-6490
Contact: Ruth Lester, Portfolio Review 860-1770

I.C.P. maintains two exhibition facilities in New York City and this location on upper Fifth Avenue's *Museum Mile* is the original one. The newer facility can be found in mid-town at 44th Street and the Avenue of the Americas. I.C.P. presents approximately 12 exhibitions annually representing the full range of photographic art.
Requirements: There are two options for presenting your work to I.C.P. Either contact Ruth Lester for an appointment at the number above or call 212-860-1773 for information on portfolio drop-offs. There are monthly portfolio reviews by the exhibitions staff.
Size: 400 running feet.
Lighting: Tungsten and incandescent.

PHOTOGRAPHY CENTER GALLERY AT 92ND ST Y ✔★

1395 Lexington Avenue
New York, New York 10128
212-415-5566 *Fax:* 212-415-5578
Contact: J. Wayne Olson

The Photography Center Gallery in Manhattan's upper eastside YMCA has established a reputation for showcasing new photographic talent. The gallery is interested in contemporary imagery by active photographers working in experimental/non-commercial modes.
Requirements: Twenty slides of recent work are requested for review and the material submitted should be accompanied by a resume.
Size: 400 square feet.
Lighting: Track.
Services: The Y Gallery hosts an opening reception. Listings in *The New York Times* and *Village Voice* publicize the exhibitions.
Expenses: Matting, framing, and shipping expenses belong to the photographer.

FOCAL POINT GALLERY ✔

321 City Island Avenue
Bronx, New York 10464
212-885-1403
Contact: Ron Terner

The Focal Point Gallery is located in a picturesque corner of the Bronx called City Island which resembles a misplaced New England fishing village. The gallery presents art in a variety of mediums and is especially interested in the work of new photographers. The gallery also hosts an annual national juried exhibition resulting in a photographer being awarded a one-person show.

Requirements: Photographers should call directly for submission information.
Size: 15′x 10′.
Lighting: Florescent.
Services: Focal Point hosts openings to which it invites members of the art media. The gallery will also offer assistance in hanging shows

BRONX MUSEUM OF THE ARTS ✔★

1040 Grand Concourse
Bronx, New York 10467
212-681-6000 *Fax:* 212-681-6181
Contact: Luis Cancel, Executive Director

The Bronx Museum of the Arts mounts 30 exhibitions annually covering all media.

Requirements: Photographers can submit sample 35mm slides with resume.
Size: 6,500 square feet.
Lighting: Incandescent.
Services: Promotional activities include receptions, quarterly bulletins, and press-releases.
Expenses: Printing and sometimes framing and matting costs are paid for by the photographer.

Additional New York area galleries, museums, and private photo/art dealers are:

American Museum of Natural History 212-769-5100
Central Park West at W. 79th Street
New York, New York 10024

Asia Society 212-288-6400
725 Park Avenue
New York, New York 10021

Barbara Fendrick Gallery 212-966-2820
568 Broadway
New York, New York 10012

Barry Friedman Ltd. 212-794-8950
1094 Madison Avenue
New York, New York 10028

Bennett Siegel Gallery 212-385-4434
140 West Broadway
New York, New York 10012

Brent Sikkema Fine Art (▲) 212-941-6210
155 Spring Street
New York, New York 10012

Burden Gallery 212-475-8790
20 E. 23rd Street
New York, New York 10010

Commerce Graphics Ltd, Inc. (▲) 201-438-9000
160 East Union Avenue
East Rutherford, New Jersey 07073

Coup de Grace 212-431-5799
579 Broadway
New York, New York 10012

Fotomann, Inc. (▲) 212-570-1223
42 East 76th Street
New York, New York 10021

Franklin Parrasch Gallery 212-925-7090
584 Broadway
New York, New York 10012

Gracie Mansion 212-941-5580
532 Broadway
New York, New York 10012

Hirschl & Adler Modern 212-744-6700
851 Madison Avenue
New York, New York 10021

Hyperion Press (▲) 212-877-2131
200 W. 86th Street
New York, New York 10012

James Danziger Gallery 212-226-0056
415 West Broadway
New York, New York 10012

Jayne H. Baum Gallery 212-219-9854
588 Broadway
New York, New York 10012

Ledel 212-966-7659
168 Mercer Street
New York, New York 10012

Lee Marks Fine Art (▲) 212-877-9354
173 W. 78th Street
New York, New York 10024

Lower East Side Tenement Museum 212-431-0233
97 Orchard Street
New York, New York 10002

Marcuse Pfeifer Gallery (▲) 212-226-2251
568 Broadway
New York, New York 10012

Massimo Audiello 212-966-8830
142 Greene Street
New York, New York 10012

Midtown Y Photography Gallery 212-674-7200
344 E. 14th Street
New York, New York 10003

Museum of the City of New York 212-534-1034
Fifth Avenue at 103rd Street
New York, New York 10029

Museum of Contemporary Hispanic Art
212-966-6699
584 Broadway
New York, New York 10012

Nahan 212-966-9313
381 West Broadway
New York, New York 10012

National Academy of Design 212-369-4880
1083 Fifth Avenue
New York, New York 10128

National Museum of Immigration 212-269-5755
Ellis Island
New York, New York 10001

Neikrug Photographica (▲) 212-288-7741
224 East 68th Street
New York, New York 10021

Nikon House 212-586-3907
620 Fifth Avenue
New York, New York 10020

One Bond/Masterworks 212-614-9880
1 Bond Street
New York, New York 10012

Photocollect (▲) 212-222-7381
740 West End Avenue
New York, New York 10024

Pyramid Gallery 212-431-3270
568 Broadway
New York, New York 10012

Robert Burge 20th Century Photographs
(212) 935-9803
200 E. 61st Street
New York, New York 10021

Robert Miller Gallery (▲) 212-980-5454
41 East 57th Street
New York, New York 10022

Sidney Janis Gallery (▲) 212-586-0110
110 West 57th Street
New York, New York 10019

Soho Photo 212-226-8571
15 White Street
New York, New York 10013

South Street Seaport Museum 212-669-9424
207 Water Street
New York, New York 10003

Stux Gallery 212-219-0010
155 Spring Street
New York, New York 10012

The 4th Street Photo Gallery 212-673-1021
67 East 4th Street
New York, New York 10003

Viridian Gallery 212-245-2882
52 W. 57th Street
New York, New York 10019

Walker, Ursitti & McGinniss 212-966-7543
500 Greenwich Street
New York, New York 10013

Zabriskie Gallery (▲) 212-307-7430
724 Fifth Avenue
New York, New York 10019

HUDSON RIVER MUSEUM

511 Warburton Avenue
Yonkers, New York 10701
914-963-4550
Admission: $3.00
Hours: Wednesday-Saturday 10-5; Sunday 12-5; Thursday evenings until 9.

The Hudson River Museum is a popular regional attraction easily reached from New York City by rail or car. The museum frequently features photographic art in its *Palisades Gallery* which is devoted to presenting new work in all media. The museum also hosts the annual juried exhibition by *The Hudson River Contemporary Artists Association*, which includes photography, painting, sculpture, and mixed media.

THE BROOKLYN MUSEUM

200 Eastern Parkway
Brooklyn, New York 11238
718-638-5000
Admission: $4.00

Hours: Wednesday-Sunday 10-5. Closed Monday and Tuesday.

The Brooklyn Museum has established a history of "firsts" when it comes to photography. In 1889 the museum became the first to collect photography and was also the only institution to offer photography as a course. Early exhibitions featured the work of Berenice Abbott, Cecil Beaton, and Andre Kertesz. In the '50s the museum was the first to recognize the significance of the photography from the Depression years with its exhibition of the *Farm Security Administration Works*. In the '70s the Brooklyn Museum's retrospective of Lewis Hine's work became the first art show to travel throughout China. Today the museum actively collects works by experimental photographers and photo documentarians.

QUEENS COLLEGE ART CENTER ✔★

65-30 Kissena Boulevard
Flushing, New York 11367
718-997-3770 *Fax:* 718-793-8049
Contact: Suzanna Simor, Director

The Queens College Art Center at the *Benjamin S. Rosenthal Library* mounts 10 exhibitions each year of which as many as 3 are devoted to photography.

Requirements: Contact via mail with samples, resume, and personal statement.
Size: 145 running feet.
Lighting: Track floods.
Expenses: Shipping, framing, and matting are the photographer's expenses. The college provides for the printing and mailing of announcements.

CAMERA MUSEUM

Extension South 2nd Avenue
Broadalbin, New York 12010
518-883-3357
Admission: $1.00

Photographers Martin and Florence Clark have created a 5 room camera museum which features antique cameras and accessories and vintage photographs of their tri-county area. Located at the southern boundary of the Adirondack Park and just to the north of Scenectady, the museum also offers vintage periodicals and magazines on photography. In addition to guided tours of the museum, the Clarks offer evening classes on all beginning phases of photography to 4-H, Scout, and senior groups. For $1.00, students receive instruction on using 4x5 cameras, developing negatives, and making enlargements and contact sheets. The $1.00 fee goes to the local ambulance corp or the fire company.

ALBANY CENTER GALLERIES ✔★

23 Monroe Street
Albany, New York 12210
518-462-4775
Contact: Leslie Urbach

The Albany Center Galleries is dedicated to the exhibiton of art by artists of the Mohawk-Hudson region. Although they usually only present one photographic exhibition each year, the Albany Center is open to viewing exceptional photographic work.

Requirements: Presented work should be "ready to be hung".
Size: 6,000 square feet.
Lighting: Track lighting.
Services: The center provides press releases, mailings, receptions, and mounting services.

TANNERY BROOK COLLECTIONS ✔

12 Tannery Brook
Woodstock, New York 12406
914-679-4706 *Fax:* 914-679-8832
Contact: Leonard I. Stein

Centrally located in the village of Woodstock, Tannery Brook offers approximately 6 exhibitions annually.

Requirements: New photographers should submit framed photographs for consideration.
Size: 1,000 square feet.
Lighting: Track and spotlights.
Services: The gallery uses the local radio and print media to promote exhibitions. The gallery also hosts opening receptions.
Expenses: All the expenses necessary to prepare work for hanging belong to the photographer.

PICTURES GALLERY ✔

Route 212
Willow, New York 12495
914-688-5865
Contact: Marty Carey

Pictures Gallery is devoted to 20th century vintage and contemporary advertising, fashion, and music images. Located about 10 miles west of the village of Woodstock, the gallery mounts 9 shows each year.

Requirements: Preceded by a telephone call or letter, slides or prints can be offered.
Size: The gallery contains 3 rooms accommodating 45 prints.
Lighting: Track lighting.
Services: Local advertising and announcement cards are used to publicize the gallery.
Expenses: Printing and shipping are the basic expenses of the photographer.

CENTER FOR PHOTOGRAPHY AT WOODSTOCK ✔★

59 Tinker Street
Woodstock, New York 12498
914-679-9957
Contact: Kathleen Kenyon, Associate Director

The Center for Photography at Woodstock is one of the northeast's outstanding photography complexes. Their creative workshops, which have featured many of the leading names in photography circles, have earned them a well-deserved following. Likewise, the center's gallery is one of the centerpieces of the ever-blooming Catskill/Hudson River arts community. The center mounts 9 exhibitions annually.

Requirements: Slides may be submitted for the review process.
Size: 2,000 square feet.
Lighting: Track.
Services: The exhibitions at the center are advertised and promoted in the national and local media. Show cards are printed for the exhibitions.
Expenses: Expenses are negotiable.

UNISON LEARNING CENTER ✔★

68 Mountain Rest Road
New Paltz, New York 12561
914-255-1559
Contact: Stuart Bigley

The Unison Learning Center Gallery exhibits all types of art and currently mounts 7 shows annually.

Requirements: Submit slides for consideration.
Size: 2,000 square feet.
Services: Promotion is handled via press-releases.

BARRETT HOUSE GALLERIES ✔★

55 Noxon Street
Poughkeepsie, New York 12601
914-471-2550
Contact: Fran Smulcheski, Association Director

Barrett House Galleries, part of the *Dutchess County Art Association*, mounts 10 exhibitions annually in all media. Photographers may submit material which addresses contemporary issues.

Requirements: Submit 15 to 20 slides with resume, reviews, statement and a SASE.
Size: There are 4 galleries and each is 11'x 15'.
Lighting: Museum standard.
Services: Barrett House works diligently at having exhibitions reviewed. The gallery lists its shows in photo periodicals and local papers and utilizes radio and TV.
Expenses: Shipping expenses only.

ADIRONDACK CENTER MUSEUM ✔★

Court Street
Elizabethtown, New York 12932
518-873-6466
Contact: James A. Kinley, Director

The Adirondack Center Museum can be found in Elizabethtown, a small town located inside the Adirondack Park and a short drive from Burlington, Vermont and Plattsburgh, New York. The museum, which features 6 or 7 new exhibitions each year, will review photography on the Adirondacks and Essex County history.

Requirements: A sample of work can be submitted to the museum's director.
Size: The main gallery is 84' linear and hall gallery 66' linear.
Lighting: Incandescent and shielded florescent.
Services: Opening receptions and membership mailings are used to promote exhibitions.
Expenses: Transportation and some publicity expenses are paid for by the photographer.

C.E.P.A. ✔★

700 Main Street, 4th Floor
Buffalo, New York 14202
716-856-2717
Contact: Gail NIcholson, Director

C.E.P.A. (Center for Exploratory & Perceptual Art) exhibits photography, film, computer imaging and installations.

Requirements: Slides with resume, press materials, and articles can be submitted for review.
Size: 210 linear feet.
Lighting: Track.
Services: The gallery produces catalogues for some shows and offers honorariums to artists. Other services may include postcard announcements and travel.

ALBRIGHT-KNOX ART GALLERY

1285 Elmwood Avenue
Buffalo, New York 14222
716-882-8700
Admission: Donation.
Hours: Tuesday-Saturday 11-5; Sunday 12-5. Closed Monday.

Buffalo's Albright-Knox Art Gallery is well-known for its exhibits of modern art, primarily 20th century painting and sculpture by American and European artists. The gallery periodically features photographic art such as the landscape photography of John Pfahl offered in the exhibition *A Distanced Land* which was presented in 1990.

INTERNATIONAL MUSEUM OF PHOTOGRAPHY

George Eastman House, 900 East Avenue
Rochester, New York 14607
716-271-3361

The International Museum of Photography is housed in Rochester's *George Eastman House* and features a permanent display illustrating the historic origins of photography and its development. The Museum also offers many temporary exhibitions and maintains an archive of nearly a half million images. It is possible to arrange viewing of the images in the archive.

LIGHT IMPRESSIONS SPECTRUM GALLERY

439 Monroe Avenue
Rochester, New York 14607
716-271-8960
Contact: Lance Speer, Director

This well-known gallery mounts up to 9 shows annually featuring the work of internationally known photographers such as Duane Michaels, Linda Connor, Jerry Ulesmann, John Sexton, and Aaron Siskind. Light Impressions also circulates exhibitions curated by gallery director Lance Speer, the most recent of which was entitled *Italy By Armchair: Stereographs & Their Antecedents.* Although not currently viewing portfolios, the gallery does continue to showcase new artists.

NORTH CAROLINA

ACKLAND ART MUSEUM

University of North Carolina
Chapel Hill, North Carolina 27599
919-966-5736
Hours: Tuesday-Saturday, 10-5; Sunday 1-5.

Upon completion of renovation, the Ackland Art Museum will welcome 1991 with expanded and improved galleries including a gallery primarily intended for displaying prints and photographs. The renovation will also provide a viewing room allowing access to those works not on display. The first photography exhibition held in the refreshed facility will be *Recent Acquisitions: Photography.* The museum has been collecting photography since the mid-seventies and currently owns approximately 1,000 works from such photographic masters as Atget, Brandt, Brassai, Hine, Siskind, and Strand.

DUKE UNIVERSITY MUSEUM OF ART

6845 College Station
Durham, North Carolina 27708
919-684-5135
Admission: Free
Hours: Tuesday-Friday 9-5; Saturday 11-2; Sunday 2-5.

Duke University's Museum of Art frequently showcases photography and maintains a permanent photography collection. The collection contains works by Robert Doisneau, Alen MacWeeney, and Elliott Erwitt. A recent photographic exhibition was devoted to *Masterpieces of Dance Photography 1849 to the Present.*

MINT MUSEUM

2730 Randolph Road
Charlotte, North Carolina 28207
704-337-2000
Admission: $2.00
Hours: Tuesday 10-10; Wednesday-Saturday 10-5; 1-6 Sunday; closed Monday.

Opened in 1936 as the first art museum in North Carolina, the Mint was originally contructed in 1836 as the first branch of the United States Mint. The building also served as a Confederate Headquarters and a hospital prior to its becoming an important cultural institution in the region. The Mint mounts photography exhibitions regularly and hosts an art biennial which represents as many as 50 new artists from North Carolina and neighboring states. Recent photography exhibitions have included: *A Celebration of Photography, The Fashionable Image,* and *Jacqueline Hayden: Dislocation/Relocation.*

OHIO

COLUMBUS MUSEUM OF ART

480 East Broad Street
Columbus, Ohio 43215
614-221-6801
Hours: Tuesday, Friday, Sunday 11-5; Wednesday 11-9; Saturday 10-5.

The Columbus Museum of Art has recently added a photographic gallery and archives to its facility. During 1991 the museum will exhibit *Poetics of the Real: American Landscape Photography* curated internally and will host *The Legendary John Brown: Prints by Jacob Lawrence* organized by the Detroit Institute of the Arts and the popular *I Dream A World: Portraits of Black Women Who Changed America.*

TOLEDO MUSEUM OF ART

2445 Monroe Street at Scottwood Avenue
Toledo, Ohio 43697
419-255-8000
Admission: Free
Hours: Tuesday-Saturday 10-4; Sunday 1-5; closed Monday.

The Toledo Museum of Art is an important regional stop for many traveling photographic exhibitions such as the Eastman House's *American Photography: 1839-1900;* Aperture's *Mothers & Daughters, That Special Quality*; and the New York Public Library's *Berenice Abbott, Photographer: A Modern Vision.* The museum maintains a permanent photography collection and also offers a seasonal series of photography workshops and classes geared for junior and senior high school students as well as beginning and studio courses for adults.

BUTLER INSTITUTE OF AMERICAN ART

524 Wick Avenue
Youngstown, Ohio 44502
216-743-1107
Admission: Free
Hours: Tuesday-Thursday 11-4; Wednesday 11-8; Sunday 12-4; closed Monday.

The Butler Institute of American Art was founded in 1919 by industrialist Joseph G. Butler and is housed in the first structure built in the U.S. to specifically house a collection of American Art. The museum's photographic collection, begun in 1955, includes almost 6,000 black and white movie stills and star close-ups; photos of early Massachusetts gravestones and dye-transfers by Daniel Farber; and a collection of *Youngstown Steel* by George Bennett. Recent photography exhibitions have included: *Steichen & His Men: A Portrait of World War II, Ohio Steel Mills: A Post Industrial Perspective* panoramic photo collages by Masumi Hayashi, and *History of Travel,* paintings (!) by William Wegman.

CINCINNATI ART MUSEUM

Eden Park
Cincinnati, Ohio 45202
513-721-5204
Hours: Tuesday-Saturday 10-5; Wednesday until 9 pm; Sunday 12-5;.

Situated in the city's beautiful Eden Park, the Cincinnati Art Museum sits atop one of seven hills overlooking the Ohio River and the colorful northern Kentucky landscape. The museum, which will be undergoing renovation of most of the facility until fall 1992, owns an extensive photography collection which includes masterworks from Mathew Brady, Eadweard Muybridge, Julia Magaret Cameron, Nadar, Man Ray, Dorthea Lange, Richard Avedon, and Cecil Beaton among many others. As the museum will be operating with an extremely limited exhibition space and schedule during the renovations, it's recommended that you call before planning a visit.

CONTEMPORARY ARTS CENTER

115 East Fifth Street
Cincinnati, Ohio 45206
513-721-0390

Cincinnati's Contemporary Arts Center, located downtown in the city's revitalized Fountain Square area, plays host to a wide variety of contemporary mediums including the photo-art of Robert Mapplethorpe. Although already well-known within the national art community, in 1990 the CAC became front-page news worldwide when local authorities tried (unsuccessfully!) to censor *Robert Mapplethorpe: The Perfect Moment* exhibit. Art remains alive and healthy in Cincinnati!

OREGON

PHOTOGRAPHIC IMAGE GALLERY ✔

208 S.W. First Street
Portland, Oregon 97204
503-224-3543
Contact: Guy Swanson

The Photographic Image Gallery presents 12 exhibitions annually and is interested in viewing traditional photography in color or b/w.

Requirements: Slides accompanied by a resume can be submitted.
Size: 1,500 square feet.
Lighting: Track.
Services: The gallery has a framing department. Promotion is via direct mail and print advertising.
Expenses: The photographer presents mounted and matted photographs for exhibition.

CAMERAWORK GALLERY ✔✮

2255 N.W. Northrup Street
Portland, Oregon 97210
503-228-6509 *Fax:* 503-228-6510
Contact: William P. Galen

Camerawork Gallery mounts 13 exhibitions each year. The entire spectrum of serious photography is of interest to the gallery.

Requirements: In person presentation should be in the form of mounted prints. Slides can be submitted for review by mail.
Size: The gallery space allows for up to 30 works.
Lighting: Incandescent.
Services: The gallery prints and mails announcements and promotes its shows via mailing lists and newspaper notices.

PHOTOZONE GALLERY ✔★

411 High Street
Eugene, Oregon 97401
503-485-2278
Contact: John Coggins

Photozone is a photographer's collective, dedicated to the study, production, exhibition, and promotion of fine arts photography. In addition to regularly showing the work of the members, there is a state-wide juried show each year.
Requirements: A body of work should be presented for critique.
Size: The gallery can accomodate 40-50 prints.
Lighting: Overhead incandescent.
Services: The gallery uses print and electronic media to publicize their activities.
Expenses: Monthly dues are paid by all members.

JACOBS GALLERY ✔★

One Eugene Centre
Eugene, Oregon 97405
503-687-5087 *Fax:* 503-683-6827
Contact: Suzanne Pepin

Eugene's Jacobs Gallery mounts from 12 to 14 exhibitions each year emphasising the work of new artists in all media.
Requirements: If you are interested in the possibility of exhibiting at Jacobs, it is necessary to first get on the gallery's mailing list. There are periodic announcements pertaining to portfolio reviews.
Size: 2,000 square feet.
Services: The gallery offers receptions and invitations.
Expenses: Half the cost of the announcements is the photographers.

Key: ✔ = Portfolios Reviewed
★ = Non-Profit Organization
▲ = Private Dealer

PENNSYLVANIA

BLATENT IMAGE/SILVER EYE ✔★

1015 East Carson
Pittsburgh, Pennsylvania 15203
412-431-1810
Contact: Jody Guy, Director

Blatent Image/Silver Eye mounts 13 exhibitions each year of contemporary photography.
Requirements: The gallery prefers prints unframed or unmatted. Slides can also be submitted. There are also portfolio reviews quarterly.
Size: 100 square feet.
Lighting: Track.
Services: In addition to the quarterly portfolio reviews, there is a slide registry for members and a gallery publication called *Photopaper.*
Expenses: One-way shipping and the cost of publicity prints are the photographer's expenses.

CARNEGIE MUSEUM OF ART ✔★

4400 Forbes Avenue
Pittsburgh, Pennsylvania 15213
412-622-1975 *Fax:* 412-622-3112
Contact: Annegreth Nill

Pittsburgh's Carnegie Museum of Art shows 2 photographic exhibitions each year of a contemporary or experimental nature.
Requirements: Slides may be offered for review after initial contact.
Size: 160 running feet.
Lighting: Incandescent.
Services: Standard museum services are available.

CONCEPT ART GALLERY ✔

1031 South Braddock Avenue
Pittsburgh, Pennsylvania 15218
412-242-9200
Contact: Sam Berkovitz

The Concept Art Gallery exhibits contemporary work in all media.
Requirements: Slides or workprints or actual portfolios may be submitted accompanied by a SASE.
Size: 2,000 square feet.
Lighting: Incandescent spots.
Services: Concept Art sponsors lectures and symposiums on selected topics. The gallery also advertises in regional magazines and uses direct mail to promote its activities.
Expenses: Printing costs.

PHILADELPHIA MUSEUM OF ART

Benjamin Franklin Parkway at 26th Street
Philadelphia, Pennsylvania 19101
215-763-8100
Admission: $5.00
Hours: Tuesday-Sunday 10-5; admission is free on Sundays until 1:00.

The Philadelphia Museum of Art periodically organizes important photographic exhibitions such as *Emmet Gowin: Photographs,* the first comprehensive survey of the master photographic printmaker's work. This exhibition will travel during 1991 and 1992 after its stay in Philadelphia.

INSTITUTE OF CONTEMPORARY ART

36th and Sansom Streets
Philadelphia, Pennsylvania 19104
215-898-7108
Hours: Tuesday-Saturday 10-5; Wednesday & Friday to 8; Sunday 12-5.

Philadelphia's Institute of Contemporary Art greets 1991 with a move into a new facility and as the recipient of the first annual *Photo Review* award for services to the field of photography. The award was presented to ICA for its long-standing commitment to contemporary photography and for its professionalism and courage in defending freedom of expression during the NEA/censorship controversy ignited by *Robert Mapplethorpe: The Perfect Moment* exhibition which was organized by the institute. ICA, which is part of the University of Pennsylvania, employs many creative devices to promote local artists such as featuring their work on the exteriors of city buses and trains.

PAUL CAVA GALLERY ✔▲

22 North 3rd Street
Philadelphia, Pennsylvania 19106
215-627-1172
Contact: Paul Cava or Carol Larson

Among the prominent exhibition showcases for contemporary art in Philadelphia, the Paul Cava Gallery has been a standout for the past fifteen years. The gallery features contemporary art in all media by both emerging and known artists. The gallery will review portfolios meeting their submission requirements.
Requirements: The initial submission should include 10 to 20 slides illustrating the photographer's range or growth. A resume should also be included.
Size: The exhibition space is 1,200 to 1,400 square feet.
Lighting: Halogen-spots and floods on tracks.
Services: The gallery also sells fine art books.
Expenses: Openings, invitations, mailings, and publicity are covered by the gallery. Some exhibition expenses are shared.

BOOK TRADER GALLERY ✔

501 South Street
Philadelphia, Pennsylvania 19147
215-925-0219
Contact: Thomas Moore, Director

The Book Trader Gallery is a long-time exhibitor of photographic art in the city of Brotherly Love. Presenting as many as 10 photographic exhibitions annually, the gallery is open to viewing the work of both new and established photographers.
Requirements: A minimum of 20 slides should be accompanied by a resume, statement, and SASE.
Size: 50 to 75 running feet.
Expenses: Many of the exhibition expenses are paid for by the photographer.

TENNESSEE

MEMPHIS BROOKS MUSEUM OF ART ✔✯

Overton Park
Memphis, Tennessee 38112
901-722-3500 *Fax:* 901-722-3522
Contact: Carole Thompson, Curator of Prints, Drawings, and Photographs

The Memphis Brooks Museum of Art offers approximately 30 exhibitions annually, of which at least 5 are photographic. Fine contemporary and vintage photography are of interest to the museum. The Photographic Circle of MBMA hosts programs and workshops.
Requirements: Submissions are by appointment only. Prints must be matted; slides are also acceptable.
Size: 80 running feet.
Services: Promotion is via the news media and member's magazine. Critiques are sometimes given by photographers of note. There is also an annual exhibition and sale of the best regional photographic art.
Expenses: Negotiable.

TEXAS

THE AFTERIMAGE ✔▲

Quadrangle #115, 2828 Routh Street
Dallas, Texas 75201
214-871-9140
Contact: Ben Breard

The Afterimage, located in Dallas' exclusive Quadrangle complex north of downtown, opened in 1971

and was one of the first art galleries devoted entirely to photographic fine art. The gallery mounts 6 or 7 new shows annually.
Requirements: As a result of its great popularity, the gallery receives many inquiries but remains open to viewing work that is innovative and salable. Visit in person or mail slides but be prepared for a possibly lengthy wait for a response.
Size: 1,500 square feet.
Lighting: Track lighting.
Services: The gallery also sells fine photography books and posters and offers an archival framing service.
Expenses: Photographer's major expense is the shipping of the art work.

DALLAS MUSEUM OF NATURAL HISTORY
Fair Park Museum Complex
Dallas, Texas 75226
214-670-8457
Admission: Free
Hours: Daily 9-5.

The Dallas Museum of Natural History features photography regularly in many of its exhibitions. Each year the *Dallas Nature Photographers Club* sponsors an exhibition of nature photography in the Museum. The works selected in this juried competition are chosen from two categories, *Nature Scenics* and *Nature Portraits*, both in color and black and white.

MODERN ART MUSEUM OF FORT WORTH
1309 Montgomery Street
Ft. Worth, Texas 76107
817-738-9215
Admission: Free
Hours: Daily 10-5; Sunday 1-5; closed Monday.

Fort Worth's Modern Art Museum occasionally exhibits photographic art. Recent shows have included *Click! 1900-1990* which featured American and European examples of photojournalism, abstract photographic art, portraits, and landscapes.

MUSEUM OF FINE ARTS, HOUSTON
1001 Bissonnet
Houston, Texas 77005
713-639-7300

Houston's Museum of Fine Arts first showed photographic art as early as 1926 when it held a juried exhibition of Texas photographers. These juried exhibitions of regional photographers were held annually until 1953. The museum began collecting photography for its permanent collection in 1965 and currently maintains over 5,000 images of which 75% are by American artists. Major collections within the photography department include: *The Edward Steichen Collection, Eliot Porter's Intimate Landscapes* portfolio and *Robert Frank's The Americans.*

HOUSTON CENTER FOR PHOTOGRAPHY ✔★
1441 West Alabama
Houston, Texas 77006
713-529-4755
Contact: Jean Caslin, Executive Director

The HCP offers a smorgasbord of photographic activities. In addition to the many exhibitions, the center produces *Spot* a photo magazine, monthly workshops, lectures, and portfolio critiques, and hosts a yearly print auction and *Photo Fiesta.*
Requirements: Emerging and mid-career artists showing work of an experimental or traditional nature may submit slides with a resume and other supporting material.
Size: 2,000 square feet.
Services: HCP has an extensive resource library and slide file available to members. Workshops and lectures are also held frequently. The center publicizes its activities via invitations and press releases.
Expenses: Matting is the primary expense for exhibited photographers.

LAGUNA GLORIA ART MUSEUM
3809 West 35th Street
Austin, Texas 78663
512-458-8191
Admission: $2.00
Hours: Tuesday to Saturday 10-5; Thursday 10-9 (free); Sunday 1-5;.

Austin's Laguna Gloria Art Museum frequently showcases the work of new, up-and-coming photo artists such as Casey Williams.

SOUTHERN LIGHT GALLERY ✔★
2201 South Washington Street
Amarillo, Texas 79178
806-371-5263 *Fax:* 806-371-5370
Contact: Robert Hirsch

The Southern Light Gallery mounts 12 new contemporary photography exhibitions each year. The gallery is interested in viewing the work of new photographers.
Requirements: Slides with a SASE are preferred. The end of March is the best time to send samples.
Size: 200 running feet.
Lighting: Track and natural lighting.

VIRGINIA

SHENANDOAH VALLEY ART CENTER ✔★
600 W. Main Street
Waynesboro, Virginia 22980
703-942-4803
Contact: Jerry Spooner, President

The Shendandoah Valley Art Center is located in Waynesboro about twenty miles west of Charlottesville. The center mounts approximately 4 new exhibitions each month featuring paintings, photography, and sculpture. The center will review the recent work of both new and established photographers.

Requirements: First request an application. The application should accompany a minimum of 10 slides of work completed within the last two years.

Size: The two exhibition spaces can accommodate 30 pictures each.

Services: There are monthly receptions for exhibiting artists and a contact service for prospective buyers. The center promotes via the regional media and mailing lists.

Expenses: Framing and shipping are the standard expenses paid by exhibiting photographers.

1708 EAST MAIN GALLERY ✔★
1708 E. Main Street
Richmond, Virginia 23223
804-643-7829
Contact: Mr. Julyen Norman

Virginia's capital city received its first artist-run, non-profit, contemporary art gallery in 1978 when the 1708 East Main Gallery opened its doors. Today the gallery presents as many as 16 to 20 exhibitions annually and is dedicated to showcasing new artists and their work.

Requirements: Request a proposal form and then submit a minimum of 10 slides illustrating contemporary, progressive, or experimental work. The gallery is mostly interested in new and emerging artists.

Size: The two galleries are 1,750 and 160 square feet.

Lighting: Tungsten spots and florescent.

Services: Exhibited artists receive a honorarium. The gallery hosts occasional *Artists Information Nights* and lectures, and also sponsors an annual Beaux Arts Ball. A quarterly newsletter, media releases, and receptions promote the gallery's activities.

Expenses: Exhibited artists pay only for shipping. The gallery covers all publicity, mailing, and opening reception.

THE WORKING GALLERY ✔
2407 Pacific Avenue #4B
Virginia Beach, Virginia 23451
804-491-8918
Contact: Rabiah Levinson

Virginia Beach's Working Gallery hosts 14 to 24 exhibitions annually and features art in all media. The gallery is interested in viewing the work of new photographers.

Requirements: Slide format is preferred.

Expenses: Some opening night expenses and shipping are incurred by the photographer.

CHRYSLER MUSEUM
Olney Road and Mowbray Arch
Norfolk, Virginia 23510
804-622-ARTS
Admission: $2.00
Hours: Tuesday-Saturday 10-4; Sunday 1-5.

The Chrysler Museum, situated in the historic section of Norfolk called Ghent, features a permanent gallery devoted solely to photography. The Alice & Sol B. Frank Photography Gallery opened in 1978 and has hosted more than 50 exhibitions since. The Chrysler has an extremely diligent photography department which curates most of the photographic exhibitions held at the Museum. The Museum actively acquires works for its permanent collection of over 1,500 images. The range of acquisitions run from Lewis Carroll to Sheila Metzner, and also include the complete two-volume set of *Gardner's Photographic Sketchbook of the Civil War.* The Chrysler also presented Robert Mapplethorpe's first museum show.

WASHINGTON

BENHAM STUDIO/GALLERY ✔
1216 First Avenue
Seattle, Washington 98101
206-622-2480
Contact: Marita Holdaway or Lisa Sharamitaro

The Benham Gallery, which shows photography exclusively, has earned a strong following as a result of showcasing promising talent. Downtown, close by the Seattle Art Museum, the gallery generally exhibits the work of new photographers from the northwest region. In August 1990 the gallery also initiated their annual *International Invitational Photography Exhibition* for university fine art students. Contact the gallery for details.

Requirements: A proposal with detailed information and several examples of finished prints should be submitted.
Size: Two spaces offer 1,000 square feet and 300 square feet.
Lighting: Track.
Services: The gallery provides mailing lists and media information for the artist to use in promoting exhibitions.
Expenses: All exhibition expenses belong to the photographer. The gallery's commission is 25%.

PHINNEY CENTER GALLERY ✔★

6532 Phinney Avenue North
Seattle, Washington 98103
206-783-2244
Contact: Ed Medeiros

Phinney Center Gallery, which mounts 12 shows annually, was created in 1983 as a showcase for the emerging artists of Washington. The center presents the *National Photography Show* each July and the *Northwest Annual*, an all media competition in October.

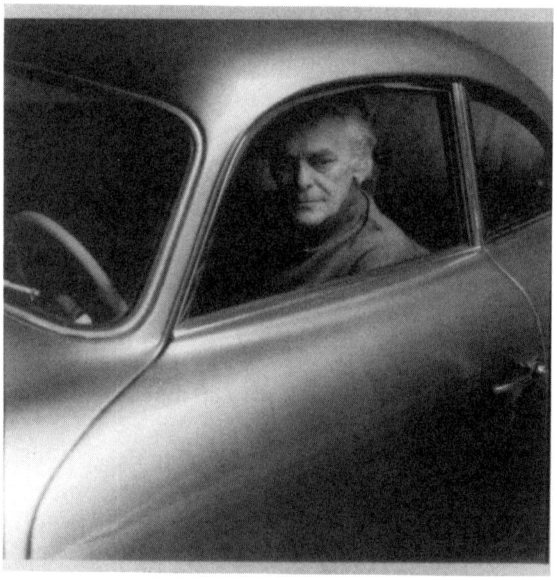

Photograph courtesy of Benham Studio Gallery

Prof Willi Schmidt, 11-3-90, *by Matthias Herrmann of The University of Applied Arts in Vienna, Austria, was a popular entry in the International Invitational Photography Exhibit '90, presented by the Benham Studio Gallery.*

Requirements: Emerging artists only should submit a resume with statement and a slide list with appropriate information. Send SASE for information on group shows, the *National Photography Show* and the *Northwest Annual Competition.*
Size: 96 linear feet of moveable panels.
Lighting: Natural, track, and flourescent.
Services: Special services include a staff to handle sales and inquiries, hanging and dismounting, a mailing list of patrons and arts organizations, and publicity and technical services.
Expenses: Expenses include $50.00 per month gallery fee, printing and postage for announcements, and refreshments for openings.

SILVER IMAGE GALLERY, INC. ✔

318 Occidental Avenue South
Seattle, Washington 98104
206-623-8116
Contact: Dan Fear

The Silver Image Gallery is interested in exhibiting contemporary photography, nudes, and traditional landscapes.
Requirements: Send SASE for information. Appointments are scheduled for a portfolio review/artist consultation. The gallery charges a $25 fee for this service which consists of 1 to 2 hours of portfolio presentation tips and basic information on the business of art.
Size: 1,000 square feet.
Lighting: Spotlights.
Services: The gallery offers a unique consultation program.

WISCONSIN

JOHN MICHAEL KOHLER ARTS CENTER ✔★

608 New York Avenue
Sheboygan, Wisconsin 53081
414-458-6144 *Fax:* 414-458-4473
Contact: Ruth DeYoung Kohler, Director

The John Michael Kohler Arts Center is in Sheboygan, 50 miles north of Milwaukee on the shores of Lake Michigan. Housed in the Kohler family home, an 1882 Italianate Villa, the center mounts approximately 15 shows each year of contemporary art and non-conventional photography. The center is especially interested in the work of emerging artists.
Requirements: The center requests submissions in transparency format.
Size: 8,525 square feet.
Lighting: Spots and floods.

Services: A wide range of classes, workshops and residencies are available for adults, students, and children.
Expenses: Freight insurance of exhibited work.

MILLER ART CENTER ✔★
107 South 4th Avenue
Sturgeon Bay, Wisconsin 54235
414-743-6578
Contact: Lorraine Mengert

Although the Miller Art Center infrequently features photographic art, the center is undertaking a campaign to broaden the scope of exhibitions and there is interest in viewing the work of new photographers. Located between Lake Michigan and Green Bay, this Sturgeon Bay art center has also begun to collect black and white photography to include in its permanent collection.
Requirements: Slides should be submitted to the center.
Size: 30′x 50′.
Services: The center promotes its activities via the local media.

PUMP HOUSE REGIONAL CENTER FOR THE ARTS ✔★
119 King Street
La Crosse, Wisconsin 54601
608-785-1434
Contact: Jerilyn Dinsmoor, Executive Director

The Pump House produces 24 shows annually. Both new and established photographers are invited to submit work in any format. However, continuity is requested.
Requirements: The jury requires slides or prints of the works to be considered. All exhibited work must be matted and framed or plexiglass/clips.
Size: Main gallery is 25′x 40′ and the balcony gallery is 15′x 8′.
Lighting: Incandescent.
Services: Exhibitions are promoted via a newsletter and the local media. A jury of three members offers brief critiques. The center does not charge a commission for works sold.
Expenses: Gallery rental fees are $60 per month for the large space and $40 for the balcony space.

WYOMING

THE ART STOP ✔
1609 Capitol Avenue
Cheyenne, Wyoming 82001
307-637-8728
Contact: Ludmila Dranchak

The Art Stop generally features the work of Wyoming artists in a variety of mediums. Interested photographers, either developing or established, may contact directly for information on joining the Art Stop Cooperative Gallery.
Requirements: Write for membership information before submitting material.
Size: Approximately 1,000 square feet.
Lighting: Florescent.
Services: All exhibitions receive official openings which are publicized via mailings and invitations.
Expenses: Photographers may pay for shipping and other items including membership fees.

LIGHT REFLECTIONS/A FREDERIC JOY GALLERY
35 East Deloney, Box 1681
Jackson, Wyoming 83007
307-733-4016

Light Reflections exhibits landscape, nature, and still-life. The gallery also collects historical photography.

International Galleries and Museums

AUSTRALIA

PHOTOACCESS EXHIBITION SPACE ✔☆
Kingsley Street Acton
Canberra Act 2601, Australia
61-6-249-7878
Contact: Projects Co-ordinator

Photo-Access is a community photographic center encompassing all areas of the art of photography. In addition to exhibition space, the center offers darkrooms, a wide range of photography courses and intensive workshops, and a vast library of international books and periodicals. Photo-Access welcomes work that is non-racist, non-sexist, and non-exploitive.
Requirements: A folio of 6 to 12 work or finished prints will be accepted for review.
Size: The exhibition space allows for a variety of gallery sizes.
Lighting: Pendulum florescent.
Services: The gallery advances funds to assist artists in mounting their exhibitions. The gallery also engages in a wide variety of promotional activities to create an awareness of its endeavors.

CAMERA LUCINDA ✔☆
317 Abercrombie Street
Chippendale, Sydney 2008, Australia
61-2-339-9551
Contact: Denis Mizzi or Steven Fasan

Camera Lucida, located in Sydney's city center, presents 26 exhibitions annually. The gallery is dedicated to showcasing the photographic art of new and developing artists.
Requirements: Do not send originals. Dupes or work prints can be sent.
Size: The gallery is a shop front.
Lighting: Florescent.
Expenses: All costs involved in transport, individual publicity and mounting the show are paid for by the photographer.

PHOTOGRAPHIC ART GALLERY ✔
6 Yalpa Road
Marino, South Australia 5049, Australia
61-8-298-7777
Contact: Leonid & Elynor Frances Olijnyk

The Photographic Art Gallery of Marino promotes the Australian landscape in all its exhibitions.
Requirements: Established photographers may submit landscapes, portraits, or flower studies, framed or ready to hang.
Services: Advertising and invitations promote the gallery.

ARTISTS SPACE GALLERY ✔
150 Park Street, North Fitzroy 3068
Melbourne, Victoria 3040, Australia
61-3-489-274
Contact: Wes Placek and Sophie Nowicka

Artists Space Gallery is Melbourne's leading photographic art gallery featuring upwards of 12 exhibitions yearly. The gallery sells contemporary photography to museums, public galleries and private collectors worldwide. Generally interested in promoting the work of emerging and mid-career photographers, the gallery is interested in historical photos from the 19th and 20th centuries, and architectural, conceptual, postmodern, and fashion photography.
Requirements: After securing an appointment, visit the gallery equipped with enough 8x10 work prints and slides to illustrate your style.
Size: 4,000 square feet.
Lighting: Natural and artificial.
Services: The gallery is actively involved in promoting the medium of photography as a major art form. Gallery promotion is limited to listings in art and photography journals.
Expenses: Costs to the photographer include space rental, announcement cards, and transport in both directions.

GERTRUDE STREET ARTISTS' SPACES INC. ✔★

200 Gertrude Street, Fitzroy
Melbourne, Victoria 3065, Australia
61-3-419-3406 *Fax:* 61-3-419-2519
Contact: Rose Lang, Director

Gertrude Street Artists' Spaces was created to support and nurture emerging artists and provide opportunities for unestablished curators and writers. This non-profit facility houses 17 studios in addition to the gallery space. Gertrude Street is particularly interested in showcasing work from emerging artists which may be considered "risk" shows in commercial spaces. Although generally open to new and emerging artists, established photographers may apply for review.

Requirements: A formal application should be submitted with accompanying slides, photographs or catalogues, and an exhibition proposal.
Size: The exhibition space is variable.
Lighting: Tracklighting with tungsten.
Services: Subsidized studios and a visiting artist's studio and residence are available. Also available is a voluntary support staff.
Expenses: One way freight within Australia is paid for by the photographer.

NATIONAL GALLERY OF VICTORIA ✔★

180 St. Kilda Road
Melbourne, Victoria 3004, Australia
61-3-618-0222 *Fax:* 61-3-614-4337
Contact: Isobel Crombie, Curator of Photography

The National Gallery of Victoria is a public institution which regularly features photographic exhibitions. All exhibitions are curated in-house.

Requirements: Contact before offering material for review. Slide format is preferred.
Size: Two galleries of 165 square meters and 80 square meters.
Lighting: Track.

ORANGE REGIONAL GALLERY ✔★

Civic Square, Byne Street
Orange, NSW 2800, Australia
61-63-615-136 *Fax:* 61-63-61500
Contact: Peter O'Neill

The Orange Regional Gallery exhibits up to 15 shows each year featuring the visual and decorative arts. The gallery will view work from new and established photographers.

Requirements: The gallery prefers to view portfolios in an in-person setting. Contact directly for additional information.
Size: 400 square meters.
Lighting: Mixed artificial.
Services: The gallery provides an on-going series of lectures, workshops, and films. The electronic and print media are used to promote exhibitions.
Expenses: The photographer's expenses vary according to the circumstances. Transportation and insurance are usually paid for by the gallery.

GALLERY 350 ✔

360 Hay Street
Subiaco 6008, Australia
61-9-381-6577 *Fax:* 61-9-388-2966
Contact: Simon Walsh

Gallery 350 exhibits art in all media and will view the photography of new and established artists.

Requirements: Contact the gallery with a letter and a sample selection of slides.
Size: 400 square meters.
Lighting: Spots.
Services: The gallery offers framing services and guarantees of purchase. Promotion is accomplished via the gallery's mailing list and local and state newspapers.
Expenses: Expenses depend on whether the work is consigned or bought outright.

ARTSPACE VISUAL ARTS CENTRE LTD. ✔★

11 Randle Street
Surry Hills, NSW 2010, Australia
61-2-212-503
Contact: Sally Couacaud

Artspace is a public gallery which specializes in changing exhibitions of contemporary art. The gallery presents up to 15 different exhibitions each year of contemporary art in all media. New and established photographers may present their work for review.

Requirements: Sample slides must be accompanied by written proposals. An information sheet outlining the proposal instructions is available.
Size: 200 square meters.
Lighting: Spots and florescent.
Services: Artspace hosts an on-going series of lectures, seminars, and workshops. The facility also offers a bookshop.

KODAK GALLERY ✔★

Mezzanine Level, 333 George Street
Sydney, NSW 2000, Australia
61-2-692-7250 *Fax:* 61-2-660-3976
Contact: Phillipa Hooper

The Kodak Gallery is located above the Kodak Shop and mounts exhibits which rotate every 3 to 4 weeks.

The gallery is interested in exhibiting all types of photographic work; the one obvious stipulation being that all photographic material used to produce the exhibited work must be *Kodak Professional Products.*

Requirements: Write for their extremely well-detailed "conditions of exhibiting" instruction sheet. Basically the gallery requires that portfolios be well organized by subject.

Size: The gallery can accommodate 35 20" x 24" framed photos.

Lighting: Spots on tracks.

Services: The gallery provides an extensive list of services including mounting assistance, framing, and opening night functions.

Expenses: Printing, matting, and framing expenses may be incurred by the photographer.

MACLEAY MUSEUM

University of Sydney
Sydney NSW 2006, Australia
61-2-692-4200

The Macleay Museum is a natural history museum which houses the Historic Photograph Collection. The photographic collections contains only black and white images taken between the years 1840 and 1959.

MORI GALLERY ✔

56 Catherine Street, Leichhardt
Sydney 2040, Australia
61-2-560-4704 *Fax:* 61-2-569-3022

Contact: Jo Holder

Sydney's Mori Gallery exhibits contemporary art and features several photographic shows annually. The gallery also represents photographic artists Robyn Stacey, Catherine Rogers, Jacky Redgate, Anne Ferran, and Julie Brown.

Requirements: The gallery will review material submitted in 35mm format only.

Size: 2,000 square feet.

Lighting: Tungsten spots.

MUSEUM OF CONTEMPORARY ART ✔

132 George Street
Sydney, NSW 2000, Australia
61-2-252-4033 *Fax:* 61-2-252-4361

Contact: Leon Paroissien, Director

Sydney's Museum of Contemporary Art, set to open in 1991, is being billed as "Australia's first public contemporary art museum and the most significant visual arts enterprise of the decade..." (*The Australian*). The museum is planned to include educational facilities, art bookshops, a cinematheque, and cafe. Although the museum's submission guidelines have not yet been supplied, the staff have replied positively to viewing the work of new and established photographers.

WOOLLOOMOOLOO GALLERY ✔

84-86 Nicholson Street, Woolloomooloo
Sydney 2011, Australia
61-2-356-4220

Contact: Elinor and Fred Wrobel

Sydney's Woolloomooloo Gallery offers exhibitions in all media and presents photographic shows at least once yearly. The art exhibited is primarily that of Australian artists.

Requirements: The gallery is interested in viewing mounted, framed work.

Size: The minimum space used is 100 square meters.

Lighting: Track spots.

Services: Ms. Wrobel is a consultant curator for the University of Melbourne's Grainger Museum. The gallery advertises in a variety of Australian newspapers and art magazines.

Expenses: Photographers pay for invitations, catalogues, postage, and advertising.

AUSTRIA

PHOTOMUSEUM DES LANDES OBER-OESTERREICH

P.O. Box 117
Bad Ischl A-4820, Austria
43-6132-4422

Photomuseum des Landes Ober-Oesterreich is the photography museum of upper Austria. Bad Ischl is located about 60 kilometers east of Salzburg.

KORALM FOTOGALERIE

Fraventalerstrasse 48
Deutschlandsberg 8530, Austria
43-34-622-396

Contact: Nauschnig Erich

Koralm Fotogalerie can be found south of Graz in the village of Deutschlandsberg. The gallery exhibits photography exclusively in the 10 to 12 shows mounted each year.

FORUM STADTPARK ✔☆

Stadtpark 1
Graz 8010, Austria
43-316-827-734 *Fax:* 43-316-825-369

Contact: Christine Frisinghelli or Manfred Willmann

Forum Stadtpark located in the town of Graz, south of Vienna near the Yugoslav border, offers from

6 to 12 contemporary photography exhibitions each year. The organization also publishes the informative quarterly, *Camera Austria*, a bilingual (German/ English) international photography journal.
Requirements: Photographers may offer Forum Stadtpark slides, prints, or catalogues for review.
Size: 200 square meters.
Services: The gallery promotes exhibitions employing the standard methods.
Expenses: Press photographs and presentation expenses are paid for by the photographer.

OSTERREICHISCHE FOTOGALERIE RUPERTINUM ✔★

Wr. Philharmoniker Gasse 9
Salzburg A-5010, Austria
43-662-8042-254 *Fax:* 43-662-80422542
Contact: Dr. Margit Zuckriegl, Photographic Department

Salzaburg's Osterreichische Fotogalerie, part of the modern art museum Rupertinum, owns the largest collection of Austrian photography with more than 6,000 pieces. Every 2 years the fotogalerie organizes an Austrian photo competition.The Rupertinum offers up to 4 major photographic exhibitions annually and is interested in work that is contemporary, historical, or Austrian.
Requirements: Contact the fotogalerie via the mail for specifics.
Size: 700 square meters.

FOTOGALERIE WIEN ✔★

Wahringer Strasse 59
Vienna 1090, Austria
43-222-408-5462
Contact: Susanne Gamauf or Josef Wais

Vienna's Fotogalerie mounts 12 contemporary or experimental photography exhibitions annually. The gallery will view the work of photographers at all levels.
Requirements: Portfolios or slides must be presented accompanied by a resume.
Size: 200 square meters.
Lighting: Color balanced florescents.
Services: The gallery furnishes catalogues and sends out announcements to its list of more than 2,500 clients.
Expenses: The photographer pays only for transport and insurance.

OESTERREICHISCHES FOTOARCHIV ✔★

Furstengasse 1
Vienna A-1090, Austria
43-222-345-397 *Fax:* 43-222-345-270
Contact: Monika Faber

Oesterreichisches Fotoarchiv im Museum Moderner Kunst (Austrian Photoarchiv of the Museum of Modern Art) mounts from 4 to 6 exhibitions annually of historic and new photography. Although specifics have not been supplied, the fotoarchiv has indicated that there is an interest in viewing portfolios.
Size: Variable.
Lighting: Artificial.

BELGIUM

GALLERY DB-S ✔

Kipdorp 4A
2000 Antwerpen, Belgium
32-3-232-4185
Contact: Marc Steculorum or Inge De Bisschop

One of the leading galleries of Antwerp's ever expanding art scene is Gallery DB-S which primarily exhibits photographic art.
Requirements: DB-S believes the primary importance is the quality of the work.
Size: The two spaces are 8x8 meters and 6x6 meters.
Lighting: Spotlights.
Services: The gallery sometimes creates posters to publicize exhibitions. Invitation cards are used for each show.
Expenses: Generally the only cost to the photographer is transportation.

MUSEUM VOOR FOTOGRAFIE ✔★

Waalse Kaai 47
B 2000 Antwerpen, Belgium
32-3-216-2211
Contact: Roger Cohen or Pool Andries

Located between Bruxelles and the dutch border, Antwerp's Museum Voor Fotografie (Photography Museum) exhibits more than 7 photographic shows each year. Recent shows have included Lee Friedlander, Brassai, and Duane Michaels retrospectives, *American Photographs 1940-1990*, and *Fantasies, Fables and Fabrications* which featured photography from the 1980s. The museum in interested in work that is international in scope and also photography with historical value.
Requirements: Slides are the best means of submitting samples.
Size: 260 square meters.
Lighting: Spotlights.

Key: ✔ = Portfolios Reviewed
★ = Non-Profit Organization
▲ = Private Dealer

RUIMTE MORGUEN ✔★

Waalse Kaai 22
2000 Antwerpen, Belgium
32-3-248-0845
Contact: Helena Derks and Marc Schepers

The Ruimte Morguen gallery, created in 1982, is interested in experimental works with photography/installations. Particularly work by new, unknown artists.

Requirements: Slides should be submitted
Size: 70 square meters.
Lighting: Halogen.
Expenses: Artist's expenses are negotiable.

ESPACE PHOTOGRAPHIQUE CONTRETYPE ✔

1 avenue de la Fonction
1060 Bruxelles, Belgium
32-2-538-4220
Contact: Jean-Louis Godefroid

Contretype mounts 8 exhibits of contemporary and vintage photography annually.

Requirements: Contretype requires a minimum of 30 samples for consideration.
Size: There are 4 separate exhibitions spaces.
Lighting: Indirect and halogen.
Services: The space offers lectures, an artshop, and lab facilities. Invitations and posters are created to promote exhibitions and a revue *Contretype* is published regularly.

MUSEE DE LA PHOTOGRAPHIE ✔★

Avenue Paul Pastur, 11
6100 Charleroi, Belgium
32-71-435-810 *Fax:* 32-71-435-810
Contact: Georges Vercheval, Director of Acquisitions

Musée de la Photographie is a museum devoted to photography which exhibits all types of photographic art. The town of Charleroi is situated 50 kilometers south of Bruxelles.

Requirements: Submissions can be made in person with a portfolio or via the mail with slides. The Museum is interested primarily in work that would be considered fine art.
Size: 1,500 square meters.
Lighting: Variable.
Services: The Museum also houses a photographic library accessible to the public.

Key: ✔ = Portfolios Reviewed
★ = Non-Profit Organization
▲ = Private Dealer

WHITE LIGHT ✔★

Europalaan
3600 Genk, Belgium
32-11-362-916
Contact: Eddy Willems

White Light Gallery, which features photography exclusively, is located in the small town of Genk, east of Bruxelles and near the borders of Germany and The Netherlands. The gallery mounts approximately 14 shows annually of mostly contemporary photography by international artists.

Requirements: There are no specific submission requirements. However, note that the gallery is generally interested in contemporary work.
Size: 35 square meters.
Lighting: Indirect tungsten.
Services: The gallery hosts workshops, and a conference room is also available. Posters and press mailings promote exhibitions.
Expenses: The transport of exhibited work and the cost for additional publicity, if necessary, is paid for by the photographer.

FOTOGALERIJ C.G.H. ✔★

Kunstlaan 5
3500 Hasselt, Belgium
32-11-229-931 *Fax:* 32-11-243-207
Contact: Jean-Pierre Grootaers

Fotogalerij C.G.H. is housed in the cultural center of Hasselt, a small town east of Bruxelles and not far from Koln and Dusseldorf, Germany. The gallery offers more than 10 exhibitions each year featuring a wide variety of photographic styles and interests.

Requirements: Information and copies of work should be sent to the gallery for their consideration.
Size: 530 square meters.
Lighting: Spots.
Services: The gallery covers many of the expenses incurred in mounting an exhibition including insurance, reception, and the printing of invitations, postcards, and posters.
Expenses: Transportation one-way.

The following galleries in Belgium also exhibit photography:

Aspects
rue du President 72
B-1050 Bruxelles, Belgium

Foto Gallerie 5.6
St. Michielsplasse 14
9000 Gent, Belgium

Galerie Stieglitz
Avenue Louise 90
B-1050 Bruxelles, Belgium

Hologram Europe
137 Avenue Voltaire
1030 Bruxelles, Belgium

Paulo Pia Galerij voor Fotografie
Kammenstraat 57
B-2000 Antwerp, Belgium

CANADA

LA CENTRALE - GALERIE POWERHOUSE ✔★

4060, Boulevard St.Laurent #205
Montreal, Quebec H2W 1Y9, Canada
514-844-3489
Contact: Carole Brovillette or Suzanne Paquet

Galerie Powerhouse exhibits contemporary visual art. The gallery will view new material and prefers to see the work of new and emerging talent.

Requirements: Submissions are the choice of the artist.
Size: 1,600 square feet.
Lighting: Halogen.
Services: Powerhouse sends out press-releases, places advertisements, and creates posters to promote exhibitions.

NATIONAL GALLERY OF CANADA

380 Sussex Drive
Ottawa, Ontario K1N 9N4, Canada
613-990-1985

The National Gallery of Canada has long been in the forefront of acknowledging photography as an art form, organizing a series of exhibitions as early as 1934. Beginning its collection in 1967, the gallery today owns over 17,000 photographs and is recognized as a major international collection. Among the many important works owned by the National are the major collections by Atget, Walker Evans, and the German photographer August Sander. Recent expansion of the museum's exhibition spaces now provides for a space devoted exclusively to the showing of photography on a continuous basis.

MUSEE DU QUEBEC

1, Avenue Wolfe-Montcalm
Parc des Champs-de-Bataille, Quebec G1R 5H3, Canada
418-643-4103
Hours: Tuesday-Sunday 10-5:45; Wednesday to 9:45; closed Monday.

The Musée du Quebec has been undergoing extensive renovation and expansion work which is scheduled for completion in the summer of '91. Although the museum maintains a limited permanent photographic collection, the facility does regularly host traveling exhibitions.

THE PHOTOGRAPHERS GALLERY ✔★

12, 23rd Street East
Saskatoon, Saskatchewan S7K 0H5, Canada
306-244-8018
Contact: Doug Townsend

The Photographers Gallery is the oldest artist-run photography gallery in Canada. Formed in 1970 by a group of photographers, the original exhibitions were mounted in department-store windows. Today the gallery is housed in a renovated downtown warehouse and offers both a main gallery for juried exhibitions and a workshop gallery for unjuried shows. Photographers Gallery is interested in exhibiting contemporary photography which furthers the contemporary practice.

Requirements: Submissions should include a maximum of 20 slides and one example of an exhibition quality print.
Services: Work production facilities are available to members as are the resource centers' library and permanent collection. The gallery also publishes its own journal, *Blackflash*.
Expenses: The photographer pays for his own transporation and one-way freight for exhibited work.

DEL BELLO GALLERY ✔

363 Queen Street West
Toronto, Ontario M5V 2A4, Canada
416-593-0884 *Fax:* 416-593-8729
Contact: Egidio Del Bello

The Del Bello Gallery, located in the heart of Toronto's gallery neighborhood, mounts 8 exhibitions annually. The gallery, which organizes a large international competition of miniature and small format art, is interested in contemporary photography.

Requirements: Contact the gallery directly for complete submission information.
Size: Approximately 850 square feet.
Lighting: Track.
Services: The gallery promotes its exhibitions via direct mail campaigns, magazine and newspaper publicity and posters.
Expenses: Shipping and framing are expenses of the photographer.

GALLERY 44 ✔★

183 Bathurst Street #202
Toronto, Ontario, M5T 2R7, Canada
416-363-5187 *Fax:* 416-360-0781
Contact: April Hickox, Director

Gallery 44-Centre For Contemporary Photography celebrated its 10th anniversary in 1990. Created to promote contemporary photography by emerging Canadian artists, the center, which includes resource and workshop facilities, is an artist-run, non-profit organization. The gallery is interested in exhibiting primarily Canadian photography which is innovative in the application of photographic materials and the examination of subject matter.

Requirements: The center has 3 yearly calls for submissions which are: January 15, May 15, and September 15. Emerging artists, and established artists whose work has not been exhibited in Toronto, may submit a statement, C.V., maximum 20 slides, 10 prints, etc.
Size: 114 running feet.
Lighting: Halogen track lighting.
Services: The center offers workshops in historic and special processes, a production facility for members, a visiting artists program, and an education program in the elementary and secondary schools. Each exhibition receives invitation and brochure support.
Expenses: Exhibitors are required to cover shipping the work one-way and their own transporation for the opening.

GALLERY TPW ✔★

80 Spadina Avenue, Suite 310
Toronto, Ontario M5V 2J3, Canada
416-362-4242 *Fax:* 416-363-7659
Contact: Kim Fullerton, Program Coordinator

Gallery TPW (Toronto Photographers Workshop) is located in downtown Toronto within a unique visual arts center. The gallery, which exhibits from 12 to 14 shows each year, specializes in photography that can be described as "critically informed or socially/politically engaged contemporary work." The gallery also houses a resource center with an extensive slide archive of TPW exhibitions and a photography bookstore.

Requirements: An eight-member exhibition committee reviews proposals three times each year. Deadlines are January 30, April 30, and September 30. Offerings must include 10-20 unframed prints or slides, a one-page summary, and a bio with support material.
Size: 120 running feet.
Services: The exhibitions are promoted in *Views* the journal of the workshop. The gallery also hosts an annual photography sale and many special projects such as traveling exhibitions, international exchanges, and lecture series.
Expenses: All preparative work to "make-ready" for installation and reproduction/press photos are paid for by the photographer.

PHOTOGRAPHY GALLERY AT HARBOURFRONT ✔★

York Quay Center, 235 Queen's Quay West
Toronto, Ontario M5V 2J3, Canada
416-362-4242
Contact: Kim Fullerton, Program Coordinator

The Photography Gallery at Harbourfront is another gallery operated by the Toronto Photographers Workshop. In existence since 1980, the gallery mounted a 10 year celebration in 1990 called *Public Exposure: One Decade* that surveyed the photographic trends on view during the gallery's first decade. Like its sister Gallery TPW, the Photography Gallery at Harbourfront presents exhibitions which address cultural and social issues.

Requirements: Contact the gallery for a submission procedures information sheet. An eight member exhibition committee reviews material 3 times a year. Deadlines are January 30, April 30, and September 30.
Size: 70 running feet or two parallel walls.

CONTEMPORARY ART GALLERY SOCIETY ✔★

555 Hamilton Street
Vancouver, B.C. V6B 2R1, Canada
604-681-2700
Contact: Bill Jeffries, Curator

The Contemporary Art Gallery Society of Vancouver is devoted to exhibiting the work of local artists in the context of national and international art. The gallery mounts 10 exhibits annually and is interested in viewing the work of new and established photographers.

Requirements: Submissions are considered in slide format with a SASE on an on-going basis.
Size: 51'x 21'.
Lighting: Reflector spots and floods.
Services: The gallery offers a frame rental service. The gallery advertises in Canadian publications and mails announcements to an international clientel.
Expenses: The photographer pays for insurance and reception drinks.

CZECHOSLAVAKIA

GALERIE 4 ✔

Kamenna 2
35001 Cheb, Czechoslavakia
42-166-22838
Contact: Zbynek Illek

Cheb is situated west of Prague on the German border. Galerie 4 produces as many as 15 photographic exhibitions annually, 80% of which are documentary.

Requirements: A small, well-chosen selection of prints or slides may be submitted. Documentary or live-action shots are preferred.
Size: The space is 4 rooms and 170 square meters.
Lighting: Natural and artificial.
Services: The gallery provides accommodations for exhibited artists, produces catalogues, and mails invitations to promote shows. A photo-library is also available.
Expenses: Transport of the work and the visiting photographer.

DENMARK

GALLERI IMAGE ✔★

Toldbodgade 8
DK-8000 Aarhus C, Denmark
45-86-202-429
Contact: Saul Shapiri or Carsten Langkilde

Galleri Image mounts from 10 to 12 shows annually featuring every aspect of photographic art. The gallery is interested in reviewing the work of both new and established photographers.

Requirements: Portfolios will be reviewed if presented in-person. Slides may also be posted for review.
Size: 100 square meters.
Lighting: Artificial.
Services: The gallery offers the space free-of-charge to exhibited photographers and creates a poster for each exhibition.
Expenses: Shipping and insurance expenses are paid for by the photographer.

Key: ✔ = Portfolios Reviewed
★ = Non-Profit Organization
▲ = Private Dealer

MUSEET FOR FOTOKUNST ✔★

Brandts Klaedefabrik
DK-5000 Odense C, Denmark
45-66-137-816 *Fax:* 45-66-137-310
Contact: Finn Thrane

Museet For Fotokunst, (Museum of Photographic Art), is located in Denmark's second city, Odense. The museum mounts approximately 10 fine art, mostly contemporary, exhibitions annually.

Requirements: Slides and samples of finished archivally matted prints can be submitted for review.
Size: 160 square meters.
Lighting: Artificial.
Services: The museum publishes a magazine, *Katalog* and promotes exhibitions via its membership and press-releases.
Expenses: Each exhibitor has a separate contract.

ENGLAND

THE ROYAL PHOTOGRAPHIC SOCIETY ✔★

The Octagon, Milsom Street
Bath BAI IDN, England
44-225-462-841 *Fax:* 44-225-448-688
Contact: Amanda Nevill

The Royal Photographic Society features all aspects of photography and offers conference facilities, lectures, workshops, children's events, and a photographic museum. Although the society is very involved in preserving vintage work, contemporary photography is also frequently on view. Recent exhibitions have included: *Cricketer* 3-D sculptures using photography by Mike Roles and *Photography Bewitched* by innovative holographer Martin Richardson.

Requirements: When possible, material for review should be presented matted and framed. Contact directly for other possibilities.
Size: The society has 4 gallery spaces.
Lighting: Variable.
Services: The society produces a wide range of one and two day workshops. The society also actively seeks sponsors for its exhibitions.

NATIONAL MUSEUM OF PHOTOGRAPHY, FILM AND TELEVISION

Prince's View
Bradford, West Yorkshire, BD50T, England
44-274-727488
Hours: Tuesday-Sunday 10:30-5:30; closed Monday.

Great Britain's National Museum of Photography, Film, and Television is situated in the town of Bradford, outside of Leeds, England. The Museum maintains a comprehensive photography center which includes numerous collections (*Kodak* and the *Daily Herald Picture Library*), permanent and temporary exhibitions showcasing historic and contemporary work, and an education division which offers workshops, seminars, and lectures.

CAMBRIDGE DARKROOM ✔☆

Dales Brewery, Gwydir Street
Cambridge B12Z, England
44-223-242-157
Contact: Claire MacDonald, Director

Cambridge Darkroom mounts up to 10 exhibitions annually featuring all aspects of the photographic medium. The gallery is interested in viewing any type of work - video, installation, film - which uses photography in an innovative manner.

Requirements: Slides and/or prints must be accompanied by a C.V. and proposal.
Size: Approximately 1,000 square feet.
Lighting: Spots on tracks.
Services: The gallery also offers darkroom facilities and non-gallery installation. Exhibitions are promoted via the national and local media.
Expenses: Expenses depend on the specific funding for each project.

BREWERY ARTS CENTER PHOTOGRAPHY GALLERY

Highgate
Kendal, Cumbria LA9 4HE, England
44-539-725-133

Located in the Lake District north of Manchester, The Brewery Arts Center Photography Gallery focuses on the work of new and emerging photographers. The center offers a variety of photography-related activities including workshops, lectures, and darkroom facilities.

PICTURE HOUSE ✔☆

113 Princess Road East
Leicester LE1 7LA, England
44-533-551-310 *Fax:* 44-533-550-132
Contact: Roger Bradley, Director or Jennie Burton, Photography Worker

The Picture House is located in Leicester about 100 miles north of London and features contemporary photography in two galleries. The Picture House policy is to present nationally produced work, particularly that of local photographers. In addition to the galleries the facility offers workshops, lectures, and educational courses.

Requirements: Interested photographers should submit a variety of sample slides.
Size: Main gallery is 69 linear feet and staircase gallery is 26.
Services: Picture House maintains a photographic archive, library, reproduction print sales, and a snack bar. There is also an annual "photo fair". To promote activities, posters and quarterly leaflets are produced.
Expenses: Photographer's expenses are negotiable.

ASSOCIATION OF PHOTOGRAPHERS GALLERY

9-10 Domingo Street
London EC1Y 0TA, England
44-71-608-1445

England's Association of Photographers maintains the Association Gallery on two floors of the organizations headquarters. The gallery features more than 20 exhibitions yearly, mainly showcasing the work of the association members. Workshops and lectures are also offered on the premises.

BLACK & WHITES GALLERY ✔

50 Monmouth Street
London WC2, England
44-71-836-4109 *Fax:* 44-71-240-6788
Contact: Charles Roff or Tiggy Williams

Black & Whites Gallery is located in London's bustling Covent Garden area and features continuously changing exhibitions of fine art photography. The gallery is an off-shoot of the company Black & Whites Publications Ltd., which specializes in the high quality reproduction of black and white photography in postcard and poster form. The company also licenses prints to magazines, calendar, and jigsaw companies. The company will consider any new projects or ideas.

Requirements: The gallery requests fine, quality, unmounted, original material for review.
Size: 400 square feet.
Lighting: Spots.
Services: Framing and special publishing services.

BLACK ART GALLERY ✔☆

225 Seven Sisters Road, Finsbury Park
London N4 2DA, England
44-81-263-1918
Contact: Shakka Dedi

The Black Art Gallery, run by OBAALA (Organisation for Black Arts Advancement & Learning Activities), is a non-commercial art-space specializing in promoting the work of Afrikan Caribbean artists. The gallery mounts 6 to 8 shows annually.

Requirements: Work by artists of African descent who find their inspiration in the black experience may submit 10 x 12 prints or transparencies plus CV and a personal statement by the artist.
Size: 45′x 20′x 9′.
Lighting: Variety.
Services: Full publicity services are available. The gallery also hosts a book and crafts shop and offers an educational program.
Expenses: Expenses may include framing, printing, and the cost of the prints.

CAMERAWORK ✔☆

121 Roman Road
London E2, England
44-81-980-6256
Contact: Kate Bush

London's Camerawork is a photographic center with gallery, darkrooms for hire, workshops and lectures, and bookshop. The gallery is interested in exhibiting socially relevant work of a contemporary nature. Recent shows have included: *Drum* a photographic chronicle of change in 1950's South Africa; *Bodies of Experience* images of the impact of HIV on society; and *Our Lady of the Iguanas* the work of Manuel Alvarez Bravo's one-time assistant, Graciela Iturbide.
Requirements: Transparencies and/or prints may be presented in a coherent fashion. The center has regularly scheduled monthly viewing days. Call first for schedule.
Size: 100 running feet.
Lighting: Spots.
Services: Camerawork provides a comprehensive educational program.
Expenses: Expenses are variable depending on the exhibition and budget.

GALLERY ✔☆

8-9 Paddington Street
London W1, England
44-71-487-2641 *Fax:* 44-71-935-3547
Contact: Alison Fisher

Gallery, situated in London's Marylebone district, mounts more than 12 exhibits annually featuring the full spectrum of photographic art.
Requirements: Portfolios should be presented for review.
Size: 8.4 x 6.4 meters.
Lighting: Concord track.

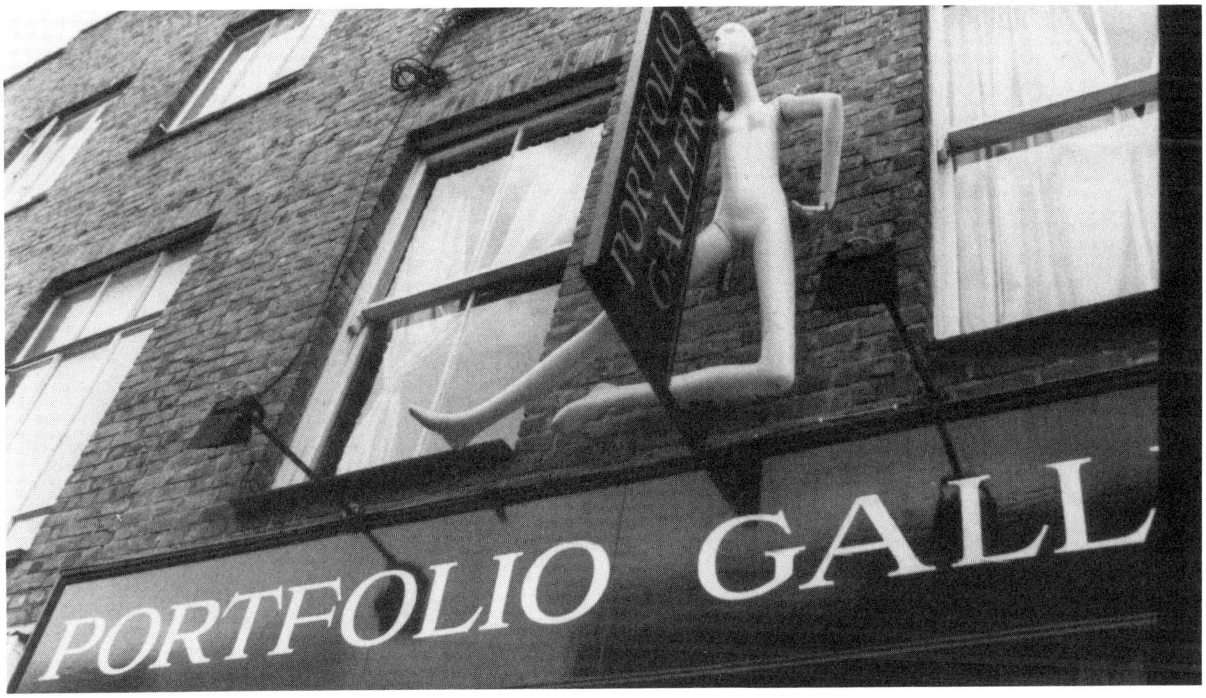

Photograph by Peter L. Gould

Located near Portobello Road's famous flea market, Portfolio Gallery features fine art photography and produces its own postcards and posters.

Services: Gallery supports its exhibitions via mailings, press releases, and advertising.
Expenses: Expenses are negotiable.

HAMILTONS GALLERY ✔▲

13 Carlos Place, Mayfair
London W1Y 5AG, England
44-71-499-9494 *Fax:* 44-071-629-9919
Contact: Andrew Cowen or Tim Jefferies

Hamiltons Gallery specializes in exhibiting 20th century photography, retrospectives, and theme shows. Although noted for exhibiting the work of stylish, established photographers such as David Bailey, Horst, Avedon, and Jean-loup Sieff, the gallery will review submitted material from both new and emerging talent.
Requirements: Samples may be offered for review in transparency or original size format.
Size: 3,500 square feet.
Services: Hamiltons Gallery has a bookshop on the premises and offers a framing service. The gallery employs a PR firm to publicize their exhibitions.

ILFORD PHOTO COMPANY

14-22 Tottenham Street
London W1P, England
44-71-636-7890

The showroom of the Ilford Photo Company frequently displays the work of outstanding photo-artists.

JANUS AVIVSON GALLERY ✔

Camden Lock
London NVI, England
44-71-482-3091 *Fax:* 44-71-284-3130
Contact: Janus Avivson

The Janus Avivson Gallery mounts 15 contemporary art exhibitions each year.
Requirements: Submitted photography should be "ready to hang".
Size: 24 square meters.
Lighting: Spotlights.
Services: The gallery receives over 1,000 visitors each weekend. Advertisements and listings are used to promote the gallery.
Expenses: Any additional advertising, framing, and transport is paid for by the photographer.

MARLBOROUGH GRAPHICS LTD ✔

42 Dover Street
London W1X 3RB, England
44-71-495-2642 *Fax:* 44-71-495-0641
Contact: Alexandra Wettstein, Director

Marlborough Graphics exhibits fine art photography.
Requirements: Marlborough will review the work of photographers. Contact for complete information before submitting material.
Size: 1,400 square feet.
Lighting: Halogen.

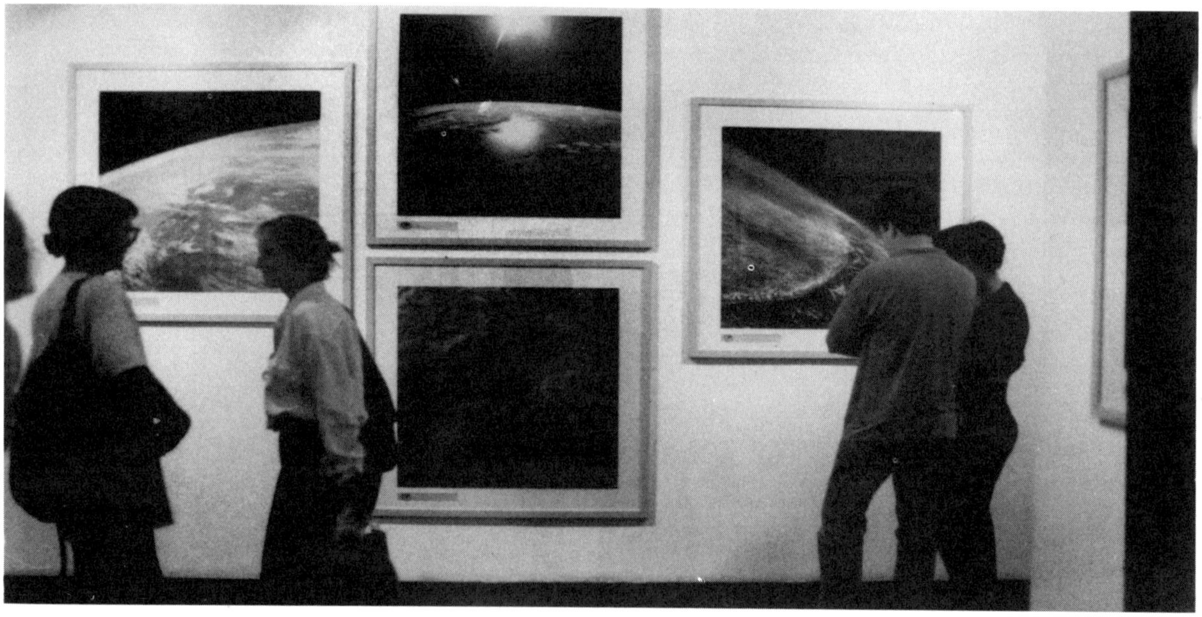

Photograph by Peter L. Gould

The Photographer's Gallery is situated at the crossroads of London, and the city's photographic community, near Leicester Square.

NATIONAL PORTRAIT GALLERY

Trafalger Square
London WC2, England
44-71-930-1522
Hours: Monday-Friday 10-5; Saturday 10-6; and Sunday 2-6.

The National Portrait Gallery periodically presents exhibitions devoted to photographic portraiture.

THE PHOTOGRAPHERS' GALLERY ✔✯▲

Halina House, 5 & 8 Great Newport Street
London WC2H 7HY, England
44-71-831-1772 *Fax:* 44-71-836-9704
Contact: Sue Davies, Director

Since its inception in January 1971, the Photographers' Gallery has successfully continued to expand its operations making it a must-stop for photographers visiting London. Centrally located near Leicester Square, the gallery's animated atmosphere attracts half a million visitors a year to view its exhibitions and visit its bookshop, reference library, and print room. The gallery is interested in exhibiting good, professional work, either straight or experimental.

Requirements: Submissions of 20-30 unmounted prints or plastic mounted slides of large work are acceptable. The gallery's Portfolio Room is reserved for exhibitions selected from portfolios by young or unknown photographers chosen by the biannual Selection Committee.

Size: The two main are 2,000' and 1,000' with 2 more at 50 sq.ft.

Lighting: Tungsten with dimmers.

Services: The gallery sometimes organizes tours of its exhibitions. Overmatting and framework are available.

PORTFOLIO GALLERY LTD ✔

345 Portobello Road
London W10 5SA, England
44-81-969-0453 *Fax:* 44-81-960-6570
Contact: Nicky Akehurst

Portfolio, which originated in an old dairy farm near the Portobello Road flea market in 1981, was founded by photographers Jayne Diggory and Gail Marcuson to showcase black and white photography. As the gallery grew, Portfolio expanded into postcard and poster publishing and now has separate gallery, shop, and publishing spaces. No longer limited exclusively to b/w, the gallery is interested in fine art photography of all types.

Requirements: The gallery will review portfolios/ slides by appointment only.

Size: 750 square feet.

Lighting: Concord.

Services: Exhibited photography has the possibility of being published in poster or postcard format. Portfolio Gallery receives excellent coverage from the press.

Expenses: Expenses are subject to review.

SLAUGHTERHOUSE GALLERY ✔

63 Charterhouse Street, Smithfield
London EC1M 6HT, England
44-71-251-5888
Contact: Marguerite Smith

The Slaughterhouse Gallery exhibits a wide range of art including sculpture, performance, mixed media and photography. The gallery will review work from new photographers.

Requirements: Slides may be offered for review.

Size: 2,000 square feet.

Services: Slaughterhouse Gallery's acitivities are promoted via the appropriate electronic and print media.

THE SPECIAL PHOTOGRAPHERS COMPANY ✔

21 Kensington Park Road
London W11 2EU, England
44-71-221-3489 *Fax:* 44-71-792-9112
Contact: Catherine Turner

The Special Photographers Company produces a minimum of 10 exhibitions annually featuring all types of photographic art from classic black/white to "manipulated and distressed" work. The company will review work from photographers at all levels. However, new photographers are generally included in mixed shows only.

Requirements: A maximum of 20 transparencies or examples of exhibition prints may be offered for review.

Size: 1,300 square feet.

Lighting: Tungsten.

Services: The company acts as agent for several top commercial photographers and employs extensive publicity campaigns to maximize media coverage. The company also is actively involved in art fairs.

Expenses: Each exhibition is negotiated individually.

VICTORIA & ALBERT MUSEUM

Cromwell Road, South Kensington
London SW7, England
44-71-938-8441
Admission: Donation
Hours: Monday-Saturday 10-5:50; Sunday 2:30-5:50.

One of the most popular and revered museums in the world, the V & A maintains a prominent collection of art photography. The Museum curates occasional traveling exhibitions culled from its collections such as *Lady Hawarden (1822-1865) A Victorian Photographer* which has been on the world's museum circuit recently. The museum's collection numbers over 300,000 images. The Henry Cole Wing of the V & A is devoted to the history of photography and the work of vintage master-photographers is on permanent display.

Additional London galleries and museums regularly featuring photographic art are as follows:

Barbican Centre Art Gallery 71-638-4141
Silk Street
London EC2, England

Birch & Conran Fine Art 71-434-1246
40 Dean Street
London W1, England

Camden Arts Center 71-435-2643
Arkwright Road
London NW3, England

Chenil Art Gallery 71-352-4689
183 Kings Road
London SW3, England

Exposure Photographic Gallery 71-736-9581
715 Fulham Road
London SW6 5UL, England

Human Products Gallery 71-969-3005
10 Chamberlayne Road, Kensal Green
London NW10, England

Ilford UK 71-636-7890
14-22 Tottenham Street
London W1P, England

The Imagination Gallery 71-323-3300
25 Store Street, South Cresent
London WC1, England

Judd Street Gallery 71-388-1985
99 Judd Street
London WC1, England

Lamont Gallery 71-981-6332
65 Roman Road
London E2, England

Light Fantastic Gallery of Holography 71-836-6423
48 South Row, Covent Garden
London WC2 England

Marlborough Fine Arts 71-629-5161
6 Albermarle Street
London W1, England

The Media Gallery 71-379-5841
10 Museum Street
London, England

Nikon Gallery 71-381-1551
20 Fulham Broadway
London SW6, England

Piers Feetham 71-381-5958
475 Fulham Road
London SW6, England

Rebecca Hossack Gallery Ltd. 71-436-4899
35 Windmill Street
London W1, England

Regent Street Gallery 71-580-2020
309 Regent Street
London W1, England

Royal Academy of Arts 71-439-4996
Burlington House, Piccadilly
London W1, England

Runkel-Hue-Williams Ltd. 71-495-7017
6/8 Old Bond Street
London W1X 3TA, England

Serpentine Gallery 71-402-6075
Kensington Gardens
London W2, England

Slaughterhouse Gallery 71-251-5888
63 Charterhouse Street
London EC1, England

Zelda Cheatle Gallery (▲) 71-836-0506
8 Cecil Court
London WCZN 4HE, England

COUNTER IMAGE ✔★

19 Whitworth Street West
Manchester M15W9, England
44-61-228-3551
Contact: Ivor Frankell, Director

Manchester's Counter Image is a center for practical work in film, video, and photography. The center offers photography classes, lectures, darkrooms for rent, portfolio sessions, and photography competitions. There are 6 exhibitions yearly and Counter Image will view photography samples, particularly from new photographers.

Requirements: Portfolios should be presented for review. If unable to submit a portfolio, contact directly for alternative possibilities.
Size: 50 square feet.
Services: Monthly portfolio reviews are given by an invited established photographer or gallery administrator. An annual competition is held for members who are invited to photograph Manchester with the reward being postcard reproduction of the winning photos.
Expenses: Expenses are variable.

FOX TALBOT MUSEUM
Lacock, Near Chippenham
Wiltshire SN15 2LG, England
44-24-973-459
Hours: Daily 11-6 from March to October.

The Fox Talbot Museum is located about 2 hours from London near the town of Bath. The Museum is housed in a 16th century barn which was previously part of the Lacock Abbey. The Fox Talbot produces various exhibitions each season either historical or contemporary in nature and also offers a series of lectures and workshops. A photographic archives, library, and bookshop are also on the premices.

FRANCE

MUSEE FRANÇAIS DE LA PHOTOGRAPHIE ✔★
78, rue de Paris
91570 Bievres, France
33-69-41-10-60 *Fax:* 33-60-19-21-11
Contact: Andre Fage

The French Museum of Photography, which is located about 5 miles south of Paris, is reached by taking the metro to the Mairie d'Issy stop and changing to the 190-a bus. The museum exhibits both contemporary and vintage work in its 6 annual shows and maintains a permanent exhibition illustrating the history of photography from its origins to the present day. The museum also hosts an annual photo fair providing exhibition space for over 200 photo artists.
Requirements: Contact the museum directly for details of their photo-fair. The museum will view work from both new and established photographers.
Size: 350 square meters.
Lighting: Spotlights.
Expenses: Photographers may pay for all or part of invitations, posters, and catalogue expenses.

CENTRE REGIONAL DE LA PHOTOGRAPHIE NORD PAS DE CALAIS ✔★
Place des Nations
Douchy 59 282, France
33-27-43-5650 *Fax:* 33-27-31-3193
Contact: Pierre Deuin

The Centre Regional de la Photographie exhibits up to 6 new shows annually. The centre will review the work of new and established photographers and is interested in contemporary, historical, and classic photography.
Requirements: Portfolios are preferred. Contact first supplying information on your offerings.
Size: 50 linear feet.
Lighting: Neon.
Services: The center produces posters and press releases and promotes its exhibitions internationally. The center also houses a photographic library and artotheque.

IMAGERIE ✔★
19 Rue Jean Savidan
Lannion 22300, France
33-96-465725
Contact: Bernard Moreau

Imagerie is the municipal gallery of Lannion which is located in Brittany adjacent to the English Channel and the Atlantic Ocean. Imagerie mounts 8 shows annually of "artistic" photography.
Requirements: The gallery is interested in looking at the work of both new and established photographers. Contact directly for details.
Size: 200 square meters.
Lighting: Spotlights.

MUSEE D'ART CONTEMPORAIN ✔★
26 rue President E Hezziot
Lyon 69001, France
33-7830-5066 *Fax:* 33-7200-8627
Contact: Isabelle Bertolotti

The Museum of Contemporary Art in France's second city, Lyon, mounts 6 photography shows annually. The museum's photography curator, Thierry Raspail, will view photography that is considered contemporary in style.
Requirements: Contact Isabelle Bertolotti before submitting any material.
Services: All the usual museum services such as posters, catalogues, TV, and publicity are available.

AGATHE GAILLARD ✔

3 rue du Pont-Louis-Philippe
75004 Paris, France
33-1-4277-3824 *Fax:* 33-1-4277-7836
Contact: Agathe Gaillard

The Agathe Gaillard Gallery, one of the best-known galleries in Europe, offers 7 shows annually. The gallery is interested in all types of photography after 1945.

Requirements: Excellent quality prints, not more than 50, can be submitted for consideration by the photographer.
Size: 120 square meters.
Lighting: Spotlights.
Expenses: The cost of producing the prints for the show. The gallery pays return shipping for exhibited work.

COMPTOIR DE LA PHOTOGRAPHIE ✔

56, rue du Faubourg Saint Antoine
75012 Paris, France
33-1-4344-1136 *Fax:* 33-1-4346-8177
Contact: Marie-Francoise George

The Comptoir de la Photographie presents from 6 to 8 contemporary photography exhibitions each year. The gallery is interested in viewing contemporary photography from new photographers.

Requirements: Make contact with the gallery before submitting work to let them know what you have to offer.
Size: 60 square meters.
Services: The gallery offers a framing service and also circulates its exhibitions. Posters are sometimes created to promote exhibitions and opening night receptions and invitation cards are the rule.
Expenses: The only expense to exhibited photographers is the cost of the prints.

ESPACE PHOTOGRAPHIQUE DE PARIS ✔★

4-8 Grande Galerie
75001 Paris, France
33-1-4026-8712 *Fax:* 33-1-4225-4205
Contact: Jean-Luc Monterosso

The Photographic Space of the city of Paris is subsidized by the cultural affairs department. At least 6 exhibibitions featuring fine art, photo-journalism, or portraiture are mounted each year. Although exhibitions are generally fixed two to three years in advance, Espace Photographique is still open to viewing work from both new and established photographers.

Requirements: There is a selection committee which will preview any material under consideration for exhibition. Arrange to leave your portfolio for review.
Size: 400 square meters.
Services: The exhibitions are given broad promotion via television, posters, and the print media.
Expenses: Expenses are negotiable.

L'ESPACE PHOTOGRAPHIE DE PARIS

Nouveau Forum des Halles, Place Carree
75001 Paris, France
33-1-4026-8712

L'Espace Photographie de la Ville de Paris is located in the popular multi-level shopping arcade, the *Forum des Halles.* The gallery offers a variety of ongoing exhibitions, generally contemporary in nature. Unfortunately, the forum has become popular as a

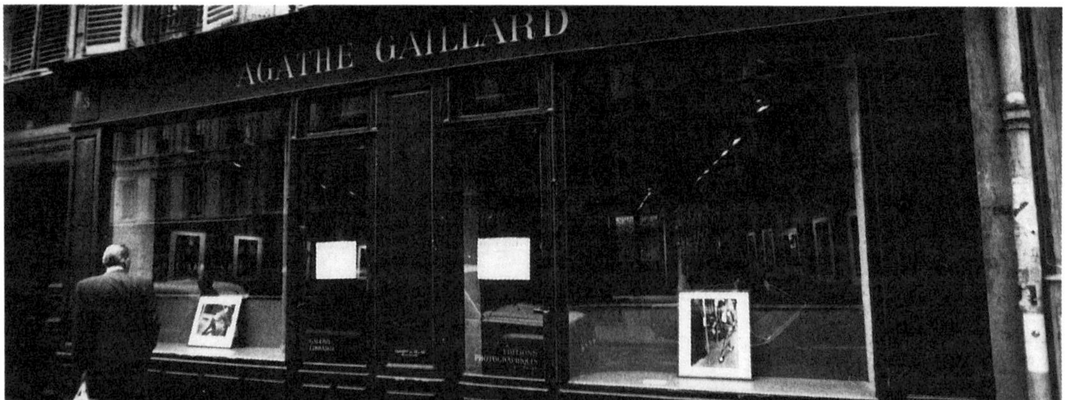

Photograph by Scott Halleran

The Agathe Gaillard Gallery has long enjoyed a reputation as a leading exhibitor of photographic art in Paris.

hang-out for unrestrained bands of youths. Proceed at your own risk and watch your cameras!

FNAC MONTPARNASSE

136 Rue de Rennes
75006 Paris, France
33-1-4548-6192

FNAC is a chain of stores located throughout Paris and beyond which sells records, concert tickets, books, and photography equipment, among many other entertainment oriented items. Several of the larger locations also offer galleries which feature photography exhibitions. This left-bank location and the popular one in the Forum at Les Halles on the right-bank regularly display the work of contemporary photographers such as William Klein and Stephane Duroy.

GALERIE DE PHOTO/BIBLIOTHEQUE NATIONALE ✔☆

Passage Colbert, 2 rue Vivienne
75002 Paris, France
33-1-4703-8392 *Fax:* 33-1-4296-8447
Contact: Jean-Claude Lemagny

The Photography Gallery in Paris' National Library mounts about 6 exhibitions annually which feature images from the French national collection. Although the gallery does not sell the photography on view, it does provide artist information for possible direct purchase. Representatives from the gallery will view portfolios and are chiefly interested in contemporary and vintage 19th century work.

Requirements: To show material to the gallery it is necessary to contact via the post or telephone one month in advance.

Services: The collection is open to the public free-of-charge. The gallery provides contact information for artists whose work is on view.

GALERIE REGINE LUSSAN ✔

7 rue de l'Odeon
75006 Paris, France
33-1-4633-3750
Contact: Regine Lussan

This well-known left-bank gallery exhibits photography on a regular basis. The gallery is interested in "aesthetic photographs."

Requirements: New and established photographers can submit portfolios for review. Contact before delivering your portfolio.

Size: 60 square feet.

Lighting: Spotlights.

Expenses: Promotion, transportation, and exhibition costs are the artists.

GALERIE URBI ET ORBI

48 Rue de Turenne
75003 Paris, France
33-1-4274-5636

Galerie Urbi et Orbi frequently exhibits contemporary and experimental photography and art in other mediums.

GRAND PALAIS

Avenue Winston-Churchill
75008 Paris, France
33-1-4289-5410
Hours: Daily, except Tuesday, 10-8; Wednesday evenings until 10.

Situated at the opposite end of the Champs-Elysee Boulevard from the Arch de Triomphe, the Grand Palais is the national gallery of France. One of many outstanding buildings created for the infamous *Paris Exhibition of 1900*, the Grand Palais is an important stop for photo-lovers visiting Paris as it is home to the *Foundation Lartique*. The Foundation houses an outstanding collection of the pioneering photographer's finest work.

MUSEE DE LA PUBLICITE

18, rue de Paradis
75010 Paris, France
33-1-4246-1309
Hours: Daily, except Tuesdays, 12-6.

Musée de la Publicité is France's Museum of Advertising. In addition to a collection of posters covering the world history of poster design from the beginning to today, there is also an extensive collection of contemporary posters many of which employ photography. The museum also houses two temporary galleries which occasionally feature shows illustrating trends in photographic advertising. Take the metro to the Gare de l'Est or Chateau-d'Eau stop.

MUSEE D'ORSAY

1, Rue de Bellechasse
75007 Paris, France
33-1-4049-4814

Although known primarily as the new home of the Impressionists following their move from the Jeu de Paume, this glorious former rail station, the Musée D'Orsay, occasionally features photographic art such as the traveling exhibition *Lady Hawarden: A Victorian Photographer.* The Museum also maintains an archives of photography dating from the beginning years through the first decades of the 20th century.

MUSEE NATIONAL DES TECHNIQUES

292, rue Saint-Martin
75141 Paris, France
33-1-4027-2371
Hours: Everyday 10-5:30; closed Mondays.

France's National Museum of Techniques, housed since 1799 in the former priory of Saint-Martin-des-Champs, features many thousands of instruments and machines which illustrate the progress of the sciences between the 16th and 20th centuries. In addition to other communication sciences, the museum devotes sections to both photography and cinematography. The museum can be reached by metro at the Reaumur-Sebastopol stop.

PALAIS DE TOKYO

13 Avenue du President Wilson
75016 Paris, France
33-1-4723-6127
Hours: Wednesday-Monday 9:45-5:15; closed Tuesday.

Previously part of Paris' Museum of Modern Art, the Palais de Tokyo is now home to the *Centre National de la Photographie*. In line for a name change, the Palais offers several vintage and contemporary exhibitions continuously.

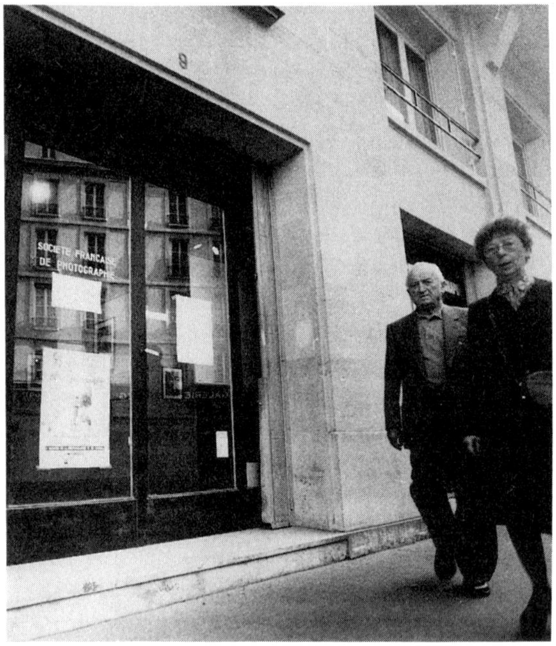

Photograph by Scott Halleran

The Société Française de Photographie, established in 1854, is one of the oldest photographic societies and continues to present both vintage and contemporary work.

SOCIETE FRANÇAISE DE PHOTOGRAPHIE ✔★

9 rue Montalembert
75007 Paris, France
33-1-4222-3717
Contact: Christiane Roger

Possibly the oldest photographic society in existence, the French Society of Photography was founded in 1854 and has been available for the public's use since 1892. The society exhibits both vintage and contemporary photography and is interested in viewing material from young photographers. Recent exhibitions have included work by French photographers Renaud Marot, Thierry Boulley, and founding member Humbert de Molard.

Requirements: The society will make available to you a lengthy guidelines sheet (in French). Be prepared to make 5 of your best photos available for addition to their permanent collection should you be lucky enough to receive an exhibition.

Services: The society prepares press dossiers and invitations for all exhibitions.

VIVIANE ESDERS ✔

40 rue Pascal
75013 Paris, France
33-1-4331-1010
Contact: Viviane Esders

Viviane Esders is a very successful commercial gallery which features contemporary photography. New and established photographers may present their work for review.

Requirements: Only prints in their intended sizes should be presented for consideration. No slides please.

Size: 60 square meters.

Services: Many of the exhibitions curated at Viviane Esders travel to festivals, museums, or institutions. The gallery provides an extensive promotional campaign around all its exhibitions.

Expenses: Prints, matting, and shipping to the gallery are costs incurred by the photographer.

ZABRISKIE ✔

37 rue Quincampoix
75004 Paris, France
33-1-4272-3547 *Fax:* 33-1-4027-9966
Contact: Editha Carpenter

Since opening in 1978, Zabriskie has developed into one of the most important photographic galleries in Paris. Situated near Beaubourg and Les Halles, the gallery exhibits contemporary as well as established artists such as William Klein and John Batho.

Requirements: New and established photographers may submit their work accompanied by a curriculum vitale and press reviews. Nouveaux realistes and surrealism are of interest to Zabriskie.
Size: 50 square meters.
Lighting: Halogen and incandescent on tracks.
Services: Advertising, invitations and catalogues are used to promote the gallery's shows.
Expenses: Preparation and transport of work, and a share of the advertising and catalogue costs are the photographer's expenses.

Photography exhibitions are also offered periodically in the following galleries and museums in Paris:

Baudoin Lebon Galerie (▲) 4272-0910
34 rue des Archives
75004 Paris, France

Charles Sablon 4548-1048
21 Avenue de Maine
75015 Paris, France

Creatis
44 Rue Quincampoix
75004 Paris, France

Espace Canon 4278-7420
117 rue Saint-Martin
75004 Paris, France

Gabrielle Maubrie 4278-0397
24 rue Ste-Croix-de-la-Bretonnerie
75004 Paris, France

Galerie de France 4274-3800
50-52 rue de la Verrerie
75004 Paris, France

Galerie Michele Chomette (▲) 4278-0562
24, rue Beaubourg
75003 Paris, France

Gutharc Ballin 4700-3210
47 rue de Lappe
75011 Paris, France

Jean-Pierre Lambert 4278-6274
3 Place du Marche Sainte Catherine
75004 Paris, France

Kodak Centre 4723-5921
38 Avenue Georges V
75008 Paris, France

Lunn Ltd. (▲) 4261-9004
11 Quai Voltaire
75007 Paris, France

Magnum 4325-9009
20, rue des Grands Augustins
75006 Paris, France

Mamiya 4325-6498
25 rue Saint-Sulpice
75006 Paris, France

Musée Carnavalet 4272-2113
23 rue de Sevigne
75003 Paris, France

Musée de l'Holographie 4296-9683
Forum des Halles
75001 Paris, France

Musée Jacquemart-Andre 4562-3994
158 Boulevard Haussmann
75008 Paris, France

Musée National des Techniques 4271-2414
270 rue Saint-Martin
75003 Paris, France

Octant 20 4260-6808
5 rue du Marche Honore
75001 Paris, France

Olympus 4297-4621
Forum des Halles, 2nd Level
75001 Paris, France

Paris Art Center 4322-3947
36 rue Falguiere
75015 Paris, France

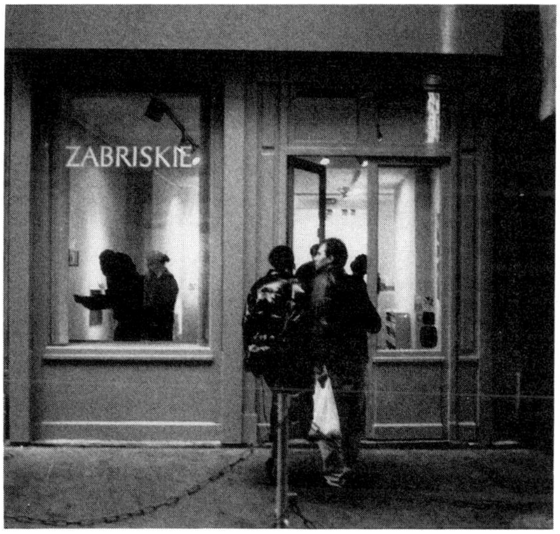

Photograph by Scott Halleran

Zabriskie Gallery, situated near the popular Beaubourg Centre, presents photography by both new and established artists.

Rohwedder 4027-8263
6 rue du Roi-Dore
75003 Paris, France

Samia Saouma 4236-4456
2 Impasse des Bourdonnais
75001 Paris, France

Studio 666 4354-5929
6 rue de Maitre Albert
75005 Paris, France

GERMANY

BRENNPUNKT - GALERIE FUR FOTOGRAFIE ✔★

Elberfelder Str. 13
D 100 Berlin 21, Germany
49-30-392-1665
Contact: Wolfgang Schiche

Brennpunkt Photography Gallery mounts 6 to 8 exhibitions annually of non-commercial photography and is interested in viewing any work which is technically perfect and innovative - from "professionals, artists, or first-class amateurs."

Requirements: Sample prints shouldn't be larger than 40 x 50 cm. or smaller than 20 x 25 cm.
Size: 7 x 6 meters.
Lighting: Spotlights.
Services: Brochures are produced to promote exhibitions.
Expenses: Photographer's expenses are generally printing costs for the brochure.

NOVA FOTODESIGN

Langenscheidtstrasse 3
1000 Berlin 62, Germany
49-30-782-4635
Contact: Frank Wolffram

Nova Fotodesign is a commercial gallery featuring photography.

MUSEUM FUR PHOTOGRAPHIE ✔★

Helmstedterstrasse 1
3300 Braunschweig, Germany
49-531-75000
Contact: Dr. Georg Kiefer or Ulrike Lahmann

Situated in central Germany, near Hannover, Braunschweig's Museum for Photography presents all categories of photographic art and is interested in viewing work from both new and established photographers. Exhibitions held in recent years include: *American Photography Today; Bernice Halpern Cutler: Pinhole Photography;* and *Andre Gelpke: The Leaning Tower of Pisa.*

Requirements: Work prints or photo copies can be submitted to the museum for consideration.
Size: 120 square meters.
Lighting: Variety.
Services: Posters, catalogues, and postcards are created for each exhibition.

FOTOMUSEUM BURGHAUSEN ✔★

Burg 1
D 8263 Burghausen, Germany
49-86-77-4734
Contact: Dr. Robert Gerlich

About an hour east of Munich and just north of Salzburg on the Austria border is the town of Burghausen. Burghausen's Photo Museum exhibits historic, amateur, and art photography and will review the portfolios of interested photographers.

Requirements: Portfolios should include a good cross-section of material with detailed information included.
Size: 500 square feet.
Services: The museum sends out press releases and invitations to the photography media and also uses regional radio to promote its exhibitions.
Expenses: Transport costs are paid for by the photographer.

GALERIE MICHAEL HELLBACH ✔

Friese St. 94
5 Cologne 1, Germany
49-203-343571
Contact: Uli Sigg

Galerie Michael Hellbach is devoted exclusively to photography. Human interest, fashion, and work demonstrating new perspectives are of interest to the gallery.

Requirements: A sample selection of recent material may be offered for review after making contact with the gallery.
Size: 140 square meters.

MUSEUM LUDWIG - PHOTOSAMMLUNG ✔★

Bischofgartenstrasse 1
Cologne, Germany
49-221-221-3619 *Fax:* 49-221-221-4114
Contact: Dr. Reinhold Misselbeck

Art photography, particularly international and 20th century is showcased in Cologne's Museum Ludwig.

Requirements: Sample work may be presented in slide or print format.

Size: 300 square meters.
Services: Museum Ludwig mails press releases and hosts press conferences to promote exhibitions.
Expenses: Variable.

TUSHITA GALLERIES
Salvatorweg 24
D-4100 Duisburg 1, Germany
49-2-03-29610
Contact: Michael Hellbach

The Tushita Galleries feature photography and other media arts. Contact the galleries directly for further information.

NIKON GALLERY ✔
Tiefenbroicher Weg 25
D4000 Dusseldorf 30, Germany
49-211-41570 *Fax:* 49-211-4157311
Contact: Hartmut Bauer

Dusseldorf's Nikon Gallery mounts approximately 8 exhibitions annually.
Requirements: Black and white or color prints, 30 x 40 cm to 50 x 60 cm.
Size: 40 square meters.
Lighting: Spotlights.
Services: Press kits and the gallery's own *Nikon News* are available for promotional purposes.

FOTOGRAFISCH SAMMLUNG IM MUSEUM FOLKWANG ✔★
Goethestrasse 41
D-4300 Essen, Germany
49-888-452 *Fax:* 49-888-450
Contact: Ute Eskildsen

The photography collection of the Museum Folkwang consists of international historic and contemporary work. The museum mounts from 6-8 new exhibitions annually and is interested in viewing work from both new and established photographers. The city of Essen is located within a half hour of both Dusseldorf and Koln.
Requirements: Sample photographs may be submitted after initial contact and should be related to the type of work the museum exhibits.
Size: 90-100 running meters.
Lighting: Lighting is variable.
Services: The museum utilizes an extensive mailing list and sends out invitations to all openings. Posters are also produced to promote shows.
Expenses: Expenses depend on the budget available for each show.

STAATLICHE GALERIE MORITZBURG HALLE ✔★
Friedemann-Bach-Platz 5
Halle/Saale 4020, Germany
37-46-37037 *Fax:* 37-46-29990
Contact: Dr. Peter Romanus or T.O. Immisch

Staatliche Galerie Mortizburg is in the town of Halle outside of Leipzig. The gallery exhibits international, historic, and contemporary photography.
Requirements: The gallery prefers to view prints in passepartout or framed.
Size: 165 square meters.
Services: The gallery completely organizes and installs its exhibitions and often produces posters, postcards, invitations, or catalogues.
Expenses: Transportation and insurance are expenses which are covered by the exhibited photographer.

MUNICH CITY MUSEUM ✔
St. Jakobs-platz 1
Munich 2, Germany
89-233-2370

Located centrally in the heart of the city's old town district, the Munich City Museum houses several museums within the walls of the late Gothic structure. In addition to the usual photographic surveys and displays found in museums devoted to a city's history, visitors will find a Museum of Photography covering the history of photographic technique. Emphasizing Munich's contribution to photography, the permanent exhibition illustrates the role of photography as document and as art. After your photography visit you'll probably be ready for another of the museum's unique offerings: The German Museum of Brewing!

NEW COLLECTION - MUSEUM OF APPLIED ARTS
Prinzregentenstrasse 3
Munich 22, Germany
89-227-844
The New Collection, the State Museum for Applied Arts in Bavaria, was founded in 1925 to extend the collection of the Bavarian National Museum into the 20th century. The New Collection, considered by some to be "a museum of good taste in our time," contains more than 22,000 works of applied art and industrial design. The frequently changing exhibits feature artifacts of modern life, furniture, architecture, and photography in all phases. The museum is located adjacent to the Bavarian National Museum at the corner of Munich's central park, The English Garden.

The following private dealers, museums, and galleries located throughout Germany sell and exhibit photographic art:

Focus Bilderladen
Dahlmannstrasse 5
1000 Berlin 12, Germany

Fotogalerie Droscher
Ellchaussee 140
D-2000 Hamburg 50, Germany

Fotowerkstatt
Lunebruger Strasse 28
Bremen, Germany

Galerie Nagel
Fasnenstrasse 42
1000 Berlin 15, Germany

Galerie Reckermann (▲) 221-212- 064
Albertusstrasse 16
5000 Koln 1, Germany

Galerie Wilde
Auf dem Derlich 6
D-5000 Koln, Germany

Kicken-Pauseback (▲) 221-515-005
Bismarckstrasse 50
5000 Koln 1, Germany

Mayer and Mayer Galerie fur Photographie
Schlosstrasse 83
D-7000 Stuttgart 1, Germany

Photogalerie Lange-Irschl
Turkenstrasse 54
8000 Munich 40, Germany

PPS Photogalerie
Hochhous 1, Feldstrasse
2000 Hamburg 4, Germany

Rudi Renner Fotogalerie
Mannhardstrasse 4
8000 Munich 22, Germany

Spectrum Photogalerie im Kunstmuseum
Hannover, Kurt-Schwitters-Platz
3000 Hamburg 1, Germany

Werkstatt fur Fotographie
Friedrichstrasse 210
1000 Berlin 36, Germany

Key: ✔ = Portfolios Reviewed
★ = Non-Profit Organization
▲ = Private Dealer

HUNGARY

MAGYAR MUNKASMOZGALMI MUZEUM ✔★

Budavari Palota "A" Epulet
Budapest 1014, Hungary
36-1-1755-984
Contact: Ilona Stemler-Balog, Department Head

Magyar Munkasmozgalmi is the Hungarian National Museum and Historical Photo Archives. The museum mainly exhibits historical, political, and documentary photography. The photography staff will view portfolios but is basically interested in the work of established photographers.

Requirements: Introduce your material via a written proposal initially.
Size: There are 5 separate galleries.
Lighting: Neon.
Services: The museum offers a cafeteria, bookshop, and lecture room.
Expenses: Expenses are negotiable.

MUCSARNOK - PALACE OF EXHIBITIONS ✔★

Dozsa Gyorgy ut 37
Budapest 1406, Hungary
36-1-142-4145 *Fax:* 36-1-122-3235
Contact: Katalin Neray, Director

Mucsarnok is a museum of visual and applied arts which regularly features photographic exhibitions.

Requirements: Sample prints, catalogues, or slides may be submitted for consideration.
Size: There are 3 galleries: 1,500, 800, and 90 square meters.
Lighting: Natural and artificial.
Services: All exhibitions are curated by art historian staff members. The museum provides the exhibition space for free and offers public relations and advertising assistance.
Expenses: Shipping, insurance, and part of the catalogue production are costs to the photographer.

PHOTO ARCHIVE OF THE WAR HISTORY MUSEUM ★

Toth Arpad Setany 40
Budapest HB 1250, Hungary
36-1-156-9970
Contact: Gyorgyi Banffyne Kalavszky

The Photo Archive of the War History Museum offers extremely specialized photography. Only photographers offering military and related subjects

should contact the museum for submission information.
Size: 220 square meters.

GODOLLOI GALERIA ✔☆

Szabadsag VT 6
Godollo H2100, Hungary
36-1-282-0977
Contact: Karoly Kincses

Godolloi Galeria is just outside the city of Budapest and is a showcase for the photographic history of Hungary. The gallery is mainly concerned with the historic aspects of photography, but is interested in viewing new work as well.
Requirements: Send a written synopsis of the exhibition prior to submitting material.
Size: 12 x 14 meters.
Lighting: Spotlight.
Services: The gallery covers all expenses and arrangements for exhibitions. Printed exhibition materials are offered for sale.

ISRAEL

SILVER PRINT, A JERUSALEM PLACE ✔

Box 4662
Jerusalem 91044, Israel
972-2-619-499 *Fax:* 972-2-382-641
Contact: Vivienne Silver

The photography exhibited at Silver Print is limited to imagery of the people, places, and things of Jerusalem and Israel. Contemporary and vintage images covering these subjects are of interest to the gallery which mounts 2 exhibitions annually. The gallery also hosts a weekly photographic walking tour of Jerusalem.
Requirements: Only regional material is of interest, either vintage or current.
Services: The gallery maintains an extensive historic archive.

ITALY

CENTRO CULTURALE EDITORIALE PASOLINI ✔☆

via Atenea 123
Agrigento, Sicily 92100, Italy
39-922-20-522
Contact: Francesco La Rocca

Sicily's Cultural Center *Pier Paolo Passolini* presents 5 photographic exhibitions annually. Contact the center directly if you have photography you'd like to show.
Size: 130 square meters.
Lighting: Neon and spotlights.

MUSEO KEN DAMY ✔☆

Corsetto S. Agata 22, Loggia Mercanzie
Brescia 25122, Italy
39-30-50295 *Fax:* 39-30-45259
Contact: Ken Damy

Located between Milano and Verona near Lake Garda, the Museo Ken Damy mounts 46 photographic exhibitions annually. The museum will view work

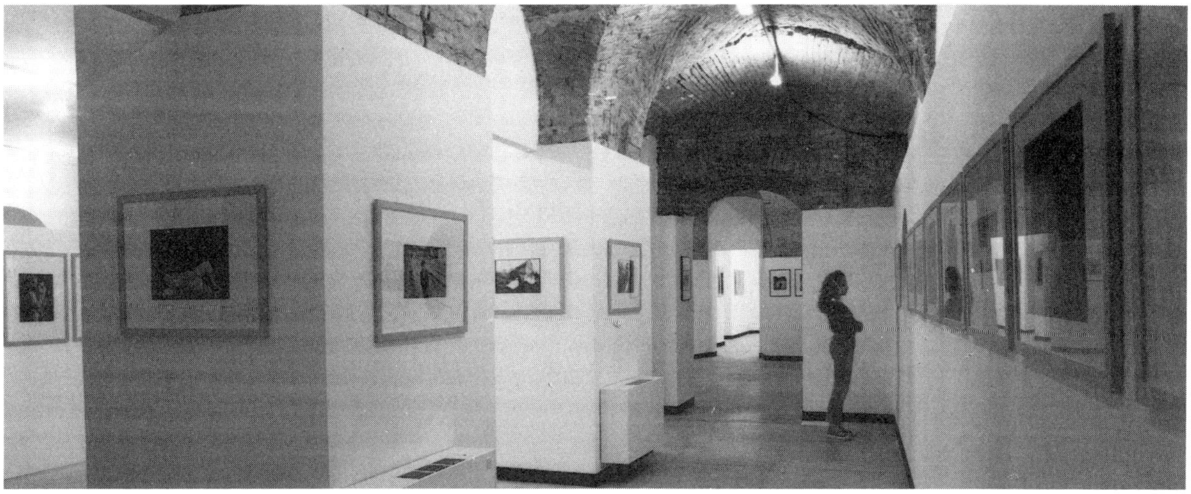

Photograph courtesy of Museo Ken Damy

Museo Ken Damy in Brescia, near Lake Garda in Northern Italy, is devoted exclusively to the art of photography.

from both established photographers and new photographers whose work illustrates upcoming trends.
Requirements: Present samples of your best work after contacting the museum.
Size: 500 square feet.
Lighting: Quartz.
Services: The museum offers a lecture series.

CENTRO DELL'IMMAGINE LA POLLERIA ✔

Palazzo Serra Gerace, V. Sottoripa 129 R
Genova 16123, Italy
39-10-284-174 *Fax:* 39-10-282-489
Contact: Franco DiGioia

Genova's Centro Dell'Immagine La Polleria Immaginaria mounts 6 or 7 exhibitions annually.
Requirements: Portfolios with passepartout are required.
Size: 200 square meters.
Lighting: Halogen.
Services: The gallery has a library. Invitation cards and posters are created for exhibitions.
Expenses: Shipping in both directions is paid for by the photographer.

GALLERIA MILANO S.A.S. ✔

Via Manin 13
Milano, Italy
39-2-290-00352 *Fax:* 39-2-290-03283
Contact: Carla Pellegrini Rocca

Galleria Milano presents 5 or 6 photographic exhibitions annually. The gallery will review work of both new and established photographers offering contemporary, avantgarde, or conceptual material.
Size: 200 square meters.
Lighting: Halogen lamps are used.
Services: The gallery produces catalogues to publicize exhibitions.
Expenses: Photographers may negotiate various expenses, primarily framing.

KEN DAMY PHOTOGALLERY ✔

Via Pastrengo 12
Milano 20100, Italy
39-2-68-86848
Contact: Ken Damy

Ken Damy maintains several galleries throughout Italy featuring creative photography. Photographers offering new trends through their work may submit samples.
Size: 110 square meters.
Lighting: Quartz.
Services: Ken Damy offers extensive promotion for his exhibitions.

MILAN ART CENTER ✔★

Via Aprica 2
Milano 201, Italy
39-2-349-1947
Contact: Ruggero Maggi

The Milan Art Center produces many photography and general art exhibitions annually. Each show is mounted for a period of 3 weeks and usually features the work of new or developing artists. The center will view material from new photographers only.
Requirements: Photography samples should be sent prior to offering a complete portfolio.
Size: 120 square meters.
Lighting: Spotlights.
Services: A special service offered by the center is the organization of group exhibitions that travel throughout Italy and abroad.
Expenses: The center will organize different aspects of an exhibition but the photographer may pay a set rate to cover invitations and other expenses.

PHOTO IMAGO ✔★

Salita di Muggia Vecchia 50
Muggia 34015, Italy
39-40-273-820
Contact: Adriano Perini

Photo Imago exhibits the work of young, European photographers. Muggia is situated on the Gulf of Trieste near the Yugoslav border.
Requirements: Submissions should include up to 20 sample slides or prints with biographical information. Landscapes, portraits, nudes, and vintage b/w are of interest.
Size: Approximately 50 linear meters.
Services: The gallery hosts opening receptions and creates posters and catalogues to promote its exhibitions.
Expenses: The galley requests two works for their collection.

DRYPHOTO ✔★

via Pugliesi 23
Prato 55407, Italy
39-574-604-939
Contact: Victoria Ciolini, Anrea Abati

Dryphoto is one of the outstanding contemporary photography galleries in Italy. The gallery mounts up to 9 exhibitions annually and does review the portfolios of photographers at all levels.
Requirements: Dryphoto prefers to view portfolios.
Size: 70 square meters.
Lighting: Spot.

Services: The gallery promotes exhibitions in photography journals and newspapers and by invitation cards.
Expenses: The photographer pays for shipping in both directions.

JAPAN

GALLERY MIN ✔

4-3-12 Himonya Meguro-ku
Tokyo 152, Japan
81-3-791-8888 *Fax:* 81-3-716-1189
Contact: Mayuhi Shinohara, Curator

Gallery Min is Tokyo's foremost contemporary photography gallery. Recently the gallery has joined with the Lowinsky Gallery in New York's Soho in a kind of "exchange artist" program devised to showcase new American and European photographers in Japan, and Japanese artists in the U.S.
Requirements: Submissions should include sample slides and prints and be accompanied by an artist's statement.
Size: 350 square feet.
Lighting: Tungsten.
Expenses: Production expenses are paid for by the artist.

TOKYO METROPOLITAN ART MUSEUM

8-36 Veno Park, Taito-Ku
Tokyo 110, Japan
81-3-3823-6921
Admission: Free
Hours: Daily 9-5; closed Mondays and holidays.

The Tokyo Metropolitan Art Museum was established in 1926 and consists of two galleries each containing multiple exhibitions. The Museum Gallery is devoted to special exhibitions curated by the curatorial staff and to temporary exhibitions showcasing the museum's contemporary Japanese collection. The second gallery, called the Rental Gallery, is used by various Japanese art organizations and features over 200 exhibitions each year. The art exhibited in both galleries is contemporary.

TOKYO METROPOLITAN MUSEUM OF PHOTOGRAPHY

Q-19-24 Ebisu, Shibuya-ku
Tokyo 150, Japan
81-3-3280-0031

1990 marked the long-awaited opening of Japan's first museum dedicated entirely to photography. Located in the Ebisu area of Tokyo, the museum's initial exhibition was a documentary show, *Tokyo: A City Perspective*, which featured the images of 20 of Japan's top photographers. In the works is the museum's quest for a world class permanent collection which already contains photographs by William Fox Talbot, the complete W. Eugene Smith retrospective *Let Truth Be The Prejudice* and Gary Winogrand's *Women Are Beautiful* series.

ZEIT-FOTO ✔

1-7-2 Muromachi-Nihonbashi Chuo-ku
Tokyo 103, Japan
81-3-246-1370 *Fax:* 81-3-279-3224
Contact: Esuro Ishihara or Mariko Fukuchi

Zeit-Foto is one of Japan's leading galleries presenting photographic art. The gallery mounts approximately 10 shows annually featuring the work of new and established photographers from Japan and other countries.
Requirements: Samples slides may be submitted for consideration.
Size: 35 square meters.
Lighting: Tungsten.
Services: The gallery sponsors touring exhibitions and hosts opening parties and prints postcards to promote shows.

The following galleries in Tokyo specialize in photography:

Canon Salon 348-2121
Shinjuku Dai-ichi Seimei Bldg. 2f Lobby
Tokyo, Japan

Dentsu Promotion Gallery 574-2544
Dentsu Bldg., 1F Ginza
Tokyo, Japan

Fuji Photo Salon 571-9411
Sukiyabashi Center 2f, Ginza
Tokyo, Japan

Ginza Gallery Nakazawa 562-5630
Namiki-dori, Ginza
Tokyo, Japan

Ginza Pocket Park 572-5555
Ginza Tokyo Gas Bldg. 2F, Ginza
Tokyo, Japan

Nikon Salon Ginza 562-5756
5-63 Chrome, Ginza
Chou-ku, Tokyo, Japan

Odakyu Gallery 342-1111
Grand Gallery 11F, Shinjuku
Tokyo, Japan

Parco Gallery 477-5873
Parco 8F, Ginza
Tokyo, Japan

Pentax Forum 348-2941
3-21-20 Nishi-Azabu
Minato-ku, Tokyo, Japan

Photo Gallery International 501-9123
Toranomon
Tokyo, Japan

Tokyo Designers Space Photo Gallery 444-5522
Studio Ebisu 2F
Tokyo, Japan

NETHERLANDS

STUDIO B.A.F. ART GALLERY ✔★
Arnhemseweg 177 A
Amersfoort, Netherlands
31-33-650-941 *Fax:* 31-33-622-248
Contact: Bernard Bakker

Studio B.A.F. Art Gallery was founded in 1987 and presents contemporary photography and audio-visual artforms. Studio B.A.F., located in the medieval city of Amersfoort near Utrecht and about 50 kilometers from Amsterdam, mounts about 10 exhibitions annually. The studio is operated entirely by volunteers and funded by private donors. The studio will review the work of new and established photographers.
Requirements: Portfolios are required for presentation.
Size: 48 square meters.
Lighting: Halogen.
Services: The gallery offers the standard promotional activities.
Expenses: Exhibited photographers must pay an exhibition fee of about $150.00 for each month the show is on.

ART GALLERY A'PERT ✔
Prinsengracht 496-S
Amsterdam 1017 KH, Netherlands
31-20-240-384
Contact: Mareu Sapinsui

The centrally located Art Gallery A'Pert specializes in modern art and regularly mounts photographic shows. The gallery is interested in "conceptual" photography.
Requirements: The gallery should be contacted directly before sending material.
Size: 7m x 8m.
Lighting: Spotlights.
Services: The gallery promotes its exhibitions internationally.

CANON IMAGE CENTRE ✔★
Leidsetraat 79
Amsterdam 1017 NX, Netherlands
31-29-254-494
Contact: Adriaan Monshouwer

The Canon Image Centre specializes in contemporary photography and exhibits about 35 shows each year. The centre is particularly interested in viewing work from young photographers.
Requirements: Contemporary work in any style and subject can be submitted via 35mm slides.
Size: 400 square meters.
Lighting: Natural and florescent.
Services: Services offered include invitation design and printing, matting and framing, and press kits.

FOTOGALERIE 2 1/2 X 4 1/2 ✔★
Prinsengracht 356
Amsterdam 1016 JA, Netherlands
31-20-260-757
Contact: Bernice Siene

Fotogalerie 2 1/2 x 4 1/2 is located along one of Amsterdam's main gallery arteries. The gallery, which presents approximately 13 photography exhibitions annually, concentrates on launching the work of beginning photographers
Requirements: Slides or prints may be submitted along with a clearly outlined proposal. The gallery is also interested in presenting the "special projects" of established photographers.
Size: 32 square meters.
Lighting: Neon.
Services: The gallery offers special payment plans for photo collectors. The gallery advertises in photo and art magazines and mails invitation cards.

GALERIE SPIEGELING ✔
Spiegelgracht 34
Amsterdam 1017 JS, Netherlands
31-20-200-650
Contact: Paul Hillebrand

Galerie Spiegeling exhibits about 6 photography shows annually and is interested in new photographers.
Requirements: Personal contact is requested if possible.
Services: Framing and passepartouts. Exhibition calendars and invitations are created for the shows.
Expenses: The photographer pays 50% of all costs.

GALERIE TORCH ✔

Prinsengracht 218
Amsterdam 1016 HD, Netherlands
31-20-260-284 *Fax:* 31-20-238-892
Contact: Adriaan van der Have or Marie Anne Dubois

Galerie Torch mounts 9 exhibitions annually of photography, painting, and installations. The gallery is most interested in viewing the work of new artists.
Requirements: Slides may be submitted for review purposes.
Services: The gallery promotes with invitations and advertisements.

GALLERY K-61 ✔

Kerkstr 61
Amsterdam 1017 GL, Netherlands
31-20-242-134 *Fax:* 31-20-205247
Contact: Mrs. Hanneke Vrind-Dumpff

Situated in the heart of Amsterdam in a 17th century building which is classified as a historial monument, Gallery K-61 offers more than 10 photographic exhibitions each year. The exhibition space is spread over three separate floors.
Requirements: Representative examples of work accompanied by curriculum vitae and press releases or clippings can be presented for consideration.
Size: 360 square meters or 90 running meters.
Lighting: Halogen or museum spotlights.
Expenses: Dependent on the exhibition and sponsoring possibilities.

MELKWEG GALERIE ✔★

Lijnbaansgracht 234 A
Amsterdam 1017 PH, Netherlands
31-20-241-777 *Fax:* 31-20-201-209
Contact: Suzanne Dechert

Melkweg (Milkyway) is a multi-media center which opened in 1970 in a former milk factory. The legendary arts center, which earned a worldwide reputation as a cultural meeting place during that era, continues to host film, theatre, and muscial performances in addition to annual festivals, workshops, and exhibitions. The Melkweg Gallery frequently exhibits contemporary photography by international artists and is interested in erotic, portrait, and reportage photography.
Requirements: Samples should be offered following contact with the gallery.
Size: Various sizes.
Lighting: Spots.
Services: There is a cafe/restaurant, tearoom and bookshop on the premises.

TECHNOLOGIE MUSEUM NINT

Tolstraat 129
Amsterdam 1074 VJ, Netherlands
31-20-664-6021
Hours: Weekdays: 10-5; weekends and holidays: 12-5.

Nint is a "hands-on" technological museum which offers a permanent holography exhibition created by the well-known artist W. Spiering.

FOTOWAND VAN PUFFELEN ✔★

Stille Veerkade 43
Den Haag 2512 BE, Netherlands
31-70-363-8938
Contact: Mr. A.H.M. van Puffelen

Mr. van Puffelen's gallery, in the Netherland's capital city "The Hague", located about 1 hour from Amsterdam, is devoted exclusively to the art of photography.
Requirements: New and established photographers should present their work in a print format in the original size or smaller.
Services: The gallery sometimes offers framing service and promotes its shows via local radio, press-releases, posters, and leaflets.
Expenses: Shipping costs in both directions.

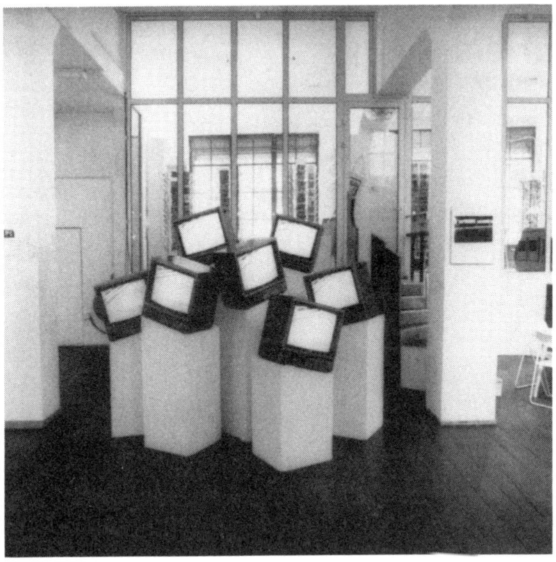

Photograph by Carol Winkel

Amsterdam's Melkweg Galerie is a multi-media center which has been in the vanguard of artistic movements for more than twenty years.

FOTOGALERIE OBJECTIEF ✔★

Walstraat 33
Enschede 7511 GE, Netherlands
31-53-322-507
Contact: Danny Scholten, Mars Vos, Erik Stok or Anna Pisula

Fotogalerie Objectief exhibits photography exclusively. Currently the gallery'is offering 10 shows annually.

Requirements: Contact directly for information. The gallery is interested in all aspects of photography.
Services: Fotogalerie Objektief produces posters and sends out invitations to promote exhibitions. Advertising is also placed in photo and art magazines and newspapers.
Expenses: Publicity photos and transport costs are paid by the photographer.

GRONINGER MUSEUM ✔★

Praediniussingel 59
Groningen NL-9711 AG, Netherlands
31-50-183-343 *Fax:* 31-50-120-815
Contact: Poul ter Hofstede

The Groninger Museum is located in the city of Groningen, north of Amsterdam and near the North Sea. The museum presents 2 photographic exhibitions annually and is interested in contemporary and "staged" photography.

Requirements: The museum prefers to view material in small formats. Reviews and biographical information should be included.
Size: 500 square meters.
Lighting: Artificial.

USVA - PHOTOGALLERY ✔★

Oude Boteringestraat 49
Groningen, Netherlands
31-50-634-659
Contact: John Mulder

The USVA Photogallery features documentary photography including landscape and portraiture. Hosting about 8 exhibitions annually, the gallery is establishing a reputation as a showcase for new, young photographers.

Requirements: A portfolio of small (18x24cm) format PE-photographs should be sent.
Size: 6 x 15 meters.
Lighting: Spotlights.
Services: USVA promotes via posters, magazine advertising, and press announcements.
Expenses: Shipping and printing costs are incurred by the photographer.

FOTOGALERIE 68 ✔★

Klinkertstraat 118
Hoensbroek, Netherlands
31-44-90-45570
Contact: P.W. Frederiks

In the southern-most tip of the Netherlands near Maastricht, you'll find the town of Hoensbroeck and Fotogalerie 68. The gallery, which has existed for 12 years already, presents 8 exhibitions annually of contemporary photography.

Requirements: Portfolios are the required mode of submitting photographs.
Services: The gallery produces posters and invitation cards for each exhibition.

VISUAL FACTS ✔★

P.C. Hooftlaan 130
Maassluis 3141 AH, Netherlands
31-18-99-20312
Contact: Jan Labree

Launched in early 1991, Visual Facts presents 4 photographic shows annually. New, trend-setting photographers are of interest to the gallery which exhibits works visualizing the "human factor" - landscapes, bodyscapes, portraits, nudes, and geographics.

Requirements: Properly mounted work only will be reviewed.
Size: 80 square meters.
Lighting: Spotlights.
Services: The gallery advertises in the local and specialized media.
Expenses: Open costs and some printing costs are paid for by the photographer.

GALERIE FOTOMANIA ✔

Van Oldenbarneveltstraat 148
Rotterdam 3012 GX, Netherlands
31-10-413-5055
Contact: Nicole Roepers or Robert Van Venetie

Galerie Fotomania specializes in Dutch art photography and mounts approximately 11 shows annually. The gallery will view the work of new and established photographers who specialize in art photography.

Requirements: Small prints or photo-copies can be submitted to the gallery to illustrate style.
Size: 60 square meters.
Lighting: Tungsten.
Services: The gallery maintains a mailing list of more than 1,000 international clients. Openings are hosted by the gallery.

Expenses: Transport costs are paid by the photographer.

MUSEUM VOOR VOLKENKUNDE

Willemskade 25
Rotterdam 3016 DM, Netherlands

Rotterdam's Museum voor Volkenkunde (Museum of Ethnology) produces several photographic exhibitions each year of historical and contemporary anthropological photography. The museum also publishes ethnological photo books such as *Burton Brothers: Photographers in New Zealand, 1866-1898* and *19th Century Portrait Photography of American Indians.*

PERSPEKTIEF ✔✭

Eendraehtsweg 21
Rotterdam 3012 LB, Netherlands
31-10-414-5766 *Fax:* 31-10-477-2072
Contact: Bob Vroege

Perspektief is one of the Netherland's leading photographic galleries and presents as many as 10 exhibitions annually covering all aspects of photographic art. The gallery is particularly interested in the work of new photographers.

Requirements: Documentation accompanied by sample slides may be sent for review. The gallery prefers to see work which illustrates "new developments" in photography and which would be considered art.
Size: 5 x 17 meters.
Lighting: Spots.
Services: The gallery employs the standard promotional activities.
Expenses: Prints for press use and framing/mounting expenses are paid for by the photographer.

TON PEEK ✔

Oudegracht 295
Utrecht 3511 PA, Netherlands
31-30-312-001
Contact: Ton Peek

The Ton Peek gallery is interested in exhibiting work which illustrates new trends in photographic art.

Requirements: Contact the gallery directly for submission requirements.
Size: 70 square meters.

Key: ✔ = Portfolios Reviewed
✭ = Non-Profit Organization
▲ = Private Dealer

NEW ZEALAND

NEW ZEALAND CENTRE FOR PHOTOGRAPHY ✔✭

27-35 Hanson Street
Wellington, New Zealand
64-4-895-109 *Fax:* 64-4-895-148
Contact: Willaim Main

The New Zealand Centre for Photography, a national venue in the capital city, mounts from 8 to 10 shows annually on every aspect of photography from snapshots to fine art.

Requirements: A selection of 35mm slides with supporting material may be offered for review.
Size: 120 linear feet.
Lighting: Natural and artificial lighting.
Services: The center has a membership of over 2,500 to which it promotes its activities.
Expenses: The photographer carries the bulk of the exhibition expenses.

NORWAY

PREUS FOTOMUSEUM ✔

Langgt. 82
3190 Horten, Norway
47-33-42737
Contact: Leif Preus

Preus Fotomuseum will review portfolios. Contact directly for submission guidelines and complete information regarding hours of operation, etc.

FOTOGALLERIET ✔

Kongensgate 6
0153 Oslo 1, Norway
47-2-424-924
Contact: Torild Gjesvik (Acting director)

Oslo's Fotogalleriet is one of the leading photographic galleries in Scandinavia. The gallery, which is run by the *Forbundet Frie Fotographer* (organization of free art phtgraphers in Norway), has just moved to this new facility which is centrally located near galleries, the Museum of Contemporary Art, and Akershus Castle. Fotogalleriet mounts up to 8 exhibitions of photography each year and will review the work of new photographers.

Requirements: The gallery prefers to view slides.
Size: Approximately 80 square meters.
Lighting: Halogen.

Services: The gallery advertises in newspapers and mails press releases, invitations, and posters to promote exhibitions.
Expenses: All expenses are negotiable.

POLAND

GALERIA FOTOGRAFII ✔☆
Rynek 44
Swidnica 58100, Poland
48-74-521-337
Contact: Andrzej Protasiuk

Galeria Fotografii mounts from 12 to 15 exhibitions annually. Situated in a small town in southeast Poland not far from the city of Wroclaw, the gallery is interested in reportage, creative, and nude photography.
Requirements: Sample prints may be submitted for review.
Size: 20 x 10 meters.
Services: The gallery produces catalogues to accompany its exhibitions.

MALA GALERIA ZPAF-CSW ✔☆
Plac Zamkowy 8
Warsaw 00277, Poland
48-22-312-339
Contact: Marek Grygiel

Warsaw's Mala Galeria specializes in exhibiting contemporary art in all media. The gallery mounts 16 exhibitions annually and is open to reviewing work from both new and established photographers.
Requirements: The gallery prefers a personal presentation of portfolio by the artist but samples can be sent by mail.
Size: 42 square meters.
Lighting: Incandescent.
Services: The gallery occasionally produces catalogues. Posters and invitation cards for openings are mailed to the gallery's clients.
Expenses: Reception and travel costs are paid for by the photographer.

FOTO MEDIUM ART GALLERY ✔
Place Nankiera 8
Wroclaw 50-140, Poland
48-22-447-840
Contact: Jerzy Olek

Foto Medium Art Gallery specializes in photographic art and will review material from both new and established photographers. The gallery also offers its work to other institutions for exhibitions.
Requirements: Submission material in either slide or print format should be accompanied by biography, reviews of past exhibitions, and the photographer's artistic manifest.
Size: 50 square meters.
Lighting: Natural and artificial lighting are used.

MUZEUM NARODOWE ☆
Pl. Powstancow Warszawy 5
Wroclaw, Poland
48-871-388-39
Contact: Adam Sobota, Photography Department

Muzeum Narodowe is a national museum which exhibits creative vintage and contemporary photography. The museum also has a large photographic collection.
Size: 200 square meters.
Lighting: Natural and artificial.

PORTUGAL

CENTRO DE ESTUDOS DE FOTOGRAFIA ✔☆
Rua Padre Antonio Vieira, A.A.C.
Coimbra 3000, Portugal
351-39-20154 *Fax:* 351-39-23505
Contact: Albano da Silva Pereira

The Portuguese center for photography studies can be found in the city of Coimbra about 150 kilometers north of Lisbon and 45 kilometers from the Atlantic coast. The center, which also maintains a photo-library, darkrooms, and publishing, mounts one or two exhibitions each month.
Requirements: Portfolios should contain well selected, quality prints. Slides may also be offered but prints are preferred.
Size: 40 square meters.
Lighting: Indirect tungsten.
Expenses: Expenses vary.

GALERIA COMICOS ✔
Rua Tenente Raul Cascais, 1B
Lisbon 1200, Portugal
351-1-677-794
Contact: Luis Serpa

Galeria Comicos is a contemporary art gallery which frequently mounts photographic exhibitions.
Requirements: Contemporary photography is preferred.
Size: 100 square meters.
Lighting: Halogen.
Expenses: Exhibited photographers pay only for the printing of the work.

MODOLO - CENTRO DIFUSOR DE ARTE ✔

34-A Calcada dos Mestres
Lisbon 4100, Portugal
351-1-685-570
Contact: Mario Teixeira da Silva

Modolo is interested in exhibiting new trends in art and photography. There is also a renewed interest in 1950s photography. The gallery has hosted recent one-man shows by photographers Bruce Charlesworth, Jochen Gerz, and Bernard Faucon.

Requirements: Portfolios or slides may be offered for review.
Size: 160 square meters.
Lighting: Halogen.
Services: The gallery services the press via invitations and press-releases. Catalogues are printed and a framing service is available.
Expenses: Freight charges for shipping the work belong to the photographer.

SCOTLAND

STILLS GALLERY ✔✯

105 High Street
Edinburgh EH1 1SG, Scotland
44-31-557-1140
Contact: Lindsay Lewis

Stills, which was the first photographic gallery in Scotland, is the *Gallery of the Scottish Photography Group*. The photography on view at Stills is generally contemporary and consists of shows originated by the gallery as well as "touring" exhibitions.

Requirements: Slides or sample prints accompanied by text may be submitted for review.
Size: 1,100 square feet.
Lighting: Spotlights with dimmers.
Services: Stills offers many services including a comprehensive bookshop, a slide making/duping service, a library of rare photography books, and a series of workshops and "talks". *Photo-Focus* is held monthly providing a forum for dialogues between artists.
Expenses: Expenses are negotiable.

COLLINS GALLERY ✔

22 Richmond Street
Glasgow G1 1XQ, Scotland
44-41-553-4145 *Fax:* 44-41-552-0775
Contact: Laura Hamilton, Curator

Glasgow's Collins Gallery exhibits fine and applied art and contemporary and historic photography. The gallery will review material on these subjects from new and established artists.

Requirements: A minimum of 6 representational slides may be submitted for review.
Size: 3,000 square feet.
Lighting: Spotlights.
Services: Special services to exhibited photographers include accommodations and loan of frames. The gallery promotes its exhibitions through private viewings, posters, local radio and the art media.
Expenses: Transport.

STREET LEVEL PHOTOGRAPHY GALLERY ✔✯

279-281 High Street
Glasgow G4 0Q5, Scotland
44-41-552-2151
Contact: Martha J. McCulloch or Catriona Grant

Street Level Photography Gallery and Workshop produces up to 12 exhibitions annually offering a broad range of creative photography. The gallery does review work from both new and established photographers.

Requirements: Photographers may submit material in slide or print formats. Biographical information should accompany the submissions.
Size: 140′ linear.
Lighting: Spotlights.
Services: The gallery provides promotional services including the distribution of posters, leaflets, and press coverage.
Expenses: Framing and mounting costs for the exhibited work are paid by the photographer.

T & R ANNAN & SONS LTD

164 Woodlands Road
Glasgow, Strathclyde G36LL, Scotland
44-41-332-0028

Although mainly a fine arts gallery selling oil and watercolor paintings, T & R Annan does sell historical photography dating from 1855. The owner, Douglas Annan, is a direct descendant of photography pioneer Thomas Annan and infrequently exhibits his great-grandfather's work which is mainly views of old Glasgow. The photographs are available for viewing and there are some prints available for purchase.

THIRD EYE CENTRE ✔✯

350 Sauchiehall Street
Glasgow G235D, Scotland
44-41-332-7521
Contact: Andrew Nairne

Glasgow's Third Eye Centre maintains a variety of gallery spaces in addition to hosting live performances. Photographic exhibitions generally offer photography considered experimental or innovative.

Requirements: A sampling of slides or transparencies should be offered initially for review.
Size: 2,800 square feet.
Lighting: Halogen and natural lighting are used.
Services: A framing service is available.

CORRIDOR GALLERY ✔☆

Fife Sports Institute, Viewfield Road
Glenrothes, Fife KY6 2RH, Scotland
44-592-756-633
Contact: Andrew Nell

Glenrothes' Corridor Gallery can be reached by traveling north across the Firth of Forth from Edinburgh. The gallery mounts 12 exhibitions annually.
Requirements: Work may be presented for review in any format.
Size: 60 linear feet.
Lighting: Track.
Services: Framing and desk-top publishing facilities are available.
Expenses: All expenses are negotiable.

CRAWFORD ARTS CENTRE ✔☆

93 North Street
St. Andrews, Fife KY16 9AL, Scotland
44-334-74610
Contact: Diana A. Sykes, Director

On the North Sea, just south of Dundee is the village of St. Andrews, home of the Crawford Arts Centre. The centre presents from 20 to 30 exhibitions each year featuring a wide range of photography as well as other media.

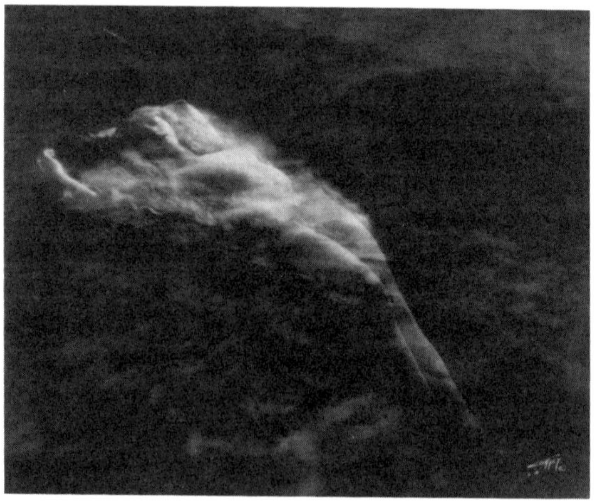

This unusual work by Edward S. Curtis, Aphrodite (Spirit of the Sea) c. 1920, far exceeded expectations at a Butterfield & Butterfield auction. Estimated to bring from $500/700, the piece brought $2,750.

Requirements: Slides should be presented for review. The center will look at work from both new and established photographers.
Size: The large gallery is 124 running feet plus 3 smaller ones.
Lighting: Track with spotlights.
Services: The center covers all exhibition promotion, installation, and private view costs. Exhibitions are promoted via the center's mailing list, posters, advertising, and press releases.
Expenses: Some mounting costs may be shared depending on the artist's requirements.

SOUTH AFRICA

BENSUSAN MUSEUM OF PHOTOGRAPHY ✔☆

c/o Africana Museum, Market Square
Johannesburg 2001, South Africa
27-836-3787 *Fax:* 27-836-6607
Contact: Mrs. E. B. Nagelgast, Curator

The Bensusan Museum of Photography is a museum devoted to all aspects of the art of photography and also maintains an extensive collection of photographic and movie equipment. The museum will move in June 1991 to a new, enhanced facility which will include an auditorium, meeting room, and kitchen. The museum mounts approximately 12 exhibitions each year and is basically interested in presenting work by South African artists or on South African subjects.
Requirements: Submitted prints should be mounted archivally on acid-free board, not larger than 1m (high) x 1,5m.
Size: The new museum will be 100 square meters
Lighting: Quartz.
Services: The museum is promoted via the local media and mailings to photographic schools and clubs.
Expenses: Mounting and hanging costs, plus opening reception and possibly security (if open after usual hours) are paid for by the photographer.

JOHANNESBURG ART GALLERY ✔

King George Street, Jarbert Park
Johannesburg 2044, South Africa
27-725-3130 *Fax:* 27-724-0003
Contact: Christopher Till

Although not devoted exclusively to the art of photography, the Johannesburg Art Gallery does own a small collection of South African and international photography. Contact the gallery directly for submission information.

SPAIN

FUNDACIO JOAN MIRO ✔★
Parc de Montjuic
Barcelona 08038, Spain
34-3-329-1908 *Fax:* 34-3-329-8609
Contact: Rosa Maria Malet

The Joan Miro Foundation was created by the artist in 1971 as both a space to house his works and also to introduce and promote the work of new contemporary artists. The foundation's building was designed by noted architect Josep Lluis Sert and is situated on a hill overlooking Barcelona in the beautiful Parc de Montjic. In addition to the foundation's many galleries, there is a library, bookshop, and restaurant. New and established photographers may submit work.
Requirements: Dossiers containing proposals for exhibitions should be sent to the director.
Size: 992 square meters.
Lighting: Natural and incandescent.
Services: The activities of the foundation are well advertised and publicized in the art media and sometimes newspapers. Posters are created for the shows.

GALERIA CIENTO ✔
Consejo de Ciento 347
Barcelona 08007, Spain
34-3-215-6365 *Fax:* 34-3-487-2588
Contact: Marisa Diez de la Fuente

Galeria Ciento exhibits all types of art.
Requirements: Contact directly for specifics.
Services: The gallery publicizes exhibitions with openings to which it invites members of the art media.
Expenses: Travel and transport. Expenses are negotiable for each exhibition.

CIRCULO DE BELLAS ARTES ✔★
Alcala, 42
Madrid 28014, Spain
34-1-531-7700 *Fax:* 34-1-531-0552
Contact: Manuel Santos or Alejandro Castellote

Circulo de Bellas Artes is a center for contemporary art which exhibits the photographic work of Spanish and international photographers. The center also conducts seminars hosted by internationally known photographers.
Requirements: A portfolio containing a minimum of 10 photographs may be submitted along with text and resume.
Size: There are two galleries each 800 square meters.
Lighting: Tungsten.
Services: Posters, postcards, and catalogues are produced. Press releases are sent to the art media.
Expenses: The cost of creating the prints for exhibition is paid for by the photographer.

RAILOWSKY FOTO-GALERIA ✔
Grabador Esteve 34
Valencia 46004, Spain
34-6-351-7218
Contact: Jose Font de Mora

The Railowsky gallery creates 12 exhibits a year. Reportage, vintage, and portraits of writers are of interest to the gallery.
Requirements: Interested photographers may submit 30 examples of their work.
Size: 60 square meters.
Services: The gallery includes a photo-library and collection of photographs. The gallery's mailing list is used to promote exhibitions via postcards, invitations, and media kits.
Expenses: Postal costs and one photograph for the gallery.

VISOR CENTRE FOTOGRAFIC ✔★
C/Corretgeria 26
Valencia, Spain
34-6-332-2399
Contact: Pep Benlloch

Visor features contemporary photography and also runs photographic workshops.
Requirements: Only recent work should be submitted for review.
Size: 50 square meters.
Lighting: Incandescent.

SWEDEN

FOTOHUSET-GALERY, SGF ✔★
Parkgatan 2
Goteborg S-411 38, Sweden
46-31-110-908
Contact: Thomas Afekenstam

Fotohuset Gallery (Photo-house) is the meeting place for the *Goteborg Photographic Society* which presents approximately 18 exhibitions annually. The society also hosts workshops and seminars. The gallery

exhibits many types of photography and is also interested in other art forms which utilize photography.
Requirements: A small representative assortment of pictures or slides must be accompanied by biographical information, an exhibition proposal with detailed information, and any press clippings.
Size: The house is 2 stories, each being about 150 square meters.
Lighting: Incandescent and neon.
Services: Posters and press-releases are mailed out to promote exhibitions. The gallery also produces a brochure twice yearly.

FOTOGRAFICENTRUM SYD ✔☆

Sit Gertrudsgatan 4
Malmo 21125, Sweden
Contact: Jan Tidman

Malmo's Fotograficentrum Syd, just a short Hovercraft ride away from Copenhagen, Denmark, presents 10 shows each year featuring documentary and art photography.
Requirements: Prints or slides can be sent for review.
Size: 35 square meters.
Lighting: Spotlights.
Services: Posters and press-releases promote the gallery.
Expenses: Framing is the main expense to photographers.

FOTOGRAFISKA MUSEET ✔☆

Skeppsholmen
Stockholm S-10327, Sweden
46-8-666-4250 *Fax:* 46-8-208-275
Contact: Leif Wigh, Curator

Fotografiska Museet is Stockholm's photography museum. Each year they mount between 10 and 15 exhibitions featuring photography from 1840 to the present.
Requirements: The museum will view work from both new and established photographers. Portfolios can be presented following contact with the museum.
Size: 200 square meters.

SWITZERLAND

NO NAME GALLERY ✔

Guterstrasse 153
Basel 4053, Switzerland
41-61-352-065
Contact: Tobias Toggweiler

Located in the northwest corner of Switzerland near the French and German border, Basel's No Name Gallery is both a gallery and photo bookstore with a young following. The gallery is interested in photography on the cutting edge of contemporary style.
Requirements: In person presentation is required with slides and catalogues and press clippings.
Size: Galleries are 40 x 50 and 60 x 80.
Lighting: Variety.
Services: Framing service and a photography and film bookstore are available.
Expenses: Promotional costs are shared with the gallery.

KUNSTMUSEUM ✔☆

Hodlerstrasse 8-12
Berne 3011, Switzerland
41-31-220-944 *Fax:* 41-31-22-7263
Contact: Thomas Pfister, Curator for Photography, Film, & Video

Kunstmuseum is Berne's museum of fine arts and mounts several photographic exhibitions yearly. The museum will view portfolios containing photographic art.
Requirements: Contact directly for precise information. The curator has indicated that photographers of all levels are welcome to submit portfolios for review.

BERNARD LETU

2 rue Calvin
Geneva 1204, Switzerland
41-22-204-757 *Fax:* 41-22-208492
Contact: Bernard Letu

The Bernard Letu gallery basically features engravings but is one of the best photo bookshops in Switzerland featuring hard-to-find international photography books.

CENTRE DE LA PHOTOGRAPHIE ✔☆

16, rue du General Dufour
Geneva 1204, Switzerland
22-29-29-35
Contact: Michele Auer

Geneva's Center for Photography was created to fill the void resulting from the closing of the city's 3 photo galleries, Obscura, Canon, and Trepied, in the early '80s. The now extremely successful center presents on-going exhibitions featuring every type of photography from the documentary style of Weegee to the contemporary work of Vasco Ascolini. 16 to 20 exhibitions are mounted annually and new photographers may submit material considered fine art.
Requirements: The center will review material only as it is intended to be hung.

Size: 100 square meters.
Services: Members receive posters, bulletins, postcards, and press-releases to keep them up to date with the projects of the center. The center also contains a videotheque and library.

GALERIE ERIC FRANCK ✔

15 Route de Flourissant
Geneva 1206, Switzerland
41-22-470-809 *Fax:* 41-22-476455
Contact: Eric Franck, Director of Acquisitions

Although the Eric Franck Gallery mounts only one photographic exhibit each year, Mr. Franck is interested in seeing new work. As the gallery specializes in contemporary art, contact him directly if you have unique, contemporary photography.
Requirements: Slide or original prints can be submitted.
Size: 150 square meters.

MUSEE DE L'ELYSEE ✔✮

18, Avenue De L'Elysee
Lausanne 1014, Switzerland
41-21-617-4821
Contact: Charles-Henri Farrod, Director

Lausanne's Musée de L'Elysee mounts 25 exhibitions annually and is interested in presenting all types of 19th and 20th century photography.
Requirements: Contact directly for information. The Musee will view portfolios from both new and established photographers.
Size: 1,000 square meters.
Lighting: Neon.
Services: The Musee produces posters and invitation cards for all exhibitions.

FOCALE ✔✮

4, Place du Chateau
Nyon 1260, Switzerland
44-22-610-966
Contact: Daniel Bavdraz

Situated between Lausanne and Geneva on Lac Leman, Nyon's Focale Gallery mounts 10 photographic exhibitions each year. The gallery is interested in viewing the work of both new and established photographers.
Requirements: About 40 work prints or sample slides illustrating a theme may be presented for review.
Size: Approximately 25 square meters.
Lighting: Halogen spotlights.
Services: The gallery hosts discussions and consultations and offers a library for public use. Posters and invitations are created to publicize the exhibitions.
Expenses: Photographer's expenses may include shipping and print costs.

Additional Swiss galleries, museums, and private dealers include:

Galerie Zur Stockeregg
Stockerstrasse 33
8022 Zurich, Switzerland

Marlborough Galerie AG
Glarnischstrasse 10
CH-8992 Zurich, Switzerland

Nikon Foto-Galerie
Schoffelgasse 3
8001 Zurich, Switzerland

Photogalerie Portfolio
21 Escaliers du Marche
1003 Lausanne, Switzerland

Photo-Galerie im Kunsthaus Zurich
Kunsthaus, Heimplatz 1
8001 Zurich, Switzerland

YUGOSLAVIA

GORENJSKI MUZEJ ✔✮

Tavcarjaeva 43
Kranj, Slovenija, Yugoslavia
38-64-21974
Contact: Cene Avgustin, Photography Curator

Kranj, which is the home of the Gorenjski Museum is in northern Yugoslavia near the Austrian border. The museum's photography unit, *Kabinet Slovenske Fotografije,* features a prominent Slovenian photography collection dating from 1839.The museum is interested in exhibiting both Slovenian and international photography.
Requirements: The selection committee meets several times a year to consider exhibition possibilities. Photographers should send catalogues or tear-sheets and press clippings for the committee to view.
Size: 90 square meters.
Services: The gallery produces a booklet for each exhibition. Promotion is via TV and newspapers.
Expenses: Transportation of photographs is paid for by the photographer.

From Weston, Mass.

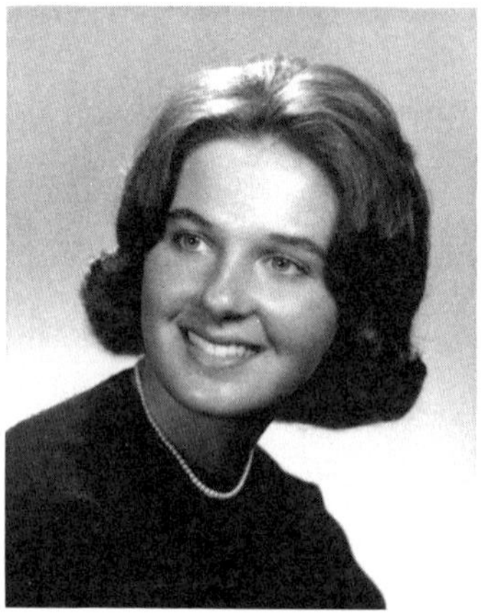

Tenneson, Joyce '67

French Club, Art Club, Foreign Exchange Student, Dean's List; activities include theater and poetry readings.

How did Joyce Tenneson get from Regis College to the pages of *L.A. Style* and *French Vogue?* By staying true to an ethereal style that's made her work a mirror of her soul. This mythic vision has

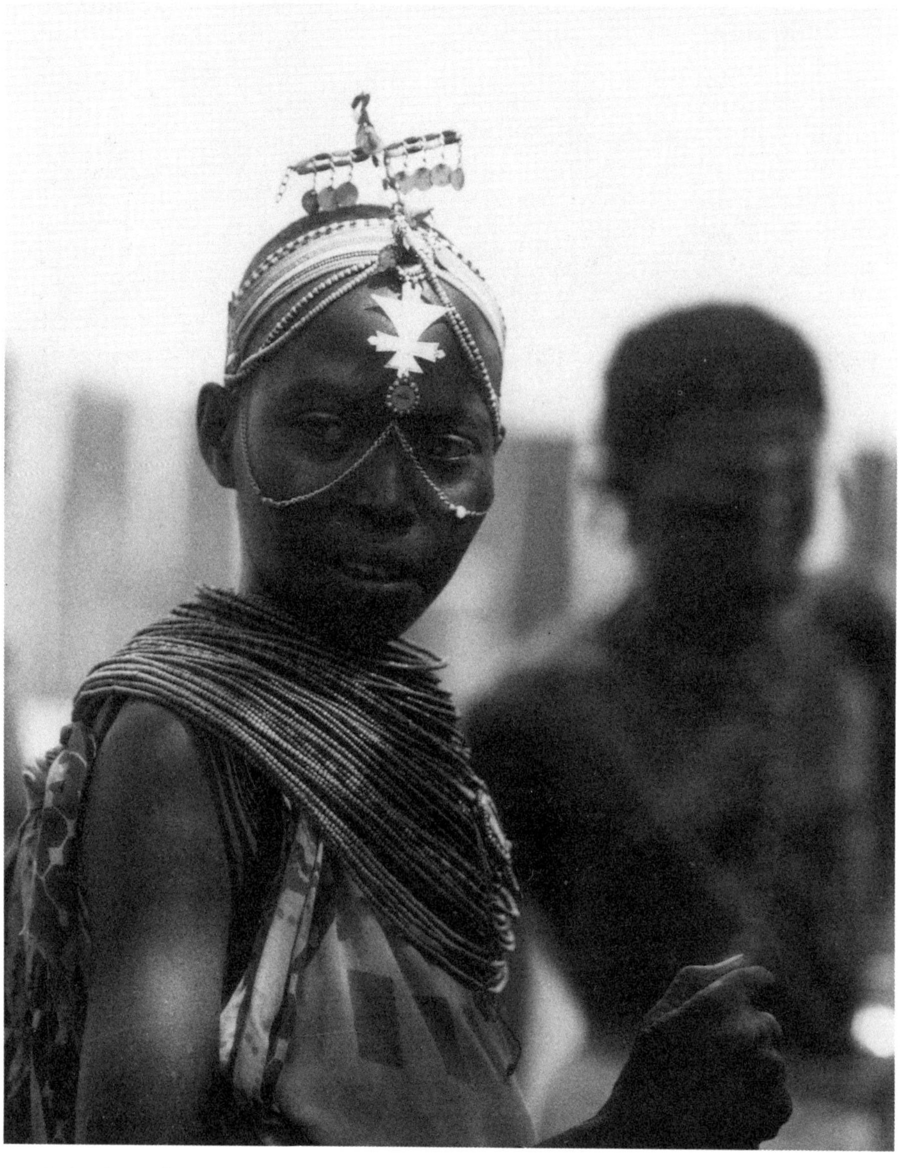

A Samburu dancer photographed in the Samburu National Park in East Africa. Photograph courtesy of East Africa Photographic Workshops.

Part II: Workshops, Seminars, and Photo-Tours

Workshop or Photo-Tour?

The choice is endless: free-wheeling, month-long photo safaris to Madagascar; intensive, one-week workshops devoted to macro-photography; and, even one day seminars on the art of glamour photography. Which experience might be the right one for you?

We'll assume you already have a general idea of what a workshop or photo-tour is. However, as I have found in researching the massive collection of material gathered for this book, the variety of subjects and locations is truly overwhelming. And although it is possible to provide detailed information here, much of the actual *experience* of attending a workshop or photo-tour depends on the degree of participation each member brings to the situation, the instructor leading the group, and the quality of the facilities and accommodations available.

There is a lot of competition to win participants in the wide-ranging world of photo-tours and safaris. The price for a two-week safari could range from $5,000 upwards depending on destination and degree of comfort. Currently the most popular international photo-tour destinations seem to be the East African countries of Tanzania and Kenya, Ecuador's Galapagos Islands, and Baja California, Mexico. Stateside, the Florida Everglades, the Rocky Mountain national parks, and the coastal waters and villages of Cape Cod vie for the traveling shooter. Although many photo-tours offer limited instruction and photographic facilities due to the usual inconveniences of travel, these group endeavors can provide an unparalleled and comfortable opportunity to shoot once-in-a-lifetime pictures. The added attraction of experienced leaders should also not be underestimated.

A wide variety of photographic workshops are available throughout the year and can be found in just about every state in the union. Often taking advantage of renowned scenic locations or highly regarded institutions, workshop offerings include instruction in such popular subjects as wildlife and landscape photography, the zone system, and glamour and studio portraiture. There are also some unique and highly-specialized workshops available such as former model Nancy Brown's Studio Workshop on beauty and illustration photography; the annual Càttle Roundup Photography Workshop for action photographers; and The Wildlife Model Workshops which allow for photographing wildlife in a controlled setting. Workshops are generally available for periods of long weekends to two weeks and more. Anything less should be considered a seminar. Photography workshops are a viable alternative to the courses offered by traditional educational institutions which usually offer on-going classes stretched out over a period of several months and often meeting only once a week. The strength of workshops is that the intensive structure allows for an in-depth, comprehensive study of a chosen subject.

The following pages contain interviews with professionals representing both workshops and photo-tours. Jim Baker, who runs the photo workshops at the Anderson Ranch in Snowmass, Colorado, elaborates on the value of the workshop experience. Chris and Jim McLarty, leaders of the East Africa Photo Safari, provide an overview on what prospective participants should look for in choosing a photo-tour.

The Workshop Low-Down from the Anderson Ranch's Jim Baker

The first thing any workshop director will tell you, is that no two workshop programs are created equal. Like the variety of popular subjects that are usually offered, the variables within a workshop program can be extremely broad. And given the fact that workshops generally bring together a diverse group of participants, what one may learn from this educational adventure is usually not what one expects to learn. As Jim Baker, Director of Photography Workshops at The Anderson Ranch Arts Center tells first-time workshop participants, "If this is your first workshop, whatever kind of experience you imagine you will have - you'll have some of that. But by the end of the week your experience will probably seem very different from what you expected."

The Anderson Ranch Arts Center, in the village of Snowmass, Colorado, near Aspen, has successfully hosted photography, and other artistic workshops, for over twenty-five years. A five-year veteran at the ranch, Jim Baker is a graduate of the Rhode Island School of Design, and spent ten years teaching at the university level before joining the Center. A photographer, who specializes in large format, color landscapes, Baker is a champion of workshops and their educational value. Subsequently his extensive experience has given him strong, heart-felt opinions on many subjects regarding the workshop experience.

Again, acknowledging that there are a multitude of worthwhile workshop programs available to photographers at every level of experience, I questioned Baker about the workshop experience in general. During our conversation I assumed the role of the natural skeptic - in this instance one who might need to be coerced into workshop participation - and Jim played the role of workshop defender and enthusiast. Not a big stretch for either of us! Hopefully the following questions and answers will guide the reader in selecting a workshop program that will prove to be a valuable and fulfilling experience.

Why choose to attend a workshop at all, why not just take a course?

In general I would say that workshops are catalysts for *change*. Whether you're a professional artist or photographer, or you just want to reaffirm your commitment to photography, because maybe you've been away from it for awhile. Perhaps you could choose to go to a community college but don't have the time, so you prefer to use your discretionary time, like two weeks in summer, to intensively immerse yourself in learning. Workshops are of short duration compared to formal education. They're very intense and so people who choose to do it like to learn in that kind of intensive situation.

Also because a workshop is a creative retreat. A way of getting away from whatever your life's been about, good or bad, and being able to look at it from a different perspective and see your career in the context of these other individuals. Not just the well-known faculty members. But the other participants who have been attracted to that workshop for very similar reasons and are collectively looking at what their concerns are and maybe saying, "Okay, I'll reaffirm where I've been going with my career or I'm gonna make a change. And I'm gonna use this new technical knowledge I've been presented with in this workshop - or the new ideas, or the new inspiration, - to take me in a new direction in my career."

Who is a good candidate to attend a workshop? And who is wrong for the experience? When we consider taking a workshop or class I think we all instinctively call up our old school days from the memory bank and remember the anxiety of being terrorized by the one misfit intent on disrupting the class.

The best people for workshops are those who are facing a change in their career. Because anybody who

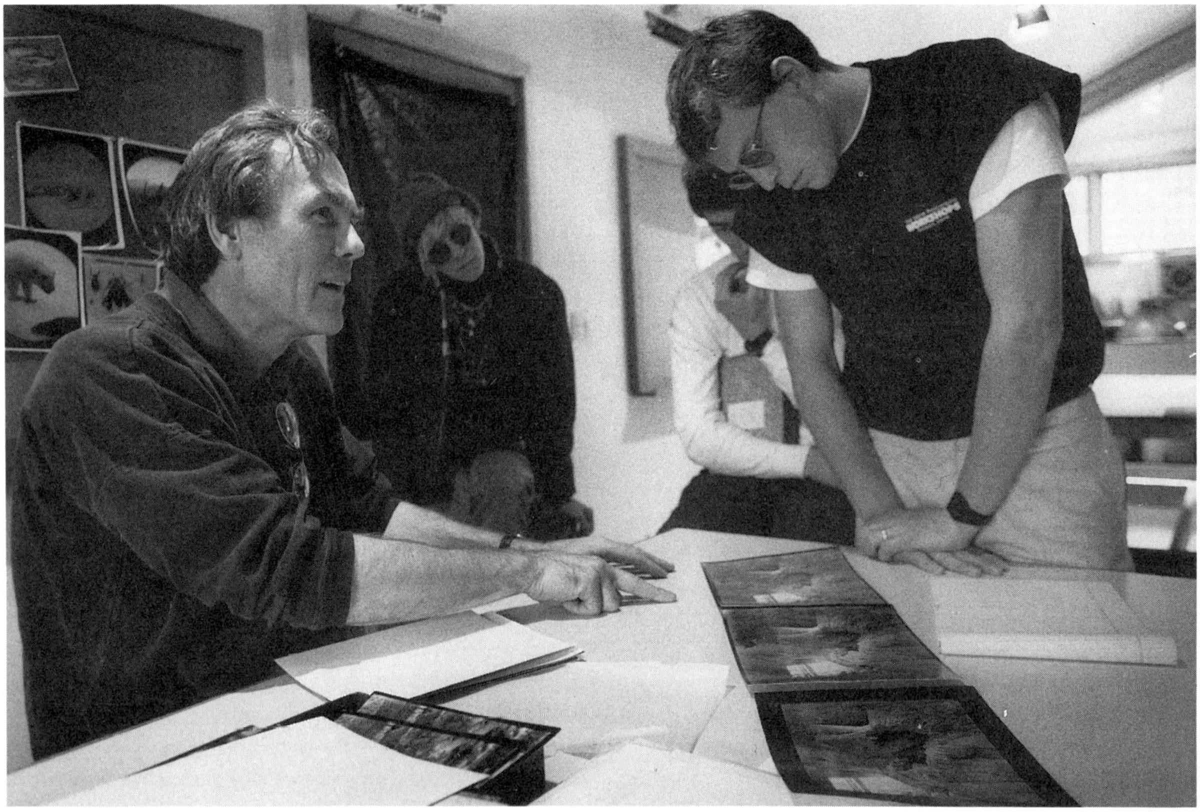

Photograph courtesy of The Anderson Ranch

Fine art photographer Emmet Gowin discusses his work with Anderson Ranch artists-in residence.

is in a professional career is somebody who is innately interested in learning, and reeducating themselves, and growing.

In contrast, anyone who is by nature very *narrow-minded* is not a good candidate for taking a workshop because very often what you learn in a workshop is not what you expect to learn. You may have come to the workshop thinking that you want to learn a particular technical process or creative skill. But during the week the instructor, or your class-mates, may point out to you that there's really something else going on and that maybe you should seize the opportunity to explore the problem from another angle. If you're not open to that you're going to be, first of all, very frustrated. Because people are going to be telling you things that you don't want to hear, and you're going to be thinking that maybe you wasted your money coming to the workshop. Then, of course it becomes a downer for the rest of the class.

Sometimes people are also kind of selfish and they have very specific ideas of what they want from the workshop. And they will do everything they can to sort of work the class toward answering their particular need instead of being sensitive to the fact that it's a group endeavor. Fortunately, that doesn't happen too often. It's my job to intervene and talk to the person or to the instructor.

Also we don't do portfolio reviews prior to the beginning of a workshop as some workshops do. We do send everyone who registers a questionnaire. And if it's clear they're not prepared to take the workshop, then I give them a call and see if I can't suggest something more appropriate. Some choose to ignore my advice and if they're clear about what they're doing, they're usually right. But there are some people who do have illusions about their ability.

Luckily, only about one in twenty people taking a workshop is taking it for the *wrong* reason. Thank God! At least here at Anderson Ranch most people come for the right reasons. And if they're not conscious of the right reasons at the beginning of the week, because perhaps they've signed on for a workshop in a totally intuitive way - that is they haven't logically determined what taking the workshop is gonna do for their life - then by the end of the week they do know why.

There are some people who get themselves into workshops and they don't know why, and we don't know why, they did it! One kind of person who does that is easy to spot and that's the person who comes strictly for affirmation. And while affirmation is important for every human being, if you want simply to show your photographs to some well-known photographer and expect him to tell you that you're doing great, and you leave the workshop without undergoing any change, then that's not good. Because that's certainly not why the people who come here to teach come to teach. They know that that's not going to do you any good. And if you don't need change there's no reason to take a workshop. If you're a great photographer or you're not a great photographer, if you're not open and ready to question your work, there's no reason to take a workshop. The primary reason the instructors teach workshops is the desire to share what they know; they want to help other photographers maybe in the same way that they've been helped. At least the ones who teach at Anderson Ranch. Of course we try and get the best photographers who are also the best teachers.

Okay, what should a first-time workshopper be looking for as he or she entertains the notion of a week-long landscape photography trip by canoe or an intensive weekend devoted to sharpening one's lighting skills? How should one go about selecting a workshop?

First of all read the descriptions in the brochures carefully. The descriptions tell you a lot about where the program's at. For instance, if you want a serious educational week, and the brochure devotes a lot of space to telling you where you can rent equipment to go hiking, or where to go for sunning at the beach, then you should know that it's probably not a very serious program in terms of a heavy-duty, intensive, learning experience. On the other hand, if you want a vacation, and you read the descriptions in the brochures and they sound really heavy to you, maybe you don't want to be *there*! You really have to read between the lines a little bit. I would certainly call with questions, and as you quiz the workshop staff - *remembering that you're a customer for a product* - you should feel like you can put any question to the person that you're talking to.

Word of mouth is by far the best way to find out about a workshop. It's probably not practical to call a workshop and request a referral. But if there is a way of contacting a prior participant, that would be the best reference.

Once it's decided a workshop's program might fit the bill, what other considerations should be made?

Facilities are important. If you're taking a workshop where you use color slide film - there are many workshops that don't have their own black and white labs so they really rely on color slide film - find out the specifics about the processing of the film; what the turn-around time is for processing. If you have to wait two days to see an assignment you shot and you only have five or seven days in the workshop, you're losing a lot of valuable time and not getting to review your work. But if there's a three or four hour turnaround with E-6 processing, then you'll be getting a lot more out of the workshop.

If they do have a black and white facility, ask about the specifics of the equipment; what they have and how it's run; what kind of assistance do they have? I always think that while certainly the most important person to the students is the instructor, the assistants are also very important because they are the intermediaries between the faculty and the students. You might want to find out how many assistants are in the workshop.

How important is it to be familiar with the instructors listed on the faculty roster?

The kind of faculty a workshop program gets tells you a lot too, and you should certainly inquire about the faculty's teaching skills in anyway that you can. Find out if they've taught there before. If they haven't, try to find out where they have taught and contact that place. If you regularly browse workshop brochures and see a teacher listed for several years and then no longer see his name, that may be a clue that he wasn't a very good teacher. And if you see someone teaching again and again in all kinds of programs, it's probably because they're *really* good teachers.

Reviewing the broad spectrum of workshop brochures and advertisements it is possible to get the impression that some of the offerings are loosely structured workshops throwing together a mismatched group of participants in a holiday-camp setting. Is it possible to truly instruct amateurs and professionals together? And how much of the workshop experience really is devoted to leisure time?

In certain selected workshops it is possible to have professionals and amateurs in the same workshops. For example, in learning dye transfer you could have professionals and amateurs together, but the ama-

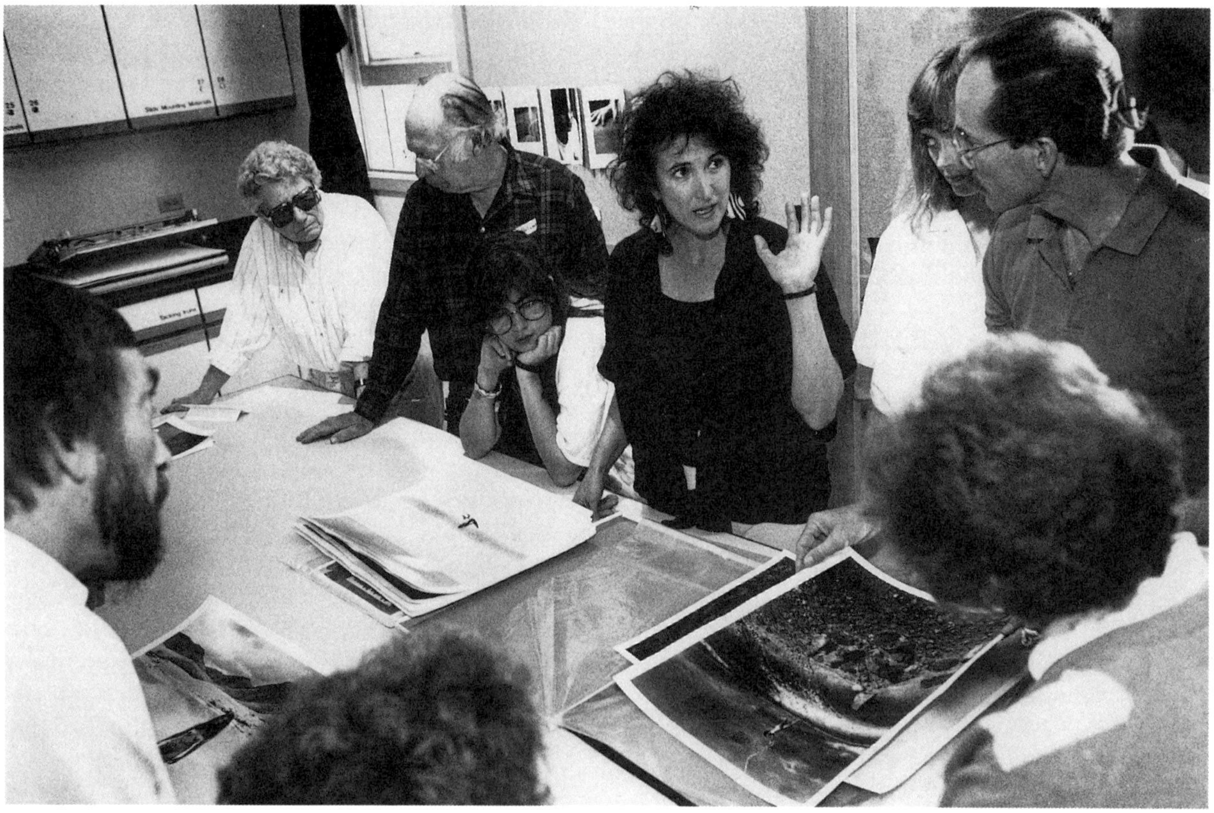

Photograph courtesy of The Anderson Ranch

Photographer Judy Dater, a popular instructor on the workshop circuit, leads a critique at the Anderson Ranch.

teurs would have to understand the basic technical processes of black and white photography, and should also maybe have some understanding of color theory. Both types of participants, because it would be a new subject to them, could take that kind of workshop. Or they could take a workshop in platinum printing or some technical process like the zone system. As long as they are both at a basic level of accomplishment that's sufficient for that particular workshop.

On the other hand, if you have a workshop with Eugene Richards or Jay Maisel, you would need a group of people who are basically on the same level. Jay, for instance, would attract a group of highly professional people and he spends a lot of time criticizing work and using it as examples to the rest of the class. So if the work is not at a high professional level then his ability to use it as examples is lessened. Occasionally a serious amateur who is really bull-headed and gets his way into the workshop turns out to be really fabulous, and sometimes even better than the professionals. Besides, what defines a professional is open to a considerable level of interpretation.

Regarding leisure time, I can only speak about the program at The Anderson Ranch. And there's almost no leisure time during the workshops here. One of the problems that one faces during a workshop is the whole issue of finding the time to bring together the people that are participating in the workshop. Some of the participants are professional photographers and might be losing client fees while they're taking the workshops and so they have to make every minute count. And so time is quite valuable to most of the people in the workshop and that's also why one-week workshops are attractive to both faculty and students.

Generally people get very little sleep during workshops. Partly because they have to cover a lot of material and partly because they tend to get very excited during these workshops. They can get quite intense and so the interaction and exchange goes well beyond the instruction time in the classroom. People tend to eat breakfast, lunch, and dinner together, spend the evenings printing in the lab, and talking until late hours with one another and the faculty. Some faculty teach mainly in the middle of the day. Others will be up early for sunrise field shoots with the students and until midnight, and they may not get a lot of sleep either. But by the end of the week they've accomplished a lot. There's a kind of focus that happens when you've intensively involved yourself with a group of like-minded individuals, on the same topic, that can only happen in that relatively short duration. It's hard to sustain that level of energy and intensity for much more than a week.

I wouldn't actually take a workshop if you want to combine it with a vacation. There may be other workshop programs where that can happen. But from my point of view, the best workshop programs, and there are a number of them around and they may be in such beautiful places as Aspen, Santa Fe, Maine, or San Francisco, generally are designed for you to be learning, not out hiking or sunning yourself.

You've mentioned the intensity of an action-packed, one-week workshop. Wouldn't programs that offer two or more weeks perhaps be too much of a good thing?

The length of the workshop should depend on the nature of the workshop. Some workshops are based on portfolio reviews and helping people see where the changes might occur in their careers, and then, them going out and deciding whether or not they want to implement those changes. That can happen in anywhere from a weekend to a week. Sometimes a workshop needs to be long enough, particularly at the intermediate level, where people have made a decision to commit themselves to photography and have been undergoing considerable change. Because they're deciding what their conviction is to photography, they may need at least a couple of weeks in order to work through the psychological - as well as the technical skills they need to deal with - in order to decide whether they want to continue and develop as professional photographers. Some technical workshops really do require more than one week. To use a previous example, if you were to thoroughly learn the dye-transfer process you would need at least two weeks to get it down right.

Tell me about the process of selecting or inviting instructors to join your faculty. How do you determine which "name" artists can deliver in the workshop environment?

There are some people who teach a lot of workshops who are incredibly good. John Sexton is a good example, or Craig Stevens. Or Eugene Richards, or Mary Ellen Mark. I could name many, many people. They evidently love to teach and are also very successful in their own careers. My faculty are often recommended by other faculty members who I respect. The people that I find to be good workshop teachers generally recommend other really good people. And because they have a good sense of what a workshop can be, and what it can accomplish, and if they're also consistently being rated highly by the participants, they usually have a pretty good sense of who else can do that too. I'll sometime hear a name come up several times in a two year period and I'll think 'I really should get this person.' After some experience, it's pretty clear to me who are the accomplished professionals teaching workshops. I also think a compassionate human being is the first prerequisite for a good faculty person. Somebody who genuinely likes helping other people. I suppose that it happens on occasion that a faculty member just gets off on the idea of teaching a workshop. But I can't imagine someone wanting to make a career of teaching workshops. I mean, they're just too much work to want to do them just to see your name on a workshop schedule. The people who work out best are the people who just really love helping people and you can see that. They really are thrilled at the end of the week if they can see they've made a difference in somebody else's life.

Do participants sometimes choose a workshop with a well-known photographer with unrealistic expectations?

First, not all workshop faculty teach the same. Some are professional teachers, some are not. The professional teacher will arrive with a well-organized curriculum and will anticipate almost any student need. Occasionally, you will get workshops with well-known artists who rarely teach, and these people, in a good workshop program, are good people who will work with you, but they may not have a set structure. The structure may come out of the express needs of the participants. They will need to actively educate themselves by determining what they need to learn and asking the instructor for that. One problem with the student who is attracted to studying with someone famous, say Jerry Uelsmann for example, is that they're sometimes intimidated by that person. One thing I would caution about - and this is very easy for me to say because I've found that these people are all very human, accessible, compassionate, and wanting to help - is the need to break through that intimidation that one naturally feels. And realize that the instructor is there for one reason only and that is to help the participant.

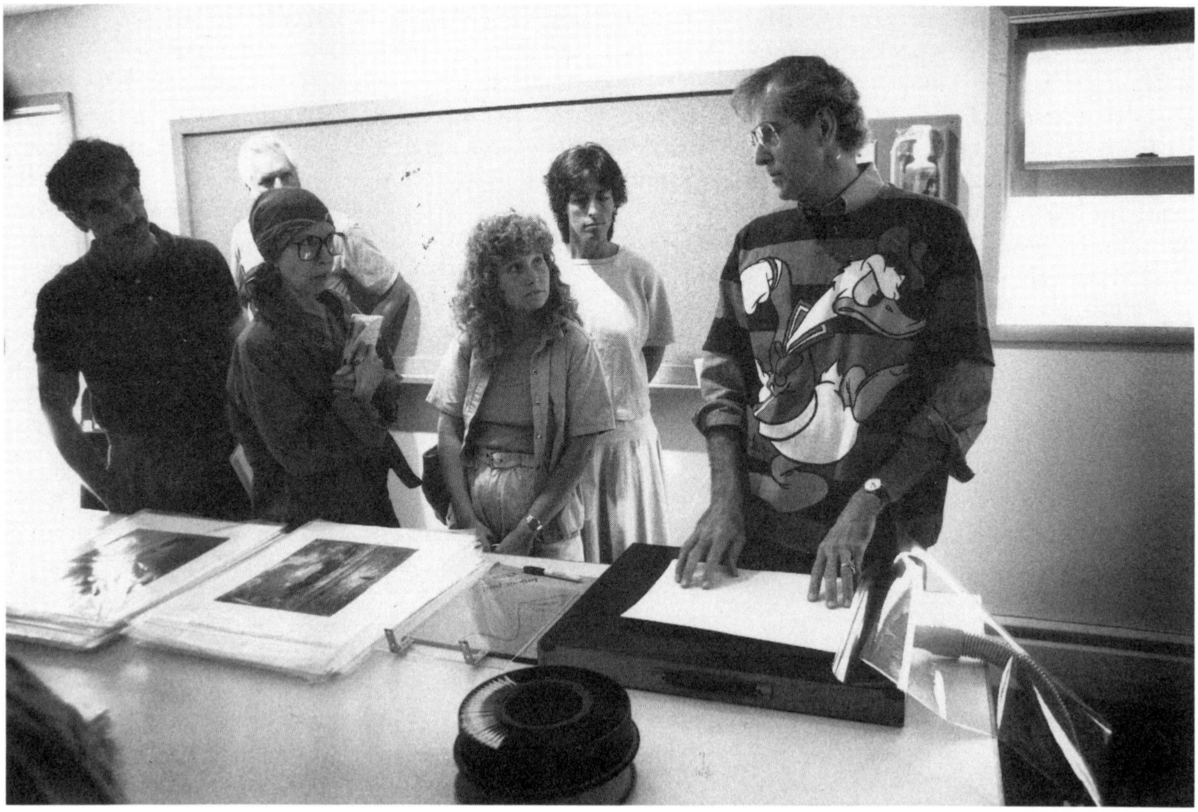

Photograph courtesy of The Anderson Ranch

Jerry Uelsmann, featuring the Donald Duck sweater, leads a photography demonstration at the Anderson Ranch.

One of the things that I've observed from behind the scenes at the workshops is the clearheadedness of the people teaching. As eccentric as occasionally some instructors are, the one thing that they're all the same about is how to make their careers work for them; how to accomplish their goals. They have very few illusions and no illusions that get in the way of their career development. This is one of the most remarkable things in workshops. Whether someone decides to be a *National Geographic* photographer or a paparazzo, generally what blocks us from doing that is our illusions or misconceptions about what it takes to accomplish that goal. What a successful person in that field can show you is how he reached his goal, or how he figured out how to get to where he wants to be - whether it's in an avant garde art approach, photojournalism, portrait photography, or whatever.

Also the participants, role is a very important one. I like to think of them as participants and not students, because I want them to think of themselves on a more equal level rather than that traditional student-teacher relationship where the teacher has all the knowledge and the student all the need. The students should really be co-participants and realize they have a lot to offer even if it's primarily in the form of questions. The most successful workshops are those where the teachers are not only teaching but the participants are teaching as well, and everybody is learning.

What is a comfortable number of participants to co-exist in a workshop setting and what is the general demographic profile at the Anderson Ranch?

Twelve participants is ideal. Some faculty can handle more than that; some a little less. We've actually lowered the number over the years. I find the energy or synergy works better with a group that size. We make a big rule of not over-booking the workshops. Sometimes you get somebody who is enormously popular and you could fill five workshops. But you have to be quite firm about that, because when you start adding people, the workshop suffers from less individual attention.

We have a wide age range from people in their seventies to college students. The average age is late thirties, evenly male and female. Nationally the groups are quite representative; people come from all over to take our workshops. Our season runs from the end of April to the beginning of October and the workshops that happen in the spring or fall are primarily landscape workshops that are either river trips or pack trips or things of that nature. The principal season runs from early June to Labour Day. We also have residency programs during the winter for mid-career people taking a sabbatical from professional life. Another program is the visiting artist program where we invite a well-known artist to pursue projects using our facilities. Usually they're artists pursuing projects in processes that they're personally not very familiar with and that they're interested in exploring. Very often these artists are the same ones teaching our workshops.

At the end of the workshop week, how should one determine the success of the experience?

A workshop group can be divided in half. First there's the professionals who take workshops and are constantly doing photography. Hopefully, they'll come away with some new ideas and new approaches to their work. So, a successful workshop will regenerate their interest in what they're already doing and open them up to new things. Sometimes the professionals would be well advised to take a workshop in something totally unfamiliar to them in the medium. Maybe they're commercial photographers and it would be really great for them to take a fine art photography workshop. That doesn't happen as often as it should, but it can be very therapeutic for somebody who needs to get dislodged from their way of thinking.

For the amateurs, and by that I mean the *serious* amateurs who have a lab at home and they print on the weekends and maybe they don't have a community to be a part of, coming to a workshop is a great way of reaffirming their dedication to photography. What is terrific about a workshop program and having all these people come together, is that they all feel photography is important. This could be true with any workshop. People need that support to realize what they're doing is valid. There's no reason why photography should be important. There's no reason why art should be important except that we decide we will make it so. That kind of affirmation is critical.

There are workshops that aren't well run or are poorly organized. People go to those workshops, put a lot of time and money on the line, have a bad experience and they don't go to any workshop again. That's tragic almost, because if they had a great experience in a good program, they might have found a new way of learning that could be quite rewarding. So, in the end, to quote John Sexton, "The only competition is a bad workshop."

The Wide-Angle of Photographic Tours: Into Africa with Chris & Jim McLarty

Unlike the workshop experience, photographic tours are often once-in-a-lifetime events, particularly when it comes to the photographic safari. Available under many guises and from practically any local travel agency, the commercial "photographic" safaris marketed to the general public today were created to replace the sporting "game" safaris which became both criminal and environmentally dangerous in the sixties. In an eagerness to maintain the economic stability brought to the wildlife rich eastern countries of Africa by tourism, the governments of some of the countries have gone to great lengths to accommodate a flourishing travel industry that, while preserving some aspects of the native culture, also threatens the dark continent with some of the worst features of westernization. Some travel operations in Africa today have become so sophisticated that travelers would be well advised not only to find out what shots are required to take before departure, but also to make sure their trip isn't a three-week tour of country clubs instead of the safari adventure of their dreams!

Although all photographic tours are not as exotic as jaunts across the Himalayas or yachting through the Galapagos Islands, there are some common problems and experiences shared by all group adventures. For whenever you mix a group of strangers, even though they may appear to share a common interest, there are sure to be conflicts and unexpected situations that arise and affect all participants. So for anyone who has ever considered a photo safari to Kenya or any other of the many types of photo-tours available, the following conversation with tour leaders Chris and Jim McLarty can be used as a guideline for preparing for whatever destination you choose.

Jim and Chris McLarty are a husband-wife photographic team who lead small groups to East Africa about three times annually. Owners of Silverline Studio, a photography and graphic-design firm in Camden, Maine, the McLarty's have extensive photographic and tour-leader credentials. Chris has taught photography in such diverse spots as Alaska and North Carolina, and Jim has led workshops at both the Maine and the Island Photographic Workshops. The couple met at the Maine Workshop and have subsequently lived, worked, and traveled together in East Africa. In 1988 they established their photo-tour company, *East Africa Photo Safaris.*

From their home base and in preparation of their next journey to East Africa, Chris and Jim told me everything I wanted to know about photographic safari adventures.

How often do you take photographers to East Africa and how large are the groups?

Jim: We like to do one in September to Kenya and that's for the fall animal migration. In the winter we've been doing them in February and March.

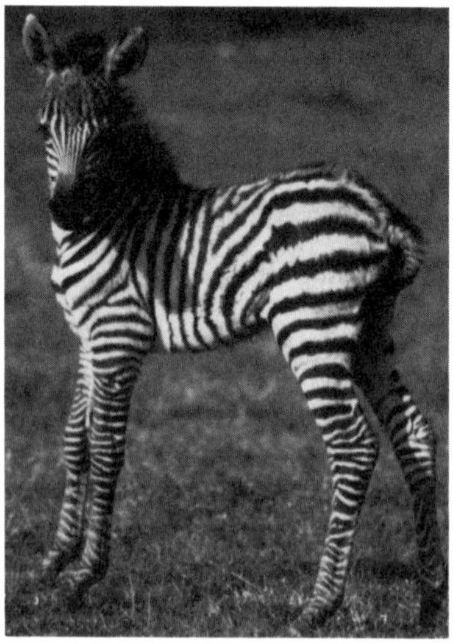

Newborn Zebra, Kenya.

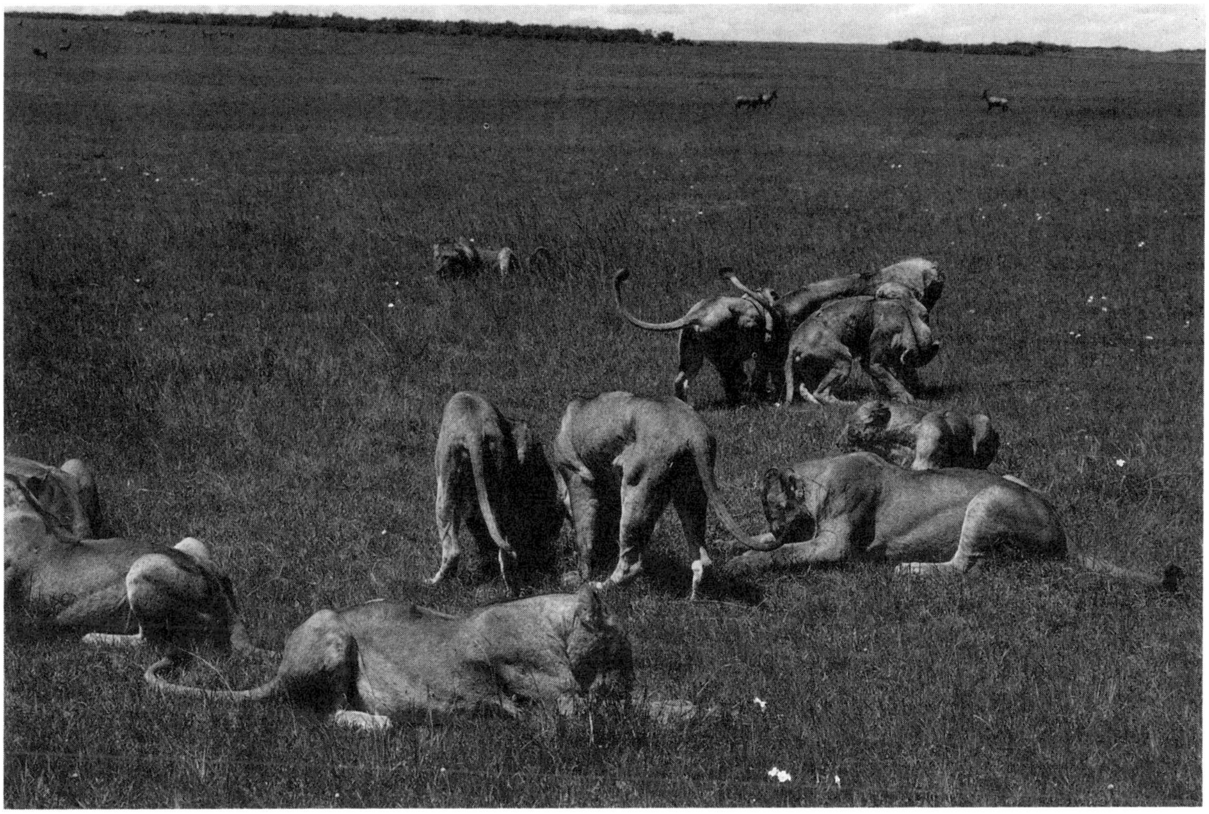

Lions lunching on a stolen kill from a Hyena in the Mara.

Our average group size is eight. We do go with as few as five, and we cut off at twelve. One thing that is important to consider is the number of people per vehicle. We use nine seater mini-vans and land-rovers. Some trips we've limited to four people per vehicle which makes a real difference.

Describe for me a typical safari day. How much time is actually devoted to photography?

Chris: We photograph on morning and afternoon game drives and we also photograph around the lodge. You can spend as much time on photography as you're inclined to.

Jim: A typical day - we try to really restrict any long day travel - we would get up from our camp and, depending on where some animals were that we'd heard about, we would leave the lodge at around 6:30 when the sun is just coming up. We'd have an early morning game drive and arrive back at camp for a late breakfast about 9:30. The afternoon would then be spent around the lodge and then around 3:30, depending again on the animals, we would go out on an afternoon drive, returning just as it's getting dark. We're usually the last vehicle in at the lodge.

What happens is most of the Kenyan and Tanzanian drivers are very conscientious and they like to please the group. But they sometimes like to get back a little earlier than we do, so we emphasize to our drivers, especially the first day, that we want to stay out there until the last little shred of light comes upon us. And we're usually back an hour later than anyone else staying there. And we're usually up an hour or so earlier. But we have a lot of time to relax and to have our classes during the day.

Chris: Game-watching is not good in the middle of the day. The inactivity of the animals and the light are not advantageous.

Jim: The light is brutal at mid-day in East Africa. So we really try to gear it around the animals and the light.

You've just mentioned classes, how much photographic instruction is possible on a photo-tour?

Chris: It depends on the tour. We don't have processing on our tours. We send out an evaluation before

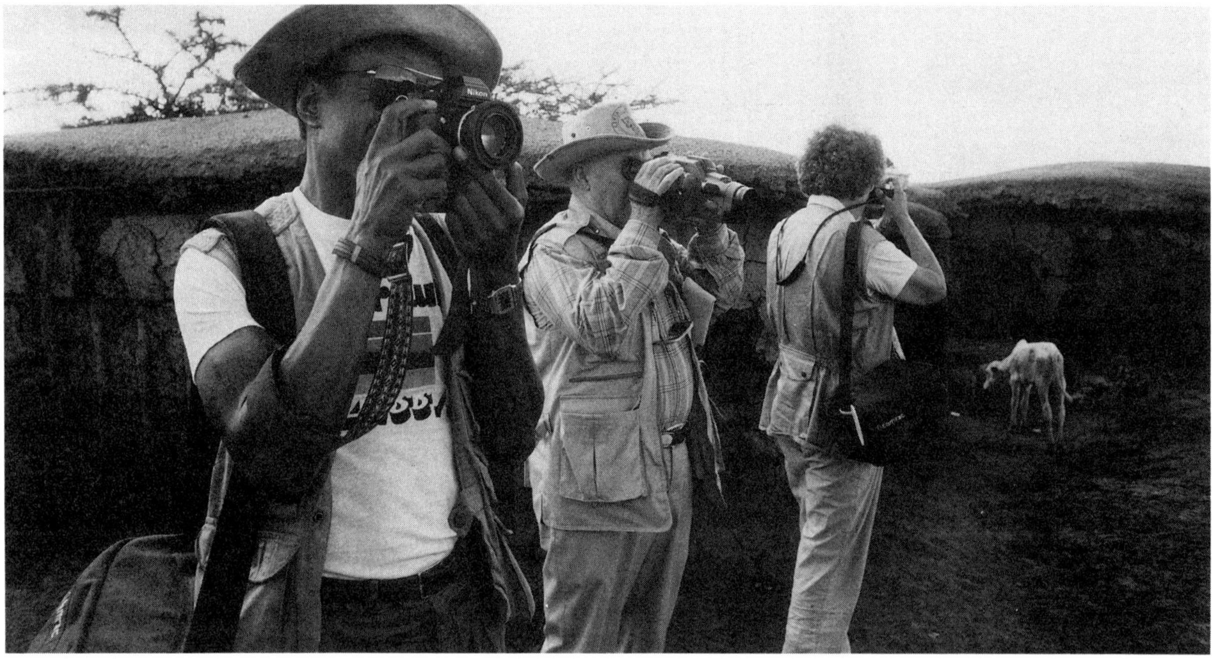

Safari participants Fred Young, Allen McClelland and Margaret Cowden photographing in a Maasai Manyatta.

departure so they can use their equipment and establish what their probable exposures are going to be, and so that they can make sure everything is in working order. We give them help on that and anything else they want to bring. When you're going that far around the world it's not like a workshop situation where you arrive and somebody has a lab set up and you go on a field-trip and you process your film and you get immediate feedback on it. So it is a bit different. The main thing is the travel. The workshop part of it is, in our case, evening lectures on composition, awareness of special lighting situations, and scenery opportunities. We do have printed material which is available to the group.

Jim: We take this material with us. We have a whole suitcase full of things that we handout once we're there and at the appropriate moment. The other thing we work out - because they can't see their daily shooting at the end of the day - is we try to work with them based on our experience of having done this before. We try to do a mental critique of what they've done during the day, and what they might have missed or done differently. And one of the things we like to let people know is that any kind of workshop or tour where you do traveling, it's easy to get into that motion of just traveling. We try to get people to think back to during the day: 'Was there anything you would have liked to photograph and just didn't?,'... so we try to get them to speak up. We give them a little time to get used to their very new and strange surroundings.

Do you offer advance guidance as to the type of equipment to bring along on the safari?

Jim: One thing we've learned is that a lot of times people going to Africa to photograph animals want to buy new lenses. Which is okay, but we really recommend that anyone who is a serious photographer should be sure to bring two bodies. A lot of people end up getting a used body as a spare. We had one student who had a camera problem and having that spare made all the difference.

Chris: We like our group members to test new equipment and to talk with us about what they're going to take. The student Jim mentioned bought an auto-winder and she had a lot of problems with it. We wouldn't necessarily recommend an auto-winder, or motor-drive, but we would recommend an extra body instead. We do talk about that before we go and we also encourage them to bring along their equipment instruction booklets.

Jim: We actually have a list that we send out, and on that list will be things like the need to bring extra batteries. Especially with the electronic cameras

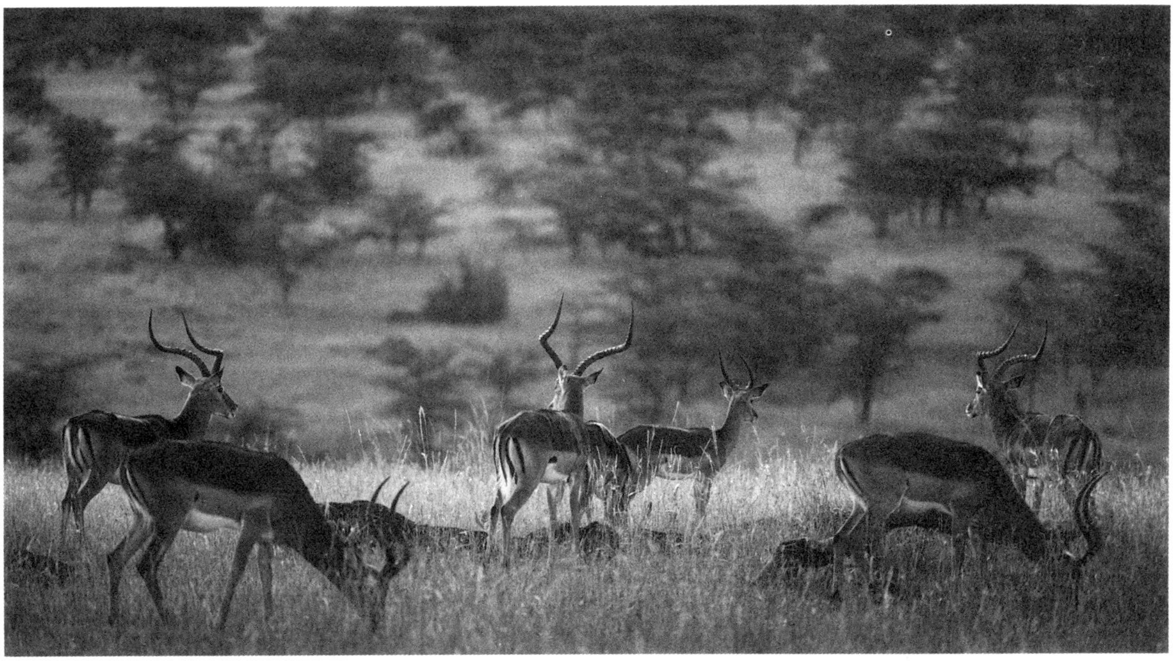

Photograph courtesy of East Africa Photo Safaris

Impala near the safari camp on the Mara River.

where you're just not going to be able to pick up batteries everywhere.

Chris: You don't want to spend a large sum of money on a trip and then slight yourself by not taking an extra battery.

Jim: And those cameras (electronic) are so dependent on the battery, and they vary a lot; they're not standarized. We carry a small repair kit and we usually carry a few different size batteries. We have actually been able to have the right battery for a few people....but we don't tell them that!

What should one be looking for when reading the brochures and selecting a photo-safari?

Jim: You should be able to talk with whomever is going to lead the trip. Before that there should be a leader. One thing we've seen time and again in our travels as we've met up with other groups, is a lot of groups don't have a leader. They are usually very lost because they have divergent interests and there's nobody to ask anything. And they're real confused. We've taken in some of these groups because, essentially, they're so lost. The other thing that sometimes happens when you go on something that may or may not be called a photo-tour or photo-safari, if there's not a leader of some description, then someone within that group is going to emerge as the leader, and it's usually the person you would least like to have as your leader.

The first thing is to go with somebody who has knowledge of the location. When you're looking at different trips you should be able to talk with that person and if that person is too busy back in the states to talk to you, *he's probably not gonna talk to you on the trip either!*

I would also look at the group size. I would try and talk with someone who has been on one of their trips. Other important considerations are the number of people per vehicle and the pace of the tour.

Chris: You also need to make sure you have enough time to do photography. Anybody who's going to go over there is going to take a camera whether they're a photographer or not.

Jim: Anything can be called a "photo-safari."

Chris: What you don't want, is to get into some sort of safari where they've got *every* seat in a vehicle filled and you can't stand up; you can't have any room to shoot; and somebody is always in your way. So we gear ours toward having plenty of room to photograph. Also you need to have a mind-set with your leader that is going to allow you to take the time to get the shot that you've come to get.

Are most itineraries pre-set and fairly inflexible, or do participants have choices along the way?

Jim: We do our own itineraries. We plan the trip. We decide how many days to spend and we consult with our agents. We don't buy a pre-planned package. Most trips to Africa are package deals; you buy two nights here, two nights there, a night here, a plane trip here, and you get this package. We make our own. If we find that people don't really like a place that much, we'll drop that and add someplace else. Every trip is a little different depending on the time of the year and other considerations. We found a private ranch where we stay. We like to get away from some of the really big lodges. They're really well-known but they also spoil the experience of Africa.

At that lodge or camp, where you may be spending a large portion of your trip, are there any animals? An example would be the Mt. Kenya Safari Club which is very famous and a very fancy resort. But there are no animals there. We just don't go there. Many people go there and they really enjoy it. They've got saunas, tennis courts, an 18-hole golf course, and you have to dress for dinner. One might want to include that as a different type of stop if you were on a month-long tour.

How about those champagne-breakfast balloon rides that always seem to be featured in the brochures?

Jim: The Mara is where they run the balloon trips and it's an option available on every trip. I have never met anyone who went on that and didn't think that it was just one of the most incredible things they had ever done in their lives. People absolutely love it. Ninety-nine percent have never been in a balloon before and they wouldn't do it here in the U.S. I guess there would be no incentive.

We also offer an optional week on the coast of Kenya that's quite different. It's almost like nothing to do with the rest of the trip. It's like going to the Caribbean for a week but with Arabic ruins and different animals.

What makes for a good mix in the group? Is there a general profile for what makes a "happy camper?"

Chris: The kind of person who would not be suitable for a photo-safari is someone who is not very patient, because you just have to go as slow as the slowest person on the trip. You go for the person who's going to be the most serious about it, you don't go for who's going to be the least serious.

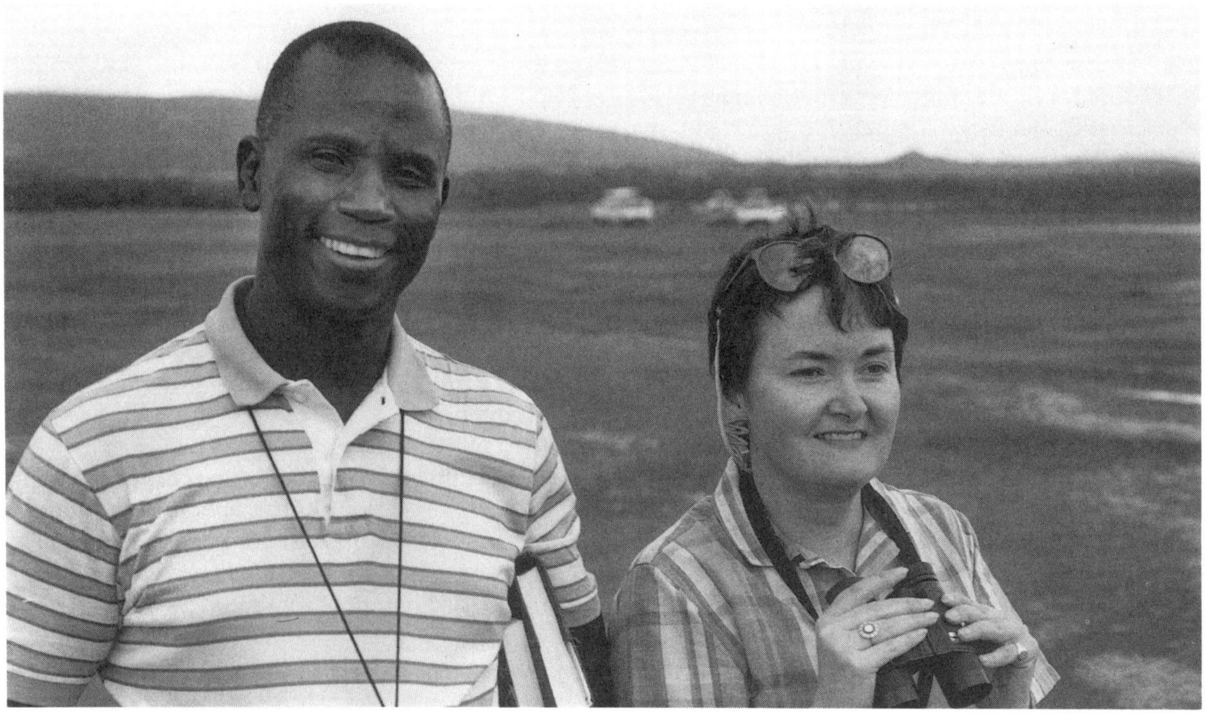

Photograph courtesy of East Africa Photo Safaris

Guide John Ledede with safari co-leader Chris McLarty.

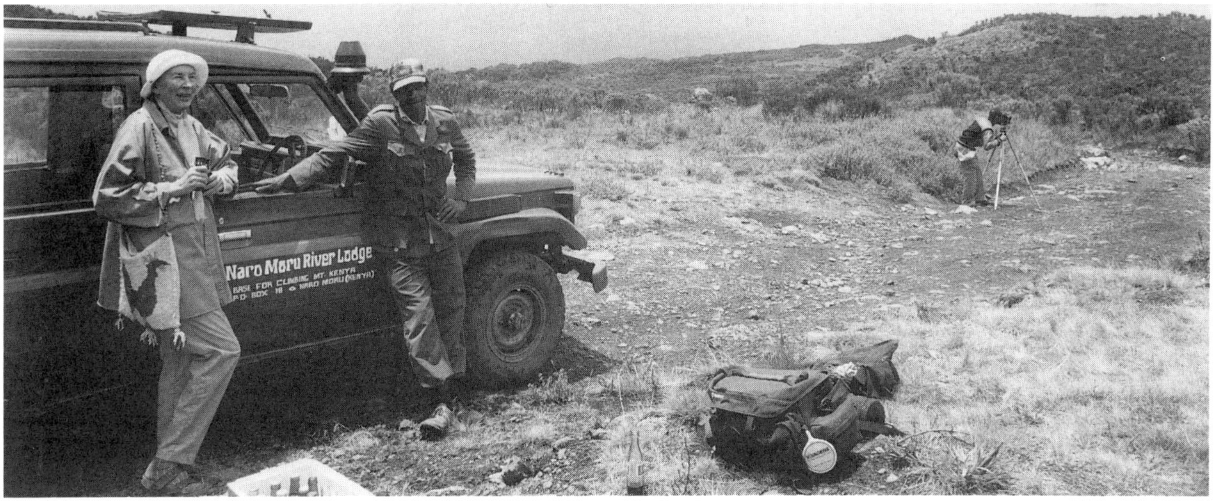

Safari-goer Dorothy Seits takes a lunch-break at 11,000 ft. on Mount Kenya.

Jim: People also come into a natural setting from different settings, a differently paced world. They're listening to phones ringing, faxes going off, modems buzzing, and they just have to change their whole outlook on the world for a few weeks. And there's a general slowing-down process. If they just go charging off, they're gonna see absolutely nothing. And that's the real temptation for everyone, to just keep moving. We try and really slow things down. If you look at how many places we go to in a three week period, we don't have as many stops as most tours. But we stay longer. We can stay up to three or four days in one area. And that gives you a chance to really do some photography. On most tours two days is a long stop, and two days is pretty much our minimum. If it's not worth two days, then we'll go someplace else that's worth two days. We stay sometimes up to six days in the Mara. We use different camps, but we're traveling very little. It may be only two hours from one stop to another.

Chris: It's the old half empty vs. the half full glass syndrome. Travel in East Africa is wonderful, - and it's really cushy. But there are some inconveniences on any trip. I would try to weed-out people who would not be patient, or who are not caring about the other participants and the things they might want to see. These people are more or less just ego-maniacs with a camera. Unfortunately, there are *jerks* everywhere and people can be more jerky with a camera than they can be normally. They sometimes use a camera as a license to be obnoxious. We try to find people that we think we would enjoy being with and that perhaps have a forgiving attitude. And who are also interested in the country in more than just seeing how many animals they can get in two weeks. We like to emphasize the culture.

Jim: We also welcome and enjoy having non-photographers. Although everything is set-up for photographers, it is also set-up for anyone interested in wildlife. It's usually a mix of couples and singles, and it's very common that the man is the photographer and the wife isn't. But she is just as important to us as he is. We have lived and worked in East Africa so we have a lot of knowledge and information about the area. If someone has an interest in the people, or something else, that's really good because it brings some diversity into the group. And it would not be as good if we had all photographers. We like everything about Africa.

How about single travelers, particularly women? Are their cultural or social restrictions which might make travel for women alone difficult?

Chris: We get a lot of single women. The thing is, if it's a single woman going to Africa, it's usually something that she's wanted to do her entire life. It's a dream come true. They just love it and they don't feel left out of couples or things like that. They're actually glad not to be encumbered by anybody else because it's such a fantasy trip. If they had somebody with them, it might be too close to reality.

As I've already mentioned, in any group there may be a jerk or two and that's the reason you need professional tour-leaders. If there are a couple of vehicles you can arrange to be in one with a group to your liking, and you can also avoid being with someone if you don't like them. And it does happen that the offending person can get dumped on by the group, but that person has also spent a good deal of money on the trip of their life. So you have to make it just as valuable for them even though they may be a pain-in-the-ass. If you don't have professional standards as a tour-leader, it can be really hard.

Jim: We restrict the number of people per vehicle and that makes it possible to have at least two vehicles, so that makes it a lot better. People find their own group within the group; we don't assign anything, we just let that evolve. You may find there's one group that's a lot more interested in photography than another. A lot of times husbands and wives will split up at this point, and maybe the more serious photographers will gather in one vehicle, and the people who are interested in other things will gather in the other. So if two people really dislike each other, they can split up and that works out real well.

Are there any special health or age restrictions on your safaris?

Jim: Basically East Africa and Tanzania are very healthy places. The main health problem that people worry about is malaria. And if you take the pills, which we recommend people do, you almost eliminate the chance of getting malaria. We've had people with slightly upset stomachs and that's it.

Chris: On one trip I took my mother for her seventieth birthday. She has emphysema, is pretty heavy, and has bad knees and she made it! It's not something where you're necessarily going to do a lot of walking. If you're in generally good health there should be no problem.

Jim: The hardest part of the trip is the flight there. We have been going the past few years with Swiss Air and they have taken exceptionally good care of us. We spend a day in Zurich on the way over. If someone couldn't do the flight, then that would disqualify them. If you can handle the flight, you can handle anything else. We go at a slower pace and we see what everyone goes to see and not just the roads and lodges.

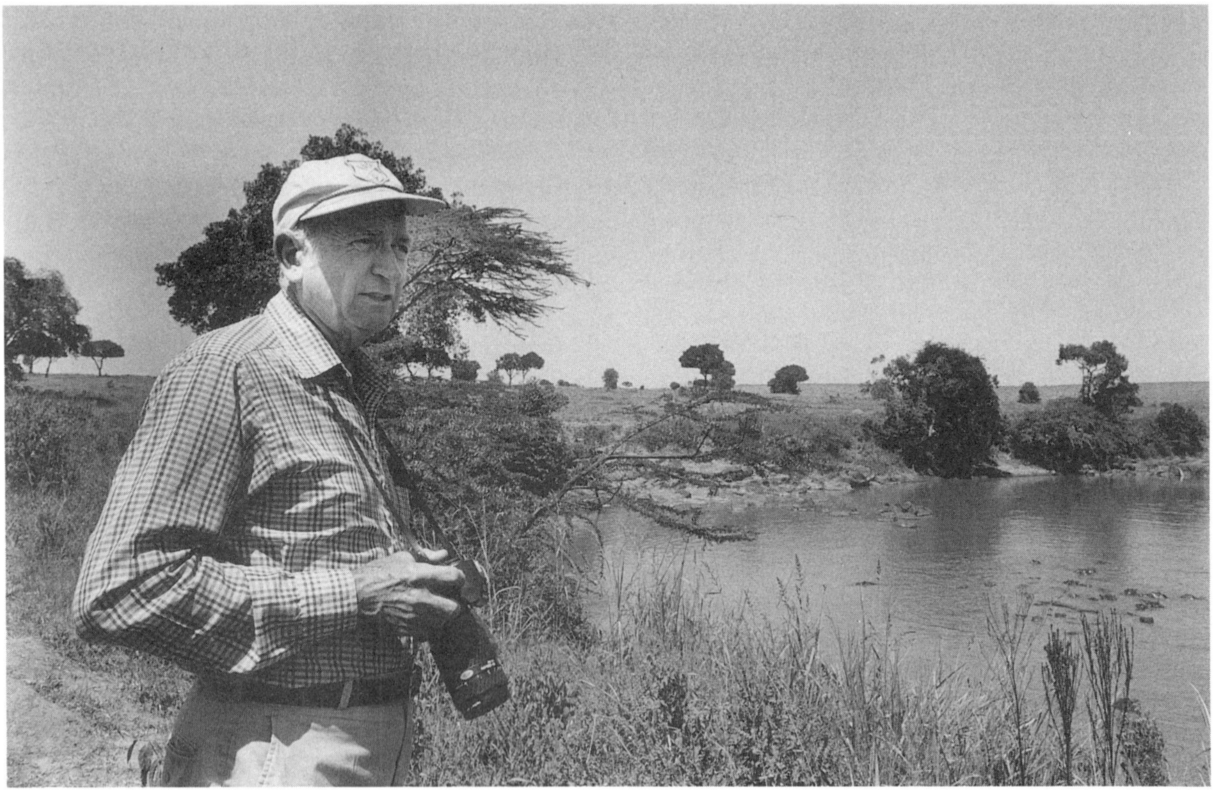

Photograph courtesy of East Africa Photo Safaris

Howard Miller reconsiders a dip in the "Hippo Pool" on the Mara River in Kenya.

Is there any danger from the wildlife? How close are you able to get to the animals?

Jim: People do get killed over there by animals. And they shouldn't. When you're in the game parks and the game areas you don't leave your vehicle. You're perfectly safe in the vehicle. People have gotten in trouble when they go into a lodge or camp, and the reality that these animals are wild doesn't sink in. They think they're in the zoo or something. You can't imagine why these people do this, but they sometimes just start walking out to get a little closer to the buffalo. There was a couple killed by buffalo even with a sign posted which said "Don't walk beyond this point." It's like people feeding marshmallows to grizzly bears; they just don't understand that these are wild animals. It's not really dangerous unless you do something incredibly stupid.

Okay, I'll play devil's advocate here. Suppose I'm smart enough to read a book; I've traveled frequently, and I think I've learned quite a lot about Africa. Why should I choose a photo-safari as opposed to winging it independently?

Chris: One thing is you probably wouldn't know where to go to get what you wanted.

Jim: There are some extremely well-known places in East Africa. But just because they are well-known doesn't mean this is really where the person wants to go. For instance, one place we haven't been going lately, and which is probably the most famous lodge in East Africa, is Tree-Tops. A lot of people want to go, but the old Tree-Tops just isn't there anymore. It's a newer place, and it's in a national park, but it's situated in a little, tiny pan-handle completely surrounded by cultivation and, it's not what it used to be. There are other lodges set back in the park and they're nicer but they're unknown. So we try to discover the unknown places.

Chris: It's harder at some of the better-known places. You may think that you're going to get to go there but sometimes they overbook and you wouldn't even be able to get in. So it's one thing to know about these special places, but it's quite another to know whether they're really worth traveling to.

Jim: Another example is, because some of these places are so well-known everyone wants to go to them. There's one in the Mara that is huge. We found a little camp that was established by Richard Leaky and the film-maker, Alan Root, which is the smallest camp in the Mara. It's a fraction of the size of the others. We really like it. I think it can accommodate about thirty as opposed to the others that can take hundreds.

So, in other words, experience is really a key factor in a successful photo-safari?

Jim: We have really good agents in East Africa that we've worked with a long time. They take really good care of us. And a key element in the process in Africa is who you're dealing with. We deal with a small company, a family-run operation, and they keep right on top of everything. Every time we pass through Nairobi, even if it's only for lunch, somebody from the organization is there to find out how things are going, or if we have any problems.

Chris: And they supply really good drivers.

Jim: We can call up and speak to any one of the family. We've been doing this for awhile and we've gotten to know a few of the local drivers and we've found some that we really like and so we request them. And that makes a big difference to have that good driver. He's the other person that is on the trip the whole way. We've had people on our trips who are still writing to their drivers!

I think the main thing we do is set the tone for the trip. We make itineraries and all that, but during the trip we set the tone of when to stop and when to move on. We're not dictatorial about this but we use our experience. I may be able to see what animals might do in ten minutes and no one on the trip would have that sort of experience. You know, if we just sit here for ten minutes that lion and zebra might meet.

We were at a lodge in northern Kenya once and there was a tour that had scheduled an early morning boat trip that they had scheduled back in America in the summertime when the sun is up at 4:30. And they scheduled this 5:30 boat trip, and they were gonna have breakfast and drive someplace. At that time in East Africa it's absolutely dark, but they actually did go out in the boat and didn't see a thing.

Give me an idea what the cost for a three-week photo-safari would be.

Chris: Of course there's a wide variety. We include air with ours, but some don't. We include almost everything. The only things not included are some lunches in Nairobi; tips to drivers; alcohol and souvenirs. Our trips run from $4,500 to $5,300 depending on where we go.

Workshop, Photo-Tour, & Seminar Listings

As with the gallery and museum listings which precede this section of the handbook, most of the individual entry information is self-explanatory and has been supplied to us as the result of an extensive questionnaire mailing. Although many of the workshops, tours, and seminars featured offer a variety of subjects and destinations, we have concentrated on providing an overview of information based on an annual schedule. For this reason, and to keep the information herein from becoming quickly obsolete, prices are not offered.

Although we have not attended the workshops or photo-tours listed here, we have made every effort to present organizations which enjoy excellent reputations and which, in many cases, have been in business for many years. Likewise, our position is not to direct readers to any particular workshop or tour, but to offer as much information on each situation as has been provided to us.

Each listing heading is followed by a symbol identifying the entry as a workshop, photo-tour, or seminar. Generally the heading denotes the title and geographic location of the workshop or tour. Sometimes the contact information will be the same as the heading, designating that the workshop is usually devoted exclusively to a particular subject or location. Different entries may also share the same contact information indicating that the host organization offers a broader selection of workshops and tours year-round. These organizations are also more likely to be introducing new workshops each season.

Due to space limitations and available information we have not been able to give in-depth background information in every instance. In general we have tried to present background pertaining to history, seasonal availability, class size, and level of experience, following the contact information.

The specialties, location, and faculty sections are self-explanatory. However, attention should be paid to the facilities/accommodations and expenses sections as these areas have direct bearing on how much you may ultimately spend to attend a workshop, tour, or seminar.

Facilities and accommodations are often an important part of the workshop or photo-tour package. The variety of situtations is infinite. Almost all photo-tours, particularly those to exotic locations, are all *inclusive* (ie: although you may have a choice between deluxe or standard sleeping arrangements the price is usually included in the cost of the tour). Meals are often included too, although there is more flexibility. Workshops, however, are a different story. Many workshops, particularly those which offer instruction out-of-doors, are held in locations which offer seasonal accommodations and are situated near state and national parks and nature reserves. In some cases the cost of accommodations is included, but more often than not, the workshop organization will provide you with a list of local motels, lodges, or bed and breakfasts from which to choose.

Facilities are another area which should not be overlooked in choosing a workshop. Many of the photo-tours to India, Africa, or on boats to Baja California or the Galapagos, do not offer even E-6 processing. So it is important to know in advance that you must test your equipment before embarking on this type of tour. Also important to know is that although workshops may offer everything from E-6 to scheduled darkroom time, the cost for these conveniences are not necessarily included in the workshop fee. In the expenses area we have stated what is not included as far as we have been informed. All workshops and photo-tours enumerate what is and is not included in their brochures or information sheets.

Above all, don't hesitate to contact an organization which you're unsure about. From my experience in talking with professional workshop leaders, most of them are very interested in fine-tuning their programs to accommodate all interests. The best learning experience is often the one where all the participants share in the learning and teaching.

The symbol next to the workshop title indicates whether the entry is a **W** = workshop, **T** = photo-tour, or **S** = seminar.

Workshops, Photo-Tours, & Seminars

ABOVE THE CLOUDS TREKKING **T**

Africa, The Andes, The Himalayas, Nepal

ABOVE THE CLOUDS TREKKING
P.O. Box 398
Worcester, Massachusetts 01602
800-233-4499
Contact: Steve Conlon, Director

Above the Clouds Trekking offers a wide variety of exotic locations and activity filled programs on its camera-oriented tours. From mountain-biking in Nepal to jeep-journeys through Yemen, the tours are designed to provide unparalleled photographic opportunities. Accompanied by local guides and professional photographers, the trips utilize a variety of room, board, and travel possibilities. Custom treks are also available.

Specialties: Landscape, travel, nature, wildlife.
Location: Tours are available to Peru, Ecuador, Patagonia, Kenya, Madagascar, Ireland, Yugoslavia, Transylvania, Spain, Turkey, Nepal, India, Sikkim, Bhutan, Japan, New Zealand, Yemen, and the Soviet Union.
Facilities: Accommodations are varied depending on the mode of travel and the destination. Lab facilities are generally not available although E-6 processing is offered in some cases.
Expenses: Accommodations and meals, guide services, and ground transportation are included in the tour fee. Airfare and personal expenses are not included.

ACREY PHOTOGRAPHIC EXPEDITIONS **W**

Yellowstone National Park

ACREY PHOTOGRAPHIC EXPEDITIONS
431 Highway 179 A-8
Sedona, Arizona 86336
602-282-2983

Noted Western photographic artist Jack Acrey conducts a series of week-long "Yellowstone In The Winter" workshops annually during the whitest months of January and February. In addition to learning Acrey's award-winning outdoor photography techniques, the special attraction of this expedition is that participants are assigned individual snowmobiles to use in discovering the frozen landscapes of Yellowstone Park.

Specialties: Winter landscape, nature, wildlife, instruction.
Location: Tours originate and end at West Yellowstone, Montana. West Yellowstone is approximately 2 hours from Bozeman, Montana which maintains the only airport in the area.
Facilities: Accommodations are at the West Yellowstone Mountain Lodge and all meals are included.
Faculty: Jack Acrey is a well-known Southwestern Fine Art photographer who resides in Sedona, Arizona.
Expenses: Transportation to and from the workshop site is not included. Workshop fee does include accommodations and meals, snowmobile rental, snowmobile clothing, park fees, and instruction.

ADULT INSTITUTES IN THE ARTS **W**

Quartz Mountain, Oklahoma

ADULT INSTITUTES IN THE ARTS
P.O. Box 18154
Oklahoma City, Oklahoma 73154
405-842-0890 *Fax:* 405-848-4538
Contact: Jon Burris, Photography Coordinator

The Oklahoma Arts Institute sponsors the 3-day Adult Institutes In The Arts every October. This intensive weekend workshop is held in the dramatic Quartz Mountains of Oklahoma and is designed for professional artists, teachers, and serious amateurs who wish to upgrade their skills in photography. Participants choose from 4 different workshop subjects guest-instructed by well-known, master photographers. Workshops are limited to 20 participants over the age of 21.

Specialties: Instruction/technical.
Location: The workshop takes place in the Quartz Mountain State Park on the western edge of the Wichita Mountains about 150 miles southwest of Oklahoma City.

Facilities: Lodge and cabin accommodations are available. Buffet and seated meals are offered. Instruction is given in both classroom and field settings.
Faculty: Guest photography instructors have included in recent years: Marie Cosindas, George Tice, John Loengard, Neil Selkirk, Morley Baer, and Ruth Bernhard among others.
Expenses: Workshop fees include instruction, accommodations, and meals.

ADVERTISING PHOTOGRAPHY SEMINAR SERIES **S**

Various cities througout the U.S.

PROFESSIONAL PHOTOGRAPHERS OF AMERICA
1090 Executive Way
Des Plaines, Illinois 60018
708-299-8161 *Fax:* 708-299-2685
Contact: Barbara Anderson or Ann Panicola

These Advertising Photography Seminars, supported by Eastman Kodak and most recently held in New York, San Francisco, Dallas, and Atlanta, consist of a full Saturday immersion in the techniques of advertising photography. All seminars are held in working studios across the nation and generally accommodate about 50 attendees.
Specialties: Advertising.
Faculty: Advertising photographers have included New York based Jack Reznicki who is noted for his people photography and who is the author of *Illustration Photography.* Dallas' True Redd is owner of an award-winning illustrative photography studio.

AFRICA: A WILDLIFE PHOTOEXPEDITION **T**

Various African locations

WORLD TRAVEL
1001 Connecticut Avenue NW, Suite 312
Washington, D.C. 20036
800-424-2896 *Fax:* 202-785-4683
Contact: Joy Goodenough

Africa: A Wildlife Photoexpedition and Workshop is offered several times annually for wildlife photographers interested in shooting in a variety of different environmental settings. Accompanied by 2 photoleaders and a zoologist, the expeditions enable participants to shoot wildlife in the typical bush veld, in the desert, and in a coastal setting. Limited to 15 photographers, the expeditions travel through well-known nature preserves and parks, 5 to a van.
Specialties: Wildlife, nature, travel.
Location: Tours begin in the Kruger National Park and travel to Sabi Sand Game Reserve, The Kalahari Gemsbok National Park, Dukier Island Seal Colony, Cape Town and more.
Facilities: Accommodations are in national park rest camps, luxury game lodges, and regional hotels. Many meals are taken with local wildlife photographers and prominent conservationists.
Faculty: Husband and wife team Lynda Richardson and Tim Wright are experienced in the African environment and regularly lead a series of seminars in wildlife photography. As a team they have also worked on special projects for the National Geograpic Society.
Expenses: Transportation to the point of departure, some meals, and film and processing are not covered by the tour fee.

AFRICAN PHOTO SAFARI **T**

Namibia, Botswana, and Zimbabwe

GARRY BLACK PHOTOGRAPHY
1083 St. Emmanuel Terrace
Gloucester, Ontario, K1C2J Canada
613-824-9295
Contact: Garry Black

Garry Black's month-long African Photo Safari has been custom designed by the nature photographer to maximize participants' photographic and travel experience. Limited to 8 photographers, this intensive package allows for visits to many locations less frequented by safari-goers. Lush rainforests, the world's highest sand dunes, and illuminated wildlife feedings, are a few of the experiences promised, with the grand finale being a visit to Victoria Falls.
Specialties: Wildlife and nature.
Location: African locations include: Namib Desert, Skeleton Coast, Etosha Pan, Chobe National Park, Hwange National Park, and Victoria Falls.
Facilities: Accommodations are in lodges, bungalows, and tented camps.
Faculty: Garry Black is a self-taught photographer who specializes in nature and wildlife photography. His clients have included Sony, Coca-Cola, and United Airlines.
Expenses: Included are: all meals and accommodations in Africa, ground transport, park entrance fees, instruction, and services of guides. Not included: airfare to Africa, personal expenses, insurance, or gratuities.

ALASKA UP CLOSE T

Alaska

ALASKA UP CLOSE
P.O. Box 32666
Juneau, Alaska 99803
907-789-9544 *Fax:* 907-463-3802
Contact: Judy Shuler

Alaska Up Close is a series of week-long photographic workshops focusing on the wildlife and landscapes of southeast Alaska. The unique wildlife workshop, "A Gathering of Eagles" is held annually in November.

Specialties: Wildlife, nature, landscape.
Location: Juneau and nearby locations.
Facilities: Motels, hotels, and bed & breakfasts are used and meals are included. Slide programs and informal discussions are held in the evenings. Daytime is devoted to hands-on instruction in the field.
Faculty: Tour leaders are professional photographers who have worked extensively in Alaska.
Expenses: Film, processing, and personal expenses are not included in the tour fee.

ALLAMAN'S MONTANA ADVENTURES T

Montana

ALLAMAN'S MONTANA ADVENTURES
West Fork Route
Darby, Montana 59829
406-821-3763
Contact: Ken Allaman

Photographer, fisherman, explorer, and historian Ken Allaman has spent over 25 years photographing the wilderness of the west. Allaman puts all his experience and talents into guiding small groups of photographers on wildlife adventures from April through October. Designed to accommodate photographers from beginner to professional levels, the photo tours are usually 5-day treks and use llamas to carry gear and food. Maximum 6 member tours keep the pace comfortable.

Specialties: Scenic, wildflower, landscape.
Location: Summer llama treks are conducted on the Idaho-Montana border of the Selway-Bitterroot Wilderness. The Selway is one of the largest wilderness areas in the U.S.
Facilities: Bunkhouses, teepees, and local motels are used for lodging.
Expenses: Film and personal items are not included.

AMERICAN PHOTOGRAPHY INSTITUTE W

New York City, New York

AMERICAN PHOTOGRAPHY INSTITUTE
721 Broadway, 8th Floor
New York, New York 10003
212-998-1930
Contact: Tom Drysdale, Chair-Photo Department

New York City's American Photography Institute is housed in the Department of Photography at Tisch School of the Arts, New York University in Greenwich Village. The institute offers both credit and non-credit 6 week courses as well as 4 -day master workshops. Applied production courses, professional seminars, advanced master classes, and open lab options offer a variety of choices covering every aspect of photography.

Location: The American Photography Institute is centrally located in Greenwich Village not far from Soho, Little Italy, or Chinatown.
Facilities: University dorms are available to workshop and course attendees. Excellent darkroom and class facilities are available as well as a photographic library and gallery.
Faculty: The faculty is selected from among the professors of NYU and master classes are taught by such well-known photographers as William Wegman and Jerry Uelsmann.
Expenses: Housing and meals are not included. A variety of lab fees may apply depending on the workshop.

AMERICAN SOUTHWEST PHOTOGRAPHY WORKSHOPS W

Arizona, New Mexico, Texas, Utah

AMERICAN SOUTHWEST
PHOTOGRAPHY WORKSHOPS
P.O. Box 220450
El Paso, Texas 79913
915-581-7959
Contact: George B. Drennan

American Southwest Photography Workshops are held yearly in the spring and fall with emphasis on fine black and white printmaking. All workshops are conducted in the field and include critiques of participant's portfolios. Workshops are limited to 8 participants per instructor.

Location: Various locations in the southwest.
Facilities: Accommodations may include trail and riverside camping or local motels. Meals and lodging are not included in the basic workshop fees.

AMPRO PHOTO WORKSHOPS **W**

Vancouver, Canada

AMPRO PHOTO WORKSHOPS
636 East Broadway
Vancouver, British Columbia V5T 1X6, Canada
604-876-5501 *Fax:* 604-876-5502
Contact: Ralph Baker

Vancouver's Ampro Photo Workshops offer something for everyone covering every aspect of photography. From one-day seminars in introductory figure photography to intensive 12-week, full-time photofinishing courses to 39-week career courses in commerical photography, Ampro welcomes beginners, intermediate, and advanced participants. Photography Basics, Studio Portrait Lighting, Prints From Slides, and Photography and The Law are just a sampling of courses available.

Specialties: Technical.

Facilities: Many motels and other housing possibilities are located near the workshop location. The workshop facility offers two classrooms, a b/w darkroom, copy stands, slide duplicating machinery, and mounting press.

Faculty: Ralph Baker is the instructor and there are five other professional instructors.

Expenses: Course fees cover instruction and some supplies. All workshop expenses are variable.

ANCHELL PHOTOGRAPHY WORKSHOPS **W**

Big Sur, California

ANCHELL PHOTOGRAPHY WORKSHOPS
1411 N. Catalina Street
Los Angeles, California 90027
213-465-8777 *Fax:* 213-464-5644
Contact: Steve Anchell or Donna Conrad

Photographer Steve Anchell conducts several weekend nude photography workshops throughout the year in Big Sur, California; Molokai, Hawaii; and Taos, New Mexico. He and his associates also conduct periodic weekend workshops on "Photographing Big Sur," week-long photo tours of the canyons of Utah, and 2-week tours to colorful destinations such as Andalusia in Spain. Most workshops feature a student/teacher ratio of 1:4 and are suitable for all levels of experience.

Specialties: Nude, landscape, scenic, fine art.

Facilities: Attendees make their own accommodation plans based on information provided by the workshop.

Faculty: Steve Anchell has conducted over 50 workshops both privately and for six universities since 1979. Nude photographer Donna Conrad and underwater/nature photographer Bob Abraham assist Anchell in some workshops.

Expenses: Accommodations and meals are payable separately from workshop fees. Travel to and from the workshop site is not included.

ANDERSON RANCH ARTS CENTER **W**

Snowmass Village, Colorado

ANDERSON RANCH ARTS CENTER
5263 Owl Creek Road, P.O. Box 5598
Snowmass Village, Colorado 81615
303-923-3181 *Fax:* 303-923-3871
Contact: James Baker

Anderson Ranch Arts Center, created in 1966, is credited with having one of the most versatile workshop programs in the U.S. The photography program offers a wide range of one and two-week workshops appropriate for a variety of skill levels. Field expeditions on a horse-pack trip, rafting the San Juan River, photographing people with Eugene Richards, or creativity and critical thinking with Andy Grundberg are a few of the choices offered during the summer sessions.

Specialties: B/w, zone system, dye transfer, nude, photojournalism, photogravure, landscape, portraiture, architectural.

Location: The Anderson Ranch Arts Center is located in the mountain resort of Snowmass, 7 miles from the Aspen, Colorado airport. The center is at an elevation of 8,200 feet and sits amid the 14,000 foot peaks of the Elk Range of the Colorado Rockies.

Facilities: Housing and meals are not included in the workshop fee but can be arranged through the center. The Fischer Photography Center is equipped with a printing lab, film processing area, Beseler enlargers, and lenses. E-6 color processing is available.

Faculty: Faculty are influential working artists and educators well-known in their fields of expertise.

Expenses: Housing, meals, processing, and film are not included in the workshop fee.

ANNAPURNA SANCTUARY PHOTO TREK **T**

The Himalayas, Nepal

WILDLAND JOURNEYS
3516 N.E. 155th
Seattle, Washington 98155
206-365-0686 *Fax:* 206-363-6615
Contact: Kurt Katay

Wildland Journeys offers 3-week trips to Nepal annually. Although climbing experience is not required, 14 days of the trip will be spent trekking through the heart of the great Annapurna Mountain

Range surrounded by magnificent peaks. Trip leader Robert Stahl, who teaches photography at the University of Washington, has garnered great experience trekking the Himalayas and is assisted by a local guide and cook.
Specialties: Scenic, landscape.
Location: Tours begin and end in Kathmandu.
Facilities: Hotels and campsites are used.
Faculty: Photographer Robert Stahl has conducted photo tours and taught photography in many exotic locations including Afghanistan, Pakistan, Nepal, and Alaska. His work has appeared in *Sierra* and *Adventure Travel* among many magazines.

ANSEL ADAMS GALLERY PHOTOGRAPHY WORKSHOP **W**

Yosemite National Park, California

ANSEL ADAMS GALLERY
PHOTOGRAPHY WORKSHOP
Yosemite Village Mall
Yosemite Naitonal Park, California 95389
209-372-4413 *Fax:* 209-372-4714
Contact: Annette Bottaro-Walklet

Ansel Adams began conducting fine art photography workshops in Yosemite National Park 50 years ago. Through time the workshops became integrated into the operation of the Gallery which is still owned and run by Adams' family today. Currently weeklong workshops featuring master photographers and shorter workshops offering specific topics such as dye transfer printing, infrared, zone system and cibachrome are available. Write to workshop headquarters for full details.
Specialties: Dye transfer printing, cibachrome, the zone system, infrared.
Location: Most of the workshops are held in Yosemite National Park.
Facilities: Accommodations range from rustic cabins without bathrooms to hotel rooms depending upon the particular workshop and season. Camping is also available. In addition to park facilities, Ansel Adams' demonstration darkroom and home are used.
Faculty: Past instructors of weeklong workshops include: Ansel Adams, John Sexton, Ernst Haas, Sally Mann, Annie Leibovitz, David Hockney, Jerry Uelsmann, and others.
Expenses: Meals, lodging, and park entry fee are not covered by the workshop fee.

Key: **W** = Workshop
T = Photo-Tour
S = Seminar

APPALACHIAN ENVIRONMENTAL ARTS CENTER **W**

Blue Ridge Mountains, North Carolina

APPALACHIAN ENVIRONMENTAL ARTS
CENTER
P.O. Box 580
Highlands, North Carolina 28741
704-526-4303
Contact: Gilbert W. Leebrick, Associate Director

The Appalachian Environmental Arts Center offers a variety of photographic workshops from May through November. The center, established by the University of North Carolina in 1983, is a photographic education and research center dedicated to creating a visual and verbal dialogue among the arts, humanities, and sciences concerning the natural environment. Workshops for a maximum of 12 participants include "Spring Wildflower," "Altered Landscape," and "Metaflora."
Specialties: Large format, printing, landscape, wildlife.
Location: Highlands is a summer resort town in southwestern North Carolina on the crest of the Blue Ridge Mountains where the Carolinas and Georgia meet, about 65 miles south of Ashland. The Nantahala National Forest and the Cullasaja Gorge are close by.
Facilities: Workshops include rooms in the Valentine House, a renovated country home near the Arts Center. Cooking facilities are available. The photographic facility is a 2,000 square foot building equipped for b/w and color work and has 4 master darkrooms.
Faculty: The center invites well-known professional photographers to instruct workshops. Many workshops also include professional biologists and environmental specialists.
Expenses: Workshop fee includes housing but not meals.

APPALACHIAN MOUNTAIN CLUB **W**

The Appalachian Mountains, New Hampshire

APPALACHIAN MOUNTAIN CLUB
Pinkham Notch Camp, Box 298
Gorham, New Hampshire 03581
603-466-2727
Contact: Walter S. Graff

The Appalachian Mountain Club conducts a weeklong "Natural Light Photography" workshop each autumn for new nature photographers who are looking for an experience-getting opportunity. Participants, limited to 12-18, explore all facets o f the mountains including timberline, forest, streams, and rocks and spend several nights in remote AMC huts. The

club, established in 1876, is the oldest conservation organization of its kind. Weekend workshops are also available.
Specialties: Nature, landscape, natural light.
Location: Pinkham Notch Camp is located in the heart of New Hampshire's White Mountain National Forest. The camp is served by Concord Trailways from Boston daily.
Facilities: The camp offers 2,3, and 4 bunk rooms. All-you-can-eat breakfasts and dinners are included in the workshop fee. Lunches are on the trail. Film processing is available.
Faculty: Philip Evans, a photographer for Friends of the Earth, teaches workshops at the AMC. He has taught photography seminars in the U.S. and Great Britain for 15 years.
Expenses: All expenses except for travel to the workshop site are included in the fee.

ARIZONA PHOTO ADVENTURES W

Various locations in Arizona

FRIENDS OF ARIZONA HIGHWAYS
P.O. Box 6106
Phoenix, Arizona 85005
602-271-5904 *Fax:* 602-254-6106
Contact: Shannon Rosenblatt, Director

Arizona Photo Adventures are offered by The Friends of Arizona Highways, a non-profit auxiliary of "Arizona Highways". The adventures are 3 and 4 day scenic workshops, limited to 20 participants, with instruction given by the "Arizona Highways" contributing photographers. Some of the workshops have included: an all-women's group into Havasupai Canyon; an exploration of Monument Valley in the footsteps of moviemaker John Ford; and autumn in Oak Creek Canyon.
Specialties: Nature, landscape, wildlife.
Facilities: Various hotel and meal combinations are available.

ARROWMONT SCHOOL OF ARTS & CRAFTS W

Gatlinburg, Tennessee

ARROWMONT SCHOOL OF ARTS & CRAFTS
556 Parkway/P.O. Box 567
Gatlinburg, Tennessee 37738
615-436-5860
Contact: Sandra Blain

The Arrowmont School of Arts & Crafts offers one and two week workshops in photography as well as painting, clay, metal, papermaking, and more. Attendees during spring and summer sessions can receive credit from the University of Tennessee at Knoxville for their endeavors. Some scholarships are also available.
Location: Arrowmont is a visual arts complex situated on seventy wooded acres adjacent to the Great Smoky Mountains National Park in eastern Tennessee.
Facilities: Studios, a book-supply store, a resource center, gallery, and auditorium are a few of the many useful facilities found in the campus setting. Accommodations are simply furnished single, double, and triple rooms. A dining room offers home cooked meals.
Expenses: Classroom materials are additional.

ART KANE PHOTO WORKSHOP W

Cape May, New Jersey

CAPE MAY INSTITUTE
1511 New York Avenue
Cape May, New Jersey 08204
609-884-7117
Contact: Art Kane Photo Workshop

Art Kane has conducted photographic workshops for over 30 years and these programs, sponsored by the Cape May Institute annually during July and August, provide one of the most comprehensive subject selections available. Kane and Yale MFA graduates teach the basic courses for beginners. Master courses and evening lectures are given by photographic artists such as Arnold Newman, Douglas Kirland, Lucien Clergue, Cole Weston, Lucille Khornak, and Jay Maisel.
Specialties: Commercial, advertising, printing, basics, portrait, fine art, sports, nude, photojournalism, nature, still-life, lighting.
Location: Cape May, New Jersey is a national historic landmark containing 600 carefully preserved Victorian houses and is America's oldest seashore resort. The town is only 3 hours by car from New York City, 4 hours from Washington, D.C, and 2 from Philadelphia.
Facilities: The workshop makes arrangements with local inns and hotels for special 6 night packages some of which also include meals. The workshop will provide details. Fully equipped darkrooms, studios and a photo supply shop are available to participants.
Faculty: Art Kane was elected to the Hall of Fame of the Art Directors Club of New York in 1986 and received the ASMP Lifetime Achievement Award in 1984. He has also published 5 books including the popular *Paper Dolls.*

Expenses: Tuition covers instruction. Lab fees with E-6 processing are additional as are b/w lab fees. Accommodations and meals are not included.

ASIAN PACIFIC ADVENTURES T

China, Japan, Thailand, Tibet, USSR

ASIAN PACIFIC ADVENTURES
826 South Sierra Bonita Avenue
Los Angeles, California 90036
213-935-3156 *Fax:* 213-935-3156
Contact: Tovya Wager or Hima Singh

Asian Pacific Adventures specializes in excursions which combine photography with activities such as bicycling or hiking or with cultural experiences. The tours accommodate from 6 to 16 participants and are for 2 to 3 weeks in length from March through December. Escorted by experienced leaders, the adventures provide a leisurely schedule suitable for outdoor and travel photography.

Specialties: Travel, outdoor, nature, landscape, documentary.
Location: Tours include: Pakistan Jeep Safari; Best of China Bike; Thailand Cycling Adventure; The Glasnost Deluxe Combo; and Indonesia: Bike & Hike the Mystical Islands of Sumatra and Bali.
Facilities: A full range of accommodations are available from camping to first class hotels.
Expenses: Airport departure taxes, photography supplies, and personal items are not included in the tours.

BACKROADS BICYCLE TOURING T

Yellowstone Park & the California Coast

BACKROADS BICYCLE TOURING
1516 5th Street
Berkeley, California 94710
415-527-1555 *Fax:* 415-527-1444
Contact: Elizabeth Gignilliat

In 1990 the well-known bicycle touring company, Backroads, initiated bicycling photo tours designed for beginning photographers and bicyclists of all ages and ability. The week-long tours include scenic routes, and a photographer-guide who gives informal lectures and demonstrations. Tours are accompanied by a fully equipped support van. Participants generally number from 16 to 23, but never more than 26.

Specialties: Landscape, basics, wildflower, night photography.
Location: 1990 locations included the Coast of Maine, California Wine country & Mendocino coast, and Utah's Zion, Bryce, and Grand Canyons.
Facilities: Maine and California tours include accommodations in inns. The Bryce/Zion/Grand Canyon tour is a camping tour.
Faculty: Tours are accompanied by 2 or 3 staff members.
Expenses: Bicycle rental fee and some meals are not included in the tour fee.

BAJA DISCOVERY FIELD PHOTOGRAPHY T

Baja California, Mexico

BAJA DISCOVERY
P.O. Box 152527
San Diego, California 92115
800-829-BAJA
Contact: Gene Warneke

Photographer Gene Warneke leads a monthly, except during the hotter months of July, August, and September, photo-tour of Baja, Mexico's land and seascapes. Limited to small groups of 8, the 8-day tour takes in the coastline, the deserts, and the peninsula's colorful towns, villages, and old missions. Participants will have the opportunity to travel and photograph the entire length of the Baja peninsula down to Cabo San Lucas.

Specialties: Landscape, nature.

Location: The tour departs by air-conditioned van from San Diego and continues through mountains, deserts, and shoreline.
Facilities: Seven nights accommodations and eight meals are included in the tour. Although there is no field lab, fully guided trips by van explore the wilderness areas.
Faculty: Gene Warneke is a professional outdoor, travel, and commercial photographer and former Oregon State University photo instructor.
Expenses: Not included in the tour fee is one-way air transportation between Cabo San Lucas and San Diego and some hotel meals.

BAJA EXPEDITIONS T
Baja California, Mexico

BAJA EXPEDITIONS
2625 Garnet Avenue
San Diego, California 92115
800-843-6967 *Fax:* 619-581-6542
Contact: Gary Cotter

Baja Expeditions offers several photo-oriented week-long tours of Mexico's Baja California area year-round. Accommodating up to 18 passengers, travel by boat provides participants ample opportunity to photograph the annual bird and gray whales' migration as well as the everchanging land and seascapes. All tours are accompanied by a professional outdoor photographer and a group leader.
Specialties: Underwater, landscape, wildlife, nature, birds, whales.
Facilities: Accommodations are on board a sailing vessel and meals are included.
Expenses: Tours are all inclusive except for tips and departure taxes.

BEYOND SANTA FE PHOTO TOURS T
Abiquiu, New Mexico

BEYOND SANTA FE PHOTO TOURS
P.O. Box 149
Abiquiu, New Mexico 87510
505-638-5620
Contact: Dugan Uekert

Beyond Santa Fe specializes in photo tours of the red rock country north of Abiquiu made famous by the paintings of Georgia O'Keefe. The tours also take in historical Spanish architecture and the ruins of the ancient Anasazi, Chama Canyon, and the mesas and cliffs of Mesa Alta. Groups vary in size from 4 to 8.
Specialties: Landscape.
Location: Abiquiu is one hour north of Santa Fe.
Facilities: Accommodations are at the Abiquiu Inn and include meals.
Faculty: Dugan Uekert is a professional photographer and guide who has 15 years experience leading excursions.
Expenses: Tour packages include all lodging, meals, and transportation from Santa Fe. Film and personal items are not included.

BHUTAN TRAVEL T
Bhutan, The Himalayas

BHUTAN TRAVEL INC.
120 E. 56th Street, #1430
New York, New York 10022
212-838-6382
Contact: Marie Brown

Bhutan Travel offers tours throughout the year to Bhutan, the remote country which is the last of the small, hidden Himalayan Kingdoms. These trips are all planned around special Bhutan festivals and events and most also include treks to close-by exotic locations. None of the trips are designed exclusively for photographers, but Bhutan Travel specializes in customized itineraries for groups of six or more.
Specialties: Wildlife, landscape, documentary.
Facilities: Hotels and tent camping are generally the accommodations used. There are no photographic facilities available in this remote and unspoiled country.

BILL & GILL PHOTO WORKSHOPS W
East Coast locations

BILL & GILL PHOTO WORKSHOPS
1220 Ocean Parkway
Brooklyn, New York 11230
718-338-6086
Contact: Gilly Safdeye or Bill Wakslicht

Bill & Gill Photo Workshops are conducted by experienced freelance photographers Bill Wakslicht and Gill Safdeye. Currently they are offering weekend photo excursions to various regional New York locations such as Mystic Seaport in Connecticut and fall foliage workshops in the Hudson River Valley. Designed for participants at any level of skill interested in continuing to learn about photography, enrollment is kept to a minimum to insure personalized attention.
Specialties: Landscape, nature, instruction, portraiture.
Facilities: Workshops include accomodations at AAA approved hotels with modern conveniences. Breakfast is usually the only meal included.

BILL THOMAS TOUCH OF SUCCESS SEMINARS **W**
Florida, the Southwest, Maine, Africa

TOUCH OF SUCCESS
P.O. Box 194
Lowell, Florida 32663
904-867-0463
Contact: Bill Thomas

Wildlife photographer Bill Thomas, best-known for his book *How To Make $50,000 a Year As A Nature Photojournalist*, conducts one-day seminars, week-long workshops, and photo safaris throughout the year. One-day seminars accommodate up to 30 participants and the workshops and safaris are available to 15. All instruction consists of lectures and photo sessions in the field and is followed up by slide critiques.
Specialties: Nature, wildlife, instruction.
Location: 1991 photo safaris are planned for South Africa and the "Polar Bear Express". Weekend and week-long workshops will include visits to the Everglades and Okefenokee in Florida; southwestern Indian country; Washington state; and Maine & Nova Scotia.
Facilities: Accommodations include comfortable and informal lodges, B&B's, cabins, and inns.
Faculty: Bill Thomas is a well-known nature/wildlife photojournalist with over 30 years experience. He is the author of more than 20 books and was the recipient of the Geographic Society Award in 1976.
Expenses: Airfare to the workshop site is not included in the fees.

BLACKHAWK ARTISTS WORKSHOP **W**
Blackhawk, Colorado

BLACKHAWK ARTISTS WORKSHOP
251 Main
Blackhawk, Colorado 80422
303-582-5235
Contact: M. Parfenoff

Blackhawk is an artist's workshop located on the site of the first Gold-Rush in the mountains of Colorado. The site is now a national historic district. All workshops are one-week sessions, designed for both beginners and advanced photographers, and are limited to 10 participants. Guest instructors, who are specialists in the subjects offered, conduct the workshops which concentrate on popular interests such as landscape and people photography.
Specialties: Outdoor, landscape, people.
Location: Blackhawk, standing at an elevation of 8,000 feet in Clear Creek Canyon, is just outside of Central City, Colorado, and is a 45 minute drive from Denver.
Facilities: Accommodations are in the residence lodge and based on double occupancy. The lodge offers dining, reading, meeting and game rooms, and a street level gallery. Accommodations can also be

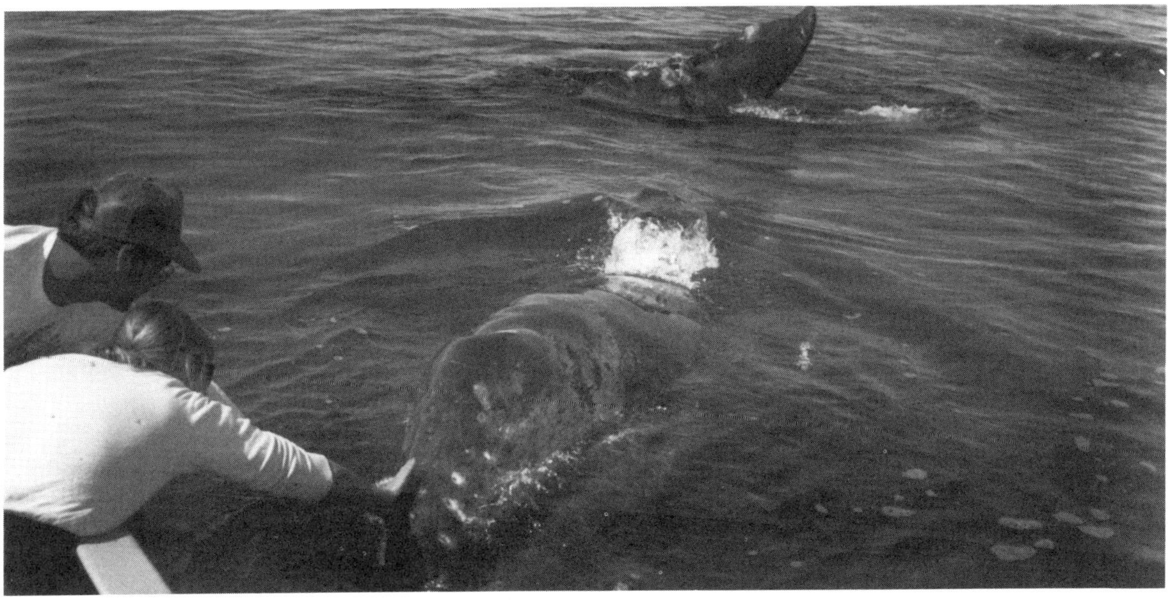

Photograph by Al Gopin.

A curious baby California Gray Whale makes friends with photographers during Baja Discovery's Gray Whale Watching Workshop in Laguna San Ignacio.

found off-campus. Darkrooms and b/w processing are available.
Faculty: Guest professionals conduct all workshops.
Expenses: Optional tuition plans are available offering on/off campus housing. All tuition fees cover meals. Photographic materials are not included.

BODIE PHOTOGRAPHY WORKSHOPS W

Bodie State Historic Park, California

BODIE PHOTOGRAPHY WORKSHOPS
345A Maher Road
Watsonville, California 95076
408-724-3575
Contact: Clinton Smith

The Bodie Photography Workshops present a rare opportunity for photographers who would like to time-travel. The California State Park System and Sierra State Parks Foundation are allowing access to the best preserved gold mining ghost town in the American West during 2 1/2 day workshops with Clinton Smith in July and August. The interiors of original, authentic buildings and artifacts dating from 1879, will be available, along with exteriors minus the tourists.
Specialties: Color photography, architecture, landscape.
Location: Bodie State Historic Park is located 12 miles north of Mono Lake and 13 miles east of the Sierra Mountains between Vining and Bridgeport, California. The elevation is 8,400 feet.
Facilities: Camping is available.
Faculty: Clinton Smith has taught many workshops for the Maine Photographic Workshops and Friends of Photography among others. His work is represented by 20 different galleries worldwide and a special segment of NBC's *Today Show* was devoted to his work.
Expenses: The woodshop fee does not cover camping, meals, or film supplies.

BROOKS INSTITUTE ONE-DAY WORKSHOPS W

Santa Barbara, California

BROOKS INSTITUTE ONE-DAY WORKSHOPS
801 Alston Road
Santa Barbara, California 93108
805-966-3888 *Fax:* 805-564-1475
Contact: Tony Corbell/Norma Santoyo

The internationally known Brooks Institute offers a variety of one-day workshops on their campus year-round. All workshops are taught by Brooks' faculty and are limited to 20 participants.

CALIFORNIA WILDLIFE PHOTOGRAPHY SAFARIS W

Various California locations

CALIFORNIA WILDLIFE PHOTOGRAPHY SAFARIS
P.O. Box 30694
Santa Barbara, California 93130
805-569-3731 *Fax:* 805-569-3731
Contact: B. "Moose" or Sharon Peterson

Wildlife research veteran B. "Moose" Peterson leads a new wildlife safari about every 6 weeks. Designed to provide access to rarely explored wildlife sites, Peterson limits his groups to 5 participants enabling him to safeguard his rare, and oftentimes endangered, photographic subjects. Safaris are generally either 2 or 5 days in length.
Specialties: Wildlife and endangered species.
Facilities: Although workshop fees do not include room and board, all locations are near motels and campgrounds.
Faculty: Peterson's photographs have appeared in such magazines as *American Artist*, *Environment West*, *Field & Stream*, *Wilderness*, and *Pacific Discovery* and has been exhibited at both the Los Angeles and San Diego Museums of Natural History.
Expenses: Workshop fees cover instruction, research material, and guide. Food, lodging, film, and transportation to the workshop site are not included.

CAMDEN PHOTOGRAPHIC WORKSHOPS W

The Adirondack Mountains, New York

CAMDEN PHOTOGRAPHIC WORKSHOPS
Wolcott Hill Studio, 59 Wolcott Hill Rd.
Camden, New York 13316
315-245-3614
Contact: Gary Allen VanRiper

Camden Photographic Workshops are one and two-day nature photography on location workshops held in the spring and autumn in the Adirondack Mountains and upstate New York. Workshops generally include slide and equipment lectures, portfolio reviews, and field sessions.
Specialties: Landscape, nature, and wildlife.
Location: Camden, New York is located one half hour from Rome and an hour from Syracuse and Utica.
Facilities: Accommodation information is available from the workshop.

Faculty: Instructor Gary Allen VanRiper is a nature photographer whose work has appeared in a variety of regional publications.
Expenses: Food and lodging are not included in the workshop fee.

CAMERA-IMAGE WORKSHOPS W
Various Western and California locations

CAMERA-IMAGE WORKSHOPS
P.O. Box 1501
Downey, California 90240
Contact: Craig Fucile or Jan Pietrzak

Camera-Image Workshops have been offered 4 times annually since 1984. The outdoor workshops teach color and b/w techniques, plus field work, demonstrations, and critiques. Accommodating 12 to 15 workshop members, all camera formats and levels are welcome.
Specialties: Technique and outdoor.
Location: Contact directly for the upcoming schedule. Recent locations have included the Sierra Nevada Mountains, the California desert, the California coast, and the canyons of southwestern Utah.
Facilities: Moderately priced motels, tent camping facilities and RVs are used. Lodging and meals are not included in the tuition fees.
Faculty: Pietrzak teaches photography at Otis/Parsons School of Design and his work has recently appeared in *Collectors Photography*, *Darkroom Photography*, and *View Camera*. Fucile has taught for over 10 years and recently organized a photography lecture series.
Expenses: Workshop fee covers tuition only.

CASS ACADEMY OF PHOTOGRAPHIC ARTS W
Hudson, Florida

ACADEMY OF PHOTOGRAPHIC ARTS
7506 New Jersey Avenue
Hudson, Florida 34667
813-863-2738 *Fax:* 813-862-3567
Contact: Veronica Cass Weiss

The Veronica Cass Academy of Photographic Arts offers week-long intensive workshops in the photo-retouching arts. Available year-round to groups of from 3 to 10, courses include negative retouching, print retouching, b/w restoration, air-brushing, and photo oil-painting, among others.
Specialties: Retouching.
Location: Hudson, Florida is located on the Gulf Coast near Weeki Wachee Springs about an hour from Tampa.
Facilities: Apartments are available for rental on the premises. All instruction is in a classroom setting.

CATTLE ROUNDUP PHOTOGRAPHY WORKSHOP W
Kremmling, Colorado

AMERICAN WILDERNESS ADVENTURES
7500 East Arapahoe Road, Suite 355
Englewood, Colorado 80112
800-322-WILD *Fax:* 303-694-9047
Contact: Jan Brooks, Program Administrator

This annual September workshop offers an unsurpassed opportunity for action photographers during the yearly cattle roundup. The week-long workshop, limited to 15 participants, is held at Latigo Ranch in Kremmling, Colorado in the heart of the Colorado Rockies.
Specialties: Action photography.
Location: The secluded and scenic Latigo Ranch lies at 9,000′ elevation in the heart of the Rocky Mountains.
Faculty: Photography instructor Sonny Rains owns a commercial studio in Dallas.
Expenses: Processing and film are not included in the workshop fee.

CENTER FOR NATURE PHOTOGRAPHY W
New York, Pennsylvania, Delaware, Italy

CENTER FOR NATURE PHOTOGRAPHY
P.O. Box 118
Riverdale, New York 10471
914-968-7163
Contact: Allen Rokach

Allen Rokach, director of the Center for Nature Photography and coordinator of the Nature Photography Program at the New York Botanical Garden, conducts one day and weekend workshops in the New York area and week-long workshops in the Rockies and Tuscany, Italy. Rokach's workshops visit many well-known garden sites during their peak blooming seasons to take advantage of a spectacular photo opportunity. In-depth instruction and critiques are offered.
Specialties: Flowers, landscape, nature.
Location: The one-day series on garden spots near New York include stops in Central Park, Olana on the Hudson, Boscobel, and Caramoor. Weekend trips are to Winterthur, and week-long tours have been offered to Tuscany, Italy, Acadia Park in Maine, and The Rockies.
Facilities: Accomodations are generally in hotels.

Faculty: Allen Rokach is a highly regarded photo educator who has taught at the Camera Club of New York, The New School, and the American Museum of Natural History. Photographers Anne Millman and Ross Horowitz assist in some workshops.
Expenses: Expenses vary according to workshop.

CHINA PHOTO WORKSHOP TOURS T

Beijing & various locations in China

CHINA PHOTO WORKSHOP TOURS
22111 Cleveland #211
Dearborn, Michigan 48124
313-561-1842 *Fax:* 313-561-1842
Contact: Dennis Cox

China Photo Workshop Tours have been offered annually since 1981. Tour groups number 8-18 participants and individual instruction is available. The itinerary varies each year.
Specialties: Photojournalism, travel, and portraiture.
Facilities: First class accommodations are used.
Expenses: Film and equipment are not included in the tours.

CITIZEN EXCHANGE COUNCIL T

Eastern Europe, Finland, & the U.S.S.R.

CITIZEN EXCHANGE COUNTIL
12 West 31st Street
New York, New York 10001
212-643-1985 *Fax:* 212-643-1996
Contact: Lea Checroni-Freid, Director of Programs

The Citizen Exchange Council's photography workshops in the U.S.S.R., for amateurs and professionals, feature person-to-person interaction with Soviet "peers" at photo-clubs and leading magazines. Exchanges of prints, informal exploration , and Soviet hospitality supplement guided sight-seeing with a full cultural program. C.E.C. is a private, non-profit and non-political cultural exchange organization with 27 years experience. Groups are limited to 20 members.
Specialties: Travel, documentary, photojournalism.
Facilities: First class hotels and some private homes are used.
Expenses: Tours are all inclusive.

Key: **W** = Workshop
T = Photo-Tour
S = Seminar

CLINTON SMITH COLOR WORKSHOPS W

Various Western locations

CLINTON SMITH COLOR WORKSHOPS
345A Maher Road
Watsonville, California 95076
408-724-3575
Contact: Clinton Smith

Workshop leader Clinton Smith leads week-long field sessions to a variety of locations throughout the United States including Death Valley, the Oregon Coast, High Sierra (Horseback Pack Trip), and the Olympic Peninsula. Most of these workshops, with concentration on color-photography, involve camping and are open to students of all levels.
Specialties: Color photography.
Facilities: Accommodations are camping only.
Faculty: Clinton Smith has taught for the Friends of Photography, Maine Photo Workshops, Appalachian Workshops, and the New School/Parsons.
Expenses: Food, film, travel, and camping accommodations are not covered by the workshop fee.

CLOSE-UP EXPEDITIONS T

Costa Rica, The Everglades, New Zealand

CLOSE-UP EXPEDITIONS
1031 Ardmore Avenue
Oakland, California 94610
415-465-8955 *Fax:* 415-465-1237
Contact: Donald Lyon

"Photography first" is the motto of Close-Up Expeditions. And in keeping with that spirit, Close-Up's photo tours are frequented by those who know that getting the best shot sometimes requires irregular eating schedules and early wake- up calls. Most of the expeditions offered are extensive, averaging about 3 weeks and limited to a small group of 5-12 participants. Most instruction is one on one and non-structured.
Specialties: Travel, landscape, wildlife, nature, documentary.
Location: Some annual tours include: English Country Life, New Zealand Spring, Switzerland Trains & Trails, Southern Spain, Classical Turkey, and Thailand & Burma.
Facilities: Accommodations are in good hotels and inns and ground transporation is generally via small vans and trains. Most meals are included.
Faculty: Professional photographic guides escort all tours.
Expenses: Airfare, medical and personal expenses are not included in the expedition fee.

COLORADO HIGH COUNTRY PHOTOGRAPHY WORKSHOP W

Salida, Colorado

ORVIL STOKES' CREATIVE VISION WORKSHOPS
317 E. Winter Avenue
Danville, Illinois 61832
217-442-3075
Contact: Orvil Stokes

Orvil Stokes, who also publishes the photography newsletter, *Photowork*, has been running workshops on the Color Zones System since 1972. This annual week-long workshop, usually held in September, is limited to 25 participants at all levels of skill and knowledge.

Specialties: Color and outdoor photography.
Location: Salida, Colorado, about 140 miles south of Denver and 100 miles west of Colorado Springs is located in Chaffee County which features 14,000' mountain peaks, groves of Aspen trees, and deserted ghost towns and goldmines.
Facilities: Workshop and lodging, with some meals, has been held at the Little River Ranch Motel and campgrounds in Salida. Some meals are in the field. The staff processes all Kodak Ektachrome film using Unicolor Rapid E-6 chemicals.
Faculty: Most sessions are with Orvil Stokes who has taught photography at universities; worked as a freelance commercial photographer; been published in leading photo journals; and developed a color exposure control system called the Color Zones System.
Expenses: Additional expenses will be film and food. Accommodations are payable separately from the workshop tuition.

COPPER CANYON PHOTO TOUR T

Copper Canyon, Mexico

SOUTHWEST SCENIC PHOTO
5387 Paseo Terraza
Tucson, Arizona 85715
602-577-6453
Contact: Joe Carder

Photographer Joe Carder escorts travelers to Mexico's fascinating Copper Canyon twice yearly. These week-long photo tours explore the remote canyon which was once rich in copper, gold, and silver, and is said to be 4 times larger and several hundred feet deeper than the U.S. Grand Canyon. The canyon is still home to the semi-nomadic Tarahumara Indians. The tour, designed to provide nightly hotel stops, will also allow for visits to smaller towns off the tourist beat.

Specialties: Nature.
Location: Copper Canyon is situated in northern Mexico and the closest well-known city is Chihuahua. The canyon exploration will involve traveling by first-class train to towns such as Los Mochis, Cerocahui, and Creel.
Facilities: Nights are spent at first class hotels and some meals are included.
Faculty: Joe Carder is a professional photographer whose experience has taken him from a position as Press Secretary at Yellowstone National Park to newspaper reporter/photographer. He is also a photography teacher and conducts other photo tours.
Expenses: The tour price includes round-trip transportation from Tucson, first class train travel in Mexico, accommodations and some meals.

DEERFIELD AT STONINGTON W

Hiawatha National Forest, Michigan

DEERFIELD AT STONINGTON
701 Elm Street
Essexville, Michigan 48732
517-893-6402
Contact: Charles & Patricia McMartin

Deerfield at Stonington offers weekend and 5-day workshops in nature and wildlife photography from June through October. Workshop headquarters are located on a cliff overlooking Lake Michigan in the Hiawatha National Forest. The natural setting of the surrounding area which includes forests, lakeshores, bogs, and a variety of wetlands, provides a multitude of field shoot subjects. Lectures and darkroom sessions round out the daily routine.

Specialties: Nature, landscape, butterfly, macro, wildflowers, wildlife, color photography.
Facilities: Participants are furnished with a list of local motel possibilities. There is also a camp-ground facility. Facilities include a master darkroom and a gang darkroom.
Faculty: Instructors are professional educators and experienced professional photographers.

DESERT BIGHORN PHOTO SAFARIS W

Southwestern Arizona

DESERT BIGHORN PHOTO SAFARIS
20 W. Keim
Phoenix, Arizona 85013
602-265-1889
Contact: Kevin Harris

Wildlife and commercial photographer Kevin Harris leads Desert Bighorn and Colorado River Photo Safaris from May through August. Groups of 2 to 6

travel to southwestern Arizona to photograph the wild Desert Bighorn Sheep in their natural habitat at the Kofa National Wildlife Institute. Personalized instruction is offered in the field and demonstrations and slide presentations are also part of the safari.
Specialties: Wildlife.
Location: The Desert Bighorn Photo Safari is held at the Kofa National Wildlife Refuge in southwestern Arizona. The Colorado River Safaris are based at the Colorado River area near Lake Mead.
Facilities: The Desert Bighorn accommodations are a fully equipped base camp at the Kofa refuge. Motels are used for the Colorado River Safaris.
Faculty: Tour director Kevin Harris is a published wildlife and commercial photographer.
Expenses: Transportation to the safari site and film are not covered by the safari fee.

DESERT PHOTO WORKSHOPS W

Arches & Canyonlands National Park, Utah

CANYONLANDS FIELD INSTITUTE
P.O. Box 68
Moab, Utah 84532
801-259-7750
Contact: David Williams

Canyonlands Field Institute presents 2 and 3-day landscape workshops from February through early October. These workshops, which are held in or near the national parks and monuments of the Colorado Plateau in southeastern Utah, all require previous experience with 35mm SLR cameras. Classroom sessions are combined with extensive field work and groups are limited to 10.
Specialties: Landscape, black & white, outdoor.
Location: Both Arches and Canyonlands National Parks are a short driving distance from the town of Moab. The parks feature unsurpassed natural beauty with sandstone spires and bright red canyons whose hues change with the seasons.
Facilities: Motels, bed and breakfasts, and camping accommodations are utilized depending on location and season.
Faculty: Tom Till is a well-known landscape photographer who has taught at the institute for 6 years; Linde Waidhofer is a nature and travel photographer who has published books on wildflowers and landscapes; and David Hiser is a *National Geographic* photographer.

Key: **W** = Workshop
T = Photo-Tour
S = Seminar

DILLMAN'S CREATIVE WORKSHOPS W

Wisconsin

DILLMAN'S CREATIVE WORKSHOPS
3305 Sand Lake Lodge Lane
Lac du Flambeau, Wisconsin 54538
715-588-3143
Contact: Dennis Robertson or Amber Weldon

Dillman's Creative Workshops offer week-long photo sessions with star photographers in an award-winning, family resort setting. This full service resort offers photography workshops from May through October and provides a plethora of recreational activities (tennis, canoeing, waterskiing, playgrounds) for family members who may be accompanying you. "Travel Photography," "The Nude & The Landscape," and "The Photographer's Canvas" are a few of the workshops available.
Specialties: Nature, portrait, photojournalism, models, travel, scenic, marketing, nudes.
Location: Dillman's is located on its own peninsula about 250 miles north of Milwaukee or 350 miles north of Chicago.
Facilities: Lake-front cabins and guesthouse rooms are available. Workshop packages also include meals. Workshop facilities include several fully outfitted studios. Field excursions are also part of the instruction offered.
Faculty: The resort staff includes workshop coordinators and features well-known guest "name" photographic instructors such as Mary Ellen Mark, Arnold Newman, Craig and Nadine Blacklock, Sandy Nykerk, and John Netherton.
Expenses: Workshop fees are inclusive except for travel to Dillmans, tax, and tips.

EARTHWATCH T

50 countries worldwide

EARTHWATCH
680 Mt. Auburn Street, P.O. Box 403
Watertown, Massachusetts 02272
617-926-8200 *Fax:* 617-926-8532
Contact: Blue Magruder

Earthwatch is a non-profit environmental conservation group which sponsors 110 scientific research projects annually. Volunteers donate skills, time, and funding to support the research. Photography skills are needed for many of the projects such as rain forest surverys, archaeological excavations, and endangered species research. All projects are overseen by scientists affiliated with educational or research institutions. Projects accommodate from 2-20 volunteers.

Specialties: Wildlife, whales, underwater, macro, architecture, nature.
Facilities: Dormitory, camping, and village homes are some of the accommodation choices.
Expenses: Airfare to the project site is not included in the research fee.

EAST AFRICA PHOTOGRAPHIC WORKSHOPS **T**
Kenya and Tanzania

EAST AFRICA PHOTOGRAPHIC WORKSHOPS
45 Rawson Avenue
Camden, Maine 04843
207-236-4244
Contact: Jim and Chris McLarty

Photographic artists Jim and Chris McLarty escort 3, 3-week photo tours to East Africa annually in February, March, and September. The photo safaris average about 7 participants per tour and are all inclusive. Their well-planned itineraries put photography first and are paced to keep the time-schedule from becoming the priority. All levels of experience are accommodated and classes on photography and African culture and history are added bonuses.
Specialties: Travel, landscape, wildlife, nature.
Location: East African locations include Kenya and the Maasai land, Tanzania, Rwanda and the trail of the Gorilla migration.
Facilities: Hotels, lodges, and camps are used and meals are included. Safari cruisers with roof hatches are used for photography in the wildlife areas. Window seats are guaranteed for all.
Faculty: The McLartys have taught photo workshops at the Maine Photographic Workshops and the Island Photographic Workshops. They also own and operate Silverline Studio in Camden.
Expenses: Personal expenses, tips, and film are not included in the tour fee.

ECOSUMMER EXPEDITIONS **T**
Arctic Islands, Belize, Iceland, Yukon

ECOSUMMER EXPEDITIONS
1516 Duranleau Street
Vancouver, BC V6H 3S4 Canada
604-669-7741 *Fax:* 604-669-3244
Contact: Richard Newbury or Don Travers

Ecosummer Expeditions offers a broad range of wild and remote travel sites for the hardy and fit. There are many expeditions to choose from all requiring an interest in education and challenge in the outdoors (ECO). Trips incorporating photo opportunities include those to Belize's barrier reef and Jaguar Preserve; New Guinea's stone-age culture in the lost world of Irian Jaya; northern Yukon's Grizzly Bear Camp; and the High Arctic Islands.
Specialties: Landscape, nature, documentary.
Facilities: Accommodations will vary according to location and include everything from inns to sleeping bags. Guides and camp cooks prepare all meals.
Faculty: Generally all trips have one guide for every 5 participants. Guest photographers accompany the photographic tours.
Expenses: Airfares and some meals are not covered by the expedition fee.

EGYPTIAN EYE PHOTOGRAPHY WORKSHOP **T**
Various Egyptian locations

EGYPTIAN EYE PHOTOGRAPHY WORKSHOP
P.O. Box 2868
San Diego, California 92112
619-595-0245
Contact: Pam Pettee

The Egyptian Eye Photography Workshops are semi-annual events designed for small groups of less than 10 serious amateurs. Special privileges provided by the tour include access to antiquity sites not generally available to photographers . Workshop discussions on photographic technique are scheduled to supplement the organized field shoots.
Specialties: Documentary, travel, scenic, landscape.
Location: Sites visited include Cairo, Abu Simbel, Aswan, and Luxor. A Nile cruise and visits to the Valleys of the King & Queen, the Pyramids at Giza, and the Egyptian Museum are included.
Facilities: Accommodations are in 5 star hotels. Most meals are included.
Expenses: Special excursions and some on site shoots are not covered by the tour fee.

FARIS WRITING/PHOTOGRAPHY SEMINARS **S**
Various U.S. cities

WRITING/PHOTOGRAPHY SEMINARS
9524 Guilford Drive, Apt A
Indianapolis, Indiana 46240
317-848-2634
Contact: Charlene Faris

Charlene Faris teaches writing and photography for beginners during two-day seminars throughout the year and offers week-long seminars at sea. The seminars provide information on beginning a freel-

ance career, establishing contact with magazines and newspapers, and recycling work. Seminars are for groups of 5 to 25 and each participant receives a workbook of information on the topics covered.
Specialties: Charlene Faris is a regularly published writer and photographer whose work has appeared in *The Saturday Evening Post*, *The Christian Science Monitor*, and *Guideposts*. She is an adjunct professor for University of Indiana and Indiana University.
Location: Seminars are held in various U.S. cities. Contact directly for up-to-date schedules.

FOLKWAYS INSTITUTE **T**
Bhutan, India, Kenya, & Nepal

FOLKWAYS INSTITUTE
14600 SE Aldridge Road
Portland, Oregon 97236
800-225-4666 *Fax:* 503-658-8672
Contact: Photography Director

The Folkways Institute offers educational photo-study tours to exotic destinations. The institute strives to create programs which emphasize life-long learning in a creative, stimulating environment, while promoting cross-cultural understanding. 1991 photo tours will take in India, Kenya, and Nepal and are limited to 8 to 15 participants. Workshop subjects include landscape, aesthetics, and people. Each tour is escorted by a seasoned professional photographer.
Specialties: Aesthetics, people, landscape, travel, wildlife.
Facilities: Tour costs generally include accommodations and meals with a wide range of housing options.
Faculty: Guides are experts on their destinations. Photography instructors include Robert Stahl and Ken Wanderer.
Expenses: Tour costs are variable but generally include accommodations, meals, and ground transportation.

FREEMAN PATTERSON/DORIS MOWRY WORKSHOPS **W**
Kingston Peninsula, Canada

FREEMAN PATTERSON/DORIS MOWRY WORKSHOPS
R.R. 2
Clifton Royal, New Brunswick E0G1N Canada
506-763-2271 *Fax:* 506-763-2389
Contact: Doris Mowry

Freeman Patterson and Doris Mowry conduct week-long workshops based on Patterson's book *Photography and the Art of Seeing*. Open to anyone from a complete novice to the professional, the organizers believe the best learning conditions exist within a mixed group. Limited to 15 participants, each day consists of instructional slide lectures, instructor led field trips, and assignments. Evaluation sessions are held daily.
Specialties: Instruction, technical, outdoor.
Location: Workshops are held at Adair's Lodge and Cabins at Kingston Creek on the Kingston Peninsula, New Brunswick, Canada. Port of entry by air is the city of St. John which is about 200 miles from Bangor, Maine.
Facilities: The lodge and log cabins, which are situated on a high hill overlooking a forest, contain kitchenettes and sitting rooms and large verandas. Meals are served in the lodge. Arrangements are made for overnight film processing.
Expenses: Room and board fees are separate from workshop tuition. Film and processing expenses are out of pocket.

FRIENDS OF PHOTOGRAPHY **W**
Carmel & San Francisco, California

THE FRIENDS OF PHOTOGRAPHY
250 Fourth Street
San Francisco, California 94103
415-495-7000
Contact: Margaret Moulton, Curator of Education

Recently relocated to San Francisco after twenty years in Carmel, The Friends of Photography continues to maintain the high standards for which the organization has become internationally known. From its new home at The Ansel Adams Center, The Friends of Photography offer a variety of 3 and 5 day workshops year-round. Recent sample workshops have included work in portraiture, architectural photography, and documentary photography.
Specialties: Fine art, portraiture, architecture, photojournalism, instruction.
Facilities: The Friends of Photography organize accommodations which are payable separately.
Faculty: Faculty are nationally and internationally recognized master photographers.
Expenses: Room and board are not covered by the workshop fee.

GALAPAGOS PHOTOGRAPHY WORKSHOP T

Galapagos Islands, Ecuador

GALAPAGOS TRAVEL
2674 N. 1st Street, Suite 112
San Jose, California 95134
800-223-3767 *Fax:* 408-434-5917
Contact: Barry Boyce

Galapagos Photography Workshops are two-week photo tours which are offered 7-8 times per year. Photographers visit the 13 Galapagos islands in a chartered yacht limited to 10-12 passengers. Licensed guides, trained at the Charles Darwin Research Station, lead twice daily shore visits and there are also two snorkeling sessions each day. Evenings are devoted to informal discussions on natural history and photography.
Specialties: Wildlife photography.
Facilities: Accommodations are in double cabins on 12 passenger yachts with complete crew.
Faculty: Barry Boyce is author of *A Traveler's Guide to the Galapagos Islands* and owns the Galapagos Travel company.
Expenses: Airfare, tips, national park entrance fees, and departure taxes are not included in the workshop price.

GERLACH & PLANCK NATURE PHOTOGRAPHY W

Upper Peninsula, Michigan

GERLACH & PLANCK NATURE PHOTOGRAPHY
P.O. Box 259
Chatham, Michigan 49816
906-439-5991
Contact: John Gerlach

John Gerlach and Rod Planck lead week-long nature photography workshops annually, July through October, near Pictured Rocks National Lakeshore in Michigan's Upper Peninsula. These extremely popular workshops emphasize the "hands-on" approach to taking pictures in a natural environment with daily dawn and evening field trips supplemented by slide programs covering such topics as exposure, close-ups, composition, film selection, and filters.
Specialties: Nature, wildlife, landscape, instruction.
Location: Workshops are based at the Buckhorn and TimberRidge Lodges about 15 miles southwest of Munising near Pictured Rocks National Lakeshore.
Facilities: Available accommodations include free campgrounds, motels, and lodges. Immediate E-6 processing is available and slide critiques are given during the week.
Faculty: Formerly a wildlife biologist, John Gerlach is a full-time nature photographer whose work has appeared in *Sierra* and *National Wildlife*. Rod Planck is a full-time wildlife photographer whose photos have graced calendars by Hallmark and Kodak.
Expenses: Lodging and meals are not included in the workshop fee.

GLACIER INSTITUTE W

Glacier National Park, Montana

GLACIER INSTITUTE
P.O. Box 1457
Kalispell, Montana 59903
406-752-5222
Contact: Kris Bruninga

The Glacier Institute is a non-profit corporation established in 1983 which provides field classes within Glacier National Park. Among the many workshops offered during the summer months are 4-day exploration classes in Advanced Photography and intensive 2-day Nature Photography courses. Basic knowledge of 35mm cameras is required.
Specialties: Nature, technique.
Location: The Glacier Institute is located just inside the west entrance to Glacier National Park near West Glacier, Montana. West Glacier is about 35 miles east of Kalispell.
Facilities: Accommodations are in rustic cabins, nearby motels, or camp sites. There are a variety of cafes and restaurants available as well as some cooking facilities at the institute.
Faculty: Photography instructors include Marshall Noice, a professional photographer who has assisted Ansel Adams, and Diane Ensign, a published nature photographer.
Expenses: Workshop fees cover instruction and field activities only.

GOLDEN GATE SCHOOL OF PROFESSIONAL PHOTOGRAPHY W

Fairfield, California

GOLDEN GATE SCHOOL
P.O. Box 187
Fairfield, California 94533
707-422-0319
Contact: Jim Inks

The Golden Gate School of Professional Photography was created in 1983 by a group of dedicated photographers whose goal was to provide affordable education to other working and aspiring photographers. Each year in June a different faculty of photographic instructors is invited to teach a selection of week-long courses which cover the full spectrum of photography, appealing to both beginners and experienced photographers. Courses cover: boudoir, wedding, portrait, etc.

Specialties: Portraiture, boudoir, glamour, environmental, commercial, wedding, photographic art, background painting.

Location: Golden Gate School uses the facilities of the College of Notre Dame in Belmont, California, a short drive from the San Francisco International Airport. The ninety acre campus includes a swimming pool and tennis courts.

Facilities: College style dormitories, two to a room are used. Single rooms are available at a higher cost. Cafeteria meals are part of the housing package and other restaurants are located near the campus.

Faculty: The school operates as a non-profit committee of the Professional Photographers of the Greater Bay Area and is administered by a Board of Trustees composed of working photographers. Instructors are chosen and invited by the board.

Expenses: Photographic materials and film processing are not covered by the workshop tuition.

GRAND MANAN PHOTO WORKSHOPS — W

Grand Manan Island, Canada

GARRY BLACK PHOTOGRAPHY
4 Highburn Crescent
Gloucester, Ontario K1B 3H8 Canada
613-824-9295
Contact: Garry Black

Nature photographer Garry Black conducts two one-week workshops on Grand Manan Island each June. A maximum of 10 participants are given full instruction from the basic technical skills to proven methods for improving photographic vision . Field trips include visits to fishing villages, wildflower fields, lighthouses, and a boat trip to the wildlife rich island, Machias Seal Island. Evaluation sessions are also offered.

Specialties: Scenics, wildlife, instruction.

Location: Grand Manan Island is the largest in the Bay of Fundy Isles and is about 35 kilometers from mainland New Brunswick via a two-hour ferry ride.

Facilities: Accommodations and meals are at the Shorecrest Lodge. Overnight film processing is available.

Faculty: Garry Black, who is a self-taught photographer, is one of Canada's leading shooters whose work has appeared in many publications and has been used by such corporations as Coca Cola, Toyota, United Airlines, and the Government of Canada.

Expenses: Tuition includes instruction, accommodations, meals, taxes, gratuities, and the boat excursion.

GRAY WHALE DISCOVERY — T

Baja California, Mexico

BAJA DISCOVERY
P.O. Box 152527
San Diego, California 92115
800-829-BAJA
Contact: Gene Warneke

This unique one-week tour is designed especially for wildlife and photography lovers and is offered only during the winter months of late January, February and March when the whales arrive at their mating grounds. In addition to photographing the whales from fiberglass fishing boats, attendees will have the opportunity to photograph Egrets, Herons, brown Pelicans, and many more species of birds and lagoon wildlife.

Specialties: Whales, birds, and wildlife.

Location: Laguna San Ignacio is located about 600 miles south of San Diego in the Baja California peninsula, Mexico on the Pacific coast. The tour departs from the Loreto, Mexico airport.

Facilities: Two nights hotel accommodations and five nights at the tented Whale Watching Camp and all camp meals are included in the tour package. Tents are equiped with floors and screened windows and solar bath facilities. A dining tent houses a full kitchen.

Faculty: Professional photographer Gene Warneke will offer assistance and instruction in photography. The Whale Camp program is led by experienced naturalists.

Expenses: Not included in the tour cost are hotel meals and roundtrip airfare between Los Angeles and Loreto, Mexico.

HARTNELL COLLEGE PHOTOGRAPHY WORKSHOPS — W

Salinas, California

HARTNELL COLLEGE
156 Homestead Avenue
Salinas, California 93901
408-755-6797
Contact: Jerri Nemiro

Hartnell College offers numerous photographic workshops covering a variety of subjects including portraiture, non-silver photography, and color pho-

tography. The college also offers workshops in the field to such destinations as Big Sur and Yosemite.
Specialties: Portraiture, landscape.
Facilities: Field workshops include camping facilities. The college has a color and b/w darkroom and a photo studio.
Expenses: Film and meals are not included in the workshop fees.

HOWARD BOND WORKSHOPS W

Ann Arbor, Michigan

HOWARD BOND WORKSHOPS
1095 Harold Circle
Ann Arbor, Michigan 48103
313-665-6597
Contact: Howard Bond

Noted photographer Howard Bond teaches 2-day workshops on "Refinements in B & W Printing" and "The Zone System for All Formats". He also offers one-day workshops on "View Camera Techniques" and leads longer field workshops on Lake Superior and the Great Sand Dunes of Colorado. Workshops generally number 9 to 16 members.
Specialties: Printing, zone system, b/w, view camera.
Location: Most workshops are held in Ann Arbor.
Facilities: Camping and cabins are used for the field trip workshops. Printing workshops necessitate darkroom use, otherwise all instruction is given in the field or lecture space.
Faculty: Howard Bond's photography has been on view in one-man exhibitions the world over including galleries in Vienna, Athens, Chicago, and Los Angeles, and the Bibliotheque Nationale in Paris, The Victoria & Albert Museum in London, and the Smithsonian.
Expenses: Meals and lodging are not included in the workshop fees.

INDIAN RIVER PHOTO WORKSHOPS W

Adirondack Park, New York

INDIAN RIVER PHOTO WORKSHOPS
P.O. Box 7
Antwerp, New York 13608
315-659-8544
Contact: Vici Zaremba

Photographic instructors Vici Zaremba and Stephen Diehl are both graduates of the prestigious Rochester Institute of Technology and lead annual spring and autumn phototours in the Adirondacks. Limited to 16 participants, both the Spring and Wildflower and Adirondack Fall workshops offer extensive field experience with plenty of technical guidance. Lectures, discussions, and one-on-one demonstrations are part of the daily routine.
Specialties: Macro, landscape, nature, wildflowers, technique.
Location: Both workshops take place in various Adirondack Park locations in northern New York. Field trips include treks along the Moose River and Black Bear Mountain, canoeing on Russian and Gull Lakes, and hikes across the Tug Hill Plateau.
Facilities: Traditional Adirondack lodges and motels are used.
Faculty: Steve Diehl is an assistant professor of Photography at RIT where he teaches nature photography, color photo design, and color printing theory. Vici Zaremba is a freelance commercial photographer. Both have been published in many photo journals.
Expenses: Lodging fees are separate from workshop fees. The program fee covers instruction, critiques, and reference material. Film and processing are not included. Lodging fees include breakfast, lunch, and one dinner.

INFOTO WORKSHOPS W

Various Locations, New York

INFOTO WORKSHOPS
The New School/66 W. 12th Street
New York, New York 11050
212-741-8972 *Fax:* 212-929-2456
Contact: Janet Grunwald

Infoto offers week-long workshops in fashion and photojournalism at the New School in Manhattan. Workshops in fine art, electronic imaging, and fashion are also held at different locations worldwide including Daytona, Florida; Sun Valley, Utah; France; Germany; and the USSR.
Specialties: Fashion, photojournalism, fine art, electronic imaging.
Location: The New School is centrally located in Manhattan's Greenwich Village and is served by a variety of subway and bus lines.
Facilities: Accommodations are not included but the workshop can arrange housing at a local YMCA. Lab facilities and studios are available for the New York City workshops. Facilities and accommodations vary at other locations.
Faculty: Faculty has included Arnold Drapkin, Ross Baughman, Mario Cabrera, and Peter Howe.

Key: **W** = Workshop
T = Photo-Tour
S = Seminar

Expenses: Accommodations and meals are not included in the tuition fee.

ISLAND PHOTOGRAPHIC WORKSHOPS — W

Coastal Islands, Maine

ISLAND PHOTOGRAPHIC WORKSHOPS
109 Bayview Street
Camden, Maine 04843
207-236-9087

Island Photographic Workshops provide a rare opportunity to creatively explore and photograph some of the 3000 coastal islands of Maine during the warm weather months. These week-long, comprehensive workshops cover many aspects of picture-taking including exposure, light meters, composition, and more. Winter workshops in Puerto Rico are also newly available.

Specialties: Macro, large format, instruction, landscape, nature.

Location: Workshop headquarters are at Port Clyde, Maine, on the coast about 100 miles from Bangor.

Facilities: Accommodations are at the Ocean House in Port Clyde, a 1824 inn overlooking the harbour, sea, and islands.

JIM BONES PHOTO-NATURALIST WORKSHOPS — W

Rio Grand River & Salt River Canyon

JIM BONES PHOTO-NATURALIST WORKSHOPS
P.O. Box 31
Terlingua, Texas 79852
800-359-4138

Contact: Steve Harris

Jim Bones' Photo-Naturalist Workshops are designed for photographers and wilderness lovers alike. The organization offers 5 workshops annually, of from 3 to 5 days, featuring wilderness river rafting with daily location walks providing a variety of landscape, wildlife, and still-life photo opportunities. The groups are limited to a maximum of 9 participants and are accompanied by guides.

Specialties: Wildlife, landscape, action, portrait, and still-life.

Location: All workshops take place on southwestern rivers with visits planned according to wildlife activity. Salt River, Arizona; the Lower and Mariscal Canyons of the Rio Grande River; and Rio Chama, New Mexico.

Facilities: Workshops are fully outfitted with river-running equipment, camps, trained staff, and meals prepared by the guides. Participants bring along their own bedrolls.

Faculty: Jim Bones has over ten years experience operating photographic workshops on the Rio Grande. He has also apprenticed with Eliot Porter and published 5 photo-anthologies on nature. An accredited naturalist also accompanies the tour.

Expenses: Fees do not include cameras, film, or bedding.

JOE MCDONALD'S WILDLIFE PHOTOGRAPHY — W

The Poconos, Yellowstone, The Everglades

JOE MCDONALD'S WILDLIFE PHOTOGRAPHY
116 7th Street
Whitehall, Pennsylvania 18052
215-433-7025

Contact: Joe McDonald

Wildlife photographer Joe McDonald offers a non-stop variety of weekend and week-long workshops and an international selection of photo-tours throughout the year. Formerly a biology and zoology high school teacher, McDonald takes special pains to make sure his students are prepared for full-day field shots by offering pre-workshop instruction. Each workshop day ends with after dinner programs on technique. Limited to 10 participants (tours may accommodate more).

Specialties: Nature, wildlife, landscape, macro, wildflowers, instruction, birds.

Location: Weekend workshops are generally held in the Pennsylvania-New Jersey area. Tours and week-long workshops are held in a variety of locations including Yellowstone in Winter, Alaska, The Galapagos, The Everglades, and Australia.

Facilities: Accommodations are not included in the workshop fee but each workshop offers a selection of recommended housing. Photo tours usually include all meals, lodging, and transportation.

Faculty: Joe McDonald is well-known as the author of *A Practical Guide to Photographing American Wildlife.* His work has appeared in most leading nature journals including *Audubon, National Wildlife, Petersen's Photographic*, and *Smithsonian.*

Key: **W** = Workshop
T = Photo-Tour
S = Seminar

JOSEPH VAN OS PHOTOSAFARIS W

Arizona, California, Oregon, Washington

JOSEPH VAN OS PHOTOSAFARIS
P.O. Box 655
Vashon, Washington 98070
206-463-5383 *Fax:* 206-463-5484
Contact: Carolyn May

For over 10 years Joseph Van Os Photosafaris have offered a variety of photography/natural history workshops and tours appropriate for beginners as well as the seasoned pro. Confined to small groups, workshops combine field trips with formal instruction. Tours provide access to remote areas and spectacular wildlife photo opportunities and allow for daily photo discussion sessions. Upcoming destinations include Columbia Gorge, Mono Lake, and Olympic National Park.

Specialties: Landscape, nature, wildlife.
Location: Week-long workshops are generally based at well-known national park and wildlife centers in the west and northwest. Photo tours take-in a variety of locations on each excursion.
Facilities: Camping and motel facilities are used.
Faculty: Experienced photographers and naturalists such as Jim Bones and John Shaw instruct the workshops.
Expenses: Room and board and travel to the workshop/tour site are not included.

JOSEPH ZAIA PHOTOVISION WORKSHOPS W

New York & various New England locations

JOSEPH ZAIA PHOTOVISION
WORKSHOPS
275 Maybury Avenue
Staten Island, New York 10308
718-356-8968
Contact: Joseph J. Zaia

Joseph Zaia has conducted workshops for over ten years geared to both beginner and advanced photographers. Workshop locations have included New York City, the Catskill Mountains, and Boothbay Harbor in Maine, as well as other locations in New England. Workshops generally are held in the spring or fall and are limited to small groups. Zaia excels at providing personalized attention with emphasis on blending technique with individual creativity.

Specialties: Technique, creative photography.
Location: Location workshops of one working week are held in Catskill, New York; Cape Ann, Massachusetts; and Boothbay Harbor, Maine.
Facilities: Hotels and guest houses are used.
Faculty: Joseph Zaia is the recipient of numerous international photography awards and has conducted photo workshops since 1979.
Expenses: Workshop fees cover instruction and accommodations. Transportation, food, film, and processing are not included.

KAZIK PAZOVSKI SCHOOL & PHOTOGRAPHY WORKSHOP W

Cincinnati, Ohio

KAZIK PAZOVSKI SCHOOL &
PHOTOGRAPHY WKSP
2340 Laredo Avenue
Cincinnati, Ohio 45206
513-281-0030
Contact: Kazik Pazovski

Kazik Pazovski offers ongoing classroom photography instruction and specialized workshops featuring prominent guest lecturers. Basic photography knowledge is required of all attendees. Classes and workshops are kept small to insure individual attention.

Specialties: Photojournalism, nature, fine art, portraiture.

Location: The school is centrally located in Cincinnati.
Facilities: Facilities include studios, darkrooms, classrooms, and a finishing room.
Expenses: Fee covers instruction only.

LAKE POWELL PHOTOGRAPHIC WORKSHOP W

Page, Arizona

WAHWEAP LODGE & MARINA
P.O. Box 1597
Page, Arizona 86040
602-645-1001 *Fax:* 602-645-5175
Contact: Steve Ward, Public Relations

The Lake Powell Photographic Workshop is a unique workshop which takes place each October on the water and in the canyons of one of Arizona's most spectacular natural sites. Surrounded by picturesque rock formations, participants hike and photograph by day, attend programs in the evening, and sleep in a houseboat "village." Intermediate to advanced amateurs or professional photographers.
Specialties: Scenics, nature, technical.
Location: Page, Arizona is about 100 miles north of Flagstaff near the Utah border and within a short driving distance of the Grand Canyon, Monument Valley, and the Navajo Indian Reservation. Lake Powell, "America's Natural Playground," is a 200 mile long lake.
Facilities: Accommodations are on 50′ houseboats, each sleeping 6, though spacious enough for 12. The boats have hot and cold running water and full shower/toilet facilities. Meals are provided by a chef and crew.
Faculty: John Telford who is Director of Photographic Services at the University of Utah leads the workshop. His photos have appeared in *National Geographic*, *People*, and *Sports Illustrated*. Representatives from Kodak and Nikon have supplemented past workshops.
Expenses: The workshop fee includes accommodations, all meals, and transportation during the workshop and applicable taxes.

LEONARD RUE ENTERPRISES S

Various U.S. locations

LEONARD RUE ENTERPRISES
138 Millbrook Road
Blairstown, New Jersey 07825
201-362-6616 *Fax:* 201-362-5808
Contact: Barbara McMickle

Leonard Rue and his son, Len Rue, Jr., present an all day wildlife photography seminar in a slide/lecture format. The seminar is geared to both amateur and professional photographers. Subjects covered include: equipment, exposure, landscapes and scenics, and how to photograph flowers, reptiles, birds, and mammals. The seminar concludes with a "Q & A" session.
Specialties: Wildlife, landscape, birds, animals.
Location: The seminars are available to groups anywhere. Contact directly for upcoming locations or to inquire about presenting the seminar.
Faculty: Leonard Lee Rue III is the author of 18 books on photography, the most recent being *How I Photo-*

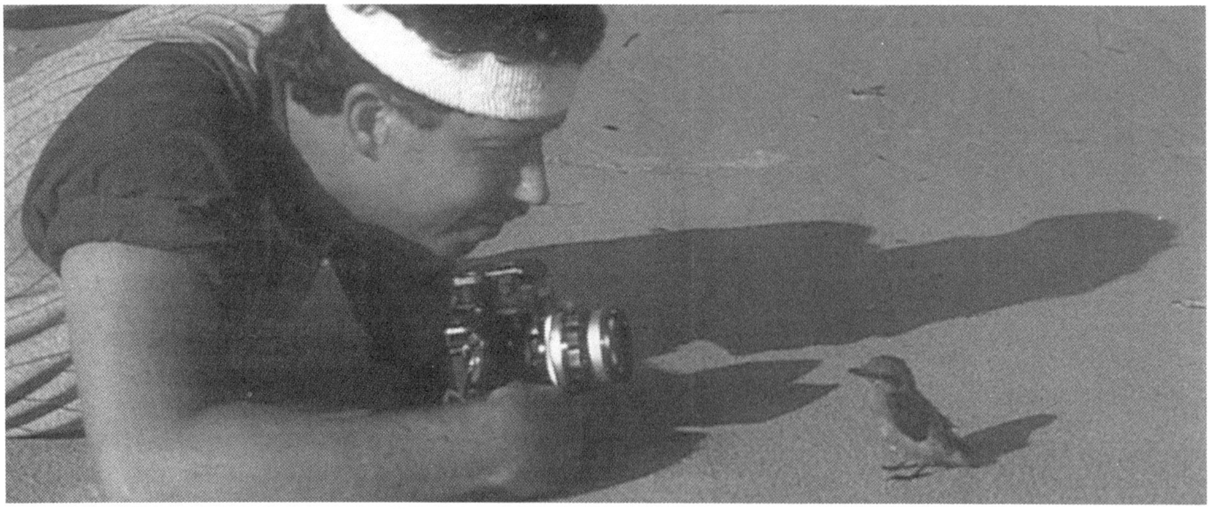

Photograph by Scott Swanson

Lost World Adventures workshop participants often enjoy close contact with their subjects as in this photograph called Close Encounters of the Bird Kind taken in Canaima National Park in Venezuela.

graph Wildlife and Nature. His work appears regularly in photographic and general consumer magazines.

LIGHTWAVE PHOTO WORKSHOPS W

Atlanta, Georgia

LIGHTWAVE PHOTO WORKSHOPS
P.O. Box 95541
Atlanta, Georgia 30347
404-248-9161
Contact: Michael Dierdorff

A new contender in the workshop sweepstakes, professional photographer Michael Dierdorff has been teaching and lecturing on photography for 11 years. One and two-day and weekend workshops will cover Beginning Photography, Advanced Photography, The View Camera, and The Nude. Weekend workshops are held in a resort setting in the North Georgia Mountains about an hour from Atlanta.

Specialties: Instruction, nudes, nature, portraiture.
Location: Weekend workshops are held at the Center for New Beginnings in the North Georgia Mountains, 9 miles from Dahlonega, Georgia and 63 from Atlanta. The center is located near the BlueRidge Mountains.
Facilities: Accommodations are at the Center for New Beginnings' resort and meals are included.
Faculty: Michael Dierdorff is the owner of Lightwave Photography in Atlanta and his work is on view at the Alias Gallery at Tula.
Expenses: Tuition fee includes instruction, meals, and lodging. Film and camera supplies are not covered by the fee.

LOS ANGELES PHOTOGRAPHY CENTER W

Los Angeles, California

LOS ANGELES PHOTOGRAPHY CENTER
412 S. Park View Street
Los Angeles, California 90032
213-383-7342
Contact: Glenna Avila, Director

The Los Angeles Photography Center offers over 100 different workshops year-round, from half-day to six weeks in length. A forerunner in city-affiliated photography centers, this center was established in 1960 and is staffed by over twenty professional photographers. The workshops offered include fine art, portraiture, photojournalism, and a variety of technical courses such as the Zone System, depth-of-field, and exposure workshops. Appropriate for all levels.

Specialties: Documentary, landscape, portraiture, technical.
Location: The Los Angeles Photography Center is located in downtown Los Angeles. There are two affiliated centers at the Peck Park Recreational Center in San Pedro and the Encino Photography Center at Encino Park.
Facilities: Darkrooms (color and b/w) with Omega enlargers, print dryers, and dry mounting press are available. The film processing room contains developing tanks and reels, and the studio shooting areas include backdrops, electronic strobes, spots, and floods.
Expenses: Workshop fees do not cover the cost of film or photographic paper.

LOST WORLD ADVENTURES T

Venezuela & Costa Rica, Central America

LOST WORLD ADVENTURES
1189 Autumn Ridge Drive
Marietta, Georgia 30066
404-971-8586 *Fax:* 404-977-3095
Contact: Scott Swanson

Lost World Adventures organizes nature and culture oriented programs in Venezuela and Costa Rica staffed by professional photographers. A variety of locations may include rain forests, mountains, and remote villages.

Specialties: Nature and outdoor photography.
Facilities: The photo tours use lodges and camping. Workshops are held "on-site".
Faculty: Professional outdoor photographer James Martin has been published in the National Geographic and Outside Magazine.
Expenses: Tour package does not cover airfare and some meals.

MACRO TOURS PHOTO WORKSHOPS W

Alaska, California, the Southwest

MACRO TOURS PHOTO WORKSHOPS
1145 Church Street/P.O. Box 460041
San Francisco, California 94114
415-826-1096
Contact: Bert Banks

Macro Tours workshops are available year-round to a variety of scenic spots offering the opportunity to photograph such special sights as the midnight sun of Alaska, autumn in the Eastern Sierras, and Marin County's carpet of wildflowers . One-day, weekend, and week-long workshops concentrate on wildlife, color slide printing, landscape, and color negative printing.

Specialties: Scenic, printing, nature.
Facilities: Motels and lodges are used for location workshops. Printing and processing workshops are held in a San Francisco facility.
Faculty: Bert Banks is the founder and leader of Macro Tours and prints much of his own work in color. He has taught photography at National Audubon, Pt. Reyes Field Seminars, and the California Institute of Integral Studies.
Expenses: Meals and transportation to the workshop location are not included in the workshop fee.

Key: **W** = Workshop
T = Photo-Tour
S = Seminar

MAINE PHOTOGRAPHIC WORKSHOPS W

Rockport, Maine

MAINE PHOTOGRAPHIC WORKSHOPS
2 Central Street
Rockport, Maine 04856
207-236-8581 *Fax:* 207-236-2558
Contact: Admissions

Perhaps the most prominent of the pioneering photographic workshops is The Maine Photographic Workshops which have been in operation for nearly 20 years. The Maine Workshops truly offer something for everyone. Three month master programs in commerical and editorial photography are available year-round, as well as a selection of shorter programs on subjects as diverse as sports and architectural photography. The *International Photo Congress* is held annually in August.

Specialties: Advertising, architecture, b/w, color, documentary, environmental, fine art, landscape, nude, people, photojournalism, printing, sports, studio, technical, travel.
Location: Rockport, Maine is located about 60 miles south of Bangor and 80 north of Portland. A two-week annual workshop is held in Fontvieille, France near Avignon each summer. "The Rencontres," summer festival of photography is held in Arles, France in July.
Facilities: A variety of accommodations are available to workshop attendees including period homes, tourist cottages, and motels. Union Hall houses a theater, gallery, library, store, and photography labs and darkrooms.
Faculty: Maine Photographic Workshops are conducted by respected professional photographers, many of whom have garnered acclaim in their areas of expertise. Recent instructors have included: Douglas Kirkland, Mary Ellen Mark, Brian Lanker, and Joyce Tenneson.
Expenses: Tuition does not cover accommodations. Some lab fees are also paid separately. Accommodation expenses cover meals in some instances.

MAKING A LIVING IN PHOTOGRAPHY S

San Rafael, California

JAY DANIEL ASSOCIATES
P.O. Box 1232
San Rafael, California 94915
415-459-1495 *Fax:* 415-459-3021
Contact: Jay Daniel

Making A Living In Photography is a series of photographic seminars conducted by Jay Daniels, a specialist in commercial, editorial, and advertising photography. The eight-week series commences

twice yearly in the spring and fall and features leading guest photographers. Subjects tackled include: "The Business Side," "Creative Studio Lighting," and "Photographing Fine Art," among others.
Specialties: Technical and business skills.
Location: In the Jay Daniel Studio in San Rafael north of San Francisco.
Facilities: There are many hotels near the seminar location.
Expenses: Either the complete seminar series or individual sessions can be purchased.

MARKETING AND SELLING YOUR PHOTOGRAPHY S

Various U.S. and Canadian locations

MARKETING & SELLING YOUR PHOTOGRAPHY
2038 Calvert Avenue
Costa Mesa, California 92626
714-556-8133
Contact: Maria Piscopo

Maria Piscopo, author of *Photographer's Guide To Marketing & Self-Promotion*, conducts full-day seminars geared to the commercial photographer, graphic designer, or art director. Subjects covered include everything from pricing to how to reach the client. Contact Ms. Piscopo for the seminar schedule.
Specialties: Instruction.
Faculty: Maria Piscopo is an art/photo rep and teaches at Cal State Long Beach and Art Center College.

MATT BRADLEY PHOTOGRAPHY WORKSHOPS W

Various locations throughout Arkansas

MATT BRADLEY PHOTOGRAPHY WORKSHOPS
15 Butterfield Lane
Little Rock, Arkansas 72212
501-224-0692 *Fax:* 501-224-0692
Contact: Matt Bradley

Photographer Matt Bradley conducts 3 weekend workshops at Arkansas State Parks annually. Geared toward the intermediate level photographer, most days are spent shooting in the field with the evenings reserved for presentations by Bradley. All workshops feature tranquil locations and a leisurely pace.
Specialties: Landscape, instruction.
Location: Locations include: Petit Jean State Park on the Arkansas River near Morrilton, the Buffalo River near the village of Ponca, and Pinnacle Mountain State Park.
Facilities: Some workshops include accommodations at park lodges.
Faculty: Matt Bradley has worked as a photojournalist for the *National Geographic* and has published three photographic books.

MESSANA PHOTO WORKSHOPS W

St. Clair Shores, Michigan

MESSANA PHOTO WORKSHOPS
22500 Rio Vista
St. Clair Shores, Michigan 48081
313-773-5815
Contact: Joseph P. Messana

The Messana Photo Workshops are celebrating their 20th season in 1991. A variety of 10 week workshops, weekend workshops, and one-time only events such as photographing the Christmas Trims in Detroit are offered. Generally the workshops are limited to 20 participants who know how to use 35mm cameras. Sponsored by the Henry Ford Centennial Library in Dearborn, the workshops meet on Saturdays at various Detroit area locations for "hands-on" instruction.
Specialties: Color slide photography, instruction, landscape, outdoor, architecture.
Facilities: Critiques and slide presentations are held at the Ford Library.
Faculty: Joseph P. Messana has been a professional photographer since 1971 and his work has appeared in over 300 publications.
Expenses: Tuition fees cover instruction only.

MICHIGAN PHOTOGRAPHY WORKSHOPS W

Various locations in Michigan

MICHIGAN PHOTOGRAPHY WORKSHOPS
28830 West 8 Mile Road
Farmington Hills, Michigan 48024
Contact: Alan Lowy

Michigan Photography Workshops are offered June through September each year and accommodate groups of 12 to 25. The two types of workshops available are "The Figure in The Environment" which is nude photography in a natural environment and "Michigan Waterfalls Autumn Workshop." These workshops are weekend and 4 day events.
Specialties: Nude, glamour, nature.
Location: Workshops are held in private locations in the western Michigan sand dunes near Ludington.
Facilities: Accommodations for the Figure/Environment workshop are at The Haven, a privately owned

resort. Meals are included. Waterfalls workshop utilizes motels in the upper peninsula.
Faculty: Alan Lowy, the Director of Michigan Photography Workshops, has been a working photographer for over 20 years. He is assisted by professional photographers C.J. Elfont and Jim Probelski.
Expenses: Film, processing, and transportation to the workshop site are not included in the workshop fee.

MIDDLEBURY WORKSHOP/ PHOTOGRAPHY W
Middlebury, Vermont

THE MIDDLEBURY WORKSHOP
RD 1, Box 371
Middlebury, Vermont 05753
802-388-6516
Contact: Leight M. Johnson

Leight Johnson, who teaches photography in Baltimore, began summer photography workshops in Vermont in 1985. The Basic I course is Monday to Friday and limited to 8 participants. Other 2-day and weekend courses offered are Basic II, Lighting in Photography, and Photographing People. These courses are strictly "learning by doing" and include lectures and critiques of finished assignments.
Specialties: B/w, basics, lighting, people.
Location: Middlebury is located in western Vermont between Burlington and Rutland. It is about a 5-hour drive from New York City and 4 hours from Boston. Passenger trains and buses also stop in Middlebury.
Facilities: Food and lodging are not included in the workshop fee. There are numerous commercial accommodations available. Classroom sessions are held in an informal meeting room. There are also darkroom facilities and a photographic library.

MISSOURI PHOTO WORKSHOP W
Various locations in Missouri

MISSOURI PHOTO WORKSHOP
University of Missouri, 3 Whitten Hall
Columbia, Missouri 65211
314-882-3296 *Fax:* 314-882-6043
Contact: Bill Kuykendall and Duane Dailey

Reving up for its 43rd edition in 1991, the Missouri Photo Workshop is an annual, week-long, advanced photojournalism workshop based on photodocumentary approach for newspaper and magazine photographers. The workshop, to which one must apply, is held in a different small town in Missouri in early October. A 20-photo portfolio, a letter of application, and a reference from a professional or teacher must accompany applications.
Specialties: Photojournalism, documentary.
Facilities: Facilities and accommodations vary each year depending on location. Lodging and meals are not included in the basic workshop fee but information is provided on the local offerings. Darkroom

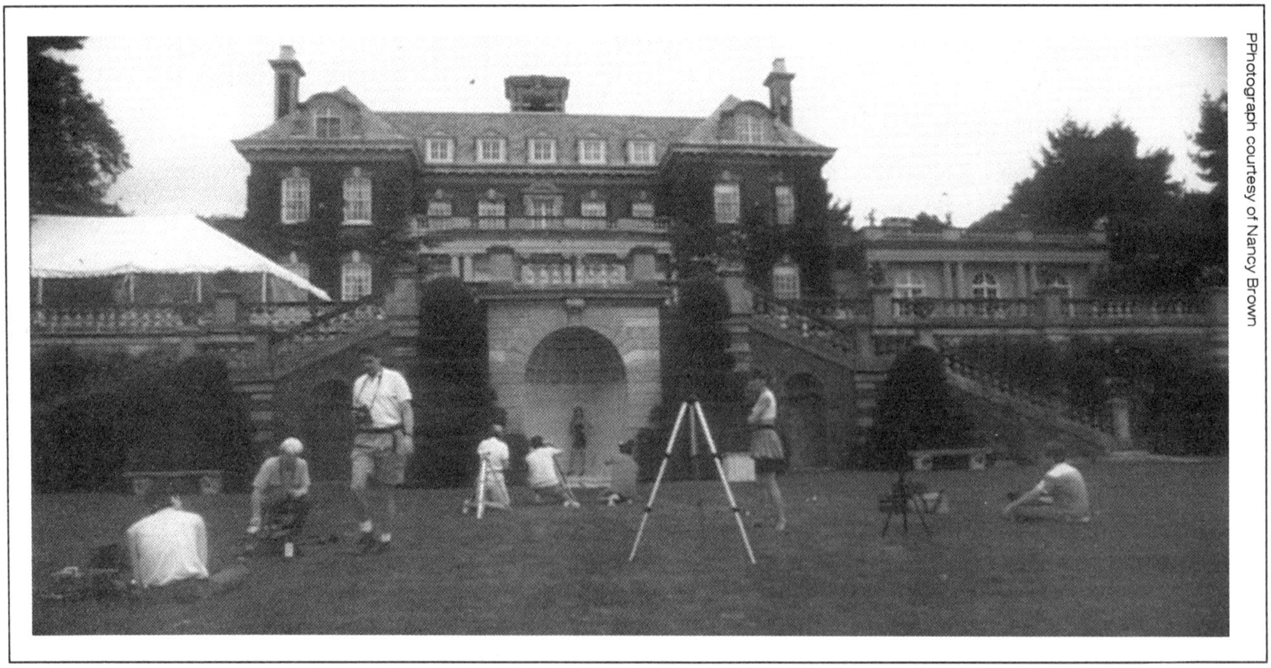

Participants in Nancy Brown's Studio Workshops often take class "on location."

processing and printing is handled by the workshop crew.
Faculty: Twelve top photo journalists are recruited annually to be instructors for the week.
Expenses: Food, lodging, and transportation are not included in the workshop fee.

NANCY BROWN STUDIO WORKSHOP W

New York City, New York

NANCY BROWN STUDIO WORKSHOP
6 W. 20th Street
New York, New York 10011
212-924-9105 *Fax:* 212-633-0911
Contact: Nancy Brown or Laura, the Studio Manager

Former model Nancy Brown teaches intensive week-long beauty and illustration workshops 3 times annually. A full team of professional photographic assistants, make-up and hair experts, and a chef assist Brown in the "hands-on" workshops which are designed to cover everything from lighting techniques to how to work with props. Restricted to 15 participants, instruction will also be offered during field trips around the city.
Specialties: Beauty, fashion, advertising, stock.
Location: Nancy Brown's Studio is located in the heart of Manhattan's photo district, also known as the Flatiron district, just off 5th Avenue.
Facilities: Nancy Brown will provide a list of recommended hotels near her studio. Breakfast and lunch at the studio are included in the tuition fee. Strobes and accessories will be provided as well as an extensive selection of props and wardrobe.
Faculty: Nancy Brown worked as a top New York City model for 19 years and has also managed her own successful photographic studio for the last 14. She counts Coty, Merle Norman, Canada Dry, Pentax, and Avon, among her many commercial clients.
Expenses: Accommodations, dinners, film, and processing are not included in the workshop fee.

NATURE IMAGES W

Everglades, Atlantic Coast, Yellowstone

NATURE IMAGES
P.O. Box 2037
West Palm Beach, Florida 33402
407-586-7332
Contact: Helen Longest-Slaughter

Nature photographer and enthusiast Helen Longest-Slaughter conducts week-long intensive work-

shops for small groups at all levels of skill or experience. Her personalized touch and well-planned itineraries have made her workshops very popular. Some of the workshops offered annually are: "The Art of Seeing" in the Everglades, "Lighthouses & Wildlife of North Carolina's Outer Banks," and "Film - The Photgrapher's Canvas" in Wisconsin's Northwoods.
Specialties: Nature, wildlife, landscape, instruction.
Facilities: Motels, lodges, cabins, and cottages are used. Lectures, demonstrations, and slide reviews are part of the daily instruction at most workshops and are held in meeting and conference rooms.
Faculty: Helen Longest-Slaughter has been photographing and writing about nature for 30 years. Her work has appeared in such photographic journals as *Popular Photography, Petersen's Photographic, Outdoor Photographer*, and *Wildlife Photography*.
Expenses: Airfare to and from the workshop location is not included. Film and processing are also not included.

NATURE PHOTOGRAPHY FIELD WORKSHOPS W
The Northwoods Lake Country, Wisconsin

NATURE PHOTOGRAPHY FIELD WORKSHOPS
2210 Branch Street
Middleton, Wisconsin 53562
608-831-2852
Contact: Jim Young

Nature Photography Field Workshops are weekend sessions conducted entirely outdoors during the spring, summer, and fall seasons. Kept to a maximum of 10 participants, the action-packed weekends often offer up to 8 shooting sessions if the weather is cooperating. Although some weekends are more geared to advanced photographers, most are considered general photography with concentration in different areas such as bird or foliage photography.
Specialties: Wildflowers, macro, birds, scenic.
Location: Workshops are held in the heart of the Wisconsin northwoods lake country about 20 miles north of Eagle River, Wisconsin.
Facilities: Accommodations are arranged individually by participants who are offered information on the local lodgings and restaurants.
Faculty: Jim Young is a professional nature photographer with over thirteen years experience. His work has appeared on the covers of Audubon, National Wildlife, and Wisconsin Trails. Young has taught at U of M Extension, Deerfield at Stonington, and Rhinelander.
Expenses: Weekend workshops fees cover instruction only.

NATURE PHOTOGRAPHY WORKSHOPS W
Pocono Mountains

P.E.E.C.
RD 2, Box 1010
Dingmans Ferry, Pennsylvania
717-828-2319
Contact: Admissions

The Nature Photography Workshops at the Pocono Environmental Education Center are held year-round and feature such well-known nature and wildlife instructors as Joe McDonald and Leonard Lee Rue III.
Specialties: Wildlife, basics, macro.
Location: P.E.E.C. is located 20 miles south of where New York, New Jersey, and Pennsylvania meet and within the boundaries of the Delaware Water Gap National Recreation Area.
Facilities: Rustic cabins with hot and cold running water.
Expenses: Most expenses are covered and workshop fees include accommodations and meals.

NATURE PHOTOGRAPHY WITH ED & LEE MASON W
St. Louis, Missouri

NATURE PHOTOGRAPHY WITH ED & LEE MASON
8410 Madeline Drive
St. Louis, Missouri 63114
314-427-6311
Contact: Ed or Lee Mason

Ed and Lee Mason have actively taught photography for over twenty years and have conducted nature workshops for fifteen. Currently they are conducting nature photography workshops at the Missouri Botanical Garden in St. Louis. Participants, limited to 25, can expect personalized instruction in both a classroom setting and in the field. The course is designed for both beginning and experienced photographers using 35mm cameras.
Specialties: Nature.
Faculty: The Masons have conducted photography workshops for the St. Louis Audubon Society, St. Louis Zoo, and the Shaw Arboretum. Their work has appeared in many regional newspapers and magazines.
Expenses: Workshop fee covers instruction only.

NEVERSINK PHOTO WORKSHOP **W**
Catskill Mountains, New York

NEVERSINK PHOTO WORKSHOP
P.O. Box 641
Woodbourne, New York 12788
914-434-0575 *Fax:* 212-929-2689
Contact: Louis Jawitz

The Image Bank's Lou Jawitz teaches weekend nature and scenic workshops in the Catskill Mountains every August. Intended for intermediate and advanced students (6 to 10 per workshop), the workshop is designed to enhance technique while expanding the participant's visual horizons. October foliage weekends are sometimes offered.
Specialties: Scenic, nature.
Location: Woodbourne, New York lies near the southern ranges of the Catskill Mountains in the heart of the resort area, about two hours north of New York City. The actual instruction is given in a restored 19th century barn on the Neversink River banks.
Facilities: The workshop fee includes accommodation in nearby bed and breakfasts and includes Saturday and Sunday lunch.
Faculty: Louis Jawitz has been a professional photographer for twenty years. His work has been shown in a one-man show at the Nikon House in New York City and he has been featured in *Popular Photography*.
Expenses: Addtional expenses are film and dinner.

NEW ENGLAND PHOTOGRAPHIC WORKSHOP, INC. **W**
New Milford, Connecticut

NEW ENGLAND PHOTOGRAPHIC WORKSHOP, INC.
30 Bridge Street
New Milford, Connecticut 06776
203-355-8578
Contact: Jo Brenzo

The New England Photographic Workshop offers year-round workshops for beginners to professionals featuring small groups and visiting instructors. Sessions with visiting professionals are generally 2 and 3 day workshops. Week-long travel workshops to a variety of destinations are also offered. In 1990 NEPH hosted a marketing seminar by Ron Engh, "Large Format Photography" with Ron Wisner, and "Handcoloring B&W Photographs" with Jill Enfield.
Specialties: Instruction, wedding, portraiture, darkroom, large format, and lighting.
Location: New Milford, Connecticut is located about 75 miles north of New York City. Workshops are held on the premises.
Facilities: Food and lodging are not included. Small, quaint inns with modest prices are within walking distance of the workshop location.
Faculty: The director is Jo Brenzo who supervises a year-round staff of 5 instructors.
Expenses: Workshop fee covers instruction only. Lab fees cover film and related expenses.

NORTH RIM - GRAND CANYON TOUR **T**
Grand Canyon, Arizona

SOUTHWEST SCENIC PHOTO
5387 N. Paseo Terraza
Tucson, Arizona 85715
602-577-6453
Contact: Joe Carder

Scenic photographer Joe Carder takes groups to the Grand Canyon's less tourist populated north rim twice yearly. These spring and fall photo tours to the "quiet side" of the natural wonder also include stops at Flagstaff's colorful monuments "Montezuma's Castle," "Tuzigoot," and "Sunset Crater." The photo tours are limited to 12 travelers and are generally for one week.
Specialties: Nature.

Location: The north rim of the Grand Canyon of the Colorado River is located about 225 miles from Flagstaff.
Facilities: Lodging is in 2-bedroom cabins.

Faculty: Group leader Joe Carder is a professional photographer whose photographic adventures have allowed for a rich diversity of experience. He has been Press Secretary for Yellowstone Park and a reporter/photographer for the *Albuquerque Tribune*.
Expenses: Tours generally include lodging and one meal per day.

NORTHEAST PHOTOGRAPHIC WORKSHOP SERIES W

New England

NORTHEAST PHOTOGRAPHIC
WORKSHOP SERIES
302 Astor Court
Delmar, New York 12054
518-439-8347
Contact: Peter Finger, Director

Director Peter Finger has been conducting workshops for over ten years and personally designs each one. Most workshops are 3 to 5 days in length, limited to 10 photographers, and are held during the warmer months. Locations include Martha's Vineyard, Nantucket, Cape Cod, the Maine Coast, the Adirondacks, the Catskills, Prince Edward Island, and Acadia National Park. Finger makes a special effort to provide outstanding scenic locations with detailed instruction.
Specialties: Landscape, nature, instruction.
Location: A variety of northeastern locations.
Facilities: Accommodations include private homes, cottages, resorts, and motels. Individual and group critiques are offered. Overnight processing of E-6 film is available.
Faculty: Peter Finger has over 15 years experience as an educator and environmentalist. His photographs have appeared in *Outdoor and Travel Photography*, *Photographic Magazine*, and *Darkroom Magazine*.
Expenses: Some meals and transportation to the workshop are not included.

NORTHLIGHT PHOTOGRAPHIC WORKSHOPS W

Hudson River Valley & New England

NORTHLIGHT PHOTOGRAPHIC
WORKSHOPS
RD 2, Box 472
Montgomery, New York 12549
914-361-1017
Contact: Brent McCullough

Outdoor photographer Brent McCullough's Northlight Photographic Workshops offer year-round field workshops throughout New York's Hudson Valley, New Jersey, and Pennsylvania. Varying in length from 1/2 day to a full week, the workshops accommodate up to 10 participants and are geared to photographers at all levels of skill. Additional out-

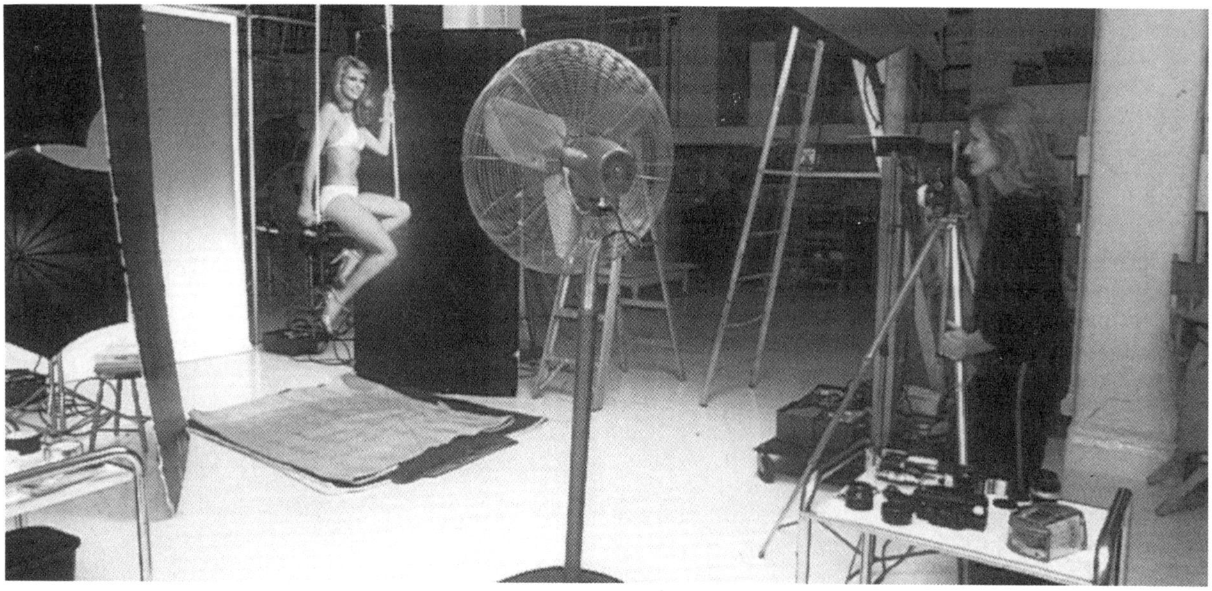

Photograph courtesy of Nancy Brown

Photographer and workshop leader Nancy Brown provides "hands-on" instruction in her Studio Workshops.

door workshops are held at a wide range of locations scheduled to coincide with nature's annual cycles.
Specialties: Architecture, fine art, documentary, photojournalism, outdoor, travel, basics.
Location: Some upcoming locations include: Sanibel Island, Florida; Vermont; Hawaii; Chincoteague, Virginia; Outer Banks, North Carolina; the Shenandoah Valley, Virginia; the Adirondack Mountains; the Maine Coast; and the White Mountains of New Hampshire.
Facilities: Country inns, resorts, and motels are generally used.
Faculty: Brent McCullough's work has appeared in the *Sierra Club* and *Audubon Nature* calendars. He has also taught at Fairleigh Dickinson University.
Expenses: Meals, lodging, and transportation are not included in the workshop fees.

OGUNQUIT PHOTOGRAPHY SCHOOL **W**
Ogunquit, Maine

OGUNQUIT PHOTOGRAPHY SCHOOL
P.O. Box 2234
Ogunquit, Maine 03907
207-646-7055
Contact: Stuart Nudelman

Ogunquit Photography School offers a summer series of intensive, 5 day-workshops that are designed to assist each participant in reaching their next level of expertise and creativity. Workshops, with 8 to 12 members, have included courses such as "Photographing Your Art," "Become A Skilled Child Photographer," and "Selling Your Photographs For Profit." Analysis of works-in-progress, group discussions, and individual assignments are part of each workshop.
Specialties: Technique, marketing, children, portrait.
Location: Ogunquit, Maine is on the Atlantic coast about 70 miles north of Boston. The area offers beaches, dunes, rocky coastline, and Perkins Cover for boat recreation.
Facilities: Hotels, motels, and camping facilities are available although not included in the workshop fee. With the exception of informal breakfast discussions with the faculty members, meals also are not included.
Faculty: The faculty includes recognized authorities in their fields of expertise such as Erika Stone, Norman Rothschild, and Joe Budne. The director, Stuart Nudelman, is also an instructor of photography at the University of Southern Maine.
Expenses: The workshop fee covers classroom instruction and fieldwork only.

OLYMPIC FIELD SEMINARS **W**
Port Angeles, Washington

OLYMPIC PARK INSTITUTE
HC 62 Box 9T
Port Angeles, Washington 98362
206-928-3720 *Fax:* 206-928-3046
Contact: Executive or Program Director

The Olympic Field Seminars have been held for seven years at the Olympic Park Institute's campus. Photography and art workshops are generally held during the summer and early autumn and make good use of the "natural classrooms" Olympic National Park offers. High alpine meadows, coastal tidewaters, and the Hoh Rain Forest provide ample opportunity for nature and wildlife photography practice. Workshops are limited to 12 members.
Specialties: Wildlife and nature.
Location: Using the city of Port Angeles as the point of entry, Olympic National Park is located about 90 miles west of Seattle.
Facilities: Participants are housed dormitory-style in the historic Rosemary Inn on Lake Crescent. Home-cooked meals are available.
Faculty: In recent seasons faculty members have included photographer Gary Braasch, author of *Secrets*

of the Old Growth Forest; Ross Hamilton, a twenty year veteran of the Olympic Peninsula; and award-winning photographic artist Jan Kepley.
Expenses: Equipment and photographic supplies are not covered by the basic tuition fees.

ON ASSIGNMENT PHOTO TOURS T

Asia, Europe, The Pacific Rim

ON ASSIGNMENT PHOTO TOURS
1380 Morningside Way
Venice, California 90291
213-392-6537 *Fax:* 213-396-4307
Contact: Albert Moldvay or Erika Fabian

On Assignment Photo Tours are personalized, custom tours conducted by former *National Geographic* photographer Albert Moldvay and author Erika Fabian. Their destinations include off-the-tourist-beat sites in Czechoslovakia, Hungary, Indonesia, Nepal, and the Pacific Rim and accommodate up to 20 travelers. Contact directly for up-coming photo tour schedules.
Specialties: Wildlife, photojournalism, travel.
Facilities: Accommodations used are top of the line. All instruction is in the field.
Faculty: Moldvay and Fabian are co-authors of an 8 city photo guidebook series, *Photographing London* (Paris, Rome, etc.). They also teach "Photographing The National Geographic Way" throughout the University of California Extensions.
Expenses: Tours are all inclusive.

OREGON PHOTO TOURS T

Oregon and The Pacific Northwest

OREGON PHOTO TOURS
745 East 8th
Coquille, Oregon 97423
503-396-5792
Contact: Tony Mason

Oregon Photo Tours offer a wide variety of little known Oregon destinations throughout the year. Designed for smallish groups of 5 or less at any skill level, the 5 to 8 day workshops allow for personalized instruction at a leisurely pace. Most workshops involve full day outdoor shoots and excursions with evenings devoted to slide presentations and critiques. Some tours offered include: "Snow in the Canyons," "Sand & Sandstone," and "Columbia River Gorge."
Specialties: Color landscape, close-up, nature, wildlife.
Location: All areas of the state of Oregon are covered.
Facilities: Motel accommodations are utilized. Workshops attendees travel by Ford Aerostar wagon.
Faculty: A native of southern Oregon, photographer Tony Mason has designed all the Oregon Photo Tours. He also teaches photography at Southwestern Oregon Community College.
Expenses: Meals and film are not included in the tour costs.

OSPREY PHOTO WORKSHOPS & TOURS WT

Argentina, West Virginia, The Galapagos

OSPREY PHOTO WORKSHOPS AND TOURS
2719 Berwick Avenue
Baltimore, Maryland 21234
301-426-5071
Contact: Irene Sacilotto

Instructor/photographer Irene Sacilotto has conducted workshops for nature centers, colleges, zoos, and wildlife conservation organizations since 1979. Throughout the year she hosts day-long and weekend nature and wildlife workshops in Canaan Valley, West Virginia and the Chesapeake Bay area near her Baltimore base. Several two and three-week photo tours are offered each year, most recently to Argentina including Patagonia, and the Galapagos Islands.
Specialties: Wildlife and nature.
Location: Various. Canaan Valley, West Virginia is about 200 miles west of Baltimore or Washington, D.C. in the central Appalachian Mountains. Battle Creek Cypress Swamp is 40 miles south of D.C. in Maryland and Kent Narrows is about 30 miles east of Baltimore.
Facilities: Accommodations are available in Canaan Valley State Park for weekend workshops. The Galapagos trip is on a chartered yacht sleeping 12 passengers. Argentina tour accommodations vary depending on location, from hotels to remote spartan ranches.
Faculty: Irene Hinke Sacilotto's wildlife photography has been used by the *Sierra Club*, *National Geographic*, and *Outdoor Photographer* and she has had exhibitions in numerous natural history museums, including the Smithsonian.
Expenses: Tour prices generally include roundtrip airfare from the tour departure city, most meals and accommodations, taxes, guide services, and instruction. Weekend workshop prices include accommodations, lectures, and field instruction.

OUTBACK PHOTO TOURS AND WORKSHOPS T

Florida & various European locations

OUTBACK PHOTOTOURS & WORKSHOPS
P.O. Box 8792
St. Petersburg, Florida 33738
813-397-3013
Contact: Bob Grytten

Outdoor photographer/writer Bob Grytten offers monthly weekend nature workshops in the St. Petersburg area from November to May and photo-tours taking in France and Italy in October. Workshops and tours are planned to accommodate 15 participants. Weekend nature sessions include field photo shoots, classroom instruction, and optional night shoots. Photo-tours travel through the French and Italian Mediterranean and Alps leisurely via private coach.

Specialties: Nature, scenic, landscape, travel.

Location: Some weekend nature workshops are held at the KOA Kampground on the shores of Long Bayou near St. Petersburg. The France-Italy photo-tour departs from Tampa and commences in Nice, France. Travel continues to Eze, Sospel, Genoa, Portofino, and Boreon.

Facilities: Lodging and meals are not included in the weekend nature workshops. A variety of accommodations, including camping, are available. The photo-tour includes deluxe lodgings and all meals.

Faculty: Bob Grytten's nature studies have been widely exhibited and have appeared in *Sailing Magazine*, *Triathlete Magazine*, and *The Florida Naturalist Magazine*, among many others.

Expenses: Photo-tours are all inclusive from the departure city except for tips and personal expenses. Meals and lodging are not included in the nature weekend workshps.

OUTDOOR PHOTOGRAPHY W

Blue Rock, Ohio

MCNUTT FARM 11/OUTDOORSMAN LODGE
6120 Cutler Lake Road
Blue Rock, Ohio 43720
614-674-4555
Contact: Patty L. McNutt

Outdoor writer-photographer Patty L. McNutt specializes in animal and outdoor photography. The small classes are offered throughout the year and both field and indoor instruction are available.

OUTER BANKS WORKSHOP W

Hatterass, North Carolina

OUTER BANKS WORKSHOP
Photo Dept., Virginia Intermont College
Bristol, Virginia 24201
703-669-6101
Contact: Jay Phyfer

The Outer Banks Workshop is offered for two weeks each May to 8 participants. Emphasis is placed on color slide photography, b/w processing, and large format photography.

Specialties: Landscape, instruction, large format.

Location: Hatterass, North Carolina is located on the Cape Hatteras National Seashore, an island peninsula about 175 miles from Raleigh.

Facilities: Accommodations are in a beach house.

Faculty: Instructors Jay Phyfer, John Scarlatta, and Joe Champagne are all on the staff of Virginia Intermont College.

Expenses: Housing and material fees are separate from tuition which offers the possibility of college credit at a special rate.

OZARK PHOTOGRAPHY WORKSHOP/FIELDTRIP W

The Ozarks and the Arkansas Delta

OZARK PHOTOGRAPHY WORKSHOP/FIELDTRIP
40 Kyle Street
Batesville, Arkansas 72501
501-793-4552
Contact: Barney Sellers

Barney Sellers, retired staff-photographer for Memphis' *Commercial Appeal*, escorts outdoor photographers and wilderness lovers on 2-day trips twice annually in October, and by appointment. Mr. Sellers instructs on the principles of composition and the use of light. He also provides help with exposure, depth of field, and focusing. Groups are generally limited to 12 members who spend the two days traveling and photographing the backroads of Arkansas.

Specialties: Outdoor, landscape, nature.

Facilities: Hotels and motels are used for overnight trips.

Faculty: Before retirement, Barney Sellers worked as a staff-photographer for the *Memphis Commercial Appeal* and has been photographing the Arkansas countryside for more than 40 years.

Expenses: Workshop fee does not cover hotels and meals.

PALO ALTO PHOTOGRAPHIC WORKSHOPS W

Palo Alto, California

PALO ALTO PHOTOGRAPHIC WORKSHOPS
854 Rorke Way
Palo Alto, California 94303
415-424-0105
Contact: Douglas Peck or Stacy Geiken

Doug Peck and Stacy Geiken offer one-day hands-on workshops on beginning photography, nature photography, and introduction to the view camera, in spring and fall. The workshops, which provide both technical and creative instruction, kick-off with morning slide and equipment demonstrations and then head outdoors for hands-on practice. Restricted to groups of 10 per instructor.
Specialties: Basics, lighting, night photography, landscape, wildlife.
Location: Palo Alto is located on California's Pacific Coast between San Francisco and San Jose.
Faculty: Doug Peck and Stacey Geiken have taught photography since the late 1970's. Both have served on the faculty of Brooks Institute of Photography.
Expenses: Workshop fees include instruction only.

PARSONS SCHOOL OF DESIGN/SPECIAL PROGRAM W

Paris, France and West Africa

PARSONS - SPECIAL PROGRAMS
66 Fifth Avenue
New York, New York 10011
212-741-8975
Contact: Francine Goldenhar, Director

Parsons School of Design offers two special photography programs each summer in Paris and the Ivory Coast of West Africa. These month-long workshops can accommodate 50 in Paris and 15 on the African photo study-trip. The French program provides lectures, discussions, field-trips, and darkroom instruction in the Parsons Paris facility. The African visit explores two separate regions and focuses on the visual traditions and cultural practices of various ethnic groups.
Specialties: Instruction, documentary, darkroom.
Location: The Parsons Paris facility is located in the 15th arrondisement on the left bank and the workshop visits various locations in Paris. The West Africa trip takes in such Ivory Coast locations as Abidjan, Bouake, and Korhogo and other traditional villages.
Facilities: In Paris dorms or 3-star hotels are used. In Africa only hotels are available. Parsons in Paris has a fully equipped darkroom. Processing and printing are completed upon return for the African tour.
Faculty: Benedict Fernandez, Chairman of Photography at Parsons and the New School runs the Paris workshop. Phyllis Galembo, Associate Professor of Fine Arts at SUNY in Albany heads the African program.
Expenses: Meals, supplies, and daily expenses are not included in the workshop fees.

PETERS VALLEY CRAFTSMEN W

Northwestern New Jersey

PETERS VALLEY CRAFTSMEN
Route 615
Layton, New Jersey 07851
201-948-5200
Contact: Jeannie Eberhardt, Executive Director

Peters Valley Craftsmen, a non-profit craft education center located in the Delaware River Gap area, celebrated its twentieth anniversary in 1990. The center, which also offers workshops in ceramics, blacksmithing, textiles, and wood, invites professionals to teach summer sessions appropriate for both beginners and advanced photography students. A program of approximately 15 different workshops is offered throughout the summer, and classes are limited to 8 to 12.
Specialties: Basics, platinum printing, portraiture, black & white, fine art, large format, landscape.
Location: Peters Valley is located west of New York City about an hour and a half by car, and northwest of Philadelpia, two and a half hours by car.
Facilities: Housing is available in several historic homes in the area. Limited kitchen facilities are available as are daily meal tickets for dining in a locally appointed country inn. Photography facilities include a full studio, and printing and darkroom space.
Faculty: The faculty varies from year to year but always includes known photography professionals.
Expenses: Lodging, transportation, and E-6 processing are not included in the basic workshop fee.

PHOTO ADVENTURE TOURS T

Russia, India, China, the Southwest

PHOTO ADVENTURE TOURS
2035 Park Street
Atlantic Beach, New York 11509
516-371-0067 *Fax:* 516-371-1352
Contact: Pamela Makaea

Photo Adventure Tours host 2-week excursions for amateurs and professionals offering a leisurely pace

and informal instruction. All the tours, which are limited to 20 participants, are accompanied by experienced photo guides/tour escorts.
Location: Current locations include Russia, Hawaii, India, Iceland, and a variety of southwestern sites.
Facilities: Depending on the tour, accommodations are generally hotels or camping.
Expenses: Departure taxes and some meals are not included in the tour fee.

PHOTO ADVENTURES W

San Francisco & Northern California

PHOTO ADVENTURES
90 Parker Avenue #303
San Francisco, California 94118
415-221-3171
Contact: Jo-Ann Ordano

Jo-Ann Ordano's Photo Adventures offers a series of weekend and daytrip workshops as well as San Francisco photowalks and night photography workshops. The workshops are held throughout the months of April to December. These programs are designed to help beginning and advanced photographers sharpen their photography skills. The workshops emphasize creative and documentary photography with a concern for the environment.
Specialties: Wildflower, night, and documentary.
Location: Weekend locations have included Yosemite, Reno, Virginia City, the Sierra Mountains, Bear Valley and Sonoma County. San Francisco photo walks have included Chinatown, the Presidio, and the Mission District.
Facilities: Participants make their own arrangements for accommodations, meals, and transportation. Instructional slide programs and demonstrations are offered.
Faculty: Jo-Ann Ordano is a photography instructor for the National Park Service at the Marin Headlands Visitor Center of the Golden Gate National Recreation Area and has recently exhibited her work at the California Academy of Sciences.
Expenses: Meals, lodging, and transportation are not included in the workshop fee.

PHOTO ADVENTURES - KENYA T

PHOTO ADVENTURES - KENYA
8 West 13th Street
New York, New York 10011
212-691-7466 *Fax:* 212-691-7466
Contact: Jason Laure

Photojournalist Jason Laure has visited over 40 African nations and divides his time between his New York City and Nairobi homes. Every summer he leads a two-week photo excursion to Kenya designed to follow the animals' schedule and to provide photographers with unsurpassed photo opportunities along the way. A special feature is a visit to a Masai tribal village which includes a rare opportunity to photograph traditional ceremonies, dancing, and village life.

Specialties: Photojournalism, nature, wildlife, travel.
Location: The Kenya Photo Adventure departs from Nairobi and continues to the Great Rift Valley, Lake Nakuru, Lake Baringo, Samburu Reserve, and the White Highlands. The tour ends in Nairobi and visits the home of Karen Blixen in the city's suburbs.
Facilities: Hotels, lodges, and tented camps are the accommodations available on the photo adventure.
Faculty: Jason Laure has traveled East Africa since 1971 and is the author of several books on Africa.

PHOTO CANOE TRIPS W

Quetico Provincial Park, Ontario, Canada

PHOTO CANOE TRIPS
18 Birch Road or Box 593
Atikokan, Ontario P0T 1C0, Canada
807-597-2621
Contact: John Stradiotto

Photo Canoe Trips depart every Monday morning and return each Friday afternoon from mid-May through September. Designed by outdoor-photographer John Straditiotto and environmentalist Martha Morris to provide personalized attention at a relaxed pace, the photo canoe trips do not require experience in canoeing. Limited to groups of 9, these tours offer a multiple of nature photography opportunities. The guides have conducted over 60 of these trips since 1975.

Specialties: Nature and outdoor photography.
Location: Quetico Provincial Park is a vast wilderness park located about 150 miles north of Duluth, Minnesota and 100 miles west of Thunder Bay.
Facilities: Tents or island cottages are available. Meals are prepared by the guides.
Faculty: John Stradiotto is an out-door photographer and author of *The Road to Canada's Wilds* and *Discovering Ontario's Parks.*
Expenses: The workshop fee covers all expenses except for film.

PHOTO FOCUS W

Coupeville, Washington

COUPEVILLE ARTS CENTER
P.O. Box 171
Coupeville, Washington 98239
206-678-3396
Contact: Judy Lynn

Situated between Seattle and Victoria, Canada, on Whidbey Island, the Coupeville Arts center offers 3 to 5 day workshops each spring in color photography, b/w, portrait, stock, picture-editing, and hand-coloring photographs.

Specialties: Technique, portrait, stock.
Location: Photo Focus in held in various locations on Whidbey Island.
Facilities: Numerous motels, bed and breakfasts, and camping facilities exist on the island. Instruction and lectures are often outdoors. There are no darkroom facilities although E-6 processing is used for some workshops.
Faculty: Bruce Barnbaum, Jay Dusard, David Hiser, and nationally known photographers.

PHOTO TOUR OF BARRANCA DEL COBRE T

Copper Canyon, Mexico

PHOTO TOUR OF BARRANCA DEL COBRE
1612 Charolais Way
Nogales, Arizona 85625
602-287-8770
Contact: Edward M. Biebel, Jr.

Photo Tours of Barranca Del Cobre & Basaseachic Falls are hosted by professional photographer Edward Biebel several times annually. The one week tours, for up to 20, travel from Nogales on the Mexican border to Los Mochis, Mexico to photograph the wonders of Copper Canyon and then journey on to Basaseachic Falls, the highest in North America. The tour also includes stops at Pacquime Ruins and Colonia Juarez.

Specialties: Landscape, nature, travel.
Facilities: Hotels and cabins are used on the tour. Most meals are included.
Expenses: Tours include most expenses except for some meals.

PHOTO TOUR OF BLANCHARD SPRINGS CAVERNS T
Ozark National Forest, Arkansas

PHOTO TOUR OF BLANCHARD SPRINGS CAVERNS
U.S. Forest Service, Box 1279
Mountain View, Arkansas 72560
501-757-2211
Contact: Pat Momich

This unique photo opportunity is offered twice yearly in March and December on a first-come, first-served basis and is limited to 10 photographers. Blanchard Springs Caverns is a spectacular, beautifully decorated limestone cave in the Ozark National Forest. The four hour tour is conducted by an experienced cave interpreter. There is a film and exhibition which precedes the tour.

Location: Blanchard Springs Caverns is located 15 miles northwest of the small town of Mountain View in the Ozark National Forest which is about 120 miles north of Little Rock.

PHOTOGRAPHER'S SAFARI T
Botswana, Kenya, Tanzania, & Zaire

THE PHOTOGRAPHER'S SAFARI
30 W. Mission #4
Santa Barbara, California 93101
805-563-0919
Contact: David Anderson

David Anderson's The Photographer's Safari specializes in the design and planning of photographic safaris to Africa. Restricted to 5 participants, the tours utilize professional safari guides, and overnight in lodges and tented camps. The tours are all inclusive.

PHOTOGRAPHIC ARTS WORKSHOPS W
Pacific Northwest, Montana, Texas

PHOTOGRAPHIC ARTS WORKSHOPS
P.O. Box 1791
Granite Falls, Washington 98252
206-691-4105
Contact: Bruce Barnbaum

Acclaimed landscape and architecture photographer Bruce Barnbaum is the director of the Photographic Arts Workshops. The workshop programs offered concentrate on photography as fine art and include sessions on landscape, portrait, architecture, and other subjects. The workshops are generally week-long and weekend events which are limited to small groups to insure personalized instruction.

Specialties: Landscape, darkroom, view camera, large format, pin-hole, portraiture, B & W.

Location: Workshops are held at various locations including the Pacific Northwest, the Canadian Rockies, Calgary, Texas, Montana, Utah, and the South Georgia Barrier Islands.

Facilities: Accommodations are not included in the workshop fees although housing information is supplied. Lodges, motels, and cabins are some of the options available. Facilities vary according to workshop. Many of the workshops combine darkroom with field work.

Faculty: Director/instructor Bruce Barnbaum is the recipient of the Sierra Club's prestigious Ansel Adams Award for Photography and Conservation. He is also the author of *Visual Symphony*. Other instructors include Jay Dusard, Martha Casanave, and Tom Carabasi.

Expenses: Accommodations, food, and transportation fees are not included.

PHOTOGRAPHIC CENTER - MONTEREY PENINSULA W
Carmel, California

PHOTOGRAPHIC CENTER - MONTEREY PENINSULA
Box 1100
Carmel, California 93921
408-625-5181 *Fax:* 408-624-5126
Contact: Roger Fremier or Gail Pierce

The Photographic Center of Monterey Peninsula was founded in 1983 with the desire to preserve the photographic tradition of the peninsula via on-going educational workshops and exhibition of photographic art in the Center Gallery. Fully living up to the original concept, the workshops offered at the center are among the most diverse anywhere. A variety of 1-day lecture/demonstration seminars, 3-day "hands-on" workshops, and 2-week photo tours are available year-round.

Specialties: Instruction, b/w, marketing, landscape, scenic, photo-painting, portraiture, printing.

Location: Carmel is located outside the city of Monterey about 100 miles south of San Francisco on the Pacific Coast.

Facilities: Accommodations and meals are included in some of the longer workshops. Photo tours are generally inclusive.

Faculty: The center's workshops are taught by well-known professional photographers such as Henry Gilpin, Brad Cole, Cole Weston, Martha Casanave and others.

Expenses: Expenses are variable depending on workshop.

PHOTOGRAPHY FIELD WORKSHOP, OREGON COAST W

Portland, Oregon

OREGON SCHOOL OF ARTS AND CRAFTS
8245 S.W. Barnes Road
Portland, Oregon 97225
503-297-5544
Contact: Joe Cantrell

This Photography Field Workshop is a daytrip workshop designed to photograph the outstanding biological and geological features between Cannon Beach and Lincoln City, an eighty mile stretch of Oregon's most scenic coastline. About a two hour drive from Portland, the program is for photographers at an intermediate level and is restricted to 15 participants.

Specialties: Nature photography.
Faculty: Instructor Joe Cantrell will demonstrate photographic techniques with 35mm and 4x5 cameras.
Expenses: Transportation, food, and film are not included in the workshop fee.

PHOTOGRAPHY STUDIES IN FRANCE W

Paris and Arles, France

PHOTOGRAPHY STUDIES IN FRANCE
8, rue Jules Valles
75011 Paris, France
33-1-4009-1858 *Fax:* 33-1-4009-8497
Contact: Deborah Bacon

Photography Studies in France offers courses in fine art photography (darkroom and studio), advertising and fashion photography, and the history of photography in both French and English. Although the courses were originally designed for "Junior Year Abroad" college students, the curriculum has been expanded and offers not only semester programs, but shorter winter and summer sessions for photography students at all levels.

Specialties: Darkroom, advertising, fashion, nudes, fundamentals, portraiture, architecture.
Location: The Paris facility of PSF is located in the Bastille arrondisement. The summer workshop is held annually in Arles, in southern France.
Facilities: PSF assists students in finding housing on a shared basis or with a French family. Costs for accommodations are not included in the fees.
Faculty: English language courses are taught by American professors from universities such as Rhode Island School of Design and the Rochester Institute of Technology. Guest instructors include such well-known names as Patrick Nagatani.
Expenses: Airfare is not included, although special rates may be available through PSF. Tuition covers instruction only.

PHYLLIS REESER PHOTOTOURS T

Europe and Southwestern U.S.

PHYLLIS REESER PHOTOTOURS
166 Rosedale Heights Drive
Toronto, Ontario M4T 1C8 Canada
416-489-4620 *Fax:* 416-363-2248
Contact: Phyllis Reeser

Phyllis Reeser has been conducting phototours since 1972. Designed for a traveling party of from 25 to 32 participants, Ms. Reeser currently is escorting groups twice yearly. Participants travel by motor coach which allows ample time f or leisurely paced photo sessions.

Specialties: Landscape, travel, nature.
Facilities: All accommodations are first class and breakfast and dinner are included.

PORT TOWNSEND PHOTO IMMERSION WORKSHOPS W

Port Townsend, Washington

PORT TOWNSEND PHOTOGRAPHY
IMMERSION WORKSHOP
225 Taylor Street
Port Townsend, Washington 98368
604-469-9804
Contact: Ron Long

The Port Townsend Photography Immersion Workshops are one-week workshops offered annually in July and September. Housed in a large 1900 Victorian home which also serves as the workshop headquarters, the 10 participants will receive daily lectures and assignments. Port Townsend and Fort Worden (the location of the film, *An Officer and A Gentleman*), provide many photographic inspirations including lighthouses, a fishing wharf, and an abundance of seabirds.

Specialties: Landscape, instruction, birds.
Location: Port Townsend is located on the Olympic Peninsula of Washington state.
Faculty: Ron Long specializes in portraiture and scientific photography. Long has been shooting in Port Townsend for 15 years.
Expenses: Accommodations and overnight film processing are not included in the workshop fee.

POWER OF PHOTOGRAPHING WOMEN W
Orlando, Florida

ILLUSIONS STUDIO
1033 E. Montana Street
Orlando, Florida 32803
407-898-0086
Contact: Jim Turner

The Power of Photographing Women For Their Personal Use is an intense 2 1/2 day workshop designed to teach a new way of looking at the business of personal photography. Glamour photographer Jim Turner teaches "beyond the camera" techniques needed to photograph women in glamour, boudoir, and classic nude styles. Marketing techniques, equipment needs, budgets, and business plans are just a few of the topics covered in these sessions offered several times annually.

Specialties: Glamour, boudoir, nudes.
Location: Workshops are held at Illusions Studio in Orlando.
Faculty: Boudoir and glamour photographer Jim Turner is credited with creating the first personal calendar for women to give to "the man in their lives." Turner has conducted workshops for over 10 years.

PROFESSIONAL PHOTOGRAPHERS OF CALIFORNIA W
Santa Barbara, California

WEST COAST SCHOOL/P.P.O.C.
743 Emory Street
Imperial Beach, California 92032
Contact: Allen Roeder

The West Coast School of the Professional Photographers of California sponsors one-week courses at the Brooks Institute in Santa Barbara on wedding, portrait, and commercial photography. Workshops are limited to 25 participants.

Specialties: Portrait, wedding, commercial.
Facilities: Motels are available locally.
Faculty: Professional photographers conduct the workshops.
Expenses: Room, board, film, and processing are not included.

Key: **W** = Workshop
T = Photo-Tour
S = Seminar

PROJECT OCEAN SEARCH W
The Oceans and Seas of the World

PROJECT OCEAN SEARCH
930 W. 21st Street
Norfolk, Virginia 23517
804-627-1144 *Fax:* 804-627-7547
Contact: Sandra Bond

Project Ocean Search is a sea/land field study program which provides expedition like experiences. The two week sessions, generally held in the summer months, accommodate up to 30 participants and take place at various locations. The 1990 sessions were held in the Fiji Islands. Coursework includes daily dives, lectures, camera maintenance, and instruction on underwater photography.

Specialties: Underwater photography.
Facilities: Accommodations are simple, usually in tents or shelters which accommodate participants' sleeping bags.
Faculty: Jean-Michel Cousteau participates in all Project Ocean Search expeditions. The staff also includes marine scientists, Cousteau Society lecturers, trained divers, and Nikon experts.
Expenses: Air travel costs to departure point and film are not included in the workshop fee.

PURCELL TEAM CAMERA SAFARIS T
Kenya and Tanzania, Africa

PURCELL TEAM CAMERA SAFARIS
5913 Skyline Heights Court
Alexandria, Virginia 22311
703-845-1104 *Fax:* 703-845-1103
Contact: Ann F. Purcell

The Purcell Team is husband and wife Carl and Ann Purcell, professional travel photographers and writers who lead this two-week camera safari every June. The Purcells have conducted these tours for several years and have planned a comprehensive itinerary which takes full advantage of the spectacular photo opportunities in East Africa. From Karen Blixen's home in Nairobi to the Mount Kenya Safari Club founded by William Holden, this is a complete photo safari event.

Specialties: Travel and wildlife photography.
Location: East African locations include Nairobi, Samburu Game Reserve, Mount Kenya, Lake Nakuru, and Masai Mara.
Facilities: Accommodations and meals are considered "luxury" class. Outstanding safari clubs are used and even the tents at Masai Mara come complete with carpets and full bathroom facilities. Frequent slide

presentations and talks are moderated by the Purcells.

Faculty: The Purcells are travel journalists/photographers who have traveled over four million miles to 89 countries and have led photo tours to Tibet, Egypt, and Norway among other places. They have conducted tours to East Africa for more than 10 years.

Expenses: Price includes roundtrip flights from Washington, D.C. via London to Nairobi, all accommodations and meals in Africa, travel by mini-bus, guide and driver tips and fees, and flights within Africa. London meals and personal incidentals not included.

REAGAN STUDIO PHOTO NUDE WORKSHOPS — W

San Francisco, California

REAGAN STUDIO
2565 Third Street, #219
San Francisco, California 94107
415-821-5747
Contact: Jim or Dale Reagan

Reagan Studio moderates a series of day-long nude workshops on location and in studio from May to October.

Specialties: Nude photography.

Location: The Reagan studio and Richmond, Santa Cruz, Watsonville, and Marin, California.

RIT PHOTOGRAPHY WORKSHOP SERIES — W

Rochester, New York

ROCHESTER INSTITUTE OF TECHNOLOGY
T & E Center, Gannett Bldg, P.O Box 9887
Rochester, New York 14623
716-475-5000
Contact: Seminar Center

Rochester Institute of Technology's Photo Workshop Series will present its eighth annual series from May through August 1991. The 15 workshops, both 2 and 5 days in length, cover a diverse array of photographic topics including advertising illustration, studio photography, and color techniques, among many others. Designed for both amateur and professional photographers, the workshops are taught by RIT instructors and allow access to the institute's facilities.

Specialties: Technical, darkroom, instruction, basics.

Location: Workshops are held in the studios and darkrooms of RIT. Field sessions are also held. Rochester is located about 70 miles east of Buffalo, New York on Lake Ontario and 350 miles north of New York City.

Facilities: RIT will provide accommodation information. The institute has 178 fully equipped darkrooms, 48 studios, and many specialty labs.

Faculty: Instructors are professional photographers who are on staff at RIT's internationally acclaimed School of Photographic Arts & Sciences.

Expenses: Workshop expenses are variable depending on the type of workshop.

ROBERT FIELDS PHOTOGRAPHIC WORKSHOPS — W

Various locations throughout California

ROBERT FIELDS PHOTOGRAPHIC WORKSHOPS
P.O. Box 3516
Ventura, California 93006
805-985-2840
Contact: Robert Fields

Robert Fields has been conducting workshops for over 6 years. Most of Fields' workshops are 3 days in length with a maximum of 8 participants plus an assistant. The location workshops offer a combination of lectures, slide reviews, and field instruction covering such topics as composition, lighting, film, technique, and filters. Workshop locations include San Francisco, Death Valley, Anza Borrego Desert, Yosemite and British Columbia, Canada.

Specialties: Landscape, macro, flower, night photography, architecture, instruction, technique.

Facilities: Most workshops include hotel or lodge accommodations.

Faculty: Instructor Robert Fields has over 11 years of photographic experience.

Expenses: Workshops do not include meals and transportation.

ROCKY MOUNTAIN SCHOOL OF PHOTOGRAPHY — W

Missoula, Montana

SOUTHEASTERN CENTER FOR THE ARTS
1935 Cliff Valley Way
Atlanta, Georgia 30329
800-874-3686 *Fax:* 404-633-1990
Contact: Jennifer Allen

The Rocky Mountain School of Photography, in cooperation with Atlanta's Southeastern Center for the Arts, conducts an intensive 9-week professional career program each summer. Classroom and field instruction are offered by a nationally recognized faculty of photographers which has featured Galen Rowell, Dennis Darling, and Cole Weston in past sessions. The Southeastern Center also conducts year-

round workshops in scenic locations and featuring master photographers.
Specialties: Nature, scenic, landscape, instruction, close-up, zone system, large-format, documentary, winter photography.
Location: The Summer intensive program is held in Missoula, Montana in the Rockies. Week-long workshop locations include New Mexico, Vermont, and Minnesota.
Facilities: Accommodations are not included in most workshops and the summer program. A recommended hotel list is available. Facilities are variable depending on location.
Expenses: Tuition fees cover instruction only.

RON ROSENSTOCK PHOTOGRAPHIC IRELAND T
Ireland

RON ROSENSTOCK PHOTOGRAPHIC EXCURSIONS
P.O. Box 915
Ithaca, New York 14851
800-633-0299 *Fax:* 607-257-3699
Contact: Mary Lee

Nature photographer Ron Rosenstock has led more than 100 groups on photographic and cultural excursions to Ireland's west country over the last 15 years. The two week tours, which are based in County Mayo, are offered almost monthly from March through October, and accommodate 11 participants. The workshops are created for photographers at all levels of accomplishment. Daily field trips to the surrounding towns and countryside are complimented by discussion sessions.
Specialties: Nature, landscape, instruction.
Facilities: Meals and accommodations are in Rosenstock's own Hillcrest House which is on the registery of the Irish Tourist Board. Breakfasts and dinners are included. Polaroid slide processing is available.
Faculty: Ron Rosenstock is a former student of Minor White and Paul Caponigro and his work has been exhibited in more than 50 shows in America and Ireland.
Expenses: Tours are all inclusive and based on double occupancy. Personal items and film are not included.

Key: **W** = Workshop
T = Photo-Tour
S = Seminar

RON SANFORD PHOTOGRAPHY WORKSHOPS W
Northern California, Ireland, Alaska

RON SANDFORD PHOTOGRAPHY WORKSHOPS
599 Oregon Street
Gridley, California 95948
916-846-4687
Contact: Ron or Nancy Sanford

Outdoor photographer Ron Sanford offers advanced photographic workshops with instruction in shooting, duping, and marketing. In addition to the workshops held in Sanford's Gridley, California studio, photo tours are planned to Baja, California and Alaska in 1991.
Specialties: Wildlife, nature, travel.
Location: Gridley is about 50 miles north of Sacramento, California.
Facilities: Motels and bed & breakfasts are used.
Faculty: Ron Sanford's wildlife and nature pictures have appeared in *European Travel & Life*, *Popular Photography*, *Newsweek*, *Backpacker*, and *Outdoor Photographer*. He has also been named *Wildlife Photographer of the Year* by the California Fish & Game Commission.

RYDER-WALKER ALPINE ADVENTURES T
The Swiss Alps and Scottish Highlands

RYDER-WALKER ALPINE ADVENTURES
87 Morese Hill Road
Millerton, New York 12546
914-373-7005
Contact: Peter and Karen Walker

Although not created exclusively for photographers, Ryder-Walker Alpine Adventures offers well-designed weeklong Alpine hikes which provide nature and scenic photographers with an abundance of beautiful locations. A variety of hikes, based on experience and capability, such as inn to inn treks across mountain ranges and tours of Mont Blanc are available. No photography instruction is given.
Specialties: Scenic and nature.
Location: Swiss hiking locations include Zermatt, the villages of Saas Fee, Wengen, and Kandersteg, the resort village of Pontresina, and Scuol. The Scottish Highlands tour takes in Skye, the Trossachs, Wester Ross, and Edinburgh.
Facilities: Four-star hotels, Relais du Silences, rustic inns, and castles are the accomodations. Generally breakfast and evening meals are included.
Faculty: Peter Walker has been leading tours in the Alps since 1975.

Expenses: Tour rates include accommodations, full breakfast and dinner, tips and taxes. Swiss Holiday Passes are included for transportation. Airfare, lunches, and personal items are not included.

SAILPLANE/BOB HITCHCOCK T

Sea of Cortez, Mexico

SAILPLANE
1615 N. Wilmot
Tucson, Arizona 85712
602-298-3743
Contact: Bobby Hitchcock

Veteran photographer and studio owner Bob Hitchcock offers photography and sailing instruction in the Sea of Cortez, Mexico, twice yearly in June and October. The week-long sails, to either The Midriff Islands or San Pedro Bay in the Sea of Cortez, on the 25' cruiser are limited to 4 participants. Hiking, snorkeling, and deep-sea fishing are also available.
Specialties: Instruction, wildlife.
Facilities: Participants sleep on the cruiser and sometimes on beaches. The staff includes a 1st mate who cooks some meals. Other meals are taken in local establishments.
Expenses: Airfare is not included in the tour fee.

SAN DIEGO STATE UNIVERSITY EXTENDED STUDIES T

Various West Coast locations

SAN DIEGO STATE UNIVERSITY
EXTENDED STUDIES
5630 Hardy Avenue
San Diego, California 92182
619-594-5152 *Fax:* 619-594-5152
Contact: Patti McGuffin

The San Diego State University College of Extended Studies offers several 3 to 5 day phototour/workshops each spring and autumn to a variety of scenic locations. These workshops, open to all camera enthusiasts, provide both informative instruction sessions and flexible schedules for exploration on one's own. The tours are led by a staff photographer/instructor and can accommodate up to 30 participants. SDSU also presents specialty seminars and courses.
Specialties: Panoramic, night, scenic.
Location: SDSU has offered a variety of west coast locations in recent seasons including: Yosemite, Catalina Island, Bryce Canyon, Zion, and the Grand Canyon. New destinations are added frequently.
Facilities: Accommodations range from cabins to mid-price hotels.
Faculty: Professional freelance photographer Ken Randall leads and instructs the groups. Previously a photojournalist for the U.S. Coast Guard, Randall's

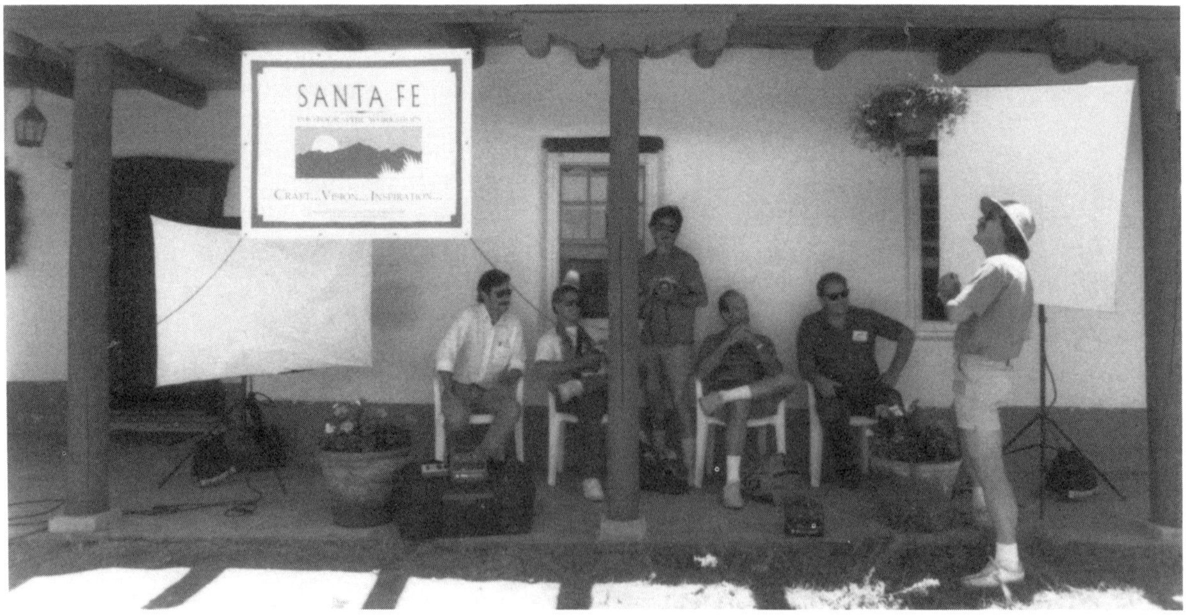

Photograph by Peter L. Gould

Santa Fe Photographic Workshop students take to the shade during one of their daily sessions.

work has appeared in the *San Diego Tribune*, *Oui*, and *Cosmopolitan*.
Expenses: Workshop fee covers accommodations, coach transport, and instruction. Film and food expenses are not covered.

SAN JUAN MAJESTY **W**

The San Juan Mountains, Colorado

GALLERY 412
412 Main Street
Grand Junction, Colorado 81501
303-245-6700
Contact: Steve Traudt

San Juan Majesty is an annual one-week workshop set amid the spectacular San Juan Mountains of southwestern Colorado. The workshop features daily field trips via 4-wheel drive to ghost towns, waterfalls, and wildflower fields. Limited to 12 participants.
Specialties: Wildlife, landscape.
Location: Ouray, Colorado, about 70 miles north of Durango, is the site of the workshop.
Facilities: Standard motels are used. Daily E-6 processing is available.
Faculty: Steve Traubt is a freelance photographer and teaches photography at Mesa State College. He is also the owner of Gallery 412 in Grand Junction.
Expenses: Film and some meals are not included in the workshop fee.

SANTA FE PHOTOGRAPHIC WORKSHOPS **W**

Santa Fe, New Mexico

SANTA FE PHOTOGRAPHIC WORKSHOPS
P.O. Box 9916
Santa Fe, New Mexico 87504
505-983-1400
Contact: Reid Callanan

The Santa Fe Photographic Workshops offer week-long, intensive instruction, geared to professional and serious amateur photographers during the months of June, July, and August. Taught by successful commercial guest photographers Karen Kuehn, Hans Neleman, Neil Selkirk, and Nick Vedros, some workshops require a portfolio review for admission. Basic workshop subjects include: studio, vision, editorial/photojournalism, advertising/corporate, and craft/architecture.
Location: The Conference Center at St. John's College is the home for the Santa Fe Workshops. The 300 acre campus, which overlooks the city, offers housing and dining facilities.

Facilities: On campus housing is available as well as local hotel/motel accommodations. The workshop includes a mandatory meal plan. A fully equipped studio, overnight film processing lab and classrooms are available to workshop members.
Expenses: Each workshop has a lab fee which covers the overnight processing of E-6 color slide film. Tuition fees cover instruction only. Meal and accommodation costs are separate.

SAWTOOTH CENTER FOR VISUAL ARTS W
Winston-Salem, North Carolina

SAWTOOTH CENTER FOR VISUAL ARTS
226 N. Marshall Street
Winston-Salem, North Carolina 27101
919-723-7395
Contact: Merry Winnett, Photo Coordinator

The Sawtooth Center For Visual Arts offers a variety of photography programs from one-day to workshops that meet in the evening for 8 consecutive weeks. Basic to advanced topics are covered including darkroom and 35mm camera techniques.
Specialties: Instruction, technique.
Location: The Sawtooth Center is located in downtown Winston-Salem.

Facilities: Available facilities include a darkroom with 10 enlargers, film-processing, and classrooms. Hotel accommodations are readily available.
Faculty: Professional photographers and IMFA trained fine-arts photographers conduct the workshops.
Expenses: Travel, food, and lodging are not included in the workshop tuitiion.

SAYLOR'S SAFARIS W
USA, Canada, Austria & The Bavarian Alps

SAYLOR'S SAFARIS
27 Dunn Place
Dumont, New Jersey 07628
201-384-7635
Contact: S.B. Saylor

Instructor/leader Sam Saylor hosts year-round weekend and extended photo safaris to a variety of scenic American, Canadian, and European locations. From the peaks of the Bavarian Alps to the bogs of New Jersey cranberry fields, Saylor offers "hands-on" instruction to small groups of 10 maximum.
Specialties: Scenic, instruction, landscape.
Facilities: Motels and guesthouses are utilized. Slide demonstrations are offered when the facilities are available.

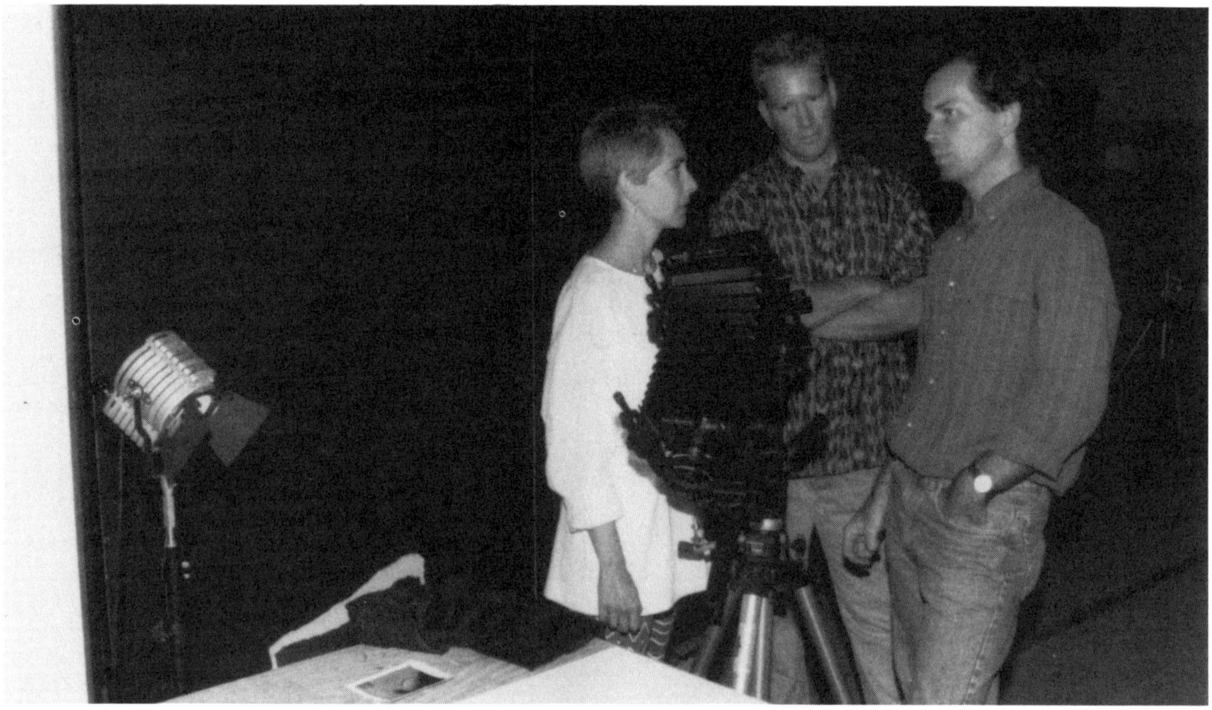

Santa Fe Photographic Workshop director Reid Callanan lends a personal touch to the workshop sessions.

Faculty: Sam Saylor is a professional photographer whose work has graced the cover of *New York Magazine* among other publications.
Expenses: Meals, with the exception of breakfast on the European tours, are not included in the basic workshop fee.

SCHOOL OF THE ARTS AT RHINELANDER W

Madison, Wisconsin

UW - MADISON SCHOOL OF ARTS/ RHINELANDER
727P Lowell Hall, 610 Langdon Street
Madison, Wisconsin 53703
608-263-3494
Contact: Kathy Berigan

The University of Wisconsin sponsors an annual arts workshop week at the Madison School of Arts at Rhinelander in late July. In addition to theatre and drama, dance and visual arts, a selection of photography courses are offered that are appropriate for beginners and advanced students. Basic photography workshops offer a hands-on approach with some field work. The advanced workshops require experience in 35mm and concentrate on a selected subject such as travel, etc.
Specialties: Instruction, basics, nature, travel.
Location: Rhinelander, Wisconsin is located 200 miles north of Madison. The area is a popular summer tourist attraction.
Facilities: A variety of accommodations will be recommended by the school upon inquiry. All classroom instruction is given in a modern junior high school.
Faculty: Photography courses are taught by instructors affiliated with the University as well as professional photographer specialists.
Expenses: The workshop fee covers instruction only. Film and processing are separate expenses.

SEDONA NATURE PHOTOGRAPHY WORKSHOPS W

Sedona, Arizona

SEDONA NATURE PHOTOGRAPHY WORKSHOPS
P.O. Box 1163
Sedona, Arizona 86336
602-282-9433
Contact: Paul Hanthcock

The Sedona Nature Photography Workshops are held twice annually. The spring workshop is usually the first week of May and the autumn workshop the second week of October. Both workshops are conducted by renowned Southwest fine-art photographer Lou DeSerio. The 3-day workshops are limited to 12 participants and include field-trips as well as classroom demonstrations.
Specialties: Fine art, nature, landscape, technical.
Location: Sedona, Arizona is a short drive south of Flagstaff.
Facilities: Workshop fees do not cover accommodations and meals. There are many hotels and restaurants serving visitors to Sedona.

SHARING NATURE PHOTO ADVENTURES W

Yosemite Park, Death Valley, & Zion Park

SHARING NATURE PHOTO ADVENTURES
41618 Tyler Foote Road
Nevada City, California 95959
916-292-3839
Contact: Robert Frutos

Professional photographer Robert Frutos leads nature-loving photographers through some of California's most scenic natural sites 10 times each year. The Sharing Nature experience offers workshops that combine the creative art of nature photography with techniques for viewing nature from a fresh perspective. Most workshops allow for 8 participants.
Specialties: Nature photography & building photographic awareness.
Location: Workshops take place in national parks in California and Nevada. Little known wildlands are also visited.
Facilities: Accommodations are in cabins, lodges, or camp sites, as determined by locale.
Faculty: Robert Frutos is a professional photographer who has been widely published.
Expenses: Workshop fees cover most expenses except for transportation to the workshop site.

SIERRA PHOTOGRAPHIC WORKSHOPS W

Alaska, Utah, Montana, & New Mexico

SIERRA PHOTOGRAPHIC WORKSHOPS
P.O. Box 33
El Portal, California 95318
415-769-0570
Contact: Lewis Kemper and Bill Neill

The Sierra Photographic Workshops, established in 1982, are offered 10 to 12 times annually in a variety of locations conducive to wildlife and landscape photography. The workshops, limited to 10 to 18 participants, provide serious instruction to photographers at any level who are interested in explor-

ing their creative potential. Programs include wildlife photo tours of a week's duration, shorter more specific workshops, and an annual 2-day marketing seminar.
Specialties: Wildlife, scenic, landscape, technique, macro, wildflowers, marketing.
Location: Wildlife photo tours visit Kalispell, Montana; Alaska; Sacramento Valley. Workshops include stays at Death Valley; Merced River Canyon; Moab, Utah; Yosemite; and Acadia, Maine.
Facilities: Accommodations and some meals are included in most workshops. The "outdoor classroom" approach is utilized.
Faculty: Lewis Kemper is the author of *The Yosemite Photographer's Handbook* and *The Yellowstone Photographer's Handbook.* William Neill has lived in Yosemite Park for 12 years and his work has appeared in many travel and photography magazines.
Expenses: Meals are not included in the tuition fee.

SMOKY MOUNTAINS NATURE & WILDLIFE — W

Smoky Mountains National Park, Tennessee

SMOKY MOUNTAINS NATURE
PHOTOGRAPHY WKSP.
205 Wayah Road
Franklin, Tennessee 28734
704-369-6044
Contact: Bill Lea or Tim Black

Photographers Bill Lea and Tim Black have over 20 years experience photographing in the Smokies. Twice each spring the two photographers offer their experience to participants in the Smoky Mountains Wildlife & Nature Photography Workshops. Limited to 18, the weekend workshops emphasize 35mm photography and the use of natural light. Specific topics usually include: how to photograph birds, flowers, mammals; exposure; close-up; composition; and purchasing equipment.
Specialties: Scenics, wildflowers, wildlife.
Location: Townsend, Tennessee in the Smoky Mountains.
Facilities: Accommodations are at the Best Western Valley View Motel in Townsend. The workshop includes slide/lecture instruction as well as field work.
Faculty: The photographic work of Tim Black and William S. Lea has appeared in *Field and Stream, Outdoor America, Mother Earth News, Southern Outdoors,* and *American Forests.*
Expenses: Meals are not included in the workshop fee.

SNAKE RIVER INSTITUTE — W

Jackson Hole & Yellowstone Park, Wyoming

SNAKE RIVER INSTITUTE
P.O. Box 7724
Jackson Hole, Wyoming 83001
307-733-2214
Contact: Michelle Sullivan, Executive Director

The Snake River Institute was established in 1988 to study the connections between nature and the arts and between nature and our lives. As might be expected, nature photography is the thrust of the photographic workshops, but workshops on "Native American Culture & Art," "Anatomy For the Artist," and "The Illustrated Journal" are also offered. Groups are limited in size to 15 maximum and all instruction is given in the field.
Specialties: Nature, scenics, composition, landscape.
Location: Workshops are held in a variety of Wyoming and Utah locations including Moab Desert and Yellowstone Park. Jackson Hole, home of the Snake River Institute, is located near the southern entrance to Yellowstone Park and is surrounded by the Grand Tetons.
Facilities: Weekend photography workshop trips generally include meals and lodging.
Faculty: Local professional photography instructors include Ed Riddell, Jan Stuart, and John Telford.
Expenses: Expenses covered vary according to workshop and location.

SOBEK'S ALSEK & TATSHENSHINI RIVERS — T

The Yukon Territory and Alaska

SOBEK'S ALSEK & TATSHENSHINI RIVERS
P.O. Box 1089
Angels Camp, California 95222
800-777-7939 *Fax:* 209-736-2646
Contact: Tricia Newkirk

Held annually in July and August, Sobek's tours to the Yukon and beyond offer an opportunity to photograph some of the most remote wilderness areas in North America. These camping tours, accompanied by professional photographer/guides, are designed for 8 to 12 participants.
Specialties: Wildlife, nature.
Location: The tours, departing from Haines, Alaska, travel through the Yukon Territory, British Columbia, and Alaska.
Facilities: This tour is strictly camping and on-site field work.
Expenses: Airfare to and from Alaska is not included.

SOCIETY EXPEDITIONS PHOTO TOURS T
Antartica, Amazon, Polynesia, Madagascar

SOCIETY EXPEDITIONS PHOTO TOURS
3131 Elliott Avenue
Seattle, Washington 98121
800-426-7794 *Fax:* 206-285-7917
Contact: John Parker, Director

Society Expeditions are year-round workshops sponsored by Leica and held in some of the world's most remote areas. Each tour has a professional photographer on board the specially designed expedition ships which function as both classroom and accommodation. Shipboard lectures and intensive fieldwork are part of the daily routine. Each tour accomodates 12 to 14 participants per instructor.
Specialties: Antartica, wildlife, nature, landscape.
Location: Destinations include: Antartica, The Amazon River, Polynesia, the U.S. Canyonlands, Indonesia, New Zealand, U.S.S.R., Madagascar, and Africa.
Facilities: Accommodations are on Zodiac vessels, expedition ships with ice-hardened hulls. All outside cabins are available.
Faculty: Photographic instructors have included: Chris Rainier, Wolfgang Kaehler, Robert Millman, Jim Zuckerman, and Boyd Norton.
Expenses: Airfare to the tour destination is not included.

SOUTH FLORIDA PHOTOGRAPHIC WORKSHOPS W
Boca Raton, Florida

SOUTH FLORIDA PHOTOGRAPHIC WORKSHOPS
1900 Corporate Boulevard N.W, Suite 205
Boca Raton, Florida 33431
407-997-9879 *Fax:* 407-994-6947
Contact: Anita C. Starkoff

Anita and Earl Starkoff oversee an action-packed workshop week annually on the campus of The College of Boca Raton during the college's spring break as well as a series of one-day workshops featuring instruction by celebrated photographers. The one-day workshops have featured Ed Slater on "Stock Photography"; Lisl Dennis on "Travel Photography" and "Corporate Photography" with Joe Gemignani. The workshop week offers a variety of 2 and 3-day workshops for all levels.
Specialties: Instruction, fashion, photojournalism, nude, lighting, infrared, large format, underwater, corporate.
Location: The one-day workshops are held at a major local hotel. The longer workshops are held on the College of Boca Raton campus.
Facilities: South Florida Photographic Workshops can provide special discounted hotel rates for participants.
Faculty: All workshops are conducted by professional name photographers.
Expenses: Accommodations and meals are not included. Appropriate lab fees are also additional.

SOUTHAMPTON MASTER PHOTOGRAPHY WORKSHOP W
Long Island, New York

LONG ISLAND UNIVERSITY
Fine Arts Office - Southampton L.I.U.
Southampton, New York 11968
516-283-4000
Contact: Fine Arts Office

The Southampton Master Photography Workshop is held each summer on the campus of Long Island University. The program offers week-long workshops on The Nude, Large Format Photography, Black & White Printing, The Portfolio, The Zone System, and many other subjects. Beginner workshop programs are also available.
Specialties: Instruction.
Location: Southampton, Long Island is situated in the heart of the renowned Hampton's seaside resort. The town is easily reached from New York City via a 2 hour car, train, or bus ride.
Faculty: Yoshi Higa is the director of the workshop. Photography instructors of note have included Ralph Gibson, Gary Schneider, Herman LeRoy Emmet, and Jim Frank.

SOUTHERN ALLEGHENIES PHOTOGRAPHIC WORKSHOP W
Bedford, Pennsylvania

SOUTHERN ALLEGHENIES PHOTOGRAPHIC WORKSHOPS
Box 658
Bedford, Pennsylvania 15522
814-623-2663
Contact: Bob Webb

The Southern Alleghenies Photographic Workshops are offered twice in the autumn and are one-week workshops devoted to landscape and nature photography. Bedford is located in southern Pennsylvania, 100 miles east of Pittsburgh and 200 miles west

of Philadelphia. Participants, limited to 6 per workshop, overnight at the historic Jean Bonnet Tavern built in 1768. Daily field trips are followed by slide critiques and informal photo discussions.
Specialties: Nature, landscape.
Expenses: Film, processing, and travel to the workshop site are not included in the workshop fee.

SOUTHWEST PHOTOGRAPHIC WORKSHOPS W

Texas and New Mexico

S.W.P.W.
P.O. Box 19272
Houston, Texas 77224
713-496-2905
Contact: Jay Forrest or Frank Armstrong

The Southwest Photographic Workshops are field-conducted workshops with emphasis on landscape photography in western Texas and southern New Mexico. Held 3 or 4 times annually, the workshops provide one instructor per 4 students with groups limited to 15. East coasters can contact S.W.P.W. at 13 Dickens Lane, Mt. Laurel, New Jersey 08054, (609) 235-5071.
Specialties: Landscape.
Location: Locations include Big Bend National Park in Texas, White Sands National Monument, Three Rivers, Gila Wilderness, and Cloud Craft in New Mexico.
Facilities: Standard commerical motels/hotels are used.
Faculty: Workshops offer a staff of four instructions: Frank Armstrong, Jay Forrest, A. Rumme, and B. Wright.
Expenses: Workshop fees cover instruction only.

SPLIT ROCK ARTS PROGRAM W

Duluth, Minnesota

SPLIT ROCK ARTS PROGRAM, U OF MN
306 Wesbrook Hall, 77 Pleasant St. SE
Minneapolis, Minnesota 55455
612-624-6800 *Fax:* 612-624-5891
Contact: Phyllis Campbell

The Split Rock Arts Program sponsored by the University of Minnesota each summer holds one-week, intensive nature and documentary workshops. The workshops, which are held on the university's Duluth campus, accommodate up to 16 participants and offer both classroom and field trip instruction by nationally known professionals.
Specialties: Nature and documentary.
Facilities: University housing is available to workshop attendees.
Faculty: Nature photography authors Craig and Nadine Blacklock and Capa Award winner Harry Mattison have instructed workshops at Split Rock in recent years.
Expenses: Room and board are not included.

ST. REGIS CANOE OUTFITTERS T

The Everglades and Adirondack Parks

ST. REGIS CANOE OUTFITTERS
Box 318, Floodwood Road at Long Pond
Lake Clear, New York 12945
518-891-1838
Contact: Dave or Kathy Cilley

St. Regis Canoe Outfitters provides fully outfitted canoeing trips suitable for outdoor and nature photographers determined to navigate difficult waters to get next to those elusive wildlife subjects. January through March a variety of Everglades expeditions through mangrove wildernesses and manatee hideouts are offered. Varying from 4 to 12 nights, the trips include camping and cook-outs. April-October similar options are available for canoeing the Adirondacks.
Specialties: Wildlife, landscape.
Location: The Everglades canoe trips are all held in Everglades National Park. The Adirondack trips are based at Floodwood Pond near Upper Saranac Lake in the Adirondacks.
Facilities: Most trips include tent-camping with a night or two in a lodge or an inn.
Faculty: Professional guides lead the trips which are limited to 8 participants. No photography professionals staff the expeditions.
Expenses: Transportation to the point of departure and photographic expenses are not included.

SUGARBUSH SOARING T

The Green Mountains of Vermont

SUGARBUSH SOARING
Airport Road, P.O. Box 123
Warren, Vermont 05673
802-496-2290
Contact: John Cunningham

Sugarbush Soaring utilizes glider and open biplane flights for aerial photography.
Specialties: Aerial photography.

TOUCHSTONE CENTER FOR CRAFTS W

Pennsylvania

TOUCHSTONE CENTER FOR CRAFTS
P.O. Box 2141
Uniontown, Pennsylvania 15401
800-753-2723
Contact: Marcene Clark, Executive Director

Touchstone Center for Crafts has been conducting workshops at its rustic mountain retreat in western Pennsylvania since 1983. Located sixty miles south of Pittsburgh, the center is also within driving distance of Cleveland, Ohio, Washington, D.C., and Morgantown, W.V. Offering both weekend and week-long workshops, the center teaches over 60 different subjects which change annually. Nature photography for beginning and intermediate levels was offered in summer 1990.

Specialties: Nature.
Facilities: Workshoppers stay in rustic cabins or camp-sites.
Faculty: Changing faculty are all professionals in their fields.

TRAVEL PHOTO WORKSHOP T

Dublin, Edinburgh, London, and Paris

TRAVEL PHOTO WORKSHOP
Saint Mary's College
Notre Dame, Indiana 46556
219-284-4631 *Fax:* 219-284-4716
Contact: Doug Tyler or Dr. Anthony Black

Saint Mary's College in Notre Dame offers a biannual, 4-week tour of Ireland, Scotland, England, and France, with focus on travel documentation. The tour is limited to 30 students and college credit may be earned. Business, history, and humanities courses are also part of the program.

Specialties: Travel photography.
Facilities: Student style accommodations are utilized. Photographers may make use of local labs.
Faculty: A faculty member in each area of expertise escorts the tour.

Key: **W** = Workshop
T = Photo-Tour
S = Seminar

TRAVEL PHOTOGRAPHY WORKSHOP IN SANTA FE W

Santa Fe, New Mexico

TRAVEL PHOTOGRAPHY WORKSHOP IN SANTA FE
P.O. Box 2847
Santa Fe, New Mexico 87501
505-982-4979
Contact: Lisl Dennis

Lisl Dennis, highly regarded travel photographer, offers her award-winning techniques during week-long travel workshops held in Santa Fe in February, April, July, and September. Using her photographs which have been featured in many books and magazines, Dennis will help develop new strategies and will offer on-location demonstrations during a day trip to Santuario de Chimay, an 18th century church and the 500-year-old Taos Indian pueblo.

Specialties: Travel.
Location: The workshop is held at the Inn On The Alameda in Santa Fe.
Faculty: Lisl Dennis is a contributor to several publications including *Popular Photography*, *Outdoor Photographer*, and *Town & Country*. She is also the author of the books *Shooting Portraits On Location* and *The Essential Image*.
Expenses: Workshop price includes: lodging, opening reception, Sunday brunch, farewell dinner, photo day-trip, instruction, and 3 photo critiques.

TRINITY ALPS PHOTOGRAPHY WORKSHOPS W

California, Maine, & Washington

TRINITY ALPS PHOTOGRAPHY WORKSHOPS
216 Marquis Place
Santa Maria, California 93454
805-928-3386
Contact: Mary Ellen Schultz

Trinity Alps Photography Workshops are all inclusive week-long workshops devoted to scenic and nature photography. Suitable for photographers at any level of expertise, participants are led on a variety of daily excursions to scenic locations and return to their first class accommodations at night. Workshops generally number about 15 participants and are offered year-round.

Specialties: Landscape, nature.
Location: Locations include the Olympic Rain Forest in Washington, autumn in Ontario, Maine's Pen-

obscot Bay, and California's remote wilderness area, the Trinity Alps.
Facilities: Meals and first class accommodations in resorts and lodges are included in the workshop fee.
Faculty: Mary Ellen Schultz has shared exhibitions with Ansel Adams and Cartier-Bresson and her work has appeared in Lady Bird Johnson's *Wildflowers Across America.* She is assisted on some tours by Les Line, editor of *Audubon Magazine.*

TWIN FALLS NATURE PHOTOGRAPHY WORKSHOP W

Twin Falls State Park, West Virginia

TWIN FALLS NATURE PHOTOGRAPHY WORKSHOP
Box 1023
Mullens, West Virginia 25882
304-294-4000
Contact: A. Scott Durham

Spring and fall nature photography workshops are held at the Twin Falls Resort State Park in southern West Virginia. Accommodating as many as 30 photographers, the workshops offer a large variety of field locations within the 4,000 acre park. A 1840 Pioneer Farm, waterfalls, and White Horse Knob are a few of the photo sites. Instruction is offered in close-up photography, equipment selection, bird photography, filter use, marketing, and composition.
Specialties: Close-up, birds, scenic, technique, instruction, marketing, composition.
Location: The closest sizable town is Beckley which can be reached via the West Virginia Turnpike. The workshop will provide detailed information on reaching the resort.
Facilities: Lodge rooms and cottages are available for attendees. Lunches are included. Conference facilities are used for lectures and demonstrations.
Faculty: Instructors include Larry West, Bill Thomas, Irene Henke Scallotto, and John Cerach.
Expenses: Travel, film, dinner, and breakfast are not included in the workshop fee.

ULTIMATE IMAGE W

Northeastern Pennsylvania

ULTIMATE IMAGE
P.O. Box 22
Lawton, Pennsylvania 18828
717-934-2226
Contact: Bob Deasy

Award-winning commercial photographer Bob Deasy conducts two-day weekend workshops on "The Art and Soul of Photography," "People and Portrait," and "Still-life and Product Photography" which offer the serious photographer new perspectives on the art and the business of photography. Spring and autumn workshops on landscape and nature photography are also available and feature the wonders of the numerous Pennsylvania mountain ranges.
Specialties: Portrait, commercial, still-life, nature, landscape, instruction.
Location: Ultimate Image workshops operate out of Bob Deasy's Blue Stone facility in Rush Township, Pennsylvania, approximately 45 minutes from Scranton or Binghamton, New York.
Facilities: Accommodations are available at the nearby historic Woodbourne Farm in Montrose, Pennsylvania.
Faculty: Bob Deasy is a commercial photographer who specializes in aerial, product, and people photography.
Expenses: Weekend fees include workshops, tours, and room.

UNIVERSITY OF CALIFORNIA - SANTA CRUZ W

California & various international sites

UNIVERSITY OF CALIFORNIA EXTENSION - SC
740 Front Street, Suite 155
Santa Cruz, California 95060
408-427-6620
Contact: Photography Workshops

The University of California Extension at Santa Cruz offers an on-going series of on-campus and on-location photographic workshops throughout the year. "Understanding the View Camera"; "Computer Imaging for Photographers"; and "A Photographic Workshop in Italy with Cole Weston" are a few examples of the variety of the extensions' offerings. Most workshops average 15-18 participants and are available to photographers at various levels of skill.
Specialties: Instruction, view camera, architecture, portrait, nude, color, landscape.
Location: Some lecture/instruction oriented workshops are held on campus. Many of the workshops are field studies at various California locations. International study tours are offered several times each year.
Facilities: A list of suggested accommodations is offered to workshop participants. Darkrooms are not available.

Faculty: Outstanding instructors have included Morley Baer, Martha Casanave, Ted Orland, and Marie Cosindas.
Expenses: Fees cover instruction only.

UNIVERSITY OF SOUTHERN MAINE W
Gorham, Maine

UNIVERSITY OF SOUTHERN MAINE ART DEPT.
37 College Avenue
Gorham, Maine 04038
207-780-5460
Contact: Rose Marasco

The University of Southern Maine, located in Gorham about 15 miles west of Portland, offers an annual photography workshop devoted to "The Photographic Book". The intensive two-week course balances classroom instruction with several field trips which cover shooting, darkroom work, book sequencing, and production. This unique session, limited to 15, is restricted to full-time B.F.A. students.
Specialties: The photographic book, instruction.
Facilities: Accomodations, both room and board, are available in a dormitory setting.
Faculty: The instructor is Rose Marasco, Assistant Professor of Photography.
Expenses: Accommodations and photo supplies are not included in the workshop fee.

VIRGIN ISLAND PHOTO CRUISE T
The Virgin Islands

VIRGIN ISLAND PHOTO CRUISE
450 Smith Road
Pittsford, New York 14534
716-624-1285
Contact: Robert F. Iannazzi

Robert F. Iannazzi hosts an annual cruise in the U.S. and British Virgin Islands each March. Limited to 14, the hands-on, week-long workshop is for serious amateurs and professional photographers interested in instruction and shooting a t a leisurely pace.
Specialties: Instruction, lighting, scenics.
Facilities: The cruise is on a luxury yacht with a crew of 8 and featuring double staterooms. Daily on-board lectures are given.
Faculty: Robert Iannazzi has over 20 years experience as a professional photographer. He has received the Master of Photography and Photographic Craftsman degrees from the Professional Photographers of America.
Expenses: Airfare to St. Thomas and ferry to Tortola are not included in the cruise fee.

VISIONQUEST PHOTOGRAPHIC ADVENTURES W
Queen Charlotte & Vancouver Islands

VISIONQUEST PHOTOGRAPHY
Box 572
Duncan, British Columbia V9L 3X9, Canada
604-746-4341
Contact: Paul Fletcher

Professional photographer, writer, and naturalist Paul Fletcher hosts weekend and 6-day workshops at Long Beach on Vancouver Island from February through September. These workshops are for photographers at all levels and individual attention is given. He also is the featured photographer on several week-long sailing tours of the Queen Charlotte Islands in August. The groups are small and personalized attention is offered to photographers at all levels of experience.
Specialties: Nature and landscape.
Location: Long Beach workshops are held on the west coast of Vancouver Island not far from the city of Vancouver. The Queen Charlotte Islands are reached by ferry from the city of Prince Rupert which is about 950 miles north of Vancouver.

Facilities: Long Beach accommodations are in ocean front cottages equipped with kitchenettes. Accommodations on the Queen Charlotte Islands cruise are on the Deva sailing ship.
Faculty: Paul Fletcher is a professional nature photographer and writer.
Expenses: Workshop fees cover accommodations and instruction. Transportation to departure points and meals are not included.

VISUAL STUDIES WORKSHOP W

Rochester, New York

VISUAL STUDIES WORKSHOP
31 Prince Street
Rochester, New York 14607
716-442-8676
Contact: James B. Wyman

Rochester's Visual Studies Workshop offers courses in photography, computer-generated imagery, video, film, photographic history and theory. Workshops are limited to 12 attendees.
Location: Visual Studies is centrally located near other cultural institutions such as The International Museum of Photography at George Eastman House and the Memorial Art Gallery.
Expenses: Workshop fees cover instruction only.

VOYAGERS PHOTO TOURS T

Africa, Australia, Belize, The Galapagos

VOYAGERS PHOTO TOURS
P.O. Box 915
Ithaca, New York 14851
607-257-3091 *Fax:* 607-257-3699
Contact: David Blanton

Voyagers Photo Tours are an on-going series of travel and nature photography excursions designed and hosted by professional photographers. Most tours, planned to accommodate from 10 to 15 photographers, are totally inclusive and allow for a well-balanced mix of informal instruction and field shoots.
Specialties: Travel, nature.
Location: Worldwide destinations include: Africa, Australia, Belize, Borneo, China, Costa Rica, Galapagos, India, and Ireland.
Expenses: Personal expenses such as laundry and telephone are not included. All transportation outside the U.S., meals, and lodging are included.

WATERHOUSE PHOTOGRAPHIC TOURS T

Cayman Islands, Florida Keys, Red Sea

WATERHOUSE PHOTOGRAPHIC TOURS
P.O. Box 2487
Key Largo, Florida 33037
305-451-2228 *Fax:* 305-451-5147
Contact: Barbara Doernbach or Maria DiPasqua

Waterhouse Photographic Tours are devoted to underwater and marine photography in various Caribbean destinations. The tours are limited to 12 to 20 participants.
Specialties: Underwater and marine.
Location: Bonaire, The Bahamas, Cayman Brac, and the Florida Keys are some of the tour locations.
Faculty: Professional underwater photographers from the Nikon School of Underwater Photography provide instruction.
Expenses: Accommodations and diving instruction are not covered by the basic fees.

WEST DEAN COLLEGE W

England

WEST DEAN COLLEGE
West Dean, Chichester
West Sussex PO18 0QZ, England
44-243-63301
Contact: College Office

West Dean College occupies West Dean House, one of the largest flint mansions in England with parts of the existing building dating to the 17th century. One of the aims of the college has been to establish a center where traditional arts and crafts could be taught to the highest professional standards. Toward that goal a variety of approximately 16 different photography courses of varying length are offered during the year.
Specialties: Flowers, technique, natural light, printing, basics, color photography.
Location: West Dean College is located near Chicester, England in West Sussex, about an hour southwest of London.
Facilities: Accommodations and meals are included in the workshop fee. Darkrooms and workrooms are available.
Faculty: Photography courses are taught by a staff numbering 3.
Expenses: Photographic materials are not included in the tuition.

WESTERN PACIFIC ACADEMY OF PHOTOGRAPHY W

Victoria, British Columbia, Canada

WESTERN PACIFIC ACADEMY OF PHOTOGRAPHY
1814 Vancouver Street
Victoria, B.C. V8T 5E3, Canada
604-383-1522 *Fax:* 604-383-1534
Contact: David Smith

The Western Pacific Academy of Photography offers a full 10-month program of applied photography designed to provide a firm foundation in both the business and the art of professional photography. All of the classes in the full time pro gram are available for audit. Courses include: wedding, portraiture, photojournalism, still life, darkroom, basic studio, large format, and others. All classes are restricted to 5 to 10 attendees.

Specialties: Instruction, large format, wedding, portraiture, basics, lighting.

Location: Victoria, Canada is located on Vancouver Island, easily accessible from Vancouver or Seattle by car ferry. The Academy is located in a central residential area.

Facilities: Housing information is available from the school. The school is equipped with two studios, a large communal darkroom, print finishing area, book/supply store, and library.

Faculty: All instructors are professional photographers highly experienced in their specialized areas.

WESTERN PHOTO ILLUMINATIONS T

Kenya, Africa and the Galapagos Islands

WESTERN PHOTO ILLUMINATIONS
P.O. Box 2206
Carson City, Nevada 89702
702-885-9195
Contact: Patrick & Inga Spence

Western Photo Illuminations hosts photographic tours each year to Kenya and the Galapagos Islands. Organized by the husband and wife photographic team, Patrick and Inga Spence, both tours are designed to give photographers unlimited opportunity to shoot and live among some of the world's outstanding wildlife and nature reserves. Workshops are limited to 10 to 12 participants.

Specialties: Wildlife, nature, Africa, Galapagos Islands.

Location: Kenya, East Africa: air travel between New York and Nairobi. Major game reserves visited are: Samburu, Buffalo Springs, Masai Mara, and Lake Nakuru. Galapagos Islands: from Miami and L.A. flights meet in Quito, Ecuador before yachting to the islands.

Facilities: Kenya: accommodations are in tent cottages with full bathroom facilities. Travel is by safari van carrying 4 passengers. Galapagos: travel and accommodations will be on a 66′ deluxe, air-conditioned yacht for seven nights - plus 1st class hotels.

Faculty: Tour organizers Patrick and Inga Spence have 5 years experience hosting photography tours and are both accomplished photographers. Patrick is a published writer/photographer of nature and travel books. Inga self publishes scenic postcards.

Expenses: Kenya safari price includes: air (from departure city) and land transportation, accommodations and most meals. Personal expenses, film and processing, and tips are not included. Galapogos: air (from L.A. or Miami), meals, accommodations are included.

WESTERN PHOTO WORKSHOPS OF TELLURIDE INC W

Telluride, Colorad

WESTERN PHOTO WORKSHOPS OF TELLURIDE
P.O. Box 968, 609 E. Columbia
Telluride, Colorado 81435
303-728-3727 *Fax:* 303-728-6836
Contact: True Redd or Charlotte Freeman

Western Photo Workshops are best-known for their 14 year workshop tradition, The Autumn Eye, which is held annually during the last days of September. Held in the small former goldmining town of Telluride and surrounded by the San Juan Mountains, the program also offers alpine wildflower workshops, technical instruction workshops, and winter workshops, among others. Some workshops require previous experience and some are appropriate for all levels of skill.

Specialties: Instruction, wildlife, wildflowers, composition, lighting, winter photography, landscape.

Location: The town of Telluride is best reached via plane from Denver or Albuquerque. Car travel is possible from the towns of Cortez or Montrose, Colorado.

Facilities: Accommodation at Skyline Ranch is included in some of the workshops. Otherwise, there is a variety of accommodations including motels, inns,

and B&Bs, from which to choose. Overnight E-6 processing is generally available.
Faculty: Director/instructor True Redd runs a advertising studio in Dallas and has recently authored the photo book *La Rose, An Intimacy of Roses.* Other instructors have included Linde Waidhofer, Sam Abell, Sarah Leen, Michael S. Yamashita, and Bill Ellzely.

WILD HORIZONS PHOTOGRAPHIC SAFARIS T

Grand Canyon, Monument Valley, Zion Park

WILD HORIZONS PHOTOGRAPHIC SAFARIS
P.O. Box 5118
Tucson, Arizona 85703
602-622-0672
Contact: Thomas Wiewandt

Wild Horizons hosts 8 photographic safaris, catering to 7 amateur photographers per trip, annually. These first-class, all-inclusive packages to scenic destinations in the American Southwest are tailor-made for individual instruction by tour leader Thomas Wiewandt. Photographic Safari offerings include "Arizona Balloon Safaris," "Spring in Arizona's Cactus Country," and "Ghost-towns & Graveyards" and more.
Specialties: Scenics, landscape, nature, wildflower.
Location: Six different destinations are featured each year. Regulars include Arizona's Cactus Country, Grand Canyon/Sedona, Bryce/Zion National Parks, Monument Valley/Canyon de Chelly, and Mono Lake & The Eastern Sierras.
Facilities: First class hotels and meals are included. Evening teaching programs are scheduled for some tours. Others allow for overnight processing and critiques.
Faculty: Group leader Thomas Wiewandt is a nature photographer and holds a Ph.D. in ecology. Mr. Wiewandt has also created four award-winning films for National Geographic and the BBC, and has published his first book, *Hidden Life of the Desert.*
Expenses: Tour packages are inclusive but do not include transportation to and from the point of the tour's departure or items of a personal nature.

WILDERNESS IMAGES OUTDOOR PHOTOGRAPHY W

Cascade Mountains, Washington

WILDERNESS IMAGES OUTDOOR PHOTOGRAPHY
702 Whitman Court
Selah, Washington 98942
509-697-6260
Contact: Gary E. Holscher

The Wilderness Images Outdoor Photography Workshops are held in the eastern foothills of the Washington Cascade Mountains. The workshops are designed for intermediate level photographers using either 35mm or medium format and are limited to 12 participants .

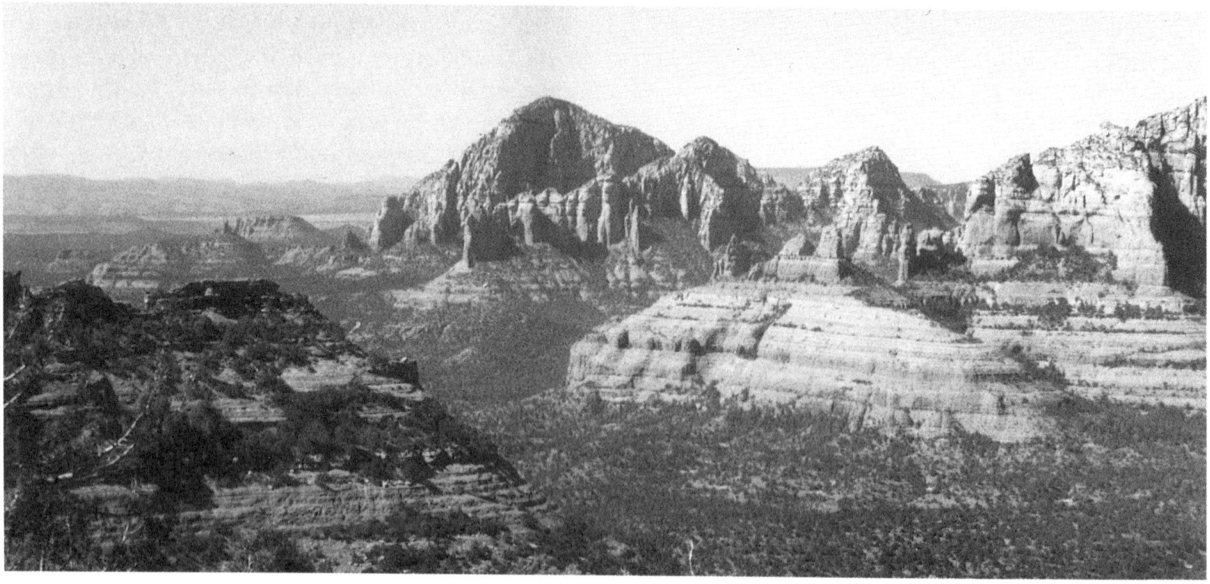
Photograph by Susan Schwinn and Ray Noonan

The spectacular vistas surrounding Sedona, Arizona, are an invitation to landscape and nature photographers.

Specialties: Outdoor, nature.
Facilities: Accommodations are at the Hidden Valley Guest Ranch and include a full range of amenities. Facilities include a conference room for lectures and slide presentations.
Expenses: Film and processing are not included in the workshop fee. Additional entertainment at the ranch is also an added expense.

WILDERNESS INSTITUTE & PHOTO TOUR W

Michigan

WILDERNESS INSTITUTE & PHOTOTOUR
P.O. Box 548
Stambaugh, Michigan 49964
906-265-4993
Contact: Joseph P. Speno

The Wilderness Institute is situated on the upper peninsula of northwestern Michigan and offers weekend and in-depth 5 day nature photography workshops. Geared to both amateur and advanced photography students, the workshops mostly take place in the field and offer limited classroom work. Limited to 8-10 attendees, workshops include: "Bald Eagle/Osprey Weekends," "Wilderness Visions," and "Pt. Pelee Birding Spectacular."
Specialties: Birds, wildflowers, ecology, wildlife.
Facilities: Students are housed at The Aerie Bed & Breakfast in Stambaugh, Michigan for workshops held at the Wilderness Institute.
Faculty: The institute's faculty is comprised of working professionals and experienced field naturalists.
Expenses: Workshops do not include film, processing, and transportation to the workshp location.

WILDERNESS LIGHT PHOTOGRAPHY WORKSHOP W

Alberta and the Canadian Rockies

WILDERNESS LIGHT
109 Lee Ridge Road
Edmonton, Alberta T6K 0N1 Canada
403-450-3279
Contact: Mark Degner

Wilderness Light offers two types of photographic workshops. Weekend workshops are held twice in June at the Sheep River Wildlife Sanctuary concentrating on wildlife and scenic with one-on-one instruction. Intensive Photographic Pack Trips of about 2 weeks are offered in July and August and afford ample opportunity for wildlife photography and exploration. Instructional sessions are given in macro-photography, night photography, creative exposure and more.
Specialties: Wildlife, scenics, nature, technical instruction.
Location: Weekend workshops: Sheep River Sanctuary is about 45 kilometers from Turner Valley, Alberta and is nestled near the peaks of Highwood Range. Pack Trips: Willmore Wilderness Area in the Alberta Rockies is a true wilderness park without tourist services.
Facilities: Weekend workshops do not include accommodations or meals. Campgrounds or the Turner Valley Inn are available. Pack Trippers are provided with wall tents equipped with stoves and solar heated showers. Bedrolls should be brought.
Faculty: Photography instructors Darwin Wiggett and Mark Degner have both conducted wildlife research and are accomplished photographers. They are joined on the pack trips by Dave and Rose Manzer who function as cooks, entertainers, and riding coaches.
Expenses: Weekend workshop fees include instruction and transportation to shooting sites. Pack Trip fees include everything but equipment, film, and transportation to and from the point of departure.

WILDERNESS PHOTOGRAPHY EXPEDITIONS T

Yellowstone National Park

WILDERNESS PHOTOGRAPHY EXPEDITIONS
402 South 5th
Livingston, Montana 59047
406-222-2302
Contact: Tom Murphy

Wildlife Photography Expeditions take place year-round and accommodate up to 8 wildlife and Yellowstone lovers. The expeditions, which are generally about one week, are accompanied by a professional instructor experienced in taking groups to remote sites in the park.
Specialties: Wildlife, landscape.
Facilities: Motels and comfortable back-country camps are used.
Faculty: Wildlife photographer Tom Murphy's work has appeared on the cover of *The New York Times Magazine*, *National Geographic World*, and *Outdoor Photographer*.
Expenses: Lodging and meals the night before and after the trip begins/ends are not included.

Key: **W** = Workshop
T = Photo-Tour
S = Seminar

WILDERNESS SEA WILDLIFE OBSERVATION TOURS T
Alaska, Mexico, Yucatan, & Costa Rica

OUTBACK EXPEDITIONS
P.O. Box 16343
Seattle, Washington 98116
206-932-7012 *Fax:* 206-935-1213
Contact: Daniel Clarke or Scott Roberge

Outback Expeditions offer commercial, professionally guided wildlife tours to a variety of interesting locations. Although the tours are not designed specifically for photographers and do not offer photographic instruction, the tours do provide access to back-country locations and involvement in a variety of recreational pastimes. Many tours are kayaks and camping, and some are with overnights in hotels. For photographers who find escorted travel a simpler approach.
Specialties: Nature, wildlife, landscape, documentary, travel.
Location: The Yucatan tour travels from Merida to Cozumel with visits to Mayan ruins. The Costa Rican journey covers beaches, jungles, volcanos and San Jose. The Alaska visit explores LeConte Glacier Bay. Additional tours cover Mexico and Canada.
Expenses: Generally airfare, taxes, and meals on land tours are not included in the tour price.

WILDLIFE EXPEDITIONS T
Wyoming

GREAT PLAINS WILDLIFE RESEARCH
P.O. Box 7580
Jackson, Wyoming 83001
307-733-2623
Contact: Tom Segerstrom

Wildlife biologist Tom Segerstrom hosts diverse 5-day wildlife and nature tours departing from Jackson Hole and traversing Yellowstone Park, the Beartooth Mountains, Cody, and Grand Teton Park. The tours, which provide opportunities to photograph and help research bald eagles, elk, bears, wild horses, the endangered black-footed ferret, prairie dog colonies, and pronghorn antelope, are available from May to September. One-day trips are available year-round.
Specialties: Wildlife.
Facilities: Accommodations are available in rustic bed and breakfasts, modern cabins, guest ranches, and Buffalo Bill Cody's famous Irma Hotel. Transportation is via a customized, 4-wheel drive Suburban.
Faculty: Tom Segerstrom has worked for the U.S. Fish & Wildlife Service and has taught wildlife ecology of the Rockies.
Expenses: One-day excursions include use of a video camera, transportation, a field meal, and guide. Five-day tours are all inclusive.

WILDLIFE MODEL WORKSHOPS W
Columbia Falls, Montana

THE WILDLIFE MODEL WORKSHOPS
P.O. Box 334
Durango, Colorado 81302
303-259-4143
Contact: Robert Winslow

The Wildlife Model Workshops offer one of the most unique photo opportunities available. Situated only 5 miles from Glacier National Park, the 3-day workshops, available to only 7 participants per session, focus on shooting wildlife models living freely in an enclosed natural setting. Portable fencing allows for a variety of natural settings and many of the healthy animals, though not domesticated, are bottle-fed and raised in captivity. June, July and September.
Specialties: Wildlife including timber wolves, mountain lions, red foxes, bobcats, coyotes, black bears, lynx, badgers, beavers, rattlesnakes, snow geese, and wild turkeys.
Location: Columbia Falls is located 5 miles from Glacier Falls National Park. The closest airport is in Kalispell, Montana.
Facilities: Motel accomodations are available and most meals are included. Overnight E-6 processing is available.
Faculty: Robert Winslow is a former photographer instructor at Idaho State University. He is also a Grand Prize winner of the National Wildlife Cover Photo Contest. Brent and Robin Allen are professional wildlife handlers who have trained many animals.
Expenses: Workshops are all inclusive.

WOMEN IN PHOTOGRAPHY CONFERENCE W
University locations throughout the U.S.

WOMEN IN PHOTOGRAPHY CONFERENCE
Bryn Mawr College
Bryn Mawr, Pennsylvania 19010
215-526-5335
Contact: Carol Campbell, Visual Resources Dept.

Women in Photography is a 3-day conference, offered periodically, which features portfolio review sessions. Held at the S.I. Newhouse School of Public Communications at Syracuse in 1986 and at Bryn Mawr College in 1989, plans for the next conference have not been made available at this writing. Contact directly for up-to-date information.

WOMEN'S STUDIO WORKSHOP W

Rosendale, New York

WOMEN'S STUDIO WORKSHOP
P.O. Box 489
Rosendale, New York 12472
914-658-9133
Contact: Ann Kalmbach

Women's Studio Workshop is a center for contemporary art activities. Year-round weekend workshops cover a spectrum of subjects including "The Constructed Photograph", "Turkish Watercolor Marbling", and "Western Papermaking". Intensive week-long workshops are offered during the summer months. Not restricted to women only, the workshop frequently offers Saturday sessions for children. Photography workshops are for beginner and advanced students.

Specialties: Instruction, technique, darkroom, silkscreen.
Location: The workshop is located in the foothills of the Catskill Mountains about a hour and a half north of New York City and a hour south of Albany.
Facilities: Recommended bed and breakfasts are located near the studio workshop.
Faculty: All workshops are taught by professional artists with extensive teaching experience.
Expenses: Workshop fees cover instruction only.

WOODSTOCK PHOTOGRAPHY WORKSHOPS W

Woodstock, New York

WOODSTOCK PHOTOGRAPHY WORKSHOPS
59 Tinker Street
Woodstock, New York 12498
914-679-9957
Contact: Kathleen Kenyon, Associate Director

The Woodstock Photography Workshops are offered weekends during the months of July, August, and September, and are taught by guest master photographers. Enrollment is limited to 15.

Location: Woodstock is located in the Catskill Mountain foothills, two hours drive north of New York City.
Facilities: A wide variety of housing possibilities are available locally. Workshop facilities include classrooms and darkrooms.
Expenses: Model and lab fees are additional as necessary.

ZONE VI WORKSHOP W

Putney, Vermont

ZONE VI WORKSHOP
RD2
Putney, Vermont 05346
802-257-5161
Contact: Fred Picker

The Zone VI Workshop is a week-long workshop held annually during the summer months for serious photographers who want to improve their technical and visual skills. Led by author Fred Picker, the workshop covers such topics as negative exposure and development, printing theory and practice, chemicals, and lenses. Exhibits, field trips, and lectures are also part of the workshop which is headquartered at The Putney School, a private boarding school during the year.

Specialties: Zone VI, technical, instruction.
Location: Putney is about 20 miles north of the Massachusetts border on the Connecticut River. The closest airport is Bradley International which is located between Hartford and Springfield and about a hour and a half drive from Putney.
Facilities: Both room and board are available at the school facility. Classrooms, lecture hall, library, dining room, and photographic laboratories are available to workshop participants. There are tennis courts, swimming holes, and horses available for free time.
Faculty: Fred Picker is assisted by a staff of 8. He is the author of the books *The Zone VI Workshop* and *The Fine Print.*
Expenses: The tuition fee covers laboratory fees, room and board, and instruction.

Geographic Index to Workshops & Photo-Tours

Workshop Specialty Index

Index